Are the Irish different?

Edited by Tom Inglis

Manchester University Press

Manchester and New York

Published by Manchester University Press
Altrincham Street, Manchester M1 7JA, UK
and Room 400, 175 Fifth Avenue, New York, NY 10010, USA
www.manchesteruniversitypress.co.uk

Distributed in the United States exclusively by
Palgrave Macmillan, 175 Fifth Avenue, New York,
NY 10010, USA

Distributed in Canada exclusively by
UBC Press, University of British Columbia, 2029 West Mall,
Vancouver, BC, Canada V6T 1Z2

British Library Cataloguing-in-Publication Data
A catalogue record for this book is available from the British Library

Library of Congress Cataloging-in-Publication Data applied for

ISBN   978 0719 0 9582 5   hardback
ISBN   978 0719 0 9583 2   paperback

First published 2014

Typeset
by Action Publishing Technology Ltd, Gloucester
Printed in Great Britain
by Bell & Bain Ltd, Glasgow

For my friend Michael Cussen
and all those who left Ireland

Contents

List of figures and tables

Figures

Table

Acknowledgements

My thanks to Susie Donnelly who helped with the organising and editing of the essays, to Tony Mason for his support and sound judgement, to John Banks for his excellent editing, to my son Arron for the cover image and to the contributors for their patience and dedication. These essays emerged from a workshop in University College Dublin in 2012 sponsored by the College of Human Sciences.

Notes on contributors

Kieran Allen is a Senior Lecturer in the School of Sociology in University College Dublin. He is the author of a number of books on contemporary Irish society, including most recently *Austerity Ireland: The Failure of Irish Capitalism* (London: Pluto Press 2013). He is also the author of a number of articles and a book on Marxist theory, including *Marx and the Alternative to Capitalism* (London: Pluto Press, 2011).

Anne Byrne is a sociologist with an interest in narrative and biography, teaching and researching in the School of Political Sciences and Sociology at NUI Galway, Ireland. Anne has published on gender, identity, inequality, stigma, rurality and on the historiography of anthropological research in rural Ireland in the 1930s. Recent publications include Anne Byrne and Deirdre O'Mahony, 'Revisiting and Reframing the Anthropological Archive', *Irish Journal of Anthropology* 16:1 (2013), pp. 8–15: and a short film: A. Byrne, D. O'Mahony and RRG, *Visualising the Anthropological Archive: A Community Collaboration* (2012), Gallivanting Media. She is a member of the Royal Irish Academy Social Sciences Committee (2012–16) and Vice-President of the Sociological Association of Ireland.

Linda Connolly is Director of the Institute for Social Science at UCC. Her research interests are in the arenas of Irish society, Irish studies, migration, gender, feminist theory, family, gender, sexualities and social movements. Her monograph *The Irish Women's Movement: From Revolution to Devolution* (Dublin: Lilliput Press, 2003) was highly commended for its meticulous research in many reviews internationally. More recently, she has served as the Managing Editor of the *Irish Journal of Sociology*, which is published twice yearly by Manchester University Press, and is in the process of completing a monograph entitled *Theorising Irish Studies*.

Michael G. Cronin is Lecturer in English at NUI Maynooth. He is the author of *Impure Thoughts: Sexuality, Catholicism and Literature in Twentieth-century Ireland*

(Manchester University Press, 2012). His essays on twentieth-century Irish fiction have appeared in *Eire-Ireland*, *Field Day Review* and *Oxford History of the Novel* (forthcoming); essays on contemporary Irish sexual politics will appear in Holohan and Tracy (eds), *Masculinity and Irish Popular Culture: Tiger's Tales* (London: Palgrave Macmillan) and in Ryan-Flood (ed.), *Gender Intimacy and Contemporary Ireland* (Routledge) in 2014. In 2013 he was guest editor of an *Irish Review* special issue on the future of Irish studies.

Ethel Crowley is a sociologist who has lectured for several years at NUI Cork, Trinity College Dublin and the Open University. Her most recent book is *Your Place or Mine? Community and Belonging in 21st Century Ireland* (Dublin: Orpen Press, 2013). She is also the author of *Land Matters: Power Struggles in Rural Ireland* (Dublin: Lilliput Press, 2006). She regularly contributes to Irish media debates on social change. She also wrote a fundraising book entitled *Daring to Dream: The Work of the Hope Foundation in India* (Cork: Hope Foundation, 2010), following a volunteering stint in Kolkata in 2009.

Michele Dillon is Professor and Chair of Sociology at the University of New Hampshire. Her publications include (with W. D'Antonio and M. Gautier) *American Catholics in Transition* (Lanham: Rowman & Littlefield, 2013), (with Paul Wink) *In the Course of a Lifetime: Tracing Religious Belief, Practice, and Change* (Berkeley: University of California Press, 2007), *Catholic Identity: Balancing Reason, Faith, and Power* (Cambridge: Cambridge University Press, 1999), *Debating Divorce: Moral Conflict in Ireland* (Lexington: University Press of Kentucky, 1993), (editor) *Handbook of the Sociology of Religion* (Cambridge: Cambridge University Press, 2003) and *Introduction to Sociological Theory* (New York: Wiley, 2014, 2nd ed.).

Martin Dowling is Lecturer in Irish Traditional Music in the School of Creative Arts in Queen's University Belfast. He completed his PhD in Irish economic and social history under Professor James S Donnelly, Jr. at the University of Wisconsin-Madison. A noted Irish fiddle player, Martin joined the traditional Irish band Samhradh Music founded by the poet and musician Michael Donaghy (1954–2004) in 1982, and later formed the trio Boxty which performed across the US Midwest. He regularly performs and teaches the Irish fiddle at festivals in Ireland, Europe and the United States. He is the author of two books on aspects of Irish social and music history.

Tony Fahey is Professor of Social Policy in the School of Applied Studies, University College Dublin. His current research focuses on the detailed analysis of family patterns in Ireland using micro-data from the census of population and from Ireland's longitudinal survey of children, *Growing Up in Ireland*. A recent publication is (with P. Keilthy and E. Polek) *Family Relationships and Family Well-being: A Study of the Families of Nine Year-olds in Ireland* (Dublin: Family support Agency, January 2013).

Bryan Fanning is a Professor and Head of the School of Applied Social Science at University College Dublin. He has written extensively on immigration and social change in Ireland and on Irish intellectual history. His books include *The Quest for Modern Ireland: The Battle of Ideas 1912–1986* (Dublin: Irish Academic Press, 2008), *New Guests of the Irish Nation* (Dublin: Irish Academic Press, 2009), *Immigration and Social Cohesion in the Republic of Ireland* (Manchester: Manchester University Press, 2011) and *Racism and Social Change in the Republic of Ireland: Second edition* (Manchester: Manchester University Press, 2012) *and Histories of the Irish Future* (2014).

Chris Haywood is Director of Postgraduate Studies in the School of Arts and Cultures at the University of Newcastle. He is currently involved in researching men, masculinities and contemporary dating practices. With Mairtin Mac an Ghaill, he has written several papers on Irish men and masculinities across generations, focusing on notions of anti-Irish racism, second generation emerging subjectivities, religious identity formation, class relations and the fragmentation of the Irish community abroad.

Mary J. Hickman is Professorial Research Fellow at the Centre for Irish Studies, St Mary's University College, London. She established the Irish Studies Centre at London Metropolitan University, where she was also Director of the Institute for the Study of European Transformations. Her latest book (with N. Mai and H. Crowley) is *Migration and Social Cohesion in the UK* (London: Palgrave Macmillan 2012) and (ed. with J. MacPherson) *Women and Irish Diaspora Identities* (forthcoming 2014). She has been Visiting Professor at New York University, Columbia University, The New School for Social Research, Victoria University, Melbourne, and University College Dublin.

Tom Inglis is Associate Professor of Sociology in University College Dublin. He writes about Irish culture, particularly in relation to religion, sexuality, the media, love and the meaning of life. He has published articles and books in these areas including *Moral Monopoly: The Catholic Church in Modern Irish Society*, 2nd ed. (Dublin: University College Dublin Press,1998); *Truth, Power and Lies: Modern Irish Society and the Case of the Kerry Babies* (Dublin: University College Dublin Press, 2003); *Global Ireland: Same Difference* (New York: Routledge, 2008); *Making Love: A Memoir* (Dublin: New Island, 2012), *Love* (London: Routledge, 2013) and *The Meanings of Life in Contemporary Ireland* (New York: Palgrave Macmillan, 2014).

Marie Keenan specialises in public policy and therapeutic responses to crime. She is a systemic and forensic psychotherapist, a lecturer in the School of Applied Social Science and a member of the Advisory Board of University College Dublin's Criminology Institute. Her most recent publications include *Child Sexual Abuse and the Catholic Church: Gender Power and Organisational Culture* (New York:

Oxford University Press, 2012) and (ed. with P. Claffey and J. Egan) *Broken Faith: Why Hope Matters* (Oxford: Lang, 2013). She is Principal Investigator of research on *Sexual Trauma and Abuse: Restorative and Transformative Possibilities* and is also collaborating with KU Leuven on a Daphne III funded project, *Developing Integrated Responses to Sexual Violence.*

Katie Liston lectures in the social sciences of sport at the University of Ulster and is a member of the Sport and Exercise Sciences Research Institute there. She has published on various aspects of the sociology of sport including national identity, migration, gender and sport in Ireland. She is also active in sociology more generally, including as managing editor of *Human Figurations*, an online multidisciplinary journal examining all aspects of the human condition. She has also achieved international sports representation and holds a number of All-Ireland titles in Gaelic football, rugby, athletics and soccer.

Mairtin Mac an Ghaill works at Newman University, Birmingham. He is author (with J. Hanafin and P. Conway) of *Gender Politics and Exploring Masculinities in Irish Education* (Dublin: National Council for Curriculum Assessment, 2004), *The Making of Men: Masculinities, Sexualities and Schooling* (Buckingham: Open University Press, 1994) and *Contemporary Racisms and Ethnicities* (Buckingham: Open University Press, 2004). He has a research interest in the Irish diaspora in Britain. With Chris Haywood, he has written several papers on Irish men and masculinities across generations, focusing on notions of anti-Irish racism, second-generation emerging subjectivities, religious identity formation, class relations and the fragmentation of the Irish community abroad.

Siniša Malešević is Professor and Head of School of Sociology at University College, Dublin. He is also a member of Royal Irish Academy and an Associated Member of the Academy of Sciences and Arts of Bosnia and Herzegovina. His recent books include *Nation-States and Nationalisms: Organisation, Ideology and Solidarity* (Cambridge: Polity, 2013), *The Sociology of War and Violence* (Cambridge: Cambridge University Press, 2010), *Identity as Ideology* (London: Palgrave, 2006), *The Sociology of Ethnicity* (London: Sage, 2004) and a co-edited volume *Nationalism and War* (Cambridge: Cambridge University Press, 2013).

Geraldine Moane received a PhD in psychology from University of California Berkeley, and is now a Senior Lecturer in University College Dublin. She has an enduring interest in the Irish psyche. She has applied feminist and liberation psychology in her work with women in disadvantaged communities and with lesbian, gay, bisexual and transgender communities. She is author of *Gender and Colonialism, a Psychological Analysis of Oppression and Liberation* (London: Palgrave Macmillan, 2011). Her awards include Fulbright and Marie Curie fellowships, and a Distinguished Publication Award for a Special Issue of *Feminism & Psychology* on 'feminist liberation psychology' (2009).

Denis O'Hearn is Professor of Sociology at Binghamton University-SUNY, visiting professor at Bogazici University-Istanbul, and a recent Keough Visiting Professor at the Keough-Naughton Institute of Irish Studies at the University of Notre Dame. He is author of numerous books and articles on economic development and imprisonment. Among his books, *The Atlantic Economy* (Manchester: Manchester University Press, 2001) won the 2003 ASA PEWS Award for Distinguished Scholarship. His (with Silvia Calamati and Laurence McKeown) *Il Diario di Bobby Sands: Storia di un ragazzo irlandese* (Roma: Castelvecchi Editore, 2011), won the 2011 Alessandro Tassoni Award and the 2013 award 'Citta di Cassino: Letterature dal Fronte'.

Seán Ó Riain is Professor of Sociology at the NUI Maynooth. His research interests are in the sociology of work and employment, comparative political economy, inequality and social change and the global information economy. Seán is the author of *The Politics of High Tech Growth: Developmental Network States in the Global Economy* (Cambridge: Cambridge University Press, 2004) and of *The Rise and Fall of Ireland's Celtic Tiger: Liberalism, Boom and Bust* (Cambridge: Cambridge University Press, 2014). He is currently directing *New Deals in the New Economy*, a five-year study of workplace bargains in Europe (www.nuim.ie/newdeals), funded by a European Research Council Consolidator Grant.

Joseph Ruane was Professor in the School of Sociology and Philosophy, University College Cork, and is currently Visiting Professor in the School of Sociology, University College Dublin. He is co-author of *The Dynamics of Conflict in Northern Ireland* (Cambridge: Cambridge University Press, 1996), co-editor of *After the Good Friday Agreement* (Dublin: University College Dublin Press, 1989), co-editor of *Europe's Old States in the New World Order: The Politics of Transition in Britain, France and Spain* (Dublin: University College Dublin Press, 2003), and author and co-author of numerous articles on conflict in Northern Ireland. He is currently conducting comparative research on Protestant–Catholic conflict in Northern Ireland, the Republic of Ireland and France.

Iarfhlaith Watson is a lecturer in University College Dublin School of Sociology and a former President of the Sociological Association of Ireland. He publishes in both Irish and English. His research is mainly in the area of the Irish language, including his book *Broadcasting in Irish* (Dublin: Four Courts, 2003), and many articles and book chapters on linguistic elitism, Irish language media and the educational advantages of speaking Irish. He has been a member of the Board of the International Visual Sociology Association, an Irish Representative on the International Social Survey Programme and has published on topics such as anti-immigrant attitudes and banal nationalism.

1

Introduction

Tom Inglis

There was a moment during the European Soccer Championships in 2012 when it seemed that Irish cultural difference was, once again, being firmly etched into the annals of global culture. Although their team had been heavily defeated by Spain, and eliminated from the competition without having won one of its matches, supporters of the team who had travelled in their thousands across Europe, instead of perhaps booing the team from the pitch, cheered and clapped them. They then began to chant and sing long after everyone else had left the stadium. Eventually the police were brought in to escort them out.

The Irish soccer supporters had gained a reputation during previous World and European soccer championships for being the best soccer supporters in the world. Everywhere they went, they tried to bring good humour and fun, to engage the locals with their banter and *craic*. In some ways they could be seen as popular Irish cultural ambassadors, spreading a different knowledge, understanding and appreciation of what it is to be Irish. Their performance could be read as a different way of dealing with loss. It mirrors what happens at many funerals. There is often laughter, music, song and dance, as well as a lot of drink, at Irish wakes. It could be argued that, if there is anything different about the Irish, it is the way they deal with desire and death.

The Irish have been characterised in many different ways, as good humoured charming, hospitable and gregarious. They love a good time. They love to tease, engage in verbal word play and spar with each other. Yet they are seen to avoid intimacy and be drawn to tragedy.[1] Many of these characteristics and other traits have been linked to the legacies of colonialism. These include a tendency to avoid confrontation, to inwardly reject but publicly comply with power, to hide success and ambition and to engage in self-deprecation.[2]

But whatever the legacies of colonialism, there have been others who, in the tradition of characterising Ireland as an island of saints and scholars, have pointed to the unique strengths of the Irish character. Richard Kearney, for example, has claimed that, over the centuries, the Irish developed a powerfully different way of thinking. In positing the unique qualities of the 'Irish Mind', he wanted 'to debunk the myth of the mindless Irish' and 'the colonialist portrayals of the Irish as brainless savages'. He argued that there is a complex, rigorous logic to Irish mythical thought that gives meaning to people's lives and that has been passed down through generations from Celtic times. 'From the earliest times, the Irish mind remained free, in significant measure, of the linear, centralising logic of the Greco-Roman culture which dominated most of Western Europe ... In contradistinction to the orthodox dualist logic of *either/or*, the Irish mind may be seen to favour a more dialectical logic of *both/and*: an intellectual ability to hold the traditional oppositions of classical reason in creative confluence.'[3]

In emphasising the dialectical logic of the Irish mind, Kearney was attempting to go beyond Matthew Arnold's concept of the Celtic Soul and to assert that the Irish, like the Celts generally, were ruled not just by reason and rationality but also by fantasy and imagination. In this view, along with an accumulated material history that makes the Irish different, there has also been an accumulation of thinking differently. In response to a number of environmental, social and cultural factors, the Irish developed ways of thinking, of perceiving, reading and understanding the world and an ability to adapt to different conditions. The Irish mind appears to have a universal, eternal quality that has enabled the Irish, not necessarily uniquely but to a greater extent than others, to think outside the standard box of Western logic of either/or. It is this ability, inherited through generations, which has been the foundation of Irish cultural difference. The Irish mind has enabled the Irish to balance and accommodate imagination and intellect, emotion and reason, poetry and science.

The idea that the Irish have some essential, inherited cultural characteristics was picked up by the Industrial Development Authority (IDA). In an international advertising campaign in 2006, it took up the theme of 'the Irish mind' that had been developed by Kearney and his colleagues. It placed adverts in numerous papers and magazines, including *The Wall Street Journal, Time* and *The Economist,* claiming that the Irish were creative, imaginative and flexible, with agile minds and a unique capacity to initiate and innovate without being directed.[4]

The chapters in this book could be seen as a good example of the Irish mind at work. They are written by human scientists who explore, in accessible, lively and innovative ways, whether the Irish are significantly different and, if so, what are the origins, nature and significance of these differences? It would be difficult, and undesirable, to try to summarise the arguments and points the various contributors make. And so, almost as an appetiser, I will try in this introduction to give just a flavour of some of their insights and understandings about Irish difference.

National difference

It is easy to talk up difference, to persuade ourselves and others that there is something unique about the Irish. We are no different from any other nation or ethnic group. It is part and parcel of maintaining ideological coherence and solidarity. We may no longer believe that we are an island of saints and scholars, exporting a unique brand of Catholicism around the world. But we still like to think of ourselves as different. Perhaps this is what the Irish soccer supporters were trying to do, to export Irish bonhomie. We are able to think differently when it comes to defeat and loss. We have the gift of the gab, a unique sense of humour and fun, and an ability to help others join with us in having 'great *craic*'. Maybe this is the new story we tell about ourselves: told and retold, acted and re-enacted, wherever the Irish gather, at home and abroad, in cafés, restaurants, pubs and clubs. It is a story told to tourists and visitors. It is a story reiterated in advertisements and in marketing strategies to promote pubs and drinking. And, like all stories, if they are told often enough they come to be believed. As the sociological dictum goes, if people believe things are real, they are real in their consequences.[5]

Of course, the notion of cultural difference is not just an Irish story, but a story of nations and ethnic groups all over the world. The story of modernity revolves around people coming to see and understand themselves as belonging to nations. When it comes to national difference, the Irish may then be the same as the French, Dutch, Spanish, Italians and every other nation in that we make mountains out of a molehill when it comes to cultural difference. But the difference may be minimal. It may well be that, as with individual sense of self, the notion that there is something unique or exceptional about national difference is an illusion of the market, the media and nation-states within the world capitalist system. It is easy to believe in images. For example, as has been suggested, we might say of the Irish that they are pub-dependent, sharp tongued and witty. They are modest and self-deprecating and like to engage in free-association humorous conversation. Again, many of these cultural traits might be linked to our colonial history. However, these cultural traits were those the anthropologist Kate Fox identified as being quintessentially English.[6]

There was no such thing as the Irish nation in the past. There were tribes. And yet now the Irish nation – and the notion of being Irish – have become taken for granted. And despite globalisation and cosmopolitanism, the notion of Ireland, being Irish and Irish cultural difference is growing. People might idolise the era of the Gaelic League, the Gaelic Athletic Association (GAA), the Catholic Church, Fianna Fáil and de Valéra's dreams as the golden years of Irishness. But the reality is that Irishness was only in its infancy then. Today it is produced and reproduced in political and economic discourse: 'we' lost the run of ourselves during the Celtic Tiger years. The sense of 'we-ness' is generated more through participation in globalised sport than it is through speaking Irish. The notion of Irish difference is reproduced through the tourist industry, the worldwide celebrations of St Patrick's Day, the export of the Irish pub, the success of Riverdance and the celebration of the Irish diaspora.

If we are to look beyond national myths, stories and images of the Irish, if we are to transcend notions of different minds and personality traits, it might be an idea to start with aspects of social life and to try to see if there are real and substantial differences in the way the Irish do economics and politics. If there is anything different about Ireland, it could be argued that it lies in the way it went from being a relatively insular, agricultural economy in the middle of the last century to becoming by the end of the century, one of the most open, advanced and globalised small economies in Europe. However, as a liberal economy on the periphery of Europe, Ireland did not develop the social contracts and internal control mechanisms that enabled core Europe economies to deal with the crises in the capitalist system. Indeed it was the combination of a dependence on foreign direct investment, a reluctance to increase taxes and, then, latterly a policy of incentivising property development that led to Ireland having the highest level of external debt among the major countries of the world. If Ireland was different within world capitalism, it was in the peculiar way it went from boom to bust.

Catholicism and colonisation

Although there were other European nations that made Catholicism a keystone of national difference, there were many factors that made the Irish project different. The idea of creating a society that had a collective vision and commitment without being socialist became an ideal of the Catholic Church during the latter half of the twentieth century. Before and after Independence, there were many who thought that Ireland could become a shining example of the type of Catholic society epitomised in de Valéra's ideal Ireland, epitomised in his St Patrick's Day speech of 1943. However, the opening up of Irish society and culture to global cultural flows and the decline of the Church's monopoly over morality meant that ideal was never realised.

The Church did, nevertheless, have a profound influence on Irish society and culture. The extent to which the Catholic Church shaped and influenced Irish politics has been the subject of much research and debate. While much of this research has focused on Church–state relations, it is important to emphasise that one of the factors that made Ireland different was the extent to which the Church shaped Irish civil society and, in particular, became the backbone of the way most Irish people saw and understood themselves and the world in which they lived. It was the way in which the Church developed and sustained links between the political parties, at local and national level, particularly within Fianna Fáil, that enabled it to become a key pillar not just in civil society generally, but in political elite society.

The power of the Catholic Church in politics stemmed from the power it developed in the modernisation of Irish society and, in particular, the controlling of sexuality, marriage and fertility. During the first half of the twentieth century, the Irish developed a particular aversion to marriage. Whereas the rest of Europe was moving to early and more numerous marriages, in Ireland fewer men and women married and, when they did so, they were older than their European counterparts. However, even though the Irish married later and less frequently, they still managed to have more children than most other Western couples. This was because many of those who did marry had large families. While this may be directly related to the delayed arrival of contraception, it may also be related to the absence of a discourse and the level of communicative competency about sexuality and fertility control between husbands and wives. In a culture in which sex was hidden and silenced, it may have been a source of shame and guilt. However, for many couples, having large families was often a means of attaining status, honour and respect.

Fewer people marrying and, when they did, marrying late gave rise to large numbers of bachelors and spinsters. As in many other aspects, it was not that the Irish were exceptional or even significantly different in the numbers of unmarried men and women, it is rather that the practice of delaying marriage combined with many not marrying at all gave rise to cultural habits that were quite different. While much has been written about bachelor groups, particularly in relation to pubs and drinking patterns, there has, until recently, been little social research on single women. The history of the Irish spinster has yet to be written. In the meantime we have to rely on literature to identify and describe their experiences.

When it comes to looking for the key to Irish cultural difference, rather than start with the mind, it might be better, then, to employ a form of historical materialism that examines what happened to Irish people as bodies operating in places. Such an approach would examine the structures, contexts and places in which people lived, particularly in homes, schools, churches and pubs. The emphasis would be on identifying, describing and analysing the practices of everyday life, how children and young people were disciplined and controlled, particularly in terms of physical punishment, and the repression of sex, desire and pleasure. This could then be related to the cultural strategies in adult life and how Irish people developed cultural traits of piety, humility and chastity.

There is much to suggest from history that the Irish had a peculiar attitude to children. Not only did so few married couples have so many children for so long, but many of these children ended up being incarcerated in industrial and reformatory schools where they were subject to physical and sexual abuse. There are many different reasons why this happened, but some of them relate specifically to the Catholic Church's teachings about sexuality, the culture of silence and the power and governance structures of the Church.

This raises questions about the robustness of Irish Catholicism. It would seem that what makes Irish Catholics similar to other European Catholics, and different from American Catholics, is that the clerical sex abuse scandals have led to a distaste for and disenchantment with the Church. Mass attendance continues to decline rapidly and there is less sense of belonging to the Church. This is in contrast to America, where Catholics seem to have withstood the challenges of the sex abuse scandals and, more generally, the undermining forces of individualisation and secularisation.

Although there is plenty of evidence to suggest that the reasons for Irish cultural difference lie in the peculiar way in which Ireland modernised and, in particular, in the central role of the Catholic Church in the modernisation process, it would be wrong to underestimate the impact and effect of colonisation. For a long time, the history of Ireland was characterised by systematic plantations and the suppression of religion, culture and language. The legacies of these colonial strategies were imprinted on Irish minds, bodies and souls for generations, particularly in relation to the way the Irish related to sex and alcohol. And yet, there is evidence from other postcolonial societies that the cultural and psychological legacies of colonial rule are often very similar. So what may make the Irish different is not so much that they developed a social, cultural, moral and personal sense of inferiority, but the ways in which they did this.

The longest-lasting impact of colonial rule in Ireland was the conflict in Northern Ireland. The legacies of the violence have been deeply imprinted on both Catholics and Protestants, Republicans and Loyalists. What perhaps made the conflict different was the nature of everyday sectarian life, the violence employed by the opposing sides and the strategies of the British state to contain the conflict. The long, deeply rooted history of sectarian conflict means that any path to reconciliation will be long and difficult. While there is plenty of evidence to show that the 1998 Good Friday agreement has achieved peace between the two communities, there is less evidence to show that the deep-rooted oppositions that festered for more than four hundred years, and are embedded in segregation and inequality, can be easily reconciled in a generation or two.

One of the outcomes of the Famine and the practice of having large families for generations was that the Irish developed a diaspora that, in comparison to those of many other European countries, is not only larger, but has spread wider and developed deeper roots in the numerous host countries to which the Irish have dispersed. If we are going to look for indications of Irish difference, it would then be useful to examine how the state relates to the diaspora – treating its members on the one hand as disenfranchised exiles and, on the other hand, as having a duty to care for the homeland – and the problems the diaspora Irish may have balancing their commitments to home with those to their new hosts. Many members of the diaspora have strong attachments to Ireland, but they are disenfranchised by the state. The difficulties of being exiled, but still feeling more at home in Ireland, of wanting to be included in the new communities of the host nation, but feeling excluded, is exemplified by the experiences of Irish gay men in Britain. Like so many other migrants, they are marginalised at home for being gay but marginalised among the gay community in Britain for being Irish.

It is perhaps this history of emigration, this movement of people in and out of places in which they have formed deep attachments, which makes the Irish different. And yet, over the past generation, the patterns of movements of people in and out of Ireland have changed dramatically. In recent years, we have returned to being a nation of emigrants. However, during the years of the Celtic Tiger, there was a quick and large influx of migrants. Quite suddenly, more than one in ten people living in Ireland were born outside of Ireland. Irish cities and towns have become a kaleidoscope of skin colour and a cacophony of foreign sounds. However, what makes Ireland different is the peculiar ways in which the state, the nation and local communities have responded to the new Irish. So it may well be that, in the near future, what makes Ireland different will be the ways in which it has become and is still becoming a multicultural society.

Cultural identity

For many nations and ethnic groups, what binds people together is that they speak the same language. The sense of 'we-ness', of bonding and belonging, of seeing and understanding the world in the same way, comes from shared forms of linguistic expression. For many years, before and after Independence, the national project was strongly linked to reviving, maintaining and developing the Irish language. If the actual numbers who speak Irish in their everyday life is an indicator, there is plenty of evidence to suggest that the language project has failed. However, in the same way that many Catholics do not go to Mass as often as they used to, but still have an affinity with being Catholic, there is also plenty of evidence to suggest that people have a strong affinity with the Irish language. They want to keep it even though they are not willing or able to speak it.

It may well be that for generations many Irish people identified the Irish language, music and sport as an inhibitor in embracing a less insular and more urbane, cosmopolitan disposition. There was little that they saw in traditional Irish culture that appealed to them. However, for many different reasons, most notably those linked to seeking cultural identity in a sea of global consumer capitalist sameness, many cosmopolitans began to see traditional difference as a form of cultural capital that can bring them honour and respect. The history of cultural distinction, of new influences and changing styles, from both inside and outside the country, is exemplified in traditional Irish music. While we might think something is completely indigenous, it is more often a mélange of local and global music flows. It was the ways in which performers were open to outside influences, particularly how they incorporated 'foreign' instruments which flowed into Ireland, and the ways in which they combined these with local and regional styles, that became central to the distinctiveness of the music.

There are many reasons for arguing that, if there is anything in contemporary Irish culture that makes the Irish different, it is the GAA. In comparison to the numbers who speak Irish or listen to traditional music, the numbers who play, participate in and follow GAA sport have grown steadily, not just in Ireland but around the world. As a primarily local and amateur sport, the GAA has thrived in an era of globalised sport, dominated by transnational media corporations, in which leading players are paid vast salaries. The key to its success is that it is stitched into family, community and parish life. Finally, if we are to understand Irish difference, particularly in relation to emigrants and immigrants, it is important to consider the meaning of 'home' for those living here and abroad. In a highly mobile society, with increasing numbers of people coming and going, the concept of home has become more complicated and nuanced not just for emigrants and the diaspora but for outsiders who have come to live and stay in Ireland. Along with the mix of colours and languages that characterise contemporary Ireland, there is an increasing creolisation of Irish culture, with elements from other cultures being mixed with indigenous ones, and of new pairings and relationships leading to new forms of cultural hybridity in food, music, dance and other forms of popular culture. It is perhaps in this sense that Ireland is no longer that different and has become the same as the rest of the West.

Critical Irish studies

Much of this introduction has been a small taste and adaptation of the different arguments and points presented in the book. Nations may be no different from individuals. They like to think of themselves as different. Maybe they have to talk up the difference if they are to survive and thrive. But there is also a need for a cool, detached description and analysis of this difference and of its origins and significance.

Although these chapters might be categorised within the realm of Irish studies, what makes them different is that they have been written by human scientists. Irish studies is a global success. But, for various reasons, it is dominated by particular themes, theories and methods. Most contributions seem to come from within the realm of literary criticism and history. There is an absence of contributions from the fields of sociology, economics, politics, psychology and so forth. If we are to understand the nature of contemporary Irish culture and society, if we are to understand how Ireland and the Irish came to be the way they are, then there is a need to extend the issues we study and the questions we ask. We need to develop the theories we use to help frame the issues and questions. And, finally, we need to expand the methods we use to identify, describe and analyse the differences we find. It may well be that the old order of Irish studies is yielding place to a new order. If this is the case, then, hopefully this book is a catalyst for such change.

Notes

1   See Monica McGoldrick, 'Irish Families', in Monica McGoldrick, Joe Giordano and Nydia
     García-Preto (eds), *Ethnicity & Family Therapy* (New York: The Guildford Press, 2005),
     p. 595. For a more detailed discussion of these characteristics, see Geraldine Moane's
     Chapter 12 below.

2   Vincent Kenny, 'The Post-Colonial Mind', *The Crane Bag*, 9:1 (1985), pp. 70–8.

3   Richard Kearney, 'Introduction', in Richard Kearney (ed.), *The Irish Mind: Exploring Intellec-
     tual Traditions* (Dublin: Wolfhound Press, 1985), pp. 33, 7, 9.

4   Michael Hennigan, 'The Irish Mind and the Knowledge Economy: Should We Bank Every-
     thing on Fuzzy Leprechaunic Political Dreams?', *Finfacts*, 3 May 2008 (www.finfacts.ie/
     irishfinancenews/article_1012308.shtml).

5   See W. I. Thomas, *The Unadjusted Girl* (Boston: Little, Brown, and Co., 1923).

6   Kate Fox, *Watching the English: The Hidden Rules of English Behaviour* (London: Hodder,
     2004).

2

Irishness and nationalisms

Siniša Malešević

Many traditional historical and literary studies of Irish nationalism insist on its unique characteristics. Some focus on the unusual mixture of ethnic and civic ideas that have historically underpinned nationalist narratives and practices in Ireland. Others point out the uncommon tendency for Irish nationalism to incorporate both left and right of the political spectrum. Many emphasise the distinct colonial legacy, the unusual geographic position, the religious specificity, the exceptionally rich and advanced cultural heritage or the distinctive cult of violence. For example Terry Eagleton insists that 'Irish have a keener sense of their history than other nations'; that 'the Irish were the first nation to recognise the potential of the popular movement for the goal of political reform' and that Ireland is 'the first modern post-colonial society'. Nevertheless this general obsession with Irish exceptionalism is most often linked to the island's political split between the North and South. In fact an overwhelming number of studies written on Irish nationhood understand nationalism through a very narrow prism – as an aspiration to national unification.[1]

Furthermore many such analyses tend to view Irish nationalism as an ideology in decline. The argument hinges on the belief that, as the question of unification becomes less pertinent in social and political discourse, nationalism is bound to weaken. More specifically they contend that, as the world becomes ever more globalised and integrated and as the Republic and Northern Ireland experience further development, both Irish and British/Unionist nationalisms are destined to wane. Hence when comparing contemporary Ireland with its 1950s counterpart it seems straightforward to most analysts that the nationalism of the 1950s was much stronger and more widespread than that experienced today.

However, this chapter challenges both of these assumptions. Firstly, I argue that despite some superficial differences Irish nationalism is not unique. In all significant sociological respects Irish nationalism is very similar to other nationalisms in

Europe and further afield. Irish nationalist ideologies and movements have originated and developed in a similar historical period and under similar structural
conditions to other European nationalisms. Instead of approaching Irish nationalism as a distinct species, its emergence and development makes sociological sense
only when viewed as a part of the broader pan-European and ultimately world
processes.

Secondly I contest the idea that nationalism in Ireland is experiencing a gradual
decline. On the contrary this chapter makes the case that, as nationalism requires
the presence of strong organisational and ideological scaffolding and well-established cross-class ties of solidarity, the existence of strong nationalism entails
intensive social development. Hence, despite the veneer of sturdy nationalist identities, post-Independence Ireland lacked the organisational and ideological
capacity for the development of a deep society-wide nationalism. Consequently
nationalist ideology and practice has actually intensified over the last several
decades and today's nationalism is much more powerful and socially embedded
than that present in de Valéra's era.

The origins of nationalisms

We live in a world where everybody is expected to possess a distinct nationality.
Moreover there is a general perception that it is normal and natural to feel a strong
sense of attachment to one's nation. To be proud of being French, Norwegian,
Greek or Irish is usually seen as a noble virtue, while being alienated from one's
nation is likely to be understood by many as a form of moral failing. More specifically in our world it is virtually impossible to opt out from nationhood: one can
change nationalities, have multiple passports, become highly proficient in several
languages and distinct cultural practices, or convert to the religion of the majority
nation; but having no nation is simply not an available option. In the contemporary world, as Gellner put it, 'a man must have a nationality as he must have a nose
and two ears'.[2]

Furthermore we inhabit a world where nationhood is deemed to be the
principal locus of one's identity, solidarity and political legitimacy. Hence it is
widely believed today that no nation should rule or dominate another nation; that
all nations should have a state of their own; that divided members of a nation
should live under a single political roof; that each member of a particular nation
should demonstrate solidarity with their co-nationals; and that in some important
respects national allegiance should supersede most other allegiances. In this
context it seems obvious to support the idea that Palestinians, Kurds, Chechens
and other 'state-less' nations should have a sovereign state of their own, or that
'separated' nations such as the Irish, Koreans or Chinese should live in a single
nation-state.

Although individuals and organised groups might differ sharply in their views on how the rights of self-determination are to be achieved and who has historical or political entitlements to a particular territory, there is near universal agreement that all nations should be free, independent and self-governing and that shared nationhood is the principal source of a state's political legitimacy.

This contemporary tendency to see nationhood as a normal, natural and ubiquitous form of group identity and solidarity obscures the fact that for much of our history human beings were nationless as they inhabited entities that were either much smaller or much larger than nation-states: from foraging bands, chiefdoms, city-states, city leagues, composite kingdoms, confederate tribal alliances to various forms of imperial orders. More importantly the historical predecessors of nation-states had no organisational mechanisms nor did they have an ideological need to foster greater cultural or political homogeneity among the inhabitants. The premodern forms of social order either were very small, less stratified, decentralised and disorganised, such as the hunting and gathering bands, or they consisted of huge, highly hierarchical and centralised entities characterised by pronounced cultural diversity, as was the case with the empires. The inhabitants of these social orders did not and could not conceptualise the world in terms of the nationalist principles of political sovereignty, cultural homogeneity and the equal moral worth of all its members. Instead they tended either to identify with, and their rulers would justify their position in relation to, belief systems that were highly localised (i.e. totemic kinship, clan- and tribe-based solidarities) or to embrace universalist creeds (i.e. mythology, religion or a particular imperial doctrine). In other words for 99.99 per cent of our existence on this planet we have lived in entities that bear no resemblance to the nation-state, and our dominant belief systems had no room for comprehending the world in nationalist terms. Expressing a deep feeling of solidarity and attachment with someone who was not a family or clan member, a trusted neighbour, a companion aristocrat or a personally well-known fellow adherent of the same religious tradition would make no sociological sense before the age of nationalism. No premodern peasant or aristocrat would ever be willing to sacrifice their lives for such an abstract, and in their world incomprehensible, concept that is a nation. Despite latter-day nationalist historiography, neither Brian Bóruma, Turlough O'Brien or any other kings of 'Irish provinces' could possibly have envisaged Ireland as a sovereign, culturally homogenous and politically unified nation. For nationhood to become a central category of one's identity, solidarity and legitimacy it was necessary for Europe and then the rest of the world to undergo dramatic and unprecedented structural transformations.

There is neither nationhood nor nationalism without large-scale organisational changes, and these are brought about with the onset of modernity. The emergence and gradual proliferation of ideas that constitute nationalism, such as popular sovereignty, cultural authenticity, self-rule and economic independence, owe a great deal to the revolutionary upheavals. These include such gigantic social transformations as industrialisation and technological and scientific advancement, the expansion of capitalism and organisational principles of the division of labour, the centralisation of state power, the development of constitutionalism and parliamentarism, the advancement of state-wide systems of transport and communication, the establishment of state monopolies on the legitimate use of force, taxation and legislation, the standardisation of vernacular languages, the establishment of society-wide educational systems, the dramatic increase in literacy rates, the formation of a substantial degree of cultural and linguistic uniformity, the expansion of institutions of 'high culture', the standardisation of chronological measures of time and the large scale-production and consumption of mass media. These structural transformations were the product of historical contingencies, changing geopolitical environments and economic bifurcations all of which have helped generate the development and expansion of diverse ideological worldviews. The immanent success of science and technology fostered a steady decline of the theological interpretations of past, present and future whereas the rise of Enlightenment, Romanticism and other intellectual movements contributed to the growth of diverse ideological articulations of one's social reality. It is no accident that all major contemporary secular ideological discourses, from liberalism, socialism, conservatism, anarchism to nationalism, originated in the wake of the French and American revolutions. The fact that nationalism established itself as the most popular and dominant ideological discourse of the modern age had a great deal to do with its rhetoric and practice of popular rule and ability to successfully penetrate the micro-universe of family, friendship and locality by embedding these feelings of micro-solidarity into a wider nationalist narrative.[3] The key issue here is that, despite its loudly proclaimed worship of authenticity, difference and particularity, nationalism was and remains a universalist, modern, doctrine that advocates the same principles throughout the globe.

Even though all nationalist doctrines strongly insist on the unique and irreplaceable qualities of their nation, this discourse itself is a product of the almost identical structural and organisational processes that came about with the inception of modernity and affected most of the world. The nationalist call for the preservation of distinctive and unique features of one's nation is a direct offshoot of the huge structural changes which provided social conditions for the emergence of nationalist movements in Europe and the Americas. Furthermore, as Gellner shows, all nationalist creeds are rooted in a deep paradox: they claim 'to defend folk culture while in fact [they are] forging a high culture'; nationalism 'claims to protect an old folk society while in fact helping to build up an anonymous mass society [...] It preaches and defends cultural diversity, when in fact it imposes homogeneity both inside and, to a lesser extent, between political units.'[4] In other words, in an important sociological sense all nationalist movements and ideologies are alike as they all arise under similar structural conditions and they all utilise almost identical rhetoric.

How unique is Irish nationalism?

Hence when viewed from this broader historical horizon there is nothing substantially unique in Irish nationalism. Irish nationalist movements developed and spread at the same time as and often in a very similar way to their European counterparts. The first proto-nationalist ideas were articulated by the representatives of cultural elites. Henry Grattan, Wolfe Tone, Robert Emmet, Thomas Davis, Terence McManus, Daniel O'Connell and others led organisations (United Irishmen, Irish Republican Brotherhood, Young Ireland etc.) that advocated exactly the same principles as their European and American colleagues. Moreover they often imitated their rhetoric, strategies and tactics in the political activism of their day. They initiated the establishment of secret societies modelled on the Italian, French, Spanish, Portuguese and Greek examples (*Carbonari, Philiki Hetairia, Carbonária* etc). In many instances the leading cultural and later political nationalists were part of broader networks of nationalist ideologues, intellectuals, artists and activists. For example the Grimm brothers and Goethe were connected with nationalist intellectuals throughout the European continent, and these well-established networks included a number of Irish intellectuals such as the grammarian John O'Donovan who became a member of the Prussian Academy on Goethe's recommendation.[5]

The Enlightenment and Romanticism inspired movements such as Young Ireland, which were directly modelled on their European counterparts such as Mazzini's Young Italy, Young Germany, Young Switzerland and later influenced further copycats such as the Young Poland, Young Turks or Young Bosnia. The establishment of the first nationalist newspapers and periodicals, choral societies, and folklore associations has followed exactly the same pan-European processes clearly visible in Germany, France or Italy. The romanticist poetry, prose and cultural activities of W.B. Yeats, Lady Gregory and John Synge, the gothic novels of Bram Stoker and the painting of Jack Yeats and Paul Henry were an integral part of the pan-European cultural nationalist aspirations spearheaded by the early aspirations of Lord Byron and Walter Scott that celebrated the authenticity, diversity and the legitimate aspirations for independence among the small nations of Europe from the Balkans to Ireland. The mythology of Celtic Ireland, which underpins much of Irish nationalism, had direct echoes in the French nationalist myths of Gaulish and Frankish origin or the German nationalist mythology of the Teutonic knights.

From its organisational inception in the late eighteenth and early nineteenth century nationalism has always been and remains a global movement and ideology. In this case, just as in other European and American cases, the emergence and expansion of nationalism was grounded in deep structural transformations. The fact that Ireland was economically less developed than France or Germany does not suggest that Irish nationalism was profoundly different from its European counterparts. It only means that in some forms of nationalist experience Ireland lagged behind and was a late developer.

However, in other aspects Irish nationalism was at the forefront of large-scale changes. For example much of Ireland was dominated by rural dwellings and kinship-based localism well into the second half of the twentieth century and the country's overall industrial output was very slow to develop. Nevertheless the island's main cities, Belfast and Dublin, were global pioneers of industrialism and mass-production in ship building, textiles and commerce. In a similar fashion, for much of the nineteenth and early twentieth century the country lacked decent roads and reliable transport systems. And yet, at the same time, Ireland was 'one of the first European countries to rail-roadise'. The island had '65 miles of track in 1845, 1000 in 1857, 2000 in 1872 and, with 3,500 by 1914, boasted one of the densest networks in the world'.[6] The standardisation of the Irish vernacular was extremely slow and patchy, with the official codification of language being finalised only in the 1950s.[7] Nevertheless Irish society was also characterised by high literacy rates in English: in the 1850s more than half of the population were literate and by 1911 this has risen to almost 90 per cent.[8] In line with most of Western Europe, Ireland had well-developed networks of mass-communication with ever expanding news outlets. For example in 1853 there were 109 newspapers and periodicals in circulation and by 1913 this number was more than doubled (230). Some newspapers had exceptionally high circulation, with the sales of the *Irish World* in the region of 20,000 and Parnell's *United Ireland* reaching a staggering 100,000 in the 1880s. Furthermore, the key vehicle of nationalist socialisation, the educational system, was firmly established in the early nineteenth century and by 1850 included 4500 schools and over half a million pupils, with these numbers doubling by 1914.[9] All these figures indicate that the emergence and expansion of nationalism were rooted in the dramatic structural transformation and the gradual modernisation of Irish social and political space. Just as in other parts of Europe and the Americas nationalist ideology was articulated and initiated by cultural and political elites and its popular expansion remained dependent on large-scale structural transformations. In the late nineteenth century the principal bearers of the nationalist torch were the ever expanding professional middle strata (solicitors, doctors, clergy, artists and teachers) and it is only in the twentieth century that nationalism became a fully fledged ideology that motivated the action of the majority of the Irish population.

The puny leviathan

There is a pronounced tendency to associate the strength of nationalism with unbridled outbursts of animosity towards others, the loud proclamations of one's national pride and the view that any significant self-criticism of the nation is a form of moral treason. Hence the omnipotence of nationalism is regularly linked to violent activities including warfare, revolutions, genocides, terrorism or the organised intimidation of non-nationals and disloyal co-nationals. When one thinks of the contemporary manifestations of nationalism the inclination is to look at the radical movements on the far right or the far left of the political spectrum: PKK, ETA, Jobbik, Golden Dawn, Tamil Tigers or Óglaigh na hÉireann. Nevertheless one should not conflate political radicalism with strength. Although extreme political organisations can occasionally stir up collective emotions and create intensive nationalist frenzy, such heightened emotional states cannot be maintained for a long time. As Durkheim demonstrated so convincingly, collective effervescence is a highly intense but rare and temporary phenomenon that simply cannot last.[10] Nationalist euphoria generated by radical organisations is usually very visible and intensive but that in itself is not a particularly reliable indicator of its strength. On the contrary, hostile defensiveness, rampant intolerance and constant accusations are often reliable signals of one's insecurity, fragility and the lack of firm and stable foundation. It is weak not strong nationalisms that are noisy and brazen. Well established, taken for granted nationalisms do not require relentless and instant mobilisation. Thus it is the habitual, banal, practices that are much more important for the reproduction and expansion of nationalism than aggressive posturing. This habitual nationalism is much more muted, less visible and characterised by ordinary routine activities. Billig emphasised the centrality of banal practices as being vital for the everyday maintenance and strengthening of nationalism. These include mundane activities such as the routine use of the plural personal pronouns ('we', 'us') in the mass media and political speeches that simply assume one's membership in a specific nation, the consumption of nationally focused and geographically demarcated television weather reports, or the passing by of the unnoticed national flags hanging on state institutions.[11] In all of these cases banal nationalism is reproduced habitually and for the most part unconsciously, thus helping preserve the nation-centric understandings of social reality.

However such habitual reproduction entails the presence of robust organisational and ideological scaffolding. The strength of a particular nationalism is often determined by its organisational capacity, infrastructural reach and its ability to provide potent ideological glue capable of projecting, and at times forging, unity and cultural homogeneity for the entire society. In other words the persistence and growth of nationalism is heavily influenced by large-scale structural transformations. These include the ever expanding state centralisation and its capacity to permeate civil society by controlling its external borders, successfully policing its territory, taxing income at source, collecting and utilising personal data, enforcing the use of identity documentation (birth certificates, passports, driving licences etc.) and providing welfare provisions among other things.[12] These organisational advancements regularly accompany and stimulate expansion of social devices for ideology creation and dissemination: standardised educational systems with near-universal literacy, mass media, legislative structures and the rich repertoire of civil society networks. The incessant growth of these organisational and ideological powers is decisive for the continuous attempt to establish and structurally embody nationhood as the dominant category and practice of everyday life.

In this context Irish nationalism had a similar trajectory to other European nationalisms. There is a general perception that in the 1930s, 1940s and 1950s Ireland was a hotbed of rampant nationalism and that the Celtic Tiger era and its aftermath represent the time when nationalism went into a gradual but certain decline. This is not the case. On the contrary Irish nationalism is significantly more dominant and influential today than it was in the early and mid-twentieth century. De Valéra's years of rule are generally seen as being characterised by fierce national- ist indoctrination, which was bolstered with the rhetoric and practice that strongly exalted the Gaelic revival, Roman Catholicism and anti-monarchist republicanism as the bulwarks against the British legacies. Moreover for much of this period a majority of Irish political organisations and civil society groupings seemed to be united in the view that Northern Ireland should and eventually would became unified with the rest of the Republic.

There is no doubt that nationalist discourses were widespread throughout society and were institutionalised in the educational system, courts, police, military, mass media and public service among others. Mid-twentieth- century Ireland was certainly dominated by the excessive nationalist rhetoric which envisaged the entire Ireland as a cosy village community populated by the frugal people. As colourfully described in de Valéra's 1943 speech, Ireland was to become an entity 'whose countryside would be bright with cosy homesteads, whose fields and villages would be joyous with the sounds of industry, with the romping of sturdy children, the contest of athletic youths and the laughter of comely maidens, whose firesides would be forums for the wisdom of serene old age'.[13] This national- ist ideal was also codified in the 1937 Constitution that emphasised the unique character of Irishness: 'The Irish nation herby affirms its inalienable, indefeasible, and sovereign right to choose its own form of government ... and to develop its life ... in accordance with its own genius and traditions'.[14]

However, the fact that the nationalist idiom was so prevalent and occasionally expressed in aggressive outburst is not in itself a reliable indicator of its strength. In fact the loud proclamations and incessant glorification of the mythological Celtic past, the purity of Irish language and traditional practices can be equally seen as a sign of insecurity and weakness, as an attempt to rescind all the ambiguities and contradictions deeply present in the nationalist project. More importantly the post-Independence Ireland lacked organisational and infrastructural capacity to make nationalism structurally embedded in the everyday life of its population. De Valéra's state apparatus was generally weak and underdeveloped. Although the Irish state inherited a solid civil service and a stable parliamentary system, the state's ability to penetrate civil society remained feeble until the late 1970s. As Garvin demonstrates convincingly, the post-Independence Ireland 'constituted a very strong society but rather weak state'.[15] The new polity had great difficulty in establishing the monopoly on the legitimate use of violence, taxation and legislation. The educational institutions overemphasised the teaching of arts and theology over science and technology and the long-term outcome of this policy was constant shortage of technical and scientific expertise. Ireland's infrastructure was particularly weak and successive governments were ill-disposed toward developing better transport and communication networks. Moreover in the 1940s, 1950s and early 1960s there was strong opposition towards building motorways and bypasses, establishing airline systems and introducing telephones, radios and television sets since they were generally seen either as unnecessary luxury or as something that might undermine the vested interest of local businesses. For example small-town shopkeepers were crucial in preventing the building of bypasses and motorway across the country as they feared the loss of 'passing trade'.[16]

The dominance of the insular worldviews that characterised the post-Independence 'Éire' was also reflected in the general animosity towards foreign investment, secular higher education and industrialisation. The introduction of heavy-handed censorship stifled the wider proliferation of 'high culture', one of the key prerequisites for the successful nationalist project. The partial consequence of this policy was the chronic underdevelopment of cultural and artistic institutions outside of Dublin and Cork. An overwhelming majority of the population remained focused on their locality and kinship-based networks, with familialism, nepotism, clientelism and patronage networks dominating political, economic and cultural life. Even the educational system, a backbone of nationalist socialisation, remained patchy, not fully standardised, and was firmly monopolised by the Church, not the nationalising state. The two pillars of the nationalist narrative of de Valéra's era were Catholicism and Gaelicisation but, whereas the former remained split between its normative universalism and everyday parochialism, the latter was not particularly successful. Despite the symbolic significance of Catholicism for Irish nationalist narrative in the early post-Independence period 'the Church was actually rather provincial, even localist and very decentralised ... Religious orders had autonomy from Irish episcopate, holding their authority from their centres in Rome or elsewhere'.[17] Similarly the project of linguistic revival and Gaelicisation of wider cultural practices had almost the exact opposite effect of what was intended as the number of fluent speakers of the (belatedly standardised) Irish language plummeted in the new Republic. With the partial exception of the GAA, the Gaelicisation project was largely a failure. Furthermore, despite the popularly shared rhetoric of cultural nationalism, the majority of the population continued to distrust state officials and often engaged in excessive anti-state diatribes. Hence de Valera's Ireland was nominally saturated with intense nationalist chatter but this nationalism was weak. It lacked a stable, secure and developed organisational and ideological grounding.

Reproducing Irishness

In contrast to its post-Independence incarnation associated with poverty, insularity and nationalism, contemporary Ireland is often depicted as being the hub of modern global trends. These include Ireland's full integration in the European and world political structures (EU, CE, UN, WTO), its highly globalised economy that attracts the leading multinational corporations and its cultural openness to international influences in art, science, technology and education, among other things. However despite these globalising effects Irish citizens, just like the rest of Europe, remain deeply committed to ideas and practices of nationhood. As various surveys show, the populations of European states are more attached to their nations today than at any other time in history and the sense of belonging to one's nation has been increasing constantly over the past three decades. For example the longitudinal Eurobarometer survey indicates that in the period between 1983 and 2005 support for the statement that one is very proud or quite proud of being Irish has increased from 89 to 98 per cent of Republic's population.[18] Nevertheless the real strength of nationalism is better gauged by looking at the changing organisational and ideological skeleton of the nation-state.

Over the past three decades the infrastructural powers of the Irish state have increased dramatically. The development of industry, education, science and technology created conditions for the expansion of state capacity and the deeper ideological penetration of nationalist ideas and practices. The Irish nation-state is much more centralised, able to police its territory, supervise its borders, tax its citizens, implement its laws and provide controlled welfare provisions than ever before. Moreover the contemporary state apparatus can easily and quickly collect and utilise vast amounts of personal information on all of its citizens: it has highly digitalised systems of control including the ever expanding surveillance devices (CCTV cameras, alarms, computer and phone supervision), it enforces the use of identity documentation such as biometric passports, ID age cards, driving licences and welfare cards that 1950s state administrators could not even dream of. The education system with the standardised curriculum and uniform assessments (such as the Junior and Leaving certificate exams) is much more controlled now by the state than the Church. The full literacy and the large-scale presence of national mass media with all-state coverage have helped reinforce the shared perceptions of an imagined community embedded in the concept of 'deep horizontal comradeship'.[19] The dominance of high-circulation national over local and regional newspapers and the exceptionally high viewing figures of RTÉ news and information programmes indicate how embedded national understandings of everyday events have become. The expanded civil society groupings have widened the debate on key social, political, economic and cultural issues and in this process have also strengthened the nation-centric understanding of social reality in Ireland. The strength of contemporary Irish nationalism is well illustrated by its banal habituality.

Unlike the 1950s when nationalism was insecure and weakly grounded in everyday life of highly localised kinship-based solidarities, today's nationalism is well grounded and constantly reproduced in everyday practices. These include the active mass public support for Irish national teams in sporting competitions (from the Soccer World and European cups, Olympics to Six Nation Rugby), the routine and largely uncontested national commemorations (from Easter Rising events to St Patrick's Day parades), the mass manufacture and use of national symbols on clothes, jewellery or makeup in everyday life (the Irish tricolour, shamrock, Claddagh rings, Celtic crosses, harps and green jerseys), the mass glorification of Irish successes in the global music and film industry (from the Irish celebrities in Hollywood blockbusters, the international recognition of Riverdance and Irish folk music to Eurovision song contests and global fame of U2 and many other Irish pop bands and singers), the worldwide branding and recognition of Irish products (from Guinness stout and whiskey to Irish stew, potatoes or green post-boxes), the packaged cultural heritage and idealised tourist destinations (from Book of Kells, Celtic mythology to the cottage landscapes of Connemara, Cliffs of Moher and medieval castles in Bunratty and Blarney). In all these instances nation-centric images and practices are normalised, naturalised, routinized and taken for granted. Just as with other European nationalisms, Irish nationalism has gained strength by becoming habitually embedded in everyday life.

Conclusion

The general propensity of all nationalist discourses is to see their nation as unique and irreplaceable. Some nationalists explicitly insist on the inherent superiority of their nation vis-à-vis the others but in most cases such argument is made indirectly by insisting on one's distinctiveness and peculiar features. So one can often come across this type of reasoning: We might not be the wealthiest, the most powerful or the most advanced nation but we possess other special characteristics that other nations lack – glorious past, moral purity, remarkable sense of national solidarity, political maturity, exceptional heroism, extraordinary sense of social justice, unique affinity to liberty, unmatched presence of fair play and civility or the distinct ability to survive and thrive in difficult circumstances. For if this was not the case there would be no sensible social justification for the existence of separate nations and their political roofs – the nation-states.

Irish nationalism is not particularly different in this respect. Despite the perceptions of many analysts that Irish nation-formation is historically unique and that contemporary Irish nationalism stands out from its European counterparts, there is nothing substantially different in nationalist rhetoric and practice in Ireland. Irish nationalism originated, developed and expanded and continues to be reproduced in line with the same processes present in other modern societies. Furthermore, just as in the rest of the world, nationalism in Ireland is not on the wane. On the contrary as the organisational and ideological structures constantly develop they provide social and institutional mechanisms for the expansion of nationalism. The fact that much of this nationalism is muted, banal and routine has misled many to confuse invisibility with insignificance. However, nationalisms are strongest when they become inconspicuous, when nationhood is universally perceived to be normal, natural and ubiquitous. Irish nationalism is no exception.

Notes

1 Terry Eagleton, *The Truth about the Irish* (Dublin: New Island Books, 1999), pp. 99, 102, 163. For good criticisms of these traditional approaches to Irish nationalism see Richard English, *Irish Freedom: The History of Nationalism in Ireland* (London: Macmillan, 2007); Robert Foster, *Modern Ireland 1600–1972* (London: Allen Lane, 1988); and Joe Lee, *Ireland 1912–1985* (Cambridge: Cambridge University Press, 1995).

2 Ernest Gellner, *Nations and Nationalism* (Oxford: Blackwell, 1983), p. 6.

3 Siniša Malešević, *Nation-states and Nationalisms* (Cambridge: Polity, 2013), pp. 55–88.

4 Gellner, *Nations and Nationalism*, p. 124.

5 Joep Leerssen, *National Thought in Europe* (Amsterdam: Amsterdam University Press, 2008).

6 Joe Lee, *The Modernisation of Irish Society 1848–1918* (Dublin: Gill & Macmillan, 2008), p. 13.

7 Tom Garvin, *Preventing the Future* (Dublin: Gill & Macmillan, 2003), p. 88; Iarfhlaith Watson, *Broadcasting in Irish* (Dublin: Four Courts Press, 2003), p. 29.

8 Lee, *Modernisation*, p. 13.

9 Lee, *Modernisation*, pp. 13, 27, 96.

10 Émile Durkheim, *The Elementary Forms of Religious Life* (New York: Oxford University Press, 1976).

11 Michael Billig, *Banal Nationalism* (London: Sage, 1995).

12 Michael Mann, *The Sources of Social Power: Vol. 3* (Cambridge: Cambridge University Press, 2012).

13 Dermott Keogh, *Twenty Century Ireland* (Dublin: Gill and Macmillan, 1994), pp. 133–4.

14 English, *Irish Freedom*, p. 329.

15. Garvin, *Preventing the Future*, p. 83.

16. Garvin, *Preventing the Future*, p.102.

17. Garvin, *Preventing the Future*, p. 160.

18. Marco Antonsich, 'National Identities in the Age of Globalisation: The Case of Western Europe', *National Identities*, 11:3 (2009), p. 286.

19. Benedict Anderson, *Imagined Communities* (London: Verso, 1983).

3

Where is Ireland in the worlds of capitalism?

Seàn Ó Riain

Capitalism is supposed to make the societies of the world more similar. Closer economic ties bring far distant societies into contact with one another while the pressures of competition and the spread of capitalist markets appear to drive economies and societies around the world towards a single model of optimal economic organisation. However, it is also clear that different countries have vastly different economies, even among capitalist societies. There are different 'worlds of capitalism'.[1]

There are two main differences. Countries differ in terms of where they fit in a global hierarchy of the capitalist economy. Some countries are located in the 'core' of the global economy, home to the control centres of leading transnational corporations and dominating trade in high technology and other rewarding industries. Others at the margins of capitalism occupy a more 'peripheral' position, exporting raw materials to the core, or offering themselves as locations for the manufacturing operations and call centres of mobile transnational corporations. Countries are, then, located 'vertically' in relation to one another, on the basis of where they fit on the ladder of capitalist power and progress.

Countries also differ dramatically in how they organise their versions of capitalism, even though they share the common features of private property, wage labour and market exchange. Alongside these common features, however, societies can be very different in how equally the rewards of capitalist activity are distributed, in the ways their businesses and labour forces are organised, and in the social protection and social investment afforded to their populations. Countries are, then, located 'horizontally' in relation to one another, as different forms of capitalism that compete and interact on the world stage of the capitalist arena.

Where does Ireland fit in these 'vertical' and 'horizontal' spaces of capitalism? Even before Ireland experienced the boom of the Celtic Tiger in the 1990s and the bust of the financial crisis since 2008, the answer was unclear.[2] Should Ireland, with its small open economy and durable liberal economic institutions, be compared to countries such as Denmark or the Netherlands in the historical core of Europe? Or did it make more sense to locate Ireland with the Mediterranean countries in the European periphery, based on their shared experience of underdevelopment and a related reliance on agriculture and weak industrial development that depended heavily on foreign investment?

Ireland did not sit easily within either of these groups. Arguably, Ireland was economically closer to the Mediterranean economies, given its structural underde-velopment, and politically closer to the European core, given its durable liberal democratic institutions. However, even this distinction oversimplified the Irish case. Economically, Ireland certainly had major structural problems of develop-ment but combined this with a significantly higher national income than in the Mediterranean economies.[3] Politically, Ireland had durable liberal democratic institutions but also shared a populist (although not militarist) political culture, with strong elements of 'brokerage' and 'clientelism'.[4]

It appeared for some time that the Celtic Tiger years had brought Ireland into the world of small open advanced capitalist European economies. This came to a screeching halt in 2008, however, as Ireland was cast back into the company of the other European peripheral economies, collectively disparaged by some as the PIIGS (Portugal, Ireland, Italy, Greece and Spain). So where does Ireland fit in global capitalism today? How does the Irish 'world of capitalism' compare to the other types of capitalist economy that we see today? How do the relationships between these different types shape Ireland's and Europe's current crisis?

Uneven development and Ireland's place within global capitalism

Ireland is famously one of the most 'globalised' economies in the world, with high levels of investment, trade, migration and financial flows. However, it is the changing form of Ireland's relationship with the global economy – and particularly with Europe – that is the most striking aspect of its recent history.

Ireland's historical links are firmly within the Anglo-American 'Atlantic economy', with close ties to both the UK and US, rooted in colonialism and migration.[5] However, these international relationships have become more complex over time. Ireland deliberately relocated itself in the global economy as part of its strategy of economic development. While it retained close ties to the UK, the Irish state firmly repositioned itself as a 'gateway to Europe' for US corporations. Ireland became a significant hub for US investment networks from the 1970s to the 2000s. However, from the early 2000s, these international ties changed as international lenders from across the UK, US and Europe were significant in funding Ireland's credit and property bubble and drove a financialisation of Ireland's economy, where flows of money became more important than productive activity.[6]

Ireland historically engaged with the international economy through its relationship with Great Britain, both as colony and as post-colonial dependent neighbour. It is this history of colonisation that makes Ireland different both from the Continental small open economies and the Mediterranean periphery. This relationship was not completely one-sided – even today, Ireland remains the sixth largest trading partner for the UK. However, the Irish economy was closely tied to a declining hegemonic global power. Where US and UK national wealth was almost the same entering the Second World War, the US exited the war with a much higher GDP per capita, and the gap between the US and UK grew significantly over the following fifty years (see Figure 3.1). Perhaps not surprisingly then, Ireland sought to turn outwards towards the international economy more broadly.

Over time, the Irish economy became increasingly Americanised. The first significant US investment came in 1971 when Digital Equipment Corporation set up a factory in Galway. In the 1980s investment was relatively evenly balanced between US, UK and other European firms (see Figure 3.2). However, the flows of investment from the UK and Europe actually declined at the same time as the massive increase in US investment in the 1990s. This Americanisation of Irish industrial activity was rooted in long-term patterns but took a dramatic turn in the 1990s boom.

Foreign investment has certainly been a central plank of Irish economic development. While this brings investment and employment, the frailty of this model of industrial development is relatively well known – including weak local linkages between foreign and domestic firms, poor spread of foreign firms' technological know-how through the broader economy and the widespread exploitation of the

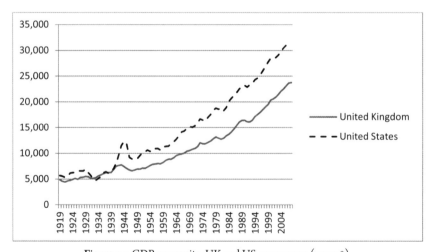

Figure 3.1 GDP per capita, UK and US 1919–2009 (1990 $)

Source: Statistics on World Population, GDP and Per Capita GDP, AD 1–2008
(Horizontal file, copyright Angus Maddison, University of Groningen)

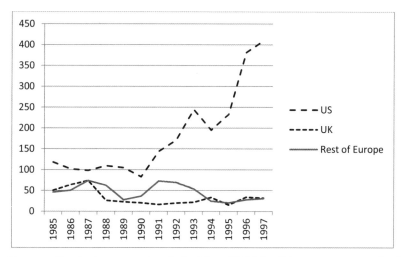

Figure 3.2 Foreign investment into Ireland from US, UK and Europe, 1985–1997 ($m)

Source: OECD Dataset on FDI Flows by Partner Country

transnational corporate structure to reduce corporations' tax payments around the world.

By far the most significant development in terms of Ireland's relationship with Europe was entry into the European Union in 1973. While ultimately loosening Ireland's ties with the UK, this initial move towards Europe was at the time heavily driven by the UK decision to join the 'Common Market'. Ireland was the first of the peripheral European countries to enter the European Union and, even among this group, Ireland was distinctive in a number of ways. The historical compromise that secured peace on the Continent after the Second World War allowed Continental European countries to co-exist for the first time without significant fear of warfare. However, Ireland was the first of the European Union members to enter the European project from outside this central European set of concerns and compromises. This in turn meant that Ireland had a different orientation to Europe, which was mediated more narrowly through a socio-economic lens.[7]

Therefore, Ireland's relationship to the global economy has shifted over time. In the words of the sociologist Joe Ruane, Ireland has shifted from being a 'simple periphery', linked directly and more or less exclusively to the UK, to a 'multiple interface periphery' located between the UK, the US and Europe.[8] While it was still in a weak position in relation to these other economies, this multiplicity of connections allowed Ireland greater opportunities to manoeuvre and reposition itself within a more diverse set of international connections. Even if each of these connections are in themselves unequal, there are strategic possibilities within international connections that states and other economic actors can use to promote various forms of economic development.

However, these multiple connections proved disastrous as Ireland's relationship with Europe changed significantly once again in the 2000s. The bubble in property and finance in Ireland was primarily funded through UK, US and European lenders. While in 2003 20 per cent of Irish banks' net liabilities were owed to international lenders, this rose to almost 80 per cent by early 2008.[9] The Irish financial crisis was intertwined with the international 'financialisation' of the global economy, as financial trading became more important and weakened investment in productive activities.[10] Ireland's bet on locating itself as a hub for the US, UK and European economics within the global economy backfired in the 2000s as Ireland became one of the places where the international financial bubble was most dramatically inflated. Ireland's 'gateway to Europe' strategy was a strategic multi-polar orientation to the world economy – but one that could promote both boom and bust.

Diverse social contracts and the 'Irish model'

However, Ireland's place within capitalism is defined not only by its relations with the centres of the global economy but also by the broader and deeper structures of its political economy and, in particular, the social contract in the society as a whole. Even within Europe, there are clear differences between the various 'worlds of capitalism'.[11] These worlds include (1) the Nordic social democracies, with high levels of equality, social spending and business competitiveness, (2) the liberal economies of Ireland and the UK which rely more heavily on markets to co-ordinate their economies, (3) the Christian democratic economies of Germany, Austria, Belgium and others which combine a concern for equality and solidarity with a strong emphasis on the family and the power of the state, and (4) the Mediterranean world of capitalism which also emphasises family-based social structures and the public sector, but from a position of weak economic development.

Table 3.1 shows a number of different elements of such social contracts in European societies.[12] These include the contribution of business to the productive economy through investment in R&D and other forms of industrial upgrading. Social spending is included as an indicator of social protection and social investment, while public deficits and fiscal balances are included as a summary measure of the balancing of this social spending with available resources. The final element is the form of organisation of labour in the workplace, as measured by the participation of workers in 'learning' organisations.

Table 3.1 shows that there are significant differences in the underlying social contracts across the various worlds of capitalism in Europe. Social spending is not surprisingly higher in the Christian democratic and social democratic countries but so too is business investment, with business R&D investment running well above the liberal and especially Mediterranean countries right across the period.

Table 3.1 Social contracts in Europe: welfare, production and macroeconomic regimes

	Average Fiscal balance, 1999–2007 (% GDP)	*Average business R&D investment, 1999–2007 (% GDP)*	*Social spending, 2002 (% GDP)*	*Percentage of all workers in 'Learning' Work Systems, 2000*
Christian Democratic				
Austria	−1.8	1.63	34.5	47.5
Belgium	−0.5	1.35	30.4	38.9
Germany	−2.2	1.74	33.4	44.3
France	−2.7	1.35	36.7	38.0
Netherlands	−0.5	1.02	27.4	64.0
Social Democratic				
Denmark	2.4	1.67	38.6	60.0
Finland	3.8	2.39	33.3	47.8
Norway	12.6	0.89	32.4	–
Sweden	1.3	2.73	38.0	52.6
Liberal				
Ireland	1.6	0.80	27.0	24.0
UK	−1.4	1.13	27.9	34.8
Mediterranean				
Greece	−5.3	0.18	–	18.7
Spain	0.2	0.56	23.7	20.1
Italy	−2.9	0.54	28.8	30.0
Portugal	−3.6	0.30	27.3	26.1

Source: Eurostat; Holm et al. (2010) (see note 13)

Furthermore the organisation of society and economy in the workplace is structured differently. Drawing on work by Holm and his colleagues, the final column shows the percentage of workers in each country who work in a 'learning' system of work, which emphasises, among other features, worker skills and learning, autonomous decision making and theme work.[13] Learning systems of work are much more prevalent in Christian democratic and social democratic economies – even more than in the apparently innovative liberal economies of the UK and particularly Ireland. Indeed, liberal economies tend to emphasise 'lean' systems of work organisation, emphasising worker input and team work but within a framework of managerial control and hierarchy. Ironically, the market-based economies appear to rely more heavily on hierarchy and managerial power.

The Nordic economies do best in terms of 'fiscal discipline', running a budget surplus. While running deficits a little larger than the social democracies, Europe's

Christian democracies also comfortably balance their books. The liberal economies of Ireland and the UK appear to do better, on the basis of their actual balance, but this masked a significant bubble as their large underlying deficits became obvious in the economic crisis that followed. The Mediterranean economies also had significant difficulties with budget deficits, which were already present in the early 2000s.

The countries with the strongest external economic performance and the greatest fiscal discipline are also those countries with the greatest social spending and business investment, and the strongest emphasis on worker input and participation in the workplace. Fiscal discipline and external competitiveness are not rooted simply in national characteristics or a continental European conservatism to be contrasted with indiscipline and recklessness in the periphery. Instead, they are rooted in the institutional features of the classic European developmental model and, even more significantly, in an underlying social contract that trades off fiscal discipline against high levels of social spending and protection and that uses both of these to underpin a dynamic and inclusive business sector.

The end of difference?

It is also telling that these differences between social contracts in different countries persisted even after decades of globalisation, European integration and market liberalisation. These trends were expected to produce a 'convergence' on the liberal market model of capitalism. Indeed a process of institutional convergence was promoted throughout the 1990s within the European Union, largely through the semi-formal 'open method of co-ordination'. However, these institutional convergences took place in a number of different areas, and to some extent moved in different directions.[14]

Most obvious is the promotion of market mechanisms through deregulation of product and labour markets. Figures 3.3 and 3.4 examine trends in such market-led processes of deregulation. Figure 3.3 refers to the degree of protection in employment afforded to employees across the different worlds of European capitalist economies. There are significant differences between the different types, with the liberal economies of the UK and Ireland having by far the lowest levels of employment protection. Christian democratic and social democratic countries of the classic European model have substantial levels of employment protection, and the highest levels of employment protection are found in the Mediterranean political economies. The 1990s through to the early 2000s was a period of significant liberalisation and deregulation of employment protection, with declining employment protection in social democracies and Christian democracies and, particularly, among Mediterranean countries. Figure 3.5 shows similar patterns of difference among countries in the degree of product market regulation within those countries. Nonetheless, it is also clear that there is a strong trend across all clusters

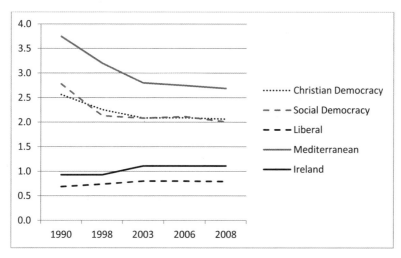

Figure 3.3 Employment protection index in European worlds of capitalism, 1990–2008 (index score)

Source: OECD

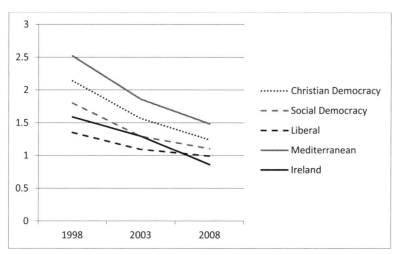

Figure 3.4 Product market regulation in European worlds of capitalism, 1998–2008 (index score)

Source: OECD

of countries towards less regulation of product markets. There is convergence on a liberal model of employment and product market regulation while significant differences between different clusters of countries and types of capitalism remain.

However, not all convergence is towards the liberal model of capitalism. A distinctively European institution – or one that has been most fully developed in

Europe – is corporatist wage bargaining where unions and employers agree wage levels and other employment-related issues for the whole economy through a central agreement, or negotiate such deals for a whole industry and not just on a firm-by-firm basis. Figure 3.5 shows there was a mild increase in wage co-ordination among European economies through the 1990s and into the 2000s. In particular Mediterranean countries and Ireland showed a much stronger trend towards centralised wage bargaining while Christian democratic and social democratic countries remained stable. The peripheral economies developed a series of 'social pacts' in the process moving closer to the institutions of the Nordic social democratic world of capitalism.[15]

Finally, the 1990s was an era when political economies around the world gave their central banks significantly greater independence from governments.[16] Central bank independence provides 'discipline' by creating an institution that is (typically) legally independent and committed to various elements of financial and fiscal discipline – including reducing inflation and maintaining the government financial balance close to surplus. Figure 3.6 shows that during the 1990s there were dramatic trends towards promotion of central bank independence. This was true across all of the worlds of capitalism. However, the greatest increases were not in liberal countries but in the Mediterranean and Irish cases, and to a slightly lesser extent the Christian democracies. Furthermore this is convergence not on a liberal model, as central bank independence is much lower in both the liberal and social democratic countries, but rather on a Christian democratic model which had by far the highest level of central bank independence in 1990 and which is now

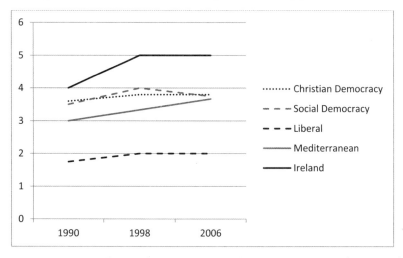

Figure 3.5 Wage co-ordination in European worlds of capitalism, 1990–2006 (index score)

Source: J. Visser *ICTWSS: Database on Institutional Characteristics of Trade Unions, Wage Setting, State Intervention and Social Pacts in 34 countries between1960 and 2010* (Amsterdam: Amsterdam Institute for Advanced Labour Studies, University of Amsterdam, 2011)

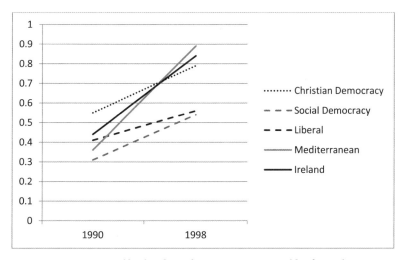

Figure 3.6 Central bank independence in European worlds of capitalism, 1990–1998 (index score)

Source: S. Polillo and M.F. Guillén "Globalization Pressures and the State: The Worldwide Spread of Central Bank Independence" *American Journal of Sociology,* 110:6 (2005), 1764–1802

clustered in a group with Ireland and the Mediterranean economies. The dramatic role of the European Central Bank in managing the affairs of national economies within Europe since the crisis is a further indication of the importance of this trend.

Formal institutional convergence therefore is a mixed story. Weakened regulation of product markets and employment brought European countries closer to the liberal world of capitalism. However, the increased independence of central banks promoted a typically Christian democratic feature of capitalism, and increasing wage co-ordination in the European periphery in the 1990s mimicked a historically strong element of social democracies. Nonetheless, significant differences between worlds of capitalism persisted, as shown in our analysis above of the social contracts of the different European countries. The Mediterranean and Irish economies sought hasty institutional convergence with the 'European model' of institutional management of the economy, arguably without the supporting institutional and normative foundations that were present in the countries where they had been longer established.

Ireland's incomplete Europeanisation and its disastrous consequences

The postwar history of Europe was centred on the creation of institutions, coalitions and contracts that could manage both the economic relations and social structural changes associated with capitalist development in Europe – and deliver

a deep process of national economic development.[17] Ireland and the other peripheral countries only partially succeeded (at best) in undertaking this task, even as
the income gap between them and the core European economies closed. This
incomplete Europeanisation became a significant problem during the Eurozone
crisis of 2008 and after.

In Europe in the 2000s, as in the US, financialisation depoliticised growth and
distribution and allowed these cracks in the European economy to be papered over
– even as it drove a further wedge between core and periphery in Europe.[18]
However, the politics of capitalisms within Europe has re-emerged with a
vengeance after the crisis. The challenges of dealing with the European crisis since
2008 have not simply involved national interests of elites or the level of attachment
of individuals to the European project – but have been heavily shaped by different
expectations in European countries of what is fair, rational and reasonable to
expect of other European nations and citizens. This has been a clash not only of
social classes and of national interests but also of long-established social contracts.

Within this unstable Europe which became the centre of the global crisis of
capitalism, the weakest point was the periphery of the Mediterranean economies
and Ireland. These countries sat in a difficult position. The development of the
welfare state, and even the administrative state, was at a much lower level than in
the continental economies whose policies and institutions were now spreading
into the periphery. They found themselves within the Euro but with only new institutions and weak social contracts to manage risks and sustain them through crises.
This was a difficult politics. However, it is also a common one that will characterise
most if not all new entrants into the EU (and potentially other regional economic
blocs). Ireland is perhaps the paradigmatic case for examining the dilemmas of
such situations as its liberal institutions were long established, and its economic
and institutional transformation went further and deeper in most respects than in
the Mediterranean economies. These were enormous strains for any European
country to face, especially those in the periphery.

Each world of capitalism in Europe relies on a different system for managing
risks. In social democratic countries the risk is internalised within the society itself
through high levels of taxation and spending, linked to strong underlying fiscal
discipline. The society insulates itself relatively effectively from the vagaries of
capitalist business cycle and crises. However, in liberal economies risk is exter-
nalised as the society tends to follow the ups and downs of the business cycle, and
indeed of boom and crisis, relying on external adjustments to escape from crisis.
These external adjustments include measures such as currency devaluation and
international borrowing to fund domestic counter cyclical measures. We can trace
many of the deepest difficulties that Europe and Ireland face in escaping the crisis
to the difficult interactions between worlds of capitalism within Europe. In particular, it can be traced to the absence of a new social contract that can combine
competing notions of risk and underpin both discipline and development.

Ireland's recovery from the economic crisis will bring it face to face once again with the question of where it will be located within the worlds of capitalism. But this is a question that is echoed in the debate around Europe as a whole. In order to protect liberal values in the broadest sense in Europe, European economies and societies will need to rediscover their own distinctive 'non-liberal' policies, institutions and social contracts.

Notes

1   Gøsta Esping-Andersen, *The Three Worlds of Welfare Capitalism* (Cambridge: Polity Press, 1990).

2   Michel Peillon, 'Placing Ireland in a Comparative Perspective', *Economic and Social Review*, 25:2 (1994), pp. 179–95.

3   Peillon, 'Placing Ireland in a Comparative Perspective'.

4   Lee Komito, 'Brokerage or Friendship? Politics and Networks in Ireland', *Economic and Social Review*, 23:2 (1992), pp. 129–42.

5   Denis O'Hearn, *The Atlantic Economy: Britain, the US and Ireland* (Manchester: Manchester University Press, 2001).

6   Seán Ó Riain, *The Rise and Fall of Ireland's Celtic Tiger: Liberalism, Boom and Bust* (Cambridge: Cambridge University Press, forthcoming 2014).

7   John O'Brennan, 'Ireland Says No Again: The 12 June 2008 Referendum on the Lisbon Treaty', *Parliamentary Affairs*, 62:2 (2009), pp. 258–77.

8   Joe Ruane, 'Ireland's Multiple Interface-periphery Development Model: Achievements and Limits', in Michael Bøss (ed.), *The Nation-state in Transformation: The Governance, Growth and Cohesion of Small States under Globalisation* (Aarhus: Aarhus University Press, 2010), pp. 213–32.

9   Phillip Lane, 'The Irish Crisis', *IIIS Discussion Paper No. 356* (Dublin: IIIS, TCD, 2011).

10 Greta Krippner, *Capitalizing on Crisis* (Cambridge, MA: Harvard University Press, 2011); Giovanni Arrighi and Beverley Silver, *Chaos and Governance in the World-system* (Minneapolis: University of Minnesota Press, 2000).

11 Esping-Andersen, *The Three Worlds of Welfare Capitalism*.

12. Ó Riain, *The Rise and Fall of Ireland's Celtic Tiger*.

13 Jacob Holm, Edward Lorenz, Bengt-ke Lundvall and Antione Valeyre, 'Organisational Learning and Systems of Labor Market Regulation in Europe', *Industrial and Corporate Change*, 19:4 (2010), pp. 1141–73.

14 Ó Riain, *The Rise and Fall of Ireland's Celtic Tiger*.

15 Aidan Regan, 'The Political Economy of Social Pacts in the EMU: Irish Liberal Market Corporatism in Crisis', *New Political Economy*, 17:4 (2012), pp. 465–91; Sabina Avdagic, Martin Rhodes and Jelle Visser (eds), *Social Pacts in Europe: Emergence, Evolution, and Institutionalization* (Oxford: Oxford University Press, 2011); Jelle Visser, *ICTWSS: Database on Institutional Characteristics of Trade Unions, Wage Setting, State Intervention and Social Pacts in 34 countries between 1960 and 2010* (Amsterdam: Amsterdam Institute for Advanced Labour Studies, University of Amsterdam, 2011).

16 Polillo and Guillén, 'Globalization Pressures and the State'.

17 Dieter Senghaas, *The European Experience: A Historical Critique of Development Theory* (Dover, NH: Berg, 1985).

18 Krippner, *Capitalizing on Crisis*.

4

Just another bubble economy?

Denis O'Hearn

Q: What is the difference between Iceland and Ireland?
A: One letter and six months.

That joke looked remarkably accurate after the Celtic 'Tiger' turned into a 'pig' (or PIIG) overnight at the end of 2008.[1] The immediate story, as in many other parts of the world after the bankruptcy of Lehmann Brothers in the United States, was a massive banking crisis and a state bailout that would prove untenable within months. Irish gross domestic product (GDP) plummeted and unemployment rates rose rapidly. By the end of 2010, a chastened Irish state signed up for its own humiliating bailout with the EU and the International Monetary Fund in order to pay for its desperate effort to keep its banks afloat. For the foreseeable future, the Irish state will pay off a multi-billion Euro loan at punitive interest rates. After all the hullaballoo of the Celtic Tiger in the 1990s about how great the Irish were, did Ireland turn out to be just another bubble economy?

The same economic pundits who got it wrong about the sustainability of the Irish growth model lined up to tell readers and television watchers why the economy suffered this massive reversal. Leading Irish economists like Morgan Kelly at University College Dublin and Patrick Honohan at Trinity College called it a 'credit bubble' or a 'banking crisis'.[2] They were as wrong about the decline as they were about the miracle. For some, their explanations were determined by their ideological predilections as neoclassical economists (or its various neoliberal versions that emerged with the so-called Washington consensus). Other commentators and experts recognised only the proximate, surface causes of the Irish collapse but were either unable or unwilling to consider deeper causes because they still believed in the Celtic Tiger. Ireland, they indicated, was just another bubble economy in a world of financial bubbles. If Ireland could only sort out the problems of corrupt banking and mismanagement that occurred during five years leading up to the crisis, its economy could get back on track. They were right – only *partly* – because Ireland did go through a rather typical economic bubble in many respects. But in other ways, they got it all fundamentally wrong because they lacked understanding of what really caused the bubble in the first place.

In truth, the Celtic Tiger was doomed from the start because of its extreme dependence on a limited group of foreign corporate investors and its membership of a regional EU federation that removed many of the state's most important economic instruments. In fact, Ireland was in terrible trouble from 2001 onwards, at least seven years before the pundits realised there was anything wrong. This is because the source of its growth – foreign direct investment – was drying up. The same mechanisms that created Irish economic growth in the 1990s also limited its longer-term stability, as the world economy went through economic cycles including periodic economic crises where there was insufficient demand for corporate output of the kind that had concentrated in Ireland.

Concurrently, the class alliances that benefited from growth – banks, financial institutions, the building sectors – required the state to underwrite growth by transferring income and wealth towards those who would reinvest rather than consume it. This starved the country of the resources that could have tied growth to social welfare, leaving the poorer sections of society even more vulnerable when the inevitable crash finally arrived. If the Irish bubble burst in 2008, it was because of extreme measures taken to reflate it after it began to deflate in the early 2000s.

Bubble economies: a potted history

What is a *bubble economy*? The term, which has a long history, is used because it refers to economies that, for one reason or another, expand too rapidly and then 'pop', causing an equal or even more rapid decline. In general, the 'pop' is associated with the unsustainable nature or patterns of expansion. Like a bubble, the economy has no firm basis and as it expands too far and too fast it eventually is unable to contain its internal elements. Thus, there are two essential aspects to a bubble: its lack of a credible infrastructure of growth and the explosive nature of its decline.

Mainstream economists define *economic bubbles* – whether speculative bubbles, market bubbles, price bubbles, financial bubbles – as 'trade in high volumes at prices that are considerably at variance with intrinsic values'.[3] Obviously, trading at such inflated prices could result from a variety of human factors including greed, unrealistic expectations of future prices or values, or even 'manias' or 'fads'. Demand may also be manufactured by misleading information or even outright lies. Corporate or business actors often put pressure on states to regulate, deregulate, or reregulate their activities in ways that enable them to manipulate markets and prices. Well-known historical examples of bubbles include the 'Tulip mania' of 1637, where tulip bulbs sold at wildly overvalued prices, and the 'South Sea bubble' of 1711–1720, where share prices of the British South Sea Company skyrocketed even though the company never made a significant profit. In our time, we have seen the 'dot.com bubble' (1997–2000), where share prices for internet companies were vastly overvalued, and, most recently, the so-called housing or sub-prime mortgage bubble that burst in 2008, causing a recession that continued for years.[4]

Beyond this usual economic survey of bubbles, there are others that are related to uneven global development and to the nature of transnational corporate investments but which are largely ignored by mainstream economists because they happen on the peripheries of world capitalism. Thus, 'dependency bubbles' may occur from the desire of transnational corporate investors to locate in places that promise the highest profitability as a result of cheap labour, government subsidies, tax havens and so forth. From the 1960s to the 1980s there appeared to be a sort of game of 'musical chairs' in this regard, wherein countries of the Third World competed vigorously for foreign investments and transnational corporations (TNCs), lacking rootedness in local places, invested and disinvested with little regard for local consequences. During this time, using Ireland as a case study, I suggested that one should distinguish between the flow-effects and stock-effects of transnational corporate investments: investment flows undeniably cause economic growth but they could also create structural economic changes (reflected in direct investment stocks) that have long-term drag effects on an economy. Indeed, such 'stock effects' could even lead to a bubble-like recession if companies disinvest without dynamic indigenous sectors that can take up the slack.[5] In another pattern, mining economies are often associated with booms from temporary construction around the establishment of a mine but once this initial phase ends the region could rapidly slump into slow or negative growth as most mining profits flow abroad and hundreds or thousands of construction workers are stranded without any prospect of employment or even the means to move out of the now-depressed area. Thus, the idea that there is a single kind of 'bubble economy' is out of the question and even within a single global recession one could expect a variety of different patterns of expansion, causes of burst and social consequences of economic decline.[6]

The recent 'sub-prime mortgage bubble' burst at different times and in different ways and patterns, depending on how a given country and certain of its economic sectors were integrated into the global economy. There was definitely a global pattern in this as in many previous bubbles. The 'bursting' of the bubble (which happened in 2008) was not a singular event but rather was the result of previous responses to previous crises. The eminent geographer David Harvey tells a compelling story about how easy credit, in the form of mortgages and credit card debt, was introduced to 'fix' a crisis in the early 2000s, which was caused by inadequate global demand for products like computers and drugs, as well as cars and electronic gadgets. According to Harvey, after a few decades of increasing inequality and falling real incomes – due to policies introduced by Thatcher and Reagan and extended by Blair, Clinton and two Bushes – there was simply inadequate money in consumers' hands to buy all the stuff that the world's corporations were producing. The extension of easy credit postponed the demand crisis of the early 2000s, yet it created a real credit bubble and conditions for a far worse crisis when the bubble burst after 2008.[8] Capitalism is like a balloon with a slow leak. Accumulation takes place in breaths, with contractions between breaths as some air escapes. Yet if businesses and policy makers blow too hard and in the wrong places to 'fix' the escape of air between breaths, the balloon may not hold.

The Irish bubble: from Tiger to PIIG

After it was named the 'Celtic Tiger' in 1994, the southern Irish economy became the global archetype of success in terms of economic growth. In a few short years, after decades cycling around two-thirds of average EU per capita income, the Republic of Ireland surpassed the EU average and eventually became, in terms of GDP per capita, the 'second richest' country in the EU. Such sharp growth success drew attention: many countries began to ask whether the 'Irish model' was a recipe for success. Irish policy makers, basking in glory after many humiliating years as the 'poor man' of Europe, answered 'yes' or, at least, 'possibly'.

In the midst of this celebration, a bare few experts – apart from myself, they included Ronnie Munck, Douglas Hamilton, Peadar Kirby, Terence McDonough and Kieran Allen – argued that the Celtic Tiger was not a model for poor countries because Irish growth was unsustainable and partly illusory, and had emerged from a strategy that caused rapidly rising inequality and failed to meet the education and healthcare needs of the Irish people. Moreover, calling Ireland a 'model' was absurd: Irish growth was based on attracting 40 per cent of high-tech foreign direct investment (FDI) into the EU, with one per cent of EU population. The UK also received another 40 per cent. As every schoolchild knows, there is only 100 per cent!

Nonetheless, many people continued to speak of the Irish model as if it could be copied and adapted. Some argued that, rather than FDI, Irish growth was primarily the result of fiscal conservatism and deregulation. After all, the Irish government had begun tackling its extreme debt problem in 1987 by drastically reducing government spending, in order to keep an investment-friendly low-tax regime. This in part opened the way for historically high flows of high-tech FDI, as US companies like Intel and Dell emerged out of the restructuring of the 1980s in an agglomerated pattern of investments that brought all major producers in computers and pharmaceuticals to Dublin and Cork. This inward flow spurred economic growth rates of about ten per cent between 1994 and 2000, which subsequently moderated and then fell (Figure 4.1).

Economic disaster hit Ireland in 2008 as quickly as success. Yet everyone should have seen it coming. FDI began falling at the turn of the century and the stock of

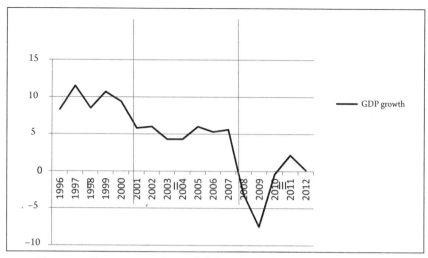

Figure 4.1 Economic growth rates (%) during and after Celtic Tiger, 1996–2012
Source: Irish Central Statistics Office

FDI fell from 130 per cent of GDP in 2001 to 67 per cent by 2006. Most Irish economists, however, preferred to see this as a sign of 'economic maturity': economic
growth continued at a respectable pace as the motor of growth shifted from foreign
industry to construction (Figure 4.2). Surely, it was said, the Irish economy, always
in danger of overheating during the Celtic Tiger period, was in for a soft landing.
Economists and policy makers breathed a sigh of relief. Few considered whether
the construction sector was sustainable. Money that had been accumulated during
the years of the Celtic Tiger, partly as the result of the government's policy of
favouring large tax cuts for the wealthy rather than provision of social services,
sought an outlet for profitable investment and found one for a few years in
construction.

  As anyone who read the 2003 IMF report could have predicted, this could not
last. The economy took a spectacular nosedive in 2008 and real GDP fell for three
straight years. Consequently, unemployment rates rose to 13 per cent in 2010 then
even further to a high of 15 per cent in 2012. Seen in retrospect, the Celtic Tiger
period and its aftermath can be seen as three distinct stages (Figure 4.1): a period
of rapid economic growth driven by transnational corporate investments mainly in
computers and pharmaceuticals (1994–2001), a period of moderate but false
growth based on housing speculation and construction (2001–8), and an intense
crisis when there was no basis for growth (2008 to present). The shifting source of
growth is seen most clearly in Figure 4.2, which compares rates of growth in
industry and construction, the former dominating until 2002 and the latter thereafter.

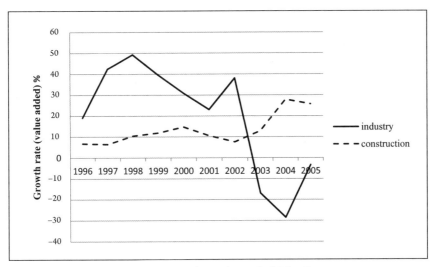

Figure 4.2 Sectoral growth at end of Celtic Tiger

Source: Irish Central Statistics Office

Debt and crisis

What is the connection between debt and growth? The discussion in Ireland always focused on government debt and on the advice of economists that government must reduce its debt as it opened up its economy to foreign direct investments. Unfortunately, this has been the basis of the EU's austerity answer to crisis, which made its depression far worse and longer even than that of the United States, although much of its severity has been hidden by the concentration of the worst crises in the EU periphery and the usual habit of blaming the victims for their failures rather than analysing national economic disaster within the framework of regional economic crisis.

With respect to Ireland, remarkably, few commentators or economists considered that an unregulated private sector with excess wealth could cause severe crisis if it was allowed access to easy credit to construct buildings that no one could rent or buy at such inflated prices. Or, speculators could create the same outcome by buying up existing properties, thus driving prices and rents even higher through their activities. While the recent plunge in Irish economic fortunes shows how vulnerable a neoliberal economy is to changes of global investment flows, it also shows that unregulated business behaviour can be a great source of economic instability during a time when a government clings to fiscal conservatism.

The Celtic Tiger years, however, added a new element to this mix: rapidly rising inequality. As the economy grew after 1994, the government enjoyed rising revenues and budget surpluses despite its low tax rates. It faced a choice of spending its surplus on social programmes, particularly in health and (especially primary) education, which were among the worst provided in Europe, or reducing taxes. It chose the latter and did so in a manner that favoured the wealthy so much that inequality rose rapidly. After 2000, new wealth sought investment outlets and, when other sources of profitable investment dried up, more and more of it went into construction and property speculation, creating a huge bubble.

The astonishing rise of private debt after 2000 is shown in Figure 4.3. Construction-based lending (by property developers, real estate speculators and household mortgage holders) rose rapidly after 2002 and drove a private debt bubble. It has since been revealed that, while driven by the Irish government's extreme promotion of inequality, the debt bubble was lubricated by deregulation of banking, which encouraged easy and, in many cases, corrupt lending practices.

Although the press tends to associate this trend with a rise in private mortgages, which was indeed a major cause of the crisis in the United States, Figure 4.4 shows clearly that the main drivers of private debt in Ireland were developers and speculators, with business lending in construction and real estate rising 800 per cent between 2000 and 2007. By contrast, mortgage lending rose less than half as quickly and GDP rose by only 80 per cent in current prices.

The resulting crisis was inevitable. Property values fell in 2007 as the interbank market froze up and the Irish banking system went into crisis. One major Irish bank was nationalised and two were bailed out. Regulators and bankers were forced to resign. A 'golden circle' of ten super-wealthy property developers who received 'secret loans' finally came to public light although the regulator apparently had known about them for some years. Construction, now the main source of Irish growth, came to a virtual halt. Seventy-five thousand new houses per year were

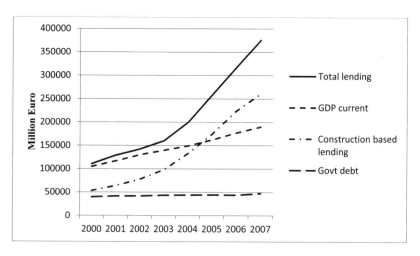

Figure 4.3 Construction-based private debt drives the Irish debt crisis

Source: Irish Central Statistics Office

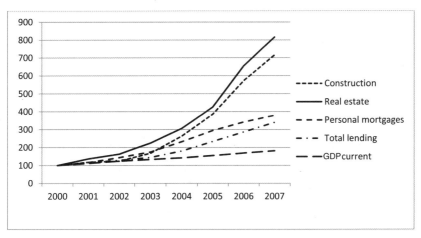

Figure 4.4 Index of private Irish debt (2000=100)
Source: Irish Central Statistics Office

built during the boom, rising to more than 90,000 in 2007 but falling to 52,000 in 2008, 18,000 in 2009 and 12,000 in 2010. Ireland was the first state in the EU to enter recession, and with the possible exception of Greece its recession has been deepest.

Conclusion

Yes, Ireland is another bubble economy. But, no, it is not *just* another bubble economy. Ireland's bubble has its own specificities, as did its expansion during the 1990s. The two were connected.

The Irish growth model was both unsustainable and unique. It created a toxic mix of dependence on FDI and rapidly rising inequality, while failing to provide for basic social welfare. In times of rapid growth, Irish governments moderated their spending so that they would not 'overheat' the economy. In time of less rapid growth or stagnation, they moderated spending because they 'could not afford' to spend. They paid attention to popular demands for health and education only when the public loudly demanded it. Then, after a short time, it was back to the status quo ante.

Now it is too late. The wealth created under the Celtic Tiger was squandered. Private indebtedness grew and now, despite its spendthrift, the Irish state has gone deep into debt after spending on bank bailouts and such. Ireland faces two debt burdens. First, its citizens and businesses, after overpaying for property, carry a huge amount of private debt. Wealth-leveraged private indebtedness reached about 250 per cent of GNP in 2008 (€400 billion). Then, public debt soared, requiring more taxation, more foreign borrowing and, ultimately, much lower

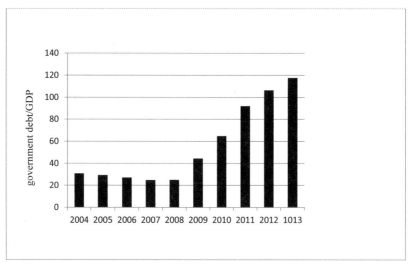

Figure 4.5 Irish government debt as % of GDP

Source: Eurostat

living standards for citizens. As of 2010, Ireland held the highest external debt among major countries of the world, in terms of external debt per capita ($515,671) and as a proportion of GDP (1224 per cent). The next most indebted country, the Netherlands, was only half as indebted per capita and one-fourth as indebted compared to GDP.[8] Second, public debt spiraled from 25 to 117.6 per cent of GDP between 2008 and 2013 (Figure 4.5).

Ireland is now in a 'classic debt deflation trap'. At the end of 2009, the average Irish household held negative equity of €43,000 and, although house prices dropped by more than a quarter since peaking in late 2006, they were still more than seven times the average income.[9] Meanwhile, interbank lending rates have risen substantially.

The proximate and widely publicised cause of Ireland's crisis is its unsustainable private and public debt (although public debt is in large part the result of Irish state pandering to debts of the wealthy and the banks). Yet the real cause is a foreign-investment-dependent growth model that has prevailed since the country was wrenched out of its inward-oriented import-substitution industrialisation regime after the Second World War. This put Ireland at the mercy of transnational corporate interests so that it might lead global growth rates during boom periods but fell into even deeper than average crisis during contractions. As David Harvey argues, crisis requires a fix. After 2000, the fix was provided by debt, which enabled regimes to pretend that they were not in crisis for nearly a decade, even though their growth rates were connected to speculation rather than real production.[10] The fix was obviously untenable, although political regimes and financial interests obviously found it useful to pretend that everything was 'business as usual'. That this pretence lasted for so long is the reason that the eventual collapse was so quick and deep. And, as severe as the crisis was in the core economies of North America and Europe, it was far worse in small dependent economies such as Ireland's.

Meanwhile, Ireland missed its chance to create a more just society while it had the wealth to attempt to do so. Perhaps the main lesson of the Celtic Tiger for other countries including the accession countries of the EU is that equality *within* countries is as important as, or even more important than, equality among countries. The chase after economic growth at any price can be deadly.

Notes

1 PIGS or PIIGS is a pejorative term for European economies in crisis including Portugal, Ireland, Italy, Greece and Spain.

2. Morgan Kelly, 'The Irish Credit Bubble', *UCD Centre for Economic Research Working Paper no. 09/32* (2009); Patrick Honohan, 'Resolving Ireland's Banking Crisis', *Economic and Social Review*, 40: 2 (2009), pp. 207–31.

3 Ronald R. King, Vernon Smith, Arlington Williams and Mark van Brening, 'The Robustness of Bubbles and Crashes in Experimental Markets', in Richard H. Day and Ping Chen (eds), *Nonlinear Dynamics and Evolutionary Economics* (New York: Oxford University Press, 1993), pp. 183–200.

4 For a list of bubbles in Britain and the United States during the nineteenth and twentieth centuries, see: International Monetary Fund, 'World Economic Outlook: Growth and Institutions', in *World Economic and Financial Surveys* (Washington, DC, April 2003), p. 65.

5 Denis O'Hearn, 'The Irish Case of Dependency: An Exception to the Exceptions?', *American Sociological Review*, 54:4 (August 1989), pp. 578–96.

6 An influential work on the footloose nature of Transnational Corporations in general was Richard J. Barnet and Ronald E. Muller, *Global Reach: The Power of Multinational Corporations* (New York: Simon and Schuster, 1974). I outlined my analysis of Ireland in O'Hearn, 'The Irish Case of Dependency'. And an important example of the literature on how mining caused underdevelopment in the Amazon is Stephen G. Bunker, *Underdeveloping the Amazon* (Chicago: University of Chicago Press, 1990).

7 See David Harvey, *The Enigma of Capital* (Oxford: Oxford University Press, 2010). Harvey's analysis is confirmed by an IMF report written in 2003 which refers to an 'equity price bust' where 'output and investment growth have fallen more than usual' (something that without doubt affected Ireland disproportionately). Crucially, the report noted that the equity price bust had been superseded by a rapid rise in house prices and, some six years before it happened, noted the strong possibility of a much more severe housing bubble and bust. See IMF *World Economic Outlook* (Washington, DC, 2003), ch. 2, 'When Bubbles Burst', esp. p. 61.

8 CIA, *The World Factbook 2011* (Washington, DC, US Central Intelligence Agency, 2010).

9 David Duffy, 'Negative Equity in the Irish Housing Market', *Economic and Social Research Institute Working Paper no. 319* (2009).

10 David Harvey, *The Enigma of Capital* (Oxford: Oxford University Press, 2010).

5

A Catholic vision of Ireland

Bryan Fanning

In his 1911 novel *The Dawn of All*, Robert Hugh Benson, an English priest who converted to Catholicism (his father had been the Archbishop of Canterbury), imagined a future where most of the world had done the same. *The Dawn of All* recounts the story of a former priest living in a future atheistic 1973, who regains consciousness in a London hospital, in an England where the Reformation and secularism have been reversed. In this vision, religion had no influence in society and priests had no relevance. In the remainder of the book Benson's imaginary future changes dramatically. It becomes one in which Catholic social and political thought has been implemented worldwide, where the great political economists of the day consult cardinals and where Ireland has been turned into the contemplative monastery of Europe.

At the beginning of the twentieth century Catholic thinkers were preoccupied with the threats that secular, liberal and socialist ideals presented to religiosity. In his 1907 novel *Lord of the World*, Benson had imagined a future world dominated since 1917 by socialism, freemasonry and secular science. In this future, England had assented to Catholic home rule in Ireland and encouraged its Catholic population to emigrate there. Catholicism had declined everywhere except in Rome and in Ireland where appearances of a woman in blue were reported at Marian shrines.[1] The ideas behind Benson's respective utopia and dystopia were in keeping with wider Catholic intellectual responses to the threat of modernity.

English Catholics like Benson and Hillaire Belloc viewed the survival of Catholicism in post-Reformation Ireland as a historical miracle. Ireland's distinctive religious history – penal laws followed by Catholic Emancipation and a devotional revolution – looked much like post-Reformation Europe in reverse. Catholic churches were mostly newer than Protestant ones and Catholic schools had been integral to the nation-building project that would lead to Irish Independence. The Protestant Church of Ireland was disestablished in 1871 and had lost much of its political influence. By the time of Independence the Catholic Church was on the cusp of a level of influence that could only be imagined as science fiction elsewhere in much of the English-speaking world.

But the Church was unwilling to depend on miracles for its future survival. In 1870 Pope Piux IX invented the doctrine of papal infallibility as a bulwark against modernism. Intellectually, the Church drew on Thomism – Aristotelian natural law philosophy as Christianised by Thomas Aquinas – for its rebuttals of liberalism and socialism. The turn of the century witnessed the rise to dominance of neo-Thomist orthodoxy in seminaries and the repression of dissident thinkers associated with modernism. The mobilisation of Thomism in the 1891 papal encyclical *Rerum Novarum* 'on the condition of the working classes' provided the basis for specific political and social prescriptions that were at once an expression of interest group politics and an ontological conflict with secular modernity.

Rerum Novarum acknowledged a spirit of revolutionary change in politics and economics and, while recognising the 'misery and wretchedness pressing so unjustly on the working classes', sought to divert an impoverished Catholic working class away from socialism.[2] But it harked back to a time before the Enlightenment when liberalism and individualism did not exist. It idealised the pre-capitalist Middle Ages as the form of society that most epitomised the Christian ideal of social solidarity.

That the Catholic ideal was a pre-Reformation one was unsurprising. But it was similar to that of Protestant conservatives opposed to the impact of industrialisation such as Thomas Carlyle who in his 1843 book *Past and Present* argued that European peasants fared better under the stable hierarchies of feudalism than their descendants were doing under industrial capitalism.[3] The Catholic critique of modernity intellectually mirrored Émile Durkheim's *The Division of Labour in Society*, which emerged in 1894 a few years after the publication of *Rerum Novarum*. Durkheim described the unravelling of traditional 'mechanistic' forms of social solidarity and their replacement by more complex 'organic' interdependencies. Mechanistic solidarity was grounded in resemblance. Individual members of society resembled each other because they cherished the same values and held the same things sacred.[4] Society was coherent because individuals led very similar lives. Durkheim's German contemporary Ferdinand Tönnies referred to this as *gemeinschaft*. This archetype had much in common with the medieval one of social cohesion beloved by neo-Thomists – people lived and died in the village in which they were born, within visual range of the same church steeple, sharing the same beliefs. Durkheim's preoccupation with the moral basis of social solidarity shared much with natural law understandings of the social order. Durkheim employed the concept of anomie to depict the ruptures in social solidarity and the sense of belonging that came with the decline of established religious moral authority.[5] The shift from traditional mechanistic interdependencies or *gemeinschaft* to new, yet to be fully realised forms of social solidarity was for Durkheim a sociological puzzle. It was understood by many European Catholic thinkers as an existential crisis.

The Catholic sociology of Catholic power

The battle for the survival of Catholic Ireland – a society that had come into being following the repeal of the Penal Laws and the Famine, and one in which the Catholic Church came to exercise what Tom Inglis calls a moral monopoly – was framed by Catholic thinkers in explicitly sociological terms for several decades after Independence.[6] For more than half a century Catholic sociology articulated influential visions of Ireland's future. These are represented here by the writings of two key figures. Fr Edward Cahill (1868–1941) was a Professor of Sociology at the Jesuit Milltown Institute: he was a close friend of his former pupil and later Taoiseach Éamon de Valéra. The last significant sociological defender of Catholic Ireland was Rev. Jeremiah Newman (1926–95), who became Professor of Sociology at Maynooth in 1953 and a longstanding editor of the doctrinally Catholic journal of sociology *Christus Rex*. Sociology for both Cahill and Newman was the science of reproducing Catholic Ireland from one generation to the next. Both emphasised the role of law in enforcing Catholic public morality and thereby enforcing social norms that were in accordance with Catholic ideals.

Cahill made the case for the kind of society fictionalised by Benson at a time when Catholic public morality was being increasingly reflected by the laws and constitution of the Irish state. Although most of the parliamentarians of the Free State were Catholics, there were limits to the extent to which the new state passed Church doctrine into law. In 1923, three private member bills put before the Dáil aimed at prohibiting divorce were blocked by William T. Cosgrave's government. Cosgrave was personally in favour of upholding the values of the Catholic majority, yet he was unwilling to prohibit divorce because this was seen to infringe upon the rights of the Protestant minority. But Catholic public morality became increasingly reflected in the laws of the state over time. The importation of contraception was prohibited by a 1935 Act and de Valéra's 1937 Constitution prohibited divorce.[7]

Cahill was in regular correspondence with de Valéra when the latter was drafting what would become the 1937 Constitution. Cahill's 701-page *Framework of a Christian State* (1932) was the most substantive post-Independence elaboration of Catholic social and political thought. He distinguished Catholic sociology from the secular kind popularised by the French positivist philosopher Auguste Comte. Catholic sociology, whilst it might make use of statistics, rested on principles of natural law which were unchanging and knowable to reason. By definition Catholic sociology excluded theories that studied religion as a social construct. To a considerable extent Catholic sociology was promoted in Irish universities to ensure that Catholic students would not be exposed to intellectual justifications of secularism.[8] *The Framework of the Christian State* was intended 'primarily for students of social science who accepted the Church's teaching'.[9] It explained and elaborated upon papal encyclicals that pontificated about the place of religion in public life, the family, education, the interrelations between capital and labour, the functions of the state and its relations with the Church.

The initial intellectual project of Catholic sociology was to combat the influence of socialism. Cahill's *Framework of a Christian State* discussed at length the history of socialist ideas, theories of surplus value and dialectical materialism. But the battle against socialism in the Irish case had long been won. On 29 January 1916, in *The Workers' Republic,* James Connolly praised a 'splendid speech' by the Capuchin priest Father Laurence in Dublin to an audience of Catholic working men and women. Connolly professed himself to be unable to identify any fundamental differences between Laurence's views and those of Irish socialists. In declaring this, he was undoubtedly trying to encourage the Catholic Irish working class to embrace socialism. Connolly echoed the language of Catholic natural law: 'We accept the family as the true type of human society. We say that as in the family the resources of the entire household are at the service of each, as in the family the strong does not prey upon the weak.'[10] Connolly, if not naive, was whistling in the dark. After his execution following the 1916 Rising, various efforts were made by Catholic intellectuals to either co-opt or dismiss him. A 1919 article 'Socialism and Catholic Teaching' in the Irish Jesuit journal *Studies* by Peter Finlay SJ argued that the programme of Connolly's Irish Republican Socialist Party was one that Leo XIII had explicitly condemned. However, in *The Social Teachings of James Connolly* (1921), the first major study of his writings by another Jesuit, Lambert McKenna, a trenchant critic of Marxism, claimed that some of Connolly's socialist principles were in accordance with Catholic social thought.[11] In the absence of a realistic socialist threat the main focus of Catholic sociology was to understand and combat any kind of voice of social change that might foster secularism.

De Valéra invited Cahill to draft a preamble to the 1937 Constitution. In their correspondence Cahill argued that 'a constitution for Ireland should be, if not confessedly Catholic (which may at present not be feasible) at least definitely and *confessedly Christian'.*[12] A number of provisions (Articles 40 to 44) covering social policy, the family, divorce, the role of women and the status of children all reflected Catholic social thought. Cahill and de Valéra's ideal Ireland had much in common. de Valéra's famous St Patrick's day speech of 1943 (see p. 17) had evoked a Catholic, anti-materialist, rural social ideal that was very much in keeping with *Rerum Novarum* and Cahill's *Framework for a Christian State.*

Cahill had emphasised the fundamental importance of rural family life to the survival of the Church and the Irish nation, a perspective which dominated Catholic social thought in Ireland until the 1960s. He argued that the urban poor were especially threatened by immorality and vice and that extreme poverty and poor housing conditions – worse in Dublin than almost anywhere in Europe – undermined family life. In 1926 more than a quarter of Dublin's families lived in one-room tenements.[13] Cahill argued that the emphasis had to be on checking rural depopulation and stabilising rural communities. He made the case for programmes that would sustain viable small farms including rural co-operatives and restrict ownership of land to people willing to live on it.[14] The root causes of emigration and urbanisation were deemed to be the concentration of the most fertile land in the ownership of the great ranchers who did not cultivate it, and insufficient protection for native producers. This was also de Valéra's diagnosis. Other causes identified by Cahill included the dreariness of rural life and the lack of Catholic rural organisatons that might improve living conditions and promote social cohesion. He also blamed the education system, the unchristian press and the cinema for inculcating distaste for rural life.

Newman's sociological focus from the late 1950s was on the impending decline of Irish Catholicism. In a 1959 book review in *Christus Rex* Newman observed that students of what was commonly called 'Sociology' in Ireland – that is as taught by him – would be very confused by how the subject was defined in other countries.[15] As editor of *Christus Rex* he kept secular theoretical sociology at bay through censorship until the last issue of the journal in 1970 before it was relaunched as *Social Studies.* In a remarkable article in the final issue he referred to a plethora of secular sociologists whose works *Christus Rex* had deliberately never discussed or reviewed.[16] Newman's own best known sociological analyses focused on rural Limerick where he grew up, and the decline in vocations at Maynooth where he took holy orders and was later in charge of the spiritual formation of seminarians. He argued that in the face of ongoing rural decline, the only way to conserve rural population was, 'paradoxical though it may seem', to develop a number of towns in each county with adequate social and cultural facilities.[17] Newman formulated an index of social provision for towns and villages in Country Limerick. This quanti-fied the availability of public utilities, different kinds of commercial activities (the presence of various kinds of shops, banks etc.), public transport, 'places of assembly' (social facilities such as churches, libraries, public houses, cinemas) and social organisations. In short Newman's proposal was to concentrate on building up a number of sustainable communities in the county. Newman's sociology extolled the virtues of *gemeinschaft,* the community life of the family and the locality, of the village, the smaller town, the owner-occupied shop, the rural church as the best incubator of priests and good Catholics.

Social change and Catholic public morality

By the time *Christus Rex* folded, Fianna Fáil, under de Valéra's successor Sean Lemass, had embraced a new nation-building project focused on economic devel-opment. The period of influence of Catholic social thought had coincided with a period of Irish Ireland, of a postcolonial cultural nation-building project which emphasised economic isolationism and efforts to promote the Irish language.

However, in a 1961 article in *Christus Rex*, Seán Lemass, by then the new Taoiseach, explicitly rejected the Catholic vision of a frugal, anti-materialistic rural-centred society championed by Cahill and de Valéra. Lemass blamed emigration on 'the insufficiency of our efforts to develop a completely attractive way of life for all elements of the national community, and adequate opportunities of employing individual talents in Ireland to earn livelihoods equivalent to those which emigrants hope to find elsewhere'. Contrary to the prevailing view in *Christus Rex*, he did not believe that emigration could be ended by urging people to willingly accept less than could be obtained elsewhere.[18]

Newman argued that spiritual life and individual faith were sustained by social habits that could be damaged by removal from a society within which religious norms prevailed. Urban life and the impersonal social structures of modernity made community intangible and made faith difficult. He argued that with the decline of Irish *gemeinschaft*, a legally enforced public morality offered the only potential bulwark against the acceleration of secularisation. The state, he argued, had a duty to Ireland's Catholic majority to enforce Catholic public morality.

The Catholic ideal, he insisted, in his book *Studies in Political Morality* (1962) was for an established Church. It should never surrender this ideal in theoretical discussions on Church–state relations. More generally it should never surrender the primacy of theology to political theory. He faulted progressive American theologians for having done so. The demands of the Church of Christ on the state, he argued, were fundamentally doctrinal; they stemmed from the uncompromising source of theological truth.[19] Catholics were required to accept Catholic doctrine. From a Catholic doctrinal perspective the focus had to be on the political implications of theological truth rather than the other way around:

> Special recognition of the church may be necessary to secure these interests to the full in a state in which the vast majority is Catholic. It is not a question of seeking what *can* be secured from the State but what *ought* to be granted if the people's spiritual interests are to be adequately looked after in so far as their government is competent to do so. On the side of the State this, in turn, re-echoes its duty of doing whatsoever is necessary in pursuit of the political common good. It is simply erroneous to suggest that the limitation of the State to catering to the exigencies of public order means that it cannot grant special recognition to the Church.[20]

In the Irish case, where the Church enjoyed a special position closer to the ideal than in many other polities, other issues came to the fore. There had, Newman insisted, to be limits to religious tolerance. The rulers in a state comprised almost entirely of Catholics had a duty to introduce legislation of the state in accordance with Catholic teaching. This included a duty to defend the religious patrimony of the people against every assault that sought to deprive them of their faith.

By the 1970s it was clear that Catholic goals in Ireland could no longer be pursued by episcopal insistence on the primacy of Church authority in

Church–state relations. The decline of vocations meant that the threats of modernity to Irish Catholicism were no longer external. There would soon be, Newman anticipated, pressure for legislation to permit divorce. He depicted this pressure as a 'minority right' issue and argued that the state in a predominantly Catholic society had a duty to protect Catholic values:

> What I am getting at is the need for a patterned sociological framework which will give support to the religious and moral beliefs of the average man and thus help him live his life in accordance with them. What he needs, if you will, is a prop to his weakness, but then this is the purpose of all society in all its domains. Political society or the State is no exception. Its legal system represents a fabric of social values that are intended to sustain the individual through social living. This is the function of a constitutional provision which prohibits divorce in a society composed predominantly of people who believe it wrong to practise it.[21]

Laws that enforced Catholic public morality protected the Catholic social fabric. In a 1969 *Christus Rex* article, he described the prohibition of divorce in Ireland as part of the framework provided by the Irish state that supported the conformism of the average man.[22] Newman argued that the emphasis of Vatican II on participation of the laity in the Church and other reforms would not ensure future high levels of religious observance in the way that had been made possible by laws underpinned by Catholic moral teaching. So defending the constitutional status quo was a priority. Social change, he believed, was inevitable. But the pace of change was fast enough without increasing it by changes to the Constitution which would, he believed further undermine Catholicism in Ireland. As he put it, in a 1969 article in *Christus Rex*:

> That diehard traditionalism is bad for society, and that there is need for a liberal stimulus to counter it, is a sound general political principle. But it should be related to society as found in the concrete. Thus the contribution of the liberal stimulus is unquestionably valuable in the context of a backward looking, quite closed, conservative society. At the other extreme, in that of a wholly liberal permissive society, there is need rather for the fostering of a sound conservativism. Today in our mixed – partly conservative and party liberal Irish society, it seems to me that one should be unusually careful about introducing a liberal stimulus in the direction of secularisation. Where has this led Britain even in our own time – from a proud empire to a giggling society?[23]

Newman believed that the pressure for divorce legislation and for secularisation went hand in hand. In the Irish case, Catholic politicians who advocated legislation on divorce tended to do so on grounds of promoting religious pluralism. But they needed to understand that in countenancing divorce they were also endorsing the secularisation of Irish society by undermining public morality. He made similar arguments against legislation in favour of contraception and abortion. He argued that the law was crucial bulwark against the erosion of Catholic public morality and that this in turn was one against the erosion of Catholic faith.

Catholic visions and the distinctive Irish case

Ireland was never a theocratic state but, according to Paul Blanshard in *The Irish and Catholic Power* (1954), it came closer to becoming one than any other Western democracy during the twentieth century. Ireland was clearly a democracy but, as put by Blanshard, an unofficial Church–state alliance permitted ecclesiastical dictatorship and political democracy to live side by side without any sense of incongruity.[24] Ireland was the only democracy where the Church enjoyed such status. By contrast, the political order Robert Hugh Benson envisaged was a highly schematic version of the vocational state: people were represented through guilds, and different professions had different coloured uniforms. Some elements of this found expression in Mussolini's Italy. But it was Salazar's Portugal that came closest to the ideal Catholic vocationalist state. Vocationalism was discussed from the 1870s by Catholic thinkers as a means of preventing the kinds of class conflict that fostered socialism. It was endorsed by an International Conference of Catholic Sociologists held in Germany in 1893.[25] As explained in a 1938 article in the *Irish Monthly* by Rev. Cornelius Lucey, who was Professor of Theology and Political Theory at Maynooth:

> The vocational guild, therefore serves a double purpose. First, it knits the employers and the workers of the same occupation together and so acts as a corrective to the class antagonism natural when only the conflicting interests of the two classes are emphasised as at present. Secondly it plans the economy of the occupation as a whole, with an eye both to the needs of the community and the good of the various bodies in the occupation. In this way it relieves the State of duties which it has ordinarily neither the competency nor the qualifications to carry out.[26]

But by then it was clear that vocationalism had only a limited influence in the Irish case. In the 1930s, it offered General O'Duffy's Blueshirt movement an off-the-shelf political programme. But the Blueshirts never gained power and the era came to be politically dominated by de Valéra and Fianna Fáil. By the time the corporatist state found political champions like O'Duffy, Ireland's most influential Catholic intellectuals had moved on. For example, Alfred O'Rahilly, a long-time supporter of vocationalism, argued that it was unnecessary in a 1935 article in *Studies* on constitutional reform.[27] Ireland, in any case, did not have a socialist problem that needed vocationalist solutions. Cahill's *Framework of a Christian State* had placed little emphasis on vocationalism per se. He was a republican nationalist who had been criticised by fellow clergy for holding IRA sympathies during the Civil War.[28] But so too were some other leading clerical proponents of Catholic social thought like the Jesuit Timothy Corcoran, the Professor of Education at University College Dublin.

Catholic social thought failed to translate into a coherent political programme in the Irish case not just because it was backed by the losing side of 1930s electoral politics. Tony Fahey has convincingly argued that the central thrust of papal social teaching, which strove to find a middle way between what the Vatican saw as the extremes of *laissez-faire* capitalism and state socialism, had only limited relevance to social conditions in Ireland: 'Outside of the industrialised north-east of the island, capitalism had failed to take off in Ireland and the socialist movement scarcely developed beyond the embryonic stage. The main targets of attack for Catholic social teaching were thus either weak or largely absent in Ireland – or were present primarily as external conditioning circumstances.'[29] Cahill and Newman saw the defence of rural life and Catholic public morality as more crucial to the survival of Catholicism than such Continental Catholic political experiments.

The Church political ideal, Newman argued in 1961, was for something like the Republic of Ireland, a Catholic society in which the Church had considerable influence upon the state and where the state established through Constitution and laws a public morality that accorded with Catholic teaching. In the case of the United States where Catholics were in the minority, the Church nevertheless held on to the ideal of a Church–state relationship that would enshrine Catholic doctrine in law. But this influence was clearly on the wane and the Church was on the cusp of losing its moral monopoly over Irish life. The tyranny of a Catholic majority at the heart of Newman's political philosophy had come to be replaced by the tyranny of a secularising majority that now needed to be resisted.

The Church also had to deal with pressures for reform from some clergy and laity. Brian Moore's 1972 novel *Catholics* imagined a future that would have horrified Newman. The book was set in what seems to be the year 1999 where, following Vatican IV, the monks on a monastery off the coast of Kerry were to be censured for practising traditional Catholicism. The Church no longer believed in miracles ('Lourdes is no longer in operation'), there had been ecumenical compromises with other faiths – a merger with Buddhism was on the cards – and the Mass was officially regarded as nothing more than a symbolic act.[30] For a time it must have looked as if liberation theology and folk masses in the post-Vatican II climate might lead to further Church reform and doctrinal comprise. However, the long papacy of Pope John Paul II and that of his successor Benedict XVI, formerly Joseph Ratzinger, were characterised by a neo-conservative doctrinal emphasis on a universally binding natural law and the teaching of absolute moral norms. The political playbook of the Catholic Church in twenty-first-century Ireland resembles the one Newman described as fitting countries where Catholics were in a minority. In such cases, he insisted, they should hold on to the ideal of a Catholic public morality, never compromising on its contents, whilst pragmatically accepting the status quo and playing a long game.

Notes

1 Robert Hugh Benson, *Lord of the World* (London: Sir Isaac Pitman and Sons Ltd, 1907); Robert Hugh Benson, *The Dawn of All* (St Louis: B. Herder, 1911).

2 *Rerum Novarum* (1891) cited in Edward Cahill, *The Framework of a Christian State* (Dublin: Gill and Son, 1932), p. 148.

3 Thomas Carlyle, *Past and Present* (London: Chapman and Hall, 1843).

4 Émile Durkheim, *The Division of Labour in Society* (London: Macmillan, 1984).

5 Émile Durkheim, *Suicide: A Study in Sociology* (New York: Free Press, 1951).

6 Tom Inglis, *Moral Monopoly: The Rise and Fall of the Catholic Church in Modern Ireland*, 2nd ed. (Dublin: University College Dublin Press, 1998).

7 John Whyte, *Church and State in Modern Ireland 1923–1979*, 2nd ed. (Dublin: Gill and Macmillan, 1980), p. 37.

8 Bryan Fanning, *The Quest for Modern Ireland: The Battle of Ideas 1912–1986* (Dublin: Irish Academic Press, 2008).

9 Edward Cahill, *The Framework of a Christian State: An Introduction to Social Science* (Dublin: M.H. Gill and Son, 1932), p. xiii.

10 James Connolly, 'The Programme of Labour', *The Workers' Republic,* 29 January (1916).

11 Lambert McKenna, *The Social Teachings of James Connolly* (Dublin: Catholic Truth Society, 1920).

12 Dermot Keogh, 'The Jesuits and the 1937 Constitution', in Bryan Fanning (ed.), *An Irish Century: Studies 1912–2012* (Dublin: University College Dublin Press, 2012).

13 Cahill, *Christian State,* p. 663.

14 Cahill, *Christian State,* pp. 321–5.

15 Jeremiah Newman, 'Review of Joseph H. Fischer, Sociology': *Christus Rex,* xiii:3 (1959), pp. 220–1.

16 Jeremiah Newman, 'Progress and Planning': *Christus Rex,* xxiii (1977), pp. 173–86; see Fanning, *The Quest for Modern Ireland,* p. 133.

17 Jeremiah Newman, 'Report of the Limerick Rural Survey', *Christus Rex,* xv:1 (1961), pp. 20–2.

18 Sean F. Lemass, 'Social Factors and Emigration', *Christus Rex,* xv:1 (1961), 16–19, pp. 19. Jeremiah Newman, *Studies in Political Morality* (Dublin: Scepter, 1962), p. 240.

19 Newman, *Studies in Political Morality,* p. 240.

20 Newman, *Studies in Political Morality,* p. 265.

21 Newman, *Studies in Political Morality,* p. 178.

22 Jeremiah Newman, 'Socio-Political Aspects of Divorce', *Christus Rex,* xxiii:1 (1969), pp. 5–15.

23 Jeremiah Newman, *Conscience Versus Law: Reflections on the Evolution of Natural Law* (Dublin: Talbot, 1971), p. 182.

24 Paul Blanshard, *The Irish and Catholic Power* (Boston: Beacon Press, 1954).

25 Cornelius Lucey, 'The Vocational Group Movement', *The Irish Monthly,* 66:778 (1938), pp. 221–37 (p. 235).

26 Lucey, 'The Vocational Group Movement', p. 227.

27 Fanning, *The Quest for Modern Ireland,* p. 104.

28 Patrick Murray, *Oracles of God: The Roman Catholic Church and Irish Politics 1922–37* (Dublin: University College Dublin Press, 2000), p. 174.

29 Tony Fahey, 'The Catholic Church and Social Policy', in Seán Healy and Brigid Reynolds (eds), *Social Policy in Ireland* (Dublin: Oak Tree Press, 1998), p. 418.

30 Brian Moore, *Catholics* (London: Cape, 1972).

6

The Irish political elite

Kieran Allen

Why don't the Irish protest? This became a familiar question after the economic crash of 2008. Diarmaid Ferriter, in his column in the *Irish Independent*, suggested that

> Historians in the future will contrast the wave of protests and mobilisations in other countries where incompetence and greed were exposed, with the absence of such activity in Ireland, even when the extent of the bankers' betrayal and contempt for their fellow citizens became public.[1]

The historians may, however, be framing their questions wrongly if they do not both acknowledge the reality of protest and examine its interpretations. There is, in fact, a myth among many academics and journalists, that Irish people have not protested. It is a myth that is sustained by the way protests have been covered in the media and debated in the public sphere.

Consider only a few fragments of evidence. At the start of the economic crisis, 15,000 pensioners surrounded Dáil Éireann and forced a government retreat on the withdrawal of medical cards. The state decided to change its 'communication' strategy and approached further cutbacks in social welfare in a more careful fashion. More than 100,000 people marched in protest at the imposition of a pension levy on public-sector workers in 2009. Later that year, 250,000 public-sector workers staged a one-day strike and were about to repeat it when their union leaders called it off. The demoralisation caused by that defeat gave the government considerable room for manoeuvre and the protest movements dropped off. After a short period, however, there was a revival around particular issues. Protests against hospital downgrades have mobilised extraordinary numbers, with 8000 marching in Roscommon, 7000 in Navan and 15,000 in Waterford. And some protests have been partially successful. Mobilisations against the cuts to disadvantaged schools; the withdrawal of personal assistants to disabled people; and cuts to home help care extracted significant concessions from the government. Even more significantly, over half of homeowners defied the law and boycotted a household charge before eventually succumbing to draconian legislation that was introduced to enforce a property tax.

This small selection of examples indicates that there is not a lack of protest but rather a different *structure and language* of protest. People may engage in protests and interpret them as futile. They may join as individuals and not belong to any sustained collective networks. Nevertheless, for whatever reason, there has not emerged in Ireland – at the time of writing – a generalised anti-austerity movement that might be comparable to the *indignado* movement in Spain or the citizens' movement in Iceland. The protests which occur are overwhelmingly sectional or focused on a single issue. More interesting questions might, therefore, be asked: Why have the Irish not developed a general anti-austerity discourse? Why have there not been sustained mobilisations against austerity?

Elsewhere, I have suggested two key reasons.[2] One was the culture of 'naïve capitalism' which developed during the Celtic Tiger period. This led to a strong propensity to seek individual solutions for social problems and produced an understanding of economics as a morality tale constructed by godlike markets. This viewpoint assumed that those who behaved according to market rules were saints and received their just rewards and those who were committed to public spending were sinners who had to be punished. The second factor was the withdrawal of the unions from an anti-austerity movement. At the start of the crisis, the Irish Congress of Trade Unions (ICTU) moved away from any serious confrontation with the state in order to resuscitate a form of shadow social partnership. Rhetorical denunciations of austerity continued, but the Croke Park Agreement, according to the Services, Industrial, Professional and Technical Union (SIPTU) leader, Jack O'Connor, 'took the best, organised section of the workforce out of the equation for social protest'.[3] This strategic shift meant that Ireland was unique among the peripheral countries in Europe for having a union movement that did not give any impetus to anti-austerity protests.

However, the level of protest in society is not simply determined by ideologies or the strategies of civil society organisations. The political elite itself plays a key role in the management of discontent and the Irish political elite have displayed some skill in diffusing mobilisation. The remainder of this chapter will focus on its role.

The political elite

By the political elite we mean the leadership of mainstream political parties, their close political confidants and the heads of the surrounding political apparatuses. They control the mainstream political parties. At its upper tiers, this layer is part of the ruling class but it is not synonymous with it. The core of a ruling class in a capitalist society is the people who control the production system and who are in pole position to set the economic agenda. Around this core are built multiple layers that form connections – both material and ideological – with them. Within these layers, the political elite undertake the more specialised task of managing social harmony. They seek to align the incessant demand for profit and accumulation with the aspirations of the mass of people. This requires considerable political skill, particularly in time of austerity. How particular political elites carry out this task differs from country to country. So, while the dynamic of capital accumulation may be prevalent everywhere, responses to its periodic crises vary according to both the discourses of non-state actors, such as unions, community organisations or wider social movements, and the strategies the political elite deploy to create social harmony and consensus.

When the political elite in Ireland confronted their worst economic crash in 2008, they responded in both an ad hoc and a strategic manner. The infamous bank guarantee scheme was, most probably, an example of the former. It was initially seen as a 'cute' move to entice credit into the Irish banking system and had all the appearance of a rash decision made under extreme crisis conditions. But once the wider contours of the Irish crisis became known, the political elite developed a broader strategy for managing discontent. A key element of this was co-opting the union leaders and, to a lesser extent, NGOs and community organisations into a form of shadow social partnership. The substance of former social partnership deals – which involved trade-offs between low wage increases and tax concessions – disappeared, but the process of 'consultation' and synchronisations of responses remained. The state embarked on a policy of wage cuts to reduce public spending and to set targets for the private sector. It hoped that similar wage cuts in this sector would improve 'competitiveness' and win greater exports. The union leaders largely acquiesced.

This strategy of co-opting union leaders was arrived at in the face of strident opposition from bodies like the Irish Small and Medium Enterprises Association and the Independent News Media who called for an end to social partnership. They pointed to the extremely weak position of union leaders who had a declining membership due to increased unemployment and suggested that they faced bitter disillusionment from their own grassroots. Yet no matter whether a Fianna Fáil-dominated or Fine Gael-dominated government was in office, the political elite stuck to a strategy of co-option rather than dismissal. In doing so they were drawing on a particular style of rule that had been deployed in the decades before.

Traditions, practices and experiences of past battles won form a sedimented framework which elites draw on to create styles of rule. These styles give a ruling elite its distinctive quality and can be an important factor in the management of social discontent. It is to these longer-term historic patterns we need now to turn.

From populism to corporatism

The Irish political system has historically been shaped by the domination of Fianna Fáil, which was one of the most successful political parties in Western democracies for two main reasons. First, it achieved an unparalled hold of office that was rivalled only by the Swedish Social Democrats. By the time of the 2007 election – the last year of its triumphal command of the Irish political scene – it had been in office for twenty-three years of the previous three decades. Second, the party's support base was drawn from all social classes and, even though it advocated right-wing policies, it was marginally skewed towards a working-class base. In 2007, for example it received more support from the skilled and unskilled working class than from professional groups. The domination of Fianna Fáil gave the Irish political system a peculiar characteristic in terms of Western European polities. In the words of John Whyte, the Irish political system was an outlier because it was built on 'politics with no social base'.[4] Understanding the nature of Fianna Fáil hegemony, therefore, is crucial to interpreting the wider political style of rule of the Irish political elite.

The historical dominance of Fianna Fáil originally arose from populist politics that appeared to fit with the aspirations of workers in a postcolonial society. When de Valéra formed the party in 1927, he described Ireland as 'an out garden for the British'.[5] It was an accurate description of Ireland's continuing neocolonial status as some 97 per cent of its exports went to Britain and these were overwhelmingly agricultural. The party's aim was to change this agro-export model and it set about constructing an industrial bloc that brought together workers and small capitalists. This meant a vigorous challenge to the big farmers and merchants who supported this form of trade and who backed the Cumman na nGaedheal party.

The nearest comparison to Fianna Fáil is with populist formations in Latin America. Di Tella defined the populist projects in that continent as:

> A political movement which enjoys the support of the mass of the urban working class and/or peasantry but which does not result from the autonomous organisational power of either. It is also supported by non-working class sectors upholding an anti-status quo ideology.[6]

This definition fitted movements formed around Peron in Argentina, Vargas in Brazil or Cardenas in Mexico. It captured both the all-class nature of their projects and the anti-status-quo ideology which challenged the landed oligarchies. When it was first formed, Fianna Fáil had a similar anti-status-quo ideology. In 2009, its leader, Micheál Martin, acknowledged this in a history of the party in Cork when he noted that the agenda of the 1926 Ard Fheis included a motion which demanded that 'profiteering' be made an offence punishable by imprisonment.[7] More broadly, the party committed itself to carrying out the radical Democratic Programme of the First Dáil which placed a strong emphasis on social justice. However, Fianna Fáil opponents among the big farmers were far weaker than their equivalents in Latin America. They wanted to continue the agro-export, neocolonial relationship with Britain but they had neither the economic nor the political strength of the landed oligarchy of Latin America. Fianna Fáil did not need to engage in significant active mobilisation beyond electioneering. There were a number of major skirmishes where Fianna Fáil activists joined with their erstwhile republican allies in defeating the Blueshirts, but that was as far as it went. There was nothing equivalent to the *decamisados* movement in Argentina, for example, where Peron was forced to build an active organised relationship with urban workers and their unions in order to defeat the oligarchy. One result of this contrast was that Fianna Fáil rhetorical radicalism was much more short-lived. Nevertheless, both the Latin American populists and Fianna Fáil shared a similar project: national development and a break from a neocolonial status.

This economic agenda of Fianna Fáil has often been ignored because political scientists tend to focus on its formal aims, which were the unification of Ireland and the restoration of the 'national language'. However, Fianna Fáil's anti-partition rhetoric never led to action and was only used as a symbolic totem to forge class unity in the twenty-six counties. The language revival campaign was effectively restricted to imposing compulsory Irish in primary schools. The central aim of Fianna Fáil was the construction of a vibrant, native capitalism and it sought to strain every resource of the state to achieve that. Crucially, it pursued a deliberate strategy to win a base among urban workers on the east coast of the country. This, sometimes, meant opposing the threat from the left and periodically invoking anti-communist rhetoric to put the left down. In a letter smuggled out of prison at the end of the civil war, de Valéra, pointed to the possibility of class politics and advised his followers to 'lean more on the economic side' and insist on raising 'a national programme for the common good not a class programme'.[8]

The Fianna Fáil project of national economic development laid the foundation for the hegemony that the wider political elite achieved over Irish society. It replaced political choices with pro-business economic strategies to overcome backwardness. Southern Irish nationalism became overwhelmingly an economic nationalism which purported to bring all social classes together to achieve the aim of national development. There was no dogmatic assertion of particular economic methods – only a broad framework which supported business and small Irish business in particular.

The first phase of this hegemonic discourse began after Fianna Fáil took office in 1932 when it embarked on a protectionist strategy to foster the growth of Irish industry and used the state to develop the necessary infrastructure. Initially, this was a modest success, as nominal capital invested in companies increased and industrial employment grew from 110,000 in 1931 to 166,000 in 1938.[9] This enabled the party to make a shift from a reliance on a declining small farming sector on the west coast to becoming the hegemonic party among Dublin workers. The second phase came with the turn in 1958 when Fianna Fáil dropped its protectionist strategy in favour of hitching the fortunes of native capitalism to foreign multinationals. It rescinded the Control of Manufacturers Act, which stipulated that Irish shareholders should own a majority stake in companies. Some on the left – such as Noel Browne – regarded the shift as a 'sell-out' of Fianna Fáil original ideals. But this was to mistake the very nature of the project – to build up native capitalism by every means possible. The foreign firms that located in Ireland mainly used the country as a platform for export elsewhere and so they offered little threat to Irish industry. The grants and tax breaks used to attract them were also enjoyed by Irish capitalists – who actually received a higher amount per job created.[10] The modest growth of Irish industry in this period combined with the influx of foreign investment allowed Fianna Fáil to revive its hegemonic position over workers because economic success appeared to lend truth to the claim that 'a rising tide lifts all boats'.

The third phase, the Celtic Tiger, was even more spectacular in its success and ultimate failure. It began fortuitously when the formation of the single EU economic market encouraged US firms to seek a location inside its borders. They chose Ireland because it was English-speaking, had a relatively educated workforce with comparatively low wages and, crucially, had a low tax regime. When the flow of US investment began to run out after the 2002 economic recession, Fianna Fáil attempted to prolong the boom by stimulating the construction industry. The long period of growth helped to shore up its voting base, which had previously shown signs of decline. The 'Teflon Taoiseach', as Bertie Ahern became known, did not have any particularly decisive or dynamic leadership qualities – he simply personified economic success. When the economy crashed, his mystique disappeared virtually overnight.

The long historic success of Fianna Fáil arose from its ability to translate the broad language of Irish republicanism into the smaller change of economic advance. It constructed a distinct twenty-six county economic nationalism that drew on postcolonial legacies to celebrate the advances of Irish capitalism and the coincidental improvement in the living standards of workers. In its early stages, there was an alliance with the bishops to link Irish identity to a deeply conservative train of Catholicism. Flying the papal flag became the substitute for flying the tricolour over the 'fourth green field'. Catholicism also offered solace when the ideals of 'competitiveness' and promoting Irish industry did not match de Valéra's idyllic promise that the population would 'not merely be wage slaves or simply spending their lives to make money for somebody else'.[11] Together, these twin pillars of twenty-six county conservatism, Fianna Fáil and the Catholic Church, held Irish society in a vice grip for decades and marginalised the left.

This style of rule became further embedded in the Irish polity after 1958 when populism gave way to a corporatist form of rule. The main reason for the transition was that the anti-status-quo rhetoric became redundant as Fianna Fáil established itself as the main party of government. Fine Gael was effectively marginalised because the space that was open to its forerunner, Cumman na nGaedheal – that is to pose as 'constitutional' nationalists as against 'extreme' republicans – had disappeared. Between 1938 and 1943, for example, the Fine Gael vote fell from a third to a quarter because it was seen as pro-British.[12] Henceforth, Fine Gael was forced to compete on the ideological terrain of economic nationalism as defined by Fianna Fáil. In addition, the post-1958 turn to foreign capital and the global economy necessitated more structured relationships with labour. The state wanted an active, collaborative relationship with the unions in order to increase productivity and competitiveness. Instead of simply relying on a more diffuse populist support base, it created a dense institutional structure.

This way of organising unions into a structure which links them to the state is usually referred to as corporatism. It normally involves establishing bodies where a limited number of key interest groups are represented. These groups – such as the unions or business interests – are encouraged to develop a consensus between them and then to discipline their own membership to accept agreements made between them. It is designed to involve labour in the management of a for-profit economy. The consensus generated at the top between the leaders of labour and business leads to greater social control of the grassroots membership of the unions.

Corporatism became the hallmark of Irish political management after an export-orientated strategy was embarked upon as the key to economic success. In 1963, for example, Seán Lemass gave clear expression to the philosophy that underlay corporatism:

> In any free democratic society, a strong well organised and competently adminis-
> tered trade union movement is essential for economic and political progress. The
> more highly developed a national economy, the more obvious does this become ...
> All of us who are concerned with ... our country's economic progress have therefore
> a vested interest in the development, the efficiency and the effectiveness of our trade
> union movement. *It cannot be the concern of its members alone – it is far too important
> for that.* (emphasis added)[13]

Lemass's pronouncement that unions are 'too important' to be left to their members indicated that the Irish state had a vested interest in shaping how they developed. This pronouncement coincided with moves to form a Commission on Industrial Organisation and the setting up of Adaptation Councils and Trade Union Advisory Boards at industry level to integrate workers into planning for extra productivity. Other institutions formed around this time included the Employer-Labour Conference and the National Industrial and Economic Council. The structures of social partnership, which emerged in their fully developed form after 1987, had, therefore, a long pre-history.

The style of elite rule that grew out of populist impulses that were later embedded in corporatist structures helped to defuse class conflict. The Irish labour movement traditionally avoided the language of the left and instead combined a mild form of social democracy with a profession of loyalty to the cause of Irish economic development. More subtle mechanisms were also developed to coincide with the integration of labour. The political elite, for example, were able to project themselves as classless. Instead of relying on support from latent instincts to respect one's betters as the British Conservative party member might have done, Irish politicians prided themselves on being 'one of the lads'. They attended the same GAA matches, drank in the same pubs and did more door to door canvassing than their equivalents elsewhere. The integration of oppositional groups also allowed for a greater informality in political decision making. The state bureaucracy – which engaged regularly with business and labour interests – learnt how to bend rules, turn blind eyes and give many nods and winks. The primary message was that those organisations who were most closely wedded to the project of social partnership could get 'things done'. The absence of clear left–right division and the overwhelming domination of twenty-six-county economic nationalism did not remove inequality and conflict in Irish society. However, they influenced how people articulated their grievances and concerns. The absence of a strong left meant that there was no language to generalise opposition or see grievances as part of a problem with 'the system'. Grievances were more likely to be articulated as sectional problems with occasional appeals to more radical nationalist traditions. Thus, hospital closures were not seen as part of a neoliberal strategy to cut back public spending – but rather as a particular attack on one's county or local area.

The consensus around a twenty-six-county economic nationalism is also linked to a strong fatalistic streak in Irish politics. Encouragement of fatalism is one of the key modes of elite rule within late capitalism as anonymous markets assume ever more control over people's lives. The elite encourage a perception that 'the economy' works like the weather – largely uninfluenced by human intervention. However, while this form of fatalism is widespread throughout late capitalism, it is particularly deep in Ireland. The smothering effects of corporatist structures have made it more difficult to articulate and mobilise around alternative agendas. While inequality produces considerable grievances, there is a strong feeling that 'nothing can be done'. Giving out and complaining on national radio phone-in shows and pub talk – these common responses bear testimony to the power of the fatalistic impulse.

After the Celtic Tiger

These, then, were some of the main features of a style of rule that the Irish political elite have built up, and they were deployed to good use when the Celtic Tiger crashed. The crisis disoriented both the elite and the mass of the population, but elites recovered more quickly and used a 'shock doctrine' effect to impose changes they considered necessary. One of the main ways they stabilised the situation was by a strategy of co-opting labour rather than seeking confrontation. Their self-satis-faction was aptly expressed by Brian Lenihan, when he noted that 'our partners in Europe ... are amazed at our capacity to take pain. In France you would have riots if you tried this.'[14] This co-option involved a considerable degree of choreography which allowed union leaders to 'let off steam' even while acquiescing to ever greater demands for sacrifice. The practice of informal networking – built up over the previous decade – was used fully to achieve this. And as each concession gave way to demands for ever more, the culture of political fatalism was deployed to full effect to spread a deep demoralisation. A style of rule which relied on co-option, informal choreography and fatalism was used as much by Fine Gael, after they became the dominant party after the 2011 election, as by their rivals in Fianna Fáil.

Fine Gael had embraced the wider Fianna Fáil hegemonic project of economic nationalism after the Second World War. Then after a major electoral defeat in 2002, it consciously presented itself as a non-ideological, catch-all party and modelled its organisation on Fianna Fáil. In the person of Enda Kenny the party found the ideal figure to unite its urban and rural wings. Although he was the longest-standing TD in the Dáil, one commentator noted that 'Kenny had not been associated with any particular national issues – he had never taken a stand on any significant topic'.[15] Fine Gaels' triumph in 2011 arose primarily because it was Fianna Fáil's traditional rival for government. Many may have voted for it because it seemed to provide the quickest and surest way of ridding them of a party that they blamed for causing the economic crash. Once it achieved victory, Fine Gael, with Labour (its junior coalition government allies), easily slotted into the style of rule that Fianna Fáil had pioneered.

However, while the political management of the crisis was impressive from the ruling elite's point of view, there are no guarantees of stability for the future. Two factors, in particular, could become impediments to the continued hegemonic stability of economic nationalism. Fine Gael does not have the same strong roots in Irish society as Fianna Fáil had and, moreover, its domination coincides with a more ostentatious display of class hierarchy. Even in 2011 its voting base was skewed towards the AB advertising category – the upper professional and business element. It won 41 per cent of this category as against 30 per cent of the C, D and E categories – skilled, semi-skilled and unskilled workers.[16] So even in its moment of triumph the party could not fully emulate Fianna Fáil's success in transcending social class.

The shift from Fianna Fáil to Fine Gael has coincided with important cultural changes in the lifestyle of the Irish rich. Before the Celtic Tiger, the flaunting of wealth and social privilege was regarded as inappropriate. The wealthy sought to blend in with local communities, supporting the local GAA clubs, attending the same churches and, crucially, sending their children to the same schools. But as mega-fortunes were made in the Celtic Tiger, there was a growing social apartheid as the wealthy developed enclaves that helped to bond them together. Increasingly they sent their children to private schools in order to achieve higher educational results and to cement new forms of identity between them.

One manifestation of this change was way the selection of cabinet ministers came to resemble the British pattern. In the past, Irish government ministers were more likely to have been educated in Christian Brothers' schools while their counterparts in Britain went to elite schools such as Eton and Harrow. Not any more. More than a fifth (22 per cent) of the Fine Gael TDs newly elected to the Dáil in 2011 went to fee-paying schools. This is just one pointer to how the structures of privilege built up during the Celtic Tiger period had important impacts. Only 8 per cent of the wider school-going population attend private, fee-paying schools, so this stratum is clearly overrepresented in the Fine Gael parliamentary party. However, the figures for the Fine Gael–Labour cabinet are even more dramatic: eight of the current fifteen ministers attended fee-paying schools.[17] It is a tangible symbol of a new style of political rule. Gone is the image of parties representing the 'plain people of Ireland' and instead there is a new elite that could be labelled 'the Celtic Tories'.

The second factor that could undermine political stability is the scale of the economic difficulties. The strategy of the political elite has been to cut labour costs and export their way out of the crisis. They assumed that the global economy would pick up quickly and that Ireland could be ahead of the curve because of its success in imposing austerity at home while managing social tension. Yet the optimistic predictions have fallen well below expectations and the theoretical edifice that lay behind this strategy – the doctrine of 'expansionary austerity' – appears much weaker.[18] Ireland's potential export markets are experiencing, at best, an anaemic recovery and in the key pharmaceutical sector – which dominates Irish exports – there are additional problems as many branded drugs are starting to fall outside their patent timeframe. One sign of the continuing stagnation is the failure of investment to pick up. At the end of the Celtic Tiger period in 2007, €48 billion was invested in the economy by the private sector but this has since declined to just €17 billion in 2012 – just over a third of the original figure.

Thus, while the political elite have been extremely skilful in drawing on a historic style of rule to manage the crisis, they must still rely on a promise that sacrifices today will bring rewards tomorrow. When those rewards appear ever more distant, there is likely to be considerable 'austerity fatigue'. And that also means that the myth of the passive Irish, who do not protest, may also be broken.

Notes

1 Diarmaid Ferriter, 'History Will Ask Why We Should Be So Docile in Face of Such Betrayal', *Irish Independent*, 1 July 2013.

2 Kieran Allen, 'Social Partnership and the Fiscal Crisis in Ireland: Acceptance or Acquiescence', in Liam Leonard and Iosif Botetzagias (eds), *Sustainable Politics and the Crisis of the Peripheries: Ireland and Greece* (Bingley: Emerald Group, 2011).

3   Jamie Smyth, 'Political Stability Helps Drive Irish Recovery', *Financial Times,* 27 January
    2012. The Croke Park agreement meant that unions accepted job cuts and changes in
    working conditions in return for a guarantee of no compulsory redundancies.

4   John Whyte, 'Ireland: Politics Without Social Bases', in Richard Rose (ed.), *Electoral
    Behaviour: A Comparative Handbook* (New York: Free Press, 1974).

5   Dáil Debates, Vol. 25, Col. 478, 12 July 1928.

6   Torcuato Di Tella, 'Populism and Reform in Latin America', in Claudio Veliz (ed.), *Obstacles
    to Change in Latin America* (Oxford: University Press, 1965), p. 47.

7. Michael Martin, *Freedom to Choose: Cork and Party Politics in Ireland 1918–1932* (Cork:
    Collins Press, 2009), p. 140.

8   Quoted in T. Ryle Dwyer, *De Valera* (Dublin: Poolbeg, 1991), p. 134.

9   John A. Murphy, *Ireland in the Twentieth Century* (Cork: Mercier, 1981), p. 86.

10 National Economic and Social Council, *A Review of Industrial Policy (Telesis Report)*
    (Dublin: NESC, 1982), pp. 187–8.

11 *Dáil Debates,* Vol. 31, Col. 397, 26 October 1927.

12 *Dáil* Debates, Vol. 31, Col. 397, 26 October 1927.

13 Irish Transport and General Workers Union (ITGWU) *Annual Report and Conference
    Proceedings* (1963), pp. 119–20.

14 Arthur Beesley, 'Europe 'Amazed' at Steps Taken in Budget – Lenihan', *Irish Times,* 27 April
    2009.

15 Kevin Rafter, *Fine Gael: Party at the Crossroads* (Dublin: New Books 2009), p. 164.

16 Rafter, *Fine Gael,* p. 182.

17 'Fee Paying Schools Have the Edge on the Battle for Seats at the Cabinet', *Irish Independent,*
    27 December 2012.

18 Carmen Reinhart and Kenneth Rogdoff, 'Growth in Time of Debt', *American Economic
    Review,* May 2010, pp. 573–8.

7

The Irish family – different or not?

Tony Fahey

William Carleton gained a reputation as a literary figure in the 1830s for his *Traits and Stories of the Irish Peasantry*, a series of whimsical but informative sketches of Irish rural folk life of his day. Much of what he wrote had to do with family life, but nothing told as much of the family patterns of his times as his own origins. He grew up the son of a Catholic tenant farmer in Co. Tyrone who, as an entry in the *Encyclopaedia Britannica* puts it, 'supported fourteen children on as many acres'. Fourteen children on fourteen acres were a lot even by the standards of Carleton's time, but they exemplify a stock image of pre-Famine Ireland – the teeming peasant family living on small potato-growing holdings, an image which Carleton's own writings did much to propagate. The enthusiasm of the Irish poor of the day for rushing into early marriage and producing large broods of children provided an early nineteenth-century variant on the theme of Irish difference, since this pattern was distinctly un-European and for British observers in particular was part of the otherness of the uncouth Irish. But in the context of the present volume, this picture also suggests to us that the question of Irish difference is in fact *two* questions, one having to do with objective contrasts as might be measured by the methods of comparative social science, the other having to do with markers of identity that are used as badges to define groups and label them as different. Badges of difference and real difference may sometimes match. However, badges work not because of the objective reality they capture but because of the images, identities and associations they conjure up and the thoughts, emotions and actions they inspire. In considering whether the Irish family is different or not, then, it is useful to consider these two meanings of difference separately and offer some thoughts on how they apply to the Irish family system, both now and as it has evolved over time.

Real difference

To look first at real difference, patterns of family life in Ireland since the pre-Famine period can be interpreted as having veered into and out of conformity with broad European trends, sometimes diverging but then swerving back into convergence. It has to be said, of course, that what we mean by 'broad European trends' is never clear-cut since there is always diversity across countries, age cohorts, socio-economic groups, religious denominations, ethnic sub-populations and so on. Even to identify a standard pattern for a single country is a simplification. If we look closely enough, we find difference everywhere – even two peas in a pod are merely similar rather than identical. What we mean by 'divergence', then, has to refer to something more than movement within a 'normal' range of variation but must imply a shift outside usual experience: it must connote the exceptional, the outlier case, and not merely the slightly different. Likewise, convergence does not mean obliteration of difference but a narrowing of gaps to the point where crossover to within the boundaries of 'ordinary difference' is made – and it is always a matter of judgement where those boundaries lie and when a crossover has occurred.

With these caveats in mind, we can focus on some key internationally compara-ble features of family life, particularly having to do with patterns of marriage and fertility, and on that basis identify four phases in the cycle of divergence and convergence of Irish family patterns relative to European norms over the past two centuries or more. These phases follow a zig-zag sequence of deviation and return to conformity which went through two full cycles in this period of over two hundred years.

The decades prior to the Famine, going back well into the eighteenth century, provided the first of these phases, a period of divergence in the direction of the exceptionally early and widespread marriage and very high fertility already mentioned. That in turn contributed to a population explosion that occurred in Ireland in this period and had no parallel elsewhere in Europe at the time – popula-tion more or less doubled between the late 1700s and the early 1840s. Given the patchiness of the records, there is some uncertainty about the exact details of these divergences and how extreme they were. K.H. Connell, Ireland's outstanding social historian of the 1950s, claimed that a wide diffusion of teenage marriage, prompted by easy access to independent albeit meagre livelihoods for young people in the subsistence potato economy, was Ireland's dominant demographic development of the late eighteenth century and its chief source of expanding popu-lation. Others have disputed that marriages were quite so young but nevertheless generally agree that they were well below the average for northern Europe (perhaps early twenties rather than teenage years, in a context where the European average age of marriage for women was close to and often greater than twenty-five years). The current consensus, in so far as there is one, is that Irish population growth in this period was exceptionally rapid, but that early marriage was not the only driver – falling infant mortality and higher fertility within marriage also made contributions.[1]

The calamity of the Famine of 1845–48 could be said to be the culmination of this phase of Irish familial and demographic exceptionalism. It was a tragic consequence of population growth built on a fragile subsistence base, and was also the last and one of the greatest of Europe's famines. As an extreme event in its own right, it was another manifestation of Irish difference and all the more remarkable for taking place in a region of what was then the richest, most advanced economy in the world – the emerging industrial giant of the UK. It may be too much to say that on its own the Famine caused the great turn towards convergence which shaped Irish family patterns in the second half of the nineteenth century: the turn was already emerging in the 1830s and took some time after the Famine to spread around the country. But undoubtedly the turn occurred, and as it proceeded did so under the long shadow cast by the disastrous events of the 1840s.

In the half century between the 1830s and 1880s, then, we get the second of our four divergence–convergence phases as Ireland moved towards a new concurrence with mainstream European patterns of family behaviour. Ireland switched from early and widespread marriage to late marriage and a high incidence of non-marriage, from high fertility to low fertility and from a marriage system where parents exerted little control over their children's couple-formation to a tightly policed regime where repression of youthful sexuality and family-controlled match-making gave a new shape and discipline to family dynamics.[2] In so doing, however, Irish difference in family patterns faded away. The Irish family system shed its outlier status and adopted standard European patterns. Late marriage, much permanent celibacy and strict social controls over sexuality (of which Christian 'moral' teaching was an important part) were defining characteristics of centuries-long patterns of human coupling in Western Europe. This was the regime that Irish families took to as the second half of the nineteenth century proceeded.

By the 1880s, once Irish women married they continued to bear children in large numbers but not to a degree that was unique, or even that unusual, in Europe at that time. By then, women spent a large proportion of their reproductive lives in a non-reproductive state of singlehood, in contrast to the early and more widespread entry into reproduction found in Ireland half a century earlier. This method of neutralising an extended early segment of women's potential span of childbearing had the effect of counter-balancing prolific childbearing after marriage took place and reducing overall birth rates to modest levels. But again, what happened in Ireland in this regard was by no means outside the normal European range. It was true that Ireland's population contracted in this period and was sharply at odds with the rolling surge of population growth then sweeping over the Western world. The continuing fall in population in Ireland from the Famine until the 1960s made for an extreme case of difference. However, emigration rather than patterns of couple formation and childbearing was the driving force behind this aspect of Irish exceptionalism. It therefore remains the case that, around the 1880s, Irish difference in family patterns could be found at the level of detail but this difference was small enough to make Ireland quite an ordinary European country as far as the broad outlines of family behaviour were concerned.

As the nineteenth century came to a close, a new of wave of the extraordinary in family behaviour swept over Europe but stopped at Ireland's shores – or at least slowed sharply and took longer to spread through the population. This had the effect of starting a new phase of exceptionalism in Irish family patterns, the third in our four-phase sequence of divergence and convergence. This phase arose not because Ireland moved away from the European norm but because the rest of the Western world moved on and left Ireland behind. The core of this new departure in Western countries was a wide diffusion of previously unknown degrees of family limitation by couples *within* marriage and a consequent sharp fall in family size (that is, in contrast to the practice of delaying marriage or avoiding it altogether which was the dominant means of limiting fertility in Europe up to that time). Across the provinces of Europe, the median decline in marital fertility in the fifty years between 1880 and 1930 was of the order of 40 per cent, and by the 1920s over half of Europeans lived in countries where the birth rate had fallen below the replacement level of 2.1 births per woman.[3] This, then, was the era in which the two-to-three-child family became a new norm for couples in Europe and smallness emerged as a defining feature of the modern family.

This dramatic shift towards strictly limited childbearing within marriage was accompanied by a gradual widening of access to marriage such that couples married younger and fewer people remained single. As this greater eagerness to marry gathered pace, it turned into a marriage boom in the 1940s and 1950s. This boom was part of what has been called the 'golden age' of Western marriage, that period in the middle decades of the twentieth century when couples married younger, nearly everyone married, few children were born outside marriage, divorce and separation were still uncommon, improved health meant that premature death of spouses became less common and thus left fewer young widows and widowers, and a standard model of working husband and stay-at-home wife was an unquestioned social ideal.[4] Surging marriage rates in these years also produced a surge in the birth rate, resulting in the baby boom of the 1940s to the early 1960s even though average family size continued to be small by Western historical standards.[5]

The Irish deviated from these evolving new patterns by clinging to large family norms for married couples and by intensifying the avoidance of marriage for everyone else. It was this continuing attachment to family patterns that were fading elsewhere in the Western world that defined this new phase of Irish divergence. By the 1930s, as the surge towards marriage was gathering speed elsewhere, marriage avoidance reached new extremes in Ireland. At the same time, marital fertility, which had fallen off a cliff in Europe, declined only slightly in Ireland. The census of population taken in 1936 revealed that one-third of men and a quarter of women aged in their early fifties had never married, indicating exceptionally high levels of 'permanent celibacy'. Marriage registration data showed that the average age of marriage among those who did take the plunge was thirty-three years for men and twenty-eight years for women, an extreme degree of lateness in marriage by contemporary European standards. These patterns, taken together, marked out Ireland in the 1930s as possibly the most marriage-averse society in human history, an outcome that is all the more remarkable when we recall that, a hundred years earlier, Irish difference under this heading had consisted in the opposite pattern of exceptionally early and widespread marriage. Moreover, couples who did marry hesitated to adopt the new preference for small families then sweeping the Western world and continued to have large numbers of children. In the 1946 census of population, among women who had married in their late twenties and had reached the end of their childbearing years by census date, over a quarter had at least seven children and a further 38 per cent had four to six children. Family sizes of this level represented some decline since the late nineteenth century, but the decline was marginal and left Ireland on an isolated path of continuing large families in the new European world of the small family.

This phase of Irish divergence continued until the 1960s, though it is important to be clear where exactly Irish difference lay. It did not consist in an exceptionally high *overall* fertility rate: at around four births per woman on average, Irish total fertility in the early 1960s was only marginally higher than in a number of other developed countries (the corresponding rates for New Zealand and the United States, for example, were 3.8 and 3.6 births per woman). The difference lay, rather, in the family patterns which produced those rates. In Ireland, these were a throwback to an earlier era in that they combined large families among those who married with no families at all among the very many who remained single. This was in contrast to the moderately sized families that were more widely and evenly distributed across the whole population found in Western countries generally. Thus, for example, although Ireland and the United States had similar levels of overall fertility in 1960, in Ireland one mother in three who gave birth in that year was having her fifth child or more while in the United States only one mother in six was doing so.[6]

The present

The emergence of a more prosperous, secular and open society in Ireland from the 1960s onwards instituted a new era of convergence on European norms in the culture and practice of family life and thus brought the last phase in our four-phase cycle of divergence and convergence. This convergence occurred in a context where family patterns throughout the Western world were themselves undergoing profound and unsettling change and thus presented a moving target for Irish families to adapt to. This was the era of the sexual revolution, which brought a more open and expressive approach to sexuality. It was accompanied by the rise of the women's movement and a revolution in gender roles. New models of parenting also came to the fore, partly spurred by new developmental concepts of childhood. These emphasised personal growth and educational attainment as goals of child-rearing and more intensive parental investments as means. These transformations created a new moral universe in which couples no longer needed to marry to have sex, women no longer were expected to think of being a wife and mother as the complete and terminal destination for their lives, fathers were expected to engage more with their children, while at the same time marriage became less of an irrevo-cable commitment that bound couples together until death did them part. There was a technological element to these revolutions in that the invention of the contraceptive pill in the 1960s, along with better access to condoms, made it easier to have sex without the worry of pregnancy and also meant that married women could better control the timing and pace of their childbearing so as to fit in with their lives outside the home. But this technological development was only one element in a freshly evolving edifice of beliefs and norms which turned many of the traditional conventions of family life on their head.

The Irish family in this period not only caught up with developments that had passed it by in the previous half century but jumped on the new wave of family change sweeping through other countries. The novelty of what happened in Ireland was heightened by economic transformation, as the centre of gravity of economic output and employment shifted from the small family farm to urban manufacturing and services, and educational credentials replaced inherited family property or job connections as the chief means to access a desirable place in the occupational structure. The family patterns associated with the small farm system thus lost their economic base at the same time as the cultural tide was turning against the austere, patriarchal traditions that had characterised rural family behaviour.

This mix of economic catch-up and cultural change provoked rapid transition. Irish families quickly becoming smaller, more democratic, less rigid in their division of gender roles, more expressive and affectionate and increasingly preoc-cupied with getting their children through to higher education. They also became more unstable and less tied to marriage, as both marital breakdown and births outside marriage increased. By the close of the 1990s, the birth rate in Ireland was hovering around two children per woman (a half of what it had been in the 1960s), almost one birth in three was to an unmarried mother (up from less than one in twenty in the early 1980s), cohabitation had become an accepted and widely practised form of union (particularly for those in their late twenties), and divorce had become an accepted fact of life. In all of this, however, Irish families also became more typical in international terms, since similar developments were occurring across a broad front of societies in the western world in the same period. The upshot was that, by the end of the twentieth century, the outlier status that had attached to family patterns in Ireland fifty years previously was gone and, as had been the case in the 1880s, Ireland was once again a commonplace European country as far belief and behaviour concerning family life were concerned.

Small difference?

Today, European comparisons highlight Irish families as distinctive on some details but not at all in an outlier position: they are located very much within the normal limits of variation found across European countries. The convergence between Irish and European patterns that had occurred in the closing decades of the twentieth century remains in place. Undoubtedly, within the pattern of overall similarly, close examination reveals many small variations, some more substantial than others, and it is of some interest to explore these. Here, we have space to take only one example, that of divorce.

Ireland was a late arrival on the divorce scene. A pre-emptive blocking clause in the 1937 Constitution, which prohibited the introduction of divorce, held back legislation until, after long and contentious debate, a national vote on the question removed the ban in 1995 and enabled a divorce law to be put into effect in 1997. The wave of divorce liberalisation which had swept Western countries some two to three decades earlier gave some indication of what to expect from this change: divorce rates usually leaped in the immediate aftermath of reform, typically going from less than one divorce per 1000 population per year prior to liberalisation to between three and five per 1000 immediately after the reforms took effect, with some settling down in those rates after the backlog of accumulated broken marriages was cleared. In the event, however, the Irish divorce rate did not quite follow suit. Starting from a zero base prior to 1997, it sputtered into life but failed to gain any real lift-off. The divorce rate peaked in Ireland in 2007 at 0.9 divorces per 1000 population, below the pre-reform threshold of one per 1000 common in other countries, and then turned downwards – there were 25 per cent fewer divorces in Ireland in 2012 than in 2007.[7]

The Irish divorce rate thus uniquely followed the trajectory of a failed rocket launch, turning nose-down towards earth soon after the smoke and noise of blast-off had cleared. Even allowing for some uncertainties about what the divorce data actually measure (since many couples in Ireland split up without seeking divorce), this experience seems to suggest that, while Irish marriages are less stable than they were, they are more stable than they are in other Western countries (bar perhaps Italy) and have reacted in an unusual way to the advent of divorce. There might be some fodder here for theories of Irish difference. There may be some underlying cultural tradition of caution about entering the state of coupledom among Irish people which makes not only for fewer shaky marriages but also for what is a distinctively low rate of entry into second marriage among those who have exited from a previous marriage. Yet, one would want to build too much into such analyses, for reasons that can be touched on as we turn to consideration of the second aspect of difference, its role as a marker of identity and a means to mark off differences with other nations.

Difference and identity

The analysis of Irish family patterns from the perspective of real difference is complex enough, but it is simpler than trying to pin down *perceptions* of difference and assess what role they play in shaping identity. The question here is not whether differences exist but which differences we pick out to distinguish between 'them' and 'us', and what beliefs, feelings and action tendencies we load on to the results. In the early days of social scientific research on how group identities are formed, it was assumed that differences used as identity markers must have substance and perhaps grow out of a formative historical background. In other words, it was taken for granted that differences would be perceived as real because they were real. As the field advanced in the 1970s and 1980s, however, studies emerged which showed that socially potent markers of identity could be constructed out of the most superficial or fleeting features that were somehow selected and imagined as hugely significant. In other words, they become real because they were perceived as real.[8] Jonathan Swift had prefigured this insight in *Gulliver's Travels* in his satirical account of the war between the Lilliputians and the Blefuscans: in Gulliver's earnest report, the war resulted from an ideological dispute between the Big-enders, who believed that boiled eggs should be cracked open at the big end, and Little-enders, who believed they should be cracked open at the little end – this being Swift's thinly veiled lampoon on the role of the Protestant–Catholic divide as ideological cover for the wars between Britain and France in his own day. Similarly, in Northern Ireland today, the Protestant–Catholic divide separates two sub-populations that could hardly be more similar in objective terms yet vehemently and sometimes murderously define themselves as different.[9]

In trying to account for the frequent disconnect between perceived and real difference, some strands of identity theory start with the premise that we have a profound cognitive need for *categorisation* – we can cope with the complexity of the real world only by assigning things and people to a manageable range of simplified categories. The simplification involved works by highlighting and exaggerating similarities between people within categories – what 'we' have in common – and overstating contrasts across categories – how we differ from 'them' – thus imposing stark imagined distinctions on what is, in fact, a jumbled, undifferentiated reality. We then construct our identities by mentally associating ourselves with groups or categories we perceive as attractive or superior and distancing ourselves from those we define as inferior. In some cases, collective crises of confidence and low self-esteem may lead to self-denigrating forms of identification. For example, groups that occupy a lowly position in the social hierarchy and are defined in disdainful terms by those above them may accept that subordinating identity and allow it to seep into their own self-awareness as if it were an objective truth.

It is well beyond the scope of this chapter to examine in detail how these processes relate to perceptions of family in Ireland. However, these strands of identity theory provide a useful warning against an avid search for distinctive features of the Irish (or any other) population and a downgrading of similarities with comparator populations, undertaken to serve a psychological need for boundary-marking and collective identity rather than as an aid to understanding. Thus, we can refer to the example given above of a possible distinctive culture of marriage and divorce in Ireland. Such distinctiveness may indeed exist and may help account for the current pattern of low divorce in Ireland, but, before we use such possible distinctiveness as a base on which to build an image of Irish differ-ence, it needs to be weighed against evidence of similarity in other aspects of family and partnership behaviour, of which there are many.

These issues gain further significance because constructed identities often have consequences for action. When Carleton wrote his accounts of the Irish peasantry, the picture he presented was indulgent and sympathetic even if it was very much a representation of the 'other' for his middle-class Anglo-minded readership (he himself had switched sides by converting to Protestantism and settling into comfortable Dublin surroundings as he made his career). During the Famine, that perception of otherness took on a baleful cast. Under the stern direction of Sir Charles Trevelyan, the British government official in charge of famine relief, mass starvation was interpreted as God's rebuke to the Irish poor for their fecklessness, especially for their reckless levels of childbearing, and as a necessary means to clear the Irish countryside of surplus population. The havoc wreaked by the Famine was allowed to become immeasurably worse as a conse-quence. Indeed, the legacy of harm might be interpreted as contributing to a debilitating inferiority complex which national revival struggled to overcome decades later. The turn to convergence in Irish family patterns in the second half of the nineteenth century outlined earlier might also be located in a similar chain of causation, since the new culture of family behaviour carried strong echoes of Victorian notions of respectability and was pursued in Ireland as a means of keeping up with the metropolis.

As a Catholic national identity was developed and consolidated in the late nine-teenth and early twentieth centuries, visible adherence to Catholic moral doctrine on family and sexuality was adopted as one marker of difference. This was pursued both positively by insiders and negatively by outsiders (as in the characterisation of the newly independent nation as a 'priest-ridden people'). Today, it seems reason-able to judge that family culture and behaviour no longer play this role in any serious way. Ireland is less Catholic than it used to be and has largely ceased to base its concepts of family morality on Catholic teaching, so that, whatever notions of Irish difference are now drawn on to define national identity, it would be hard to argue that a distinctive family morality, whether Catholic or otherwise, is one of them. Even where fine differences exist, as in the case of divorce patterns and marital stability referred to earlier, explanation by reference to a Catholic effect is hard to sustain since other Catholic societies (such as Portugal, Spain and Austria) do not show similar effects. On the other hand, reflecting the complexity of how identities may be constructed, the very absence of difference between Ireland and the European mainstream may now in itself be adopted by many as a defining feature, a reflection of Irish modernity. Perhaps too the Ireland of the not too distant past has become an important 'other' that provides a foil for such conceptions. The past is a foreign country, it has been said. It may well be that our own past history of family patterns is now one of the 'foreign' contrasts that we rely on to help us define who we are today.

Notes

1　The most recent survey of research on these issues since the appearance of K.H. Connell's pioneering study, *The Population of Ireland, 1750–1845* (Oxford, 1950), is William Macafee, 'The pre-Famine Population of Ireland: A Reconsideration', in Brenda Collins, Phillip Ollerenshaw and Trevor Parkhill (eds), *Industry, Trade and People in Ireland, 1650–1950: Essays in Honour of W.H. Crawford* (Belfast: Ulster Historical Trust, 2005), pp. 69–86.

2　For a comprehensive analysis and overview of this phase of Irish family history, see Timothy Guinnane *The Vanishing Irish: Households, Migration and the Rural Economy in Ireland, 1850–1915* (Princeton: Princeton University Press, 1997).

3　Ansley Coale and Roy Treadway, 'A Summary of the Changing Distribution of Overall Fertility, Marital Fertility, and the Proportion Married in the Provinces of Europe', in Ansely Coale and Susan Cotts Watkins (eds), *The Decline of Fertility in Europe* (Princeton: Princeton University Press, 1986), pp. 31–181. See also Tomas Frejka and John Ross, 'Paths to Subreplacement Fertility: The Empirical Evidence', *Population and Development Review*, 27 (Suppl.: Global Fertility Transition, 2001), pp. 213–54. On the surprise and anxiety in Western countries caused by new lows in fertility in the interwar years, see Jay van Bavel, 'Sub-replacement Fertility in the West before the Baby Boom: Past and Current Perspectives', *Population Studies*, 64:1 (2010).

4　Goran Therborn, *Between Sex and Power: Family in the World 1900–2000* (London: Routledge, 2003), pp. 162–70.

5　For an analysis of the mid-century baby boom in Western countries which reveals its puzzling features, see Jay van Bavel and D.S. Rehrer, 'The Baby-boom and Its Causes: What We Know and What We Need to Know', *Population and Development Review*, 39:2 (2013), pp. 257–88.

6　For a general account of the Irish family from national Independence until the 1990s, see Finola Kennedy, *Cottage to Creche: Family Change in Ireland* (Dublin, Institute of Public Administration, 2001). On the details of Irish fertility, see Tony Fahey, 'Trends in Irish Fertility Rates in Comparative Perspective', *Economic and Social Review*, 32:2 (2001). For more recent trends, see Peter Lunn, Tony Fahey and Carmel Hannan, *Family Figures: Family*

Dynamics and Family Types in Ireland, 1986–2006 (Dublin: Economic and Social Research Institute, 2010).

7 See Tony Fahey, 'Small Bang? The Impact of Divorce Legislation on Marital Breakdown in Ireland', *International Journal of Law, Policy and the Family*, 26:2 (2012); T. Fahey, 'Divorce Patterns and Trends: An Overview', in John Eekelaar and Robert George (eds), *Routledge Handbook of Family Law and Policy* (London: Routledge, 2014).

8 For much of the seminal work in this field, see Henri Tajfel, *Human Groups and Social Categories: Studies in Social Psychology* (Cambridge: Cambridge University Press, 1981).

9 Tony Fahey, Bernadette Hayes and Richard Sinnott, *Consensus and Conflict. A Study of Values and Attitudes in the Republic of Ireland and Northern Ireland* (Dublin: Institute of Public Administration, 2005).

8

Single women in story and society

Anne Byrne

The family has been central to Irish culture and society, evincing an anxious preoccupation with marital and familial relationships. Familism is associated with
patriarchal systems in which the family is a valued social institution, supporting
traditional performances of gender and sexuality in heterosexual marriage. A
thorough understanding of the relations of 'blood and marriage' was crucial to a
1930s American anthropological study of Irish family and community life.[1]
Arranged marriage or 'match-making' was still in evidence, ensuring the transfer of
the family name and farm property from one generation to the next, advancing the
status of the newly connected families, while developing new kin networks.
Though families made provision for, or educated offspring who neither inherited
land nor received a dowry, many were forced through economic necessity to leave
home to make a living elsewhere. The late nineteenth and twentieth centuries were
eras of emigration of single women and men, high rates of singleness in the population, late age of marriage and high fertility within marriage – distinctive patterns
largely ascribed to impartible farm inheritance, a 'stem family system' in which one
child would inherit, marry and produce the next generation. Given the strict
control of sexuality and sexual relations among the unmarried, the strictures of a
life of enforced celibacy was as significant as economic factors in motivating
emigration. For 'bachelors' and 'spinsters' who remained at home, opportunities
for sexual relationships were limited, despite, or perhaps because of, the advances
of 'modernisation', bringing with them differing expectations of marital intimacy,
dependency relations and gender equality for example. The new state set a
marriage 'bar' in the 1930s, that prevented female civil servants from continuing
their employment after marriage. This sent out signals to women that waged work
and family making should not and could not be combined. But women also understood that education and meaningful work could be a basis for self-fulfilment,

though at some cost to becoming a wife and mother. Intimacy and independence are set at odds.

John B. Keane's novel *The Chastitute*, captures the growing despair and decline of a 'love hungry farmer'.[2] John Bosco is a 'marriageable bachelor' with land, unable to find a woman who might marry him. A familiar figure, but an account of his life and how he might be reconciled to his bachelorhood is rarely heard. In a society in which 'marriage avoidance' is a strategy for increasing prosperity, the unmarried received poorer treatment. Sociological studies from the 1960s place bachelors as marginalised, at risk and unhappy.[3] However the marginalisation thesis is challenged in an ethnographic study that argues that identification with a masculine stereotype of men as 'tough, confident and self-reliant' goes some way in adapting to bachelorhood in rural Clare.[4] Compared to bachelor men, how are single, never married women portrayed in sociological accounts and literary fiction? How do their gendered stereotypes serve them?

Sociological models of rural communities in the 1970s placed men – including bachelors – at the centre of their analyses, married women and children at the outer perimeters, with unmarried women hovering at the limits of community. Women's lower social and economic status circumscribed their future options. To be unmarried without children was undesirable and there was little or no positive cultural support for the single life. Young women lived a life of 'unrelieved drudgery' in which they had to work as hard as their mothers on the farm in return for their keep. There were few comforts and fewer opportunities for socialising away from family and community.[5] What are the points of contact or distance between empirical studies and fiction? How are single women portrayed? Two particular stories of single women, authored by men, are examined here to consider fictional stereotypes of singlehood and womanhood. How they inspire, edit or illuminate women's lives is of some interest.

Literary spinsters

William Trevor's short story 'The Ballroom of Romance' (1972), set in the 1950s, concerns a turning point in the life of Bridie, a single woman caring for her widowed father, labouring on the family farm, tending to cows and hens.[6]

> Although her father still called her a girl, Bridie was thirty-six. She was tall and strong; the skin of her fingers and palms were stained, and harsh to touch … since childhood she'd torn away at the rough scotch grass that grew each spring among her father's mangolds and sugar beet; since childhood she'd harvested potatoes in August … wind had toughened the flesh of her face, sun had browned it; her neck and nose were lean, her lips touched with early wrinkles.

Every Saturday for twenty years, Bridie cycles seven miles to the dance, dreaming of a boy she once loved, now hoping for a man that 'would do'. 'Dano Ryan would have done, Bridie often thought, because he was a different kind of bachelor, he had a lonely look about him as if he was tired of being on his own ... Dano Ryan would have done because she felt he wouldn't mind coming to live in the farmhouse while her one-legged father was still about the place.' Bridie nurtures quiet hope of relationship and fantasises about Dano sitting at the table with her father, eating a meal she has cooked, watching them both as they set out to work on the farm while she creates a comfortable home. The night of the dance, Bridie realises that Mrs Griffin 'was arranging to marry him', the widow woman, with whom Ryan lodged. She wants to weep, to let others know how she feels about the loss of love, the death of her mother and the mould of her life as her father's carer. The sympathetic attention and comfort of others is not available to Bridie. She wishes that Dano would 'look at her in his decent way and to stroke with his road-mender's fingers the backs of her hands'. Her dignity, stoicism and dutiful loyalty to her father work to conceal her feelings, stop her tears and silence her voice.

The younger women selectively pursue eligible men, avoiding the three middle-aged bachelors, who 'were wedded already, to stout and whiskey and laziness, to three old mothers somewhere up in the hills'. Contempt is expressed for Madge Dowling, who 'should accept her condition – her age, her squint and poor complexion – and not make herself ridiculous going out after men'. In seeing herself as others perceive Madge, 'dancing on beyond her time', Bridie appraises her future. On his mother's death, Bowser Egan, having spent his inheritance on drink, would come looking for her. She would marry him, a more rational choice perhaps than indicated by the final line of the story, 'because it would be lonesome being by herself in the farmhouse'.

Trevor's single woman is restricted by her place in the social system, by her familial obligations and by her performance of conventional womanhood. In the story, Bridie does not have a surname of her own. Her conversation is polite and respectful, her inner feelings are kept in check, an acquiescent victim of circumstances. There is no opportunity given to her to speak out against the social norms that valorise marriage. There is no event in the story that might query the social blaming of single people for their singlehood. There is no moment for Bridie in which she might consider a meaningful life as a single woman. If spinsterhood was an acceptable alternative to marriage, perhaps its 'deviant' status might not have had such a strong pull.

The Lonely Passion of Judith Hearne by Brian Moore (1955) begins with Judith, a woman in her early forties, settling into another, cheaper, boarding house in Belfast of the 1950s.[7] Her means are meagre, having a modest legacy from her aunt, Judith gives piano lessons to a dwindling number of students and economises by rigourous management of her appetite. Her friends are few; Edie another single woman, ill in a nursing home, and Moira who is married. Judith presents herself as a woman 'rejected' by men, ashamed of her singlehood but who hopes to marry some day. In the new boarding house, there might be somebody 'charming'.

Looking in the mirror she sees herself as a desirable woman, '[h]er gaze deceiving, transforming her to her imaginings, changed the contour of her sallow-skinned face, skilfully re-fashioning her long pointed nose ... Her dark eyes, eyes which skittered constantly in imagined fright, became wide, soft, luminous. Her frame, plain as a cheap clothes rack, filled now with soft curves ...'

Judith becomes enamoured with James Madden, a widower, home from America, looking for a new start in life and business. Unsure of his first impressions of her, Judith's vulnerability claims her. 'Alone with this lonely stranger, she waited for his fumbled excuses, his departure ... He would see her shyness, her stiffness. And it would frighten him, he would remember he was alone with her. He would listen politely to whatever inanity she could manage to get out and then he would see the hysteria in her eyes, the hateful hotflush in her cheeks. And he would go as all men had gone before him.' Judith is bound by middle-class convention, by appearances, by religious observation and by dutiful obligation to the memory of her aunt whom she looked after. Madden mistakenly believes that Judith is a wealthy woman and is attentive. She responds, believing he will soon propose marriage. Marriage was the opportunity to escape, 'to go off, off to something better, something that might lead to something wonderful'. Realising that Judith's wealth is illusory, Madden rejects her. She turns to the comfort of alcohol and her final unraveling begins. Having lost faith in the Church and in her confessor who does not listen to her, she is alone. To Moira and her family, she is an object of pity. Evicted from the boarding house for her drinking, she speaks the truth of her life to Moira, telling her 'everything is finished', her life has no longer any meaning. She tells of her twenty-year wait for marriage, how Mr Right changes from tall, dark and handsome to 'anybody, anybody who might be eligible' and, after that, anybody will do. 'You're up for auction, a country auction, where the auctioneer stands up and says what am I bid? ... and somebody comes along, laughable and you take him. If you can get him. Because it's either that or back on the shelf for you. Back to your furnished room and your prayers. And your hopes.' Turned down by Madden, she would accept him still. As a single woman, she is unwanted, rejected by society, 'too old', 'too ugly', 'left on the shelf'. Judith feels the stigma of her singlehood. In these fictional portrayals of Bridie and Judith, the only possible flight from single-ness is through marriage. Failure to marry is failure to claim adulthood. Judith at least is given the opportunity of speech. 'What am I doing with my life? I ask you ... A single girl with no kin, what am I doing? O Moira, you always were the lucky one, a husband and children around you, you'll never know what it's like to be me.' Fiction such as this brings us closer to understanding the bite of conformity and difference, the personal and social effects of stigma and deviance and the conse-quences of losing one's entitlement to choose. Framed around the conflict of single identity and woman identity, the social norms of marriage and motherhood dominate these stories.

How to be single, how to talk about singleness, how to respond to the perception of others is a complicated business as is any portrayal of the single life. As with Judith and Bridie, lifelong singlehood was a way of life for a large number of people in an era of limited opportunities for women. The economic dependence of women on men was the norm, and the framing of womanhood through marriage and family a national endeavour. The flight from singleness into marriage was filled with urgency; to be married was respectable, to be single was second best. The failure to marry and mother was felt as a personal failure and a source of shame. Despite the knowledge of the effect of social factors – lack of a suitable partner, lack of means to marry, the need to care for others or the need to earn money – single people were blamed for being single and made to feel that their singleness was a mark of difference. Against this frame, the fictional portraits are not inaccurate. Moore and Trevor write about the emotional weight of singlehood; readers may have been more empathic to the single life as a consequence. None the less the hopeful possibility of living an acceptable life as a single woman is written out of these stories.

The recognition that the duties and strictures of Catholic marriage, obedience to husband and selfless motherhood might not be the best option for a 'modern girl' surfaces later in Irish fiction. For example, in Maeve Kelly's novel *Florrie's Girls*, Cos cedes the farm to her brother, refuses marriage to a neighbour and emigrates, because there is a bigger world out there, filled with people, ideas, music and the opportunity to live life in a different pattern.[8]

Sociological analyses of singleness

Sociology and fiction may be more similar than different. However while fiction has the capacity to draw the reader close to the time and place of a story world, and acquaint the reader with characters, their thoughts and perceptions, the intent of the author is to tell a good story. Sociology is also concerned with stories of people's lives and relationships. But it is sociology's questioning of assumptions about how the world works, its capacity for reflection on the ways things are, combined with a systematic approach to gathering and interpreting evidence about society and culture that gives it a different intent and designates it as a human science. Consider the work of sociologists concerned with the organisation and structure of family life across time and cultures. The ideal of 'family' and its durable real-world manifestations can be far apart, as Pierre Bourdieu points out.[9] Regardless, the 'family' represents a particular vision of a stable social world, prescribing relationships between women and men, children and parents. Family relationships based on love and acts of generosity rather than calculation become the internal (mental) and external (social) plumb line against which all other rela-tionships are evaluated. Individual interests are identified with collective interests; to question the norm of family life requires courage. Bourdieu described the expe-riences of single women pressurised to conform as 'social suffering', evident in the story of Bridie and Judith. In a sociological study of singleness in 1990s Ireland, Cara, an interviewee, expresses the difficulty of accepting single identity.

> I would love ... if being single was OK. If society would allow people to be single ... that must come from in here first and I probably have a conditioning that makes it difficult even for me to allow single to be OK. So I can't accept it myself. (Cara, 39 years)[10]

There are more terms for single women than men, indicating a differential access to power and control. The bachelor is always 'eligible', but can choose not to marry; the 'spinster' by contrast is no longer 'eligible'. 'Maiden aunt' places a woman within a family and sexual system. Similarly 'Old maid' combines servitude with celibacy. '*Sceach sa bearna*', an Irish term for 'stopgap', 'makeshift' or substitute, describes an unmarried woman as a helpmate who labours in the home of her married sibling. 'Bachelorette', the female diminutive of the more positive appellation of bachelor, refers to a transitory and exuberant moment in a woman's life, perhaps. The category 'single' is problematic, referring to the unmarried, divorced, separated, widowed, cohabiters with and without children. The category can be further complicated by sexuality, race or class; for example, in a familistic society, is it more difficult to be heterosexual and single, or lesbian or gay and single, both being some distance from the norm? Researchers compare the married to the unmarried, the ever married to the never married, the always single to the single again. New terms are devised to lessen the inherent normativity in the categories; for example 'solo woman' or 'socially single' may have less conceptual bias than 'unpartnered', 'unmarried' or 'single'.

Currently close to half the Irish population aged over fifteen is 'statistically single' (never married) but many will legally marry or live in same-sex or opposite-sex couple relationships for most of their lives. To be 'socially single' indicates that one is currently on one's own, not part of a couple, though this might change. To be 'sociologically single' depends on whether singleness is defined as temporary or permanent, voluntary or involuntary.[11] *Voluntary temporary singles* postpone marriage for other activities (education, career, personal goals), *voluntary stable singles* choose to be single and wish to remain so (widowed, religious orders, carers), *involuntary temporary singles* are actively seeking a partner to marry while *involuntary stable singles* would have liked to marry but the opportunity has passed or is not available. These positions are translated into common usage as 'single-and-looking' (the majority) and 'single-at-heart' (a minority). People move in and out of singleness or coupled relationships across the life span, and singleness can take on different meanings and weight as one ages. The personal and social significance of being single is further inflected by one's personal dispositions, one's relationship biography, as much as the normative expectations of the cultural era in which we live out our lives. Nonetheless the word 'single' continues to carry a burden; the nature of this burden is worth thinking about.

Commonly perceived as a 'problem', singleness is a frequent topic for empirical inquiry and everyday curiosity. Advice on how to live a meaningful life as a single person is a popular genre in Ireland. The possibilities for happiness and intimacy have been colonised by 'coupledom', with little consideration given to the satisfaction that can arise from close friendships, sibling relationships or the pleasure that comes from simply being alone. Conversely, assuming that those in partnerships are happier than those who are not partnered has been scientifically challenged, with study participants reporting an increase in life satisfaction following the dissolution of an unhappy marriage.[12] In Irish fiction, much concerned with the harsh portrayal of women's lives, married women are portrayed as far from happy. Consider the extent of the accommodations to endure constricting marriages from one end of the century to another – author Kate O'Brien's character Caroline Lanigan in the novel *Without my Cloak,* whose husband is oblivious to her sexual desire but whom she cannot leave, is one such example, as is the betrayed female protagonist in Anne Enright's *The Portable Virgin.*[13]

We learn much about how a society works by the effects of normativity on human relationships and life choices. Normative values express collective judgements about what is desirable, shaping how society ought to be structured, encouraging attachments to particular institutions and practices, discouraging others. Normative statements are prescriptive concerning gender, sexuality, race, class, age, ability, ethnicity or 'marital' status for example. We are largely unaware of the ideological force of normativity; in the interest of solidarity, we abide by social norms with little reflection on their regulatory effects. When we 'bump up' against a norm we begin to understand its constraints. A single women who finds herself explaining once again to a stranger or relative at a wedding why she is not married is someone experiencing being different to the norm and is required to provide an explanation for it.

Normative expectations are attached to strong social identities that flow from marital status; it is expected that a woman of a certain age ought to be married and, if married, a mother. Normative identities are valued while non-normative identities can be targets for social stigma and self-stigma. Erving Goffman describes how stigma works to reinforce the status quo, distinguishing stigmatised from stigmatisers.[14] Goffman identifies three types of stigma: personal, physical and social. The possession of an undesirable attribute is enough to 'spoil' one's social identity. Depending on how attached they are to the more valued social identity, persons who are stigmatised may experience a loss in social status, rejection, discrimination or worse and can suffer from lowered self-esteem and depression.

An analysis of midlife development data of three thousand adults (twenty-five to seventy-four years) in 1995 in the United States, indicated that unmarried men and women were more likely to report interpersonal discriminatory treatment than married persons. Single women reported being treated with less respect, reporting having been more harassed and threatened compared to married women. People who were never married and unpartnered felt the stigma of being single more than the formerly married.[15] Multiple studies of unmarried adults demonstrate the deleterious effects of interpersonal discrimination on one's sense of self. The appraisals of others are especially significant to us. If one is consistently regarded negatively, it is likely that these negative attitudes will become part of one's self-evaluation.

People whose social identities are 'spoiled' may work to adjust their identities in an effort to be acceptable to others or they may attempt to 'pass' as 'normal'. To prevent further intrusiveness, a woman may wear a wedding ring when travelling alone to symbolically 'pass' as married. The ring itself is a status symbol, identifying oneself as a member of the preferred group. Stigmatising attributes vary across cultures and eras, but stigma as a social process is ubiquitous and is linked to stereotyping. The targeted groups are perceived to be a disturbance to the social order and the beliefs that sustain it.

Negative generalisations of others can produce strong emotional responses and depend on whether the stigmatised person is perceived as in control of their circumstances or not. It is notoriously difficult to adjust stereotypical responses, despite new information or interaction with individual members of a stereotyped group. Stigma, stereotyping, negative (and positive) appraisals of others point to the presence of powerful conventions at work in society and culture.

Arguably the stereotypes produced by society are themselves a form of fiction. The lonely and isolated spinster, the sexy single or the independent career-minded woman are examples of contradictory fictions that have to be navigated and negotiated by single women. This is no easy task for anybody seeking to combine independence and intimacy. Research studies suggest that single women have to work hard to avoid being stereotyped and stigmatised, particularly in familistic societies such as the United States, Britain and Ireland. While younger single women are immune from negative appraisals, once the local age of marriage has passed, perceptions become increasingly pejorative. Women are castigated if perceived as responsible for their unmarried state or are actively choosing to be single – explaining the majority preference for presenting oneself as 'single-and-looking' perhaps? The preoccupation with heterosexual coupling, marriage or 'matrimania' and the constant devaluing of the single status is, according to the American sociologist Bella dePaulo, a form of 'singlism', prevalent in society and scientific investigations of single people. 'Singlism' is the stereotyping of, stigmatising of and discrimination against people who are single, despite survey evidence that suggests that single people and married people are more alike than different.[16]

The solo woman

Single Blessedness was anonymously authored in 1852 with the subtitle *Or Single Ladies and Gentleman against the Slanders of the Pulpit, Press and Lecture Room*. It was written in response to 'public scorn and odium by the voice and pen' for single people. The author asserts the right of single people to speak out and contest the representation of the 'single class' as a 'lost race' or 'an inferior order of beings'.[17] Written and performed more than a century and a half later, *Singlehood* by Una McKevitt, is a play based on fifty interviews with Irish 'singletons' who champion singlehood.[18] This is a rare example in which personal experiences of being single are central to the dramatisation, and articulated in a public space. Chiming with contemporary research, autonomy and independence are highly valued, as is living alone. The word 'freedom' is repeated, freedom from being 'in a crappy relation-ship', freedom to 'come and go as you want', freedom to 'do the dishes, clean up, wash your socks when you want', freedom from being affected 'by somebody else's feelings and emotions'. Intimate relationships are considered but without compro-mising cherished independence. Rewriting the script of singlehood, accenting the positives and enabling single people's voices to reach a wider audience are forms of politics and may help to diminish singlism.

In a recent series 'The Single Files' in *The Irish Times*, being single in contempo-rary Ireland was explored for older and younger singles, men and women, ever and never married, with and without children.[19] While most of those interviewed were 'single-and-looking' with fewer 'single-at-heart', single stigma does not seem to be as prevalent. Single people feel less marginalised and more willing to speak out about the many ways to live as a single person. There is more acceptance now of living as a single person. Opportunities for education, paid work and economic independence, and improved reproductive control combined with the ideological support of the women's movement for sexual and economic equality have benefited all women. The seismic shift in women's lives in Ireland from the 1960s onwards is part of the reason for the changes in attitudes to single women and men. As Lily, an interviewee, comments.

> I could list at least two or three dozen women who are not married between the ages of thirty and fifty ... I believe we were the kids of the sixties and we found a certain independence, not totally reliant on having appendages of a husband ... there is a certain amount of independence among us ... there is a certain belief in independ-ence. (Lily, forty-three years).[20]

Lily wants neither to be an appendage nor to have one. Women are actively making different choices concerning marriage and motherhood that were not possible in the first half of the century. Single women are clearly not 'anti-family', providing much emotional and practical care for their own and other people's families. Part-nership status does not have the same significance as it once had; single women who 'opt in' to single motherhood are one such example, making a break between marriage and maternity. Contesting the cultural norm of the nuclear family based on heterosexual marriage, single women develop deep attachments, family, friend-ship and sexual relationships, according to own desires and preferences. This distinguishes single women (the single-at-heart at least) from others. The picture that emerges from sociological research is that, while single women's own responses to the single status varies across the life span, most are autonomous, independent, resourceful, resilient, well adjusted and happy with their lives. The 'shadow of marriage' is not as long as it used to be.

Those who are sympathetic to and have some insight into the lives of those who are stigmatised achieve the status of 'wise persons', according to Goffman, providing support and encouragement for the 'marginalised'. Single women themselves can be included in the 'wise person' category; evidence from research shows that those relationships that diminish or erode single autonomy and identity are carefully avoided, while those that support singleness are nurtured, demonstrating a capacity for creating new forms of interdependency.[21] A recognition that womanhood is no longer 'a one size fits all' category but is variable and diverse is confirmed by evidence about single women's lives in Ireland, the US and UK.[22] We need more research about the actual realities of single women's lives – historically and now – as well as more fictional accounts of the relational possibilities, values and choices that imaginatively stretch personal, social and political being. Irish women writers are challenging stereotypes and misconceptions of womanhood, troubling gender relations and crucially separating 'woman' from 'nation'.[23] An analysis of Irish (women's) writing about single women would go some way to shorten the distance between Irish sociology and Irish studies, a journey that has been initiated by Irish women's studies feminist scholars.[24] Perhaps placing 'solo women' central to imaginative writing or as narrators of their own lives may first have to be rehearsed on stage like the aforementioned *'Singlehood'*? More people are choosing to be ever single in Ireland, postponing marriage, dissolving marriages, and choosing to be un/never/married. Being happy with oneself and making self-determined choices not only enables 'solo women' to pursue the creative, practical and relational passions that animate a life but may also inspire others to question the dominant version of pro-family ideology and the too narrow conceptions of womanhood, in a rapidly changing society. If we were to rewrite Bridie's and Judith's stories, might we too re-imagine them as 'tough, confident and self-reliant'? What else might we write?

Notes

1 Conrad Arensberg and Solon Kimball, *Family and Community in Ireland* (Co. Clare: CLASP, 2001).

2 John B. Keane, *The Chastitute* (Cork: The Mercier Press, 1981).

3 For an assessment of sociological studies on single men and women in the first half of the twentieth century, see Anne Byrne, 'Single Women in Irish Society: A Re-examination of the Sociological Evidence', in Anne Byrne and Madeleine Leonard (eds), *Women in Irish Society: A Sociological Reader* (Belfast: Beyond the Pale, 1997), pp. 415–30.

4 Chris Curtin and Tony Varley, 'Marginal Men? Bachelor Farmers in a West of Ireland

Community', in Chris Curtin, Pauline Jackson, Barbara O'Connor (eds), *Gender in Irish Society* (Galway: Galway University Press, 1987), pp. 287–308.

5   Patrick McNabb, '"Demography" and "Social Structure"', in Jeremiah Newman (ed.), *Limerick Rural Survey 1958–1964* (Tipperary: Muintir na Tire Publications, 1964), and Eithne Viney, 'Women in Rural Ireland', *Christus Rex*, 24 (1968), pp. 333–42.

6   William Trevor, 'The Ballroom of Romance', *in The Stories of William Trevor* (London: Penguin, 1983). The quotes come from pp. 186, 190, 196, 189, 188, 197, 199. A film of the same name was made in 1982 and directed by Pat O'Connor, see www.imdb.com/title/tt0327464/.

7   Brian Moore, *The Lonely Passion of Judith Hearne* (online: Back Bay Books, 1955, 1983), pp. 21, 26, 90, 199, 199, 198. A film of the same name was made in 1988 and directed by Jack Clayton, see www.imdb.com/title/tt0093431.

8   For a discussion of 'the modern girl', see Louise Ryan, 'Negotiating Modernity and Tradition: Newspaper Debates on the "modern girl" in the Irish Free State', *Journal of Gender Studies*, 7:2 (1998), pp. 181–97; Maeve Kelly, *Florrie's Girls* (London: Michael Joseph, 1989).

9   Pierre Bourdieu, 'On the Family as a Realised Category', *Theory, Culture and Society*, 13:3 (1996), pp. 19–26.

10 Anne Byrne, 'Developing a Sociological Model for Researching Women's Self and Social Identities', *European Journal of Women's Studies* (Special Issue on Identities), 10:4 (2003), pp. 443–64.

11 Peter J. Stein, *Single* (New York: Spectrum Books, 1976).

12 Greitmeyer investigates the robustness of the single stereotype based on personality characteristics and finds it wanting; see Tobias Greitemeyer, 'Stereotypes of Singles: Are Singles What We Think?', *European Journal of Social Psychology*, 39:3 (2009), pp. 368–83.

13 For a perceptive analysis of Kate O'Brien's women characters, see Sharon Tighe Mooney, 'Nun, Married, Old Maid: Kate O'Brien's Fiction, Women and Irish Catholicism', PhD thesis, Maynooth, Ireland, 2009. See also Kate O'Brien, *Without My Cloak* (London: Virago Modern Classics, 1987), and Anne Enright, *The Portable Virgin* (London: Vintage, 1998).

14 Erving Goffman, *Stigma: Notes on the Management of a Spoiled Identity* (Englewood Cliffs, NJ: Prentice-Hall, 1963).

15 Anne Byrne and Deborah Carr, 'Caught in the Cultural Lag: The Stigma of Singlehood', *Psychological Inquiry: An International Journal for the Advancement of Psychological Theory*, 16:2, 3 (2005), pp . 84–91.

16 For research on single people in the US see Bella dePaulo, *Singled Out: How Singles Are Stereotyped, Stigmatised and Ignored and Still Live Happily Ever After* (New York: St Martin's Griffin, 2006).

17 Anonymous, *Single Blessedness; Or Single Ladies and Gentleman against the Slanders of the Pulpit, Press and Lecture Room* (Boston: C.S. Francis and Co., 1852).

18 Una McKevitt, *Singlehood*, http://unamckevitt.blogspot.ie/ 2012.

19 Laura Slattery and Joe Humphreys, 'The Single Files', *Irish Times*, 16–21 February 2013.

20 Anne Byrne, 'Women Unbound: Single Women in Ireland', in Virginia Yans-McLoughlin and Rudy Bell (eds), *Women Alone* (New Brunswick, NJ: Rutgers University Press, 2008), pp. 29–73.

21 Anne Byrne, 'Women Unbound'.

22 For a UK study see Roona Simpson, *Contemporary Spinsterhood in Britain: Gender Partnership Status and Social Change* (online: VDM Verlag, 2005).

23 For analyses of Irish women's fiction see Anne Owens Weekes, 'Ordinary Women: Themes

in Contemporary Fiction by Irish Women', *Colby Quarterly*, 31:1 (1995), pp. 88–99; Margaret Kelleher, 'The Field Day Anthology and Irish Women's Literary Studies', *Irish Review*, 30 (2003), pp. 82–94; Heather Ingam, *Twentieth Century Fiction by Irish Women* (Farnham: Ashgate, 2007).

24 Linda Connolly, 'The Limits of Irish Studies: Historicism, Culturalism, Paternalism', *Irish Studies Review*, 12:2 (2004), pp. 139–62.

9

The Irish body

Tom Inglis

The forms of physical abuse reported by witnesses to the Committee included punching, flogging, assault and bodily attacks, hitting with the hand, kicking, ear pulling, hair pulling, head shaving, beating on the soles of the feet, burning, scalding, stabbing, severe beatings with or without clothes, being made to kneel and stand in fixed positions for lengthy periods, made to sleep outside overnight, being forced into cold or excessively hot baths and showers, hosed down with cold water before being beaten, beaten while hanging from hooks on the wall, being set upon by dogs, being restrained in order to be beaten, physical assaults by more than one person, and having objects thrown at them. (Ryan Commission on Child Abuse)[1]

In the opening to his book on the history of discipline and punishment in the West, Foucault gave a graphic description of what the French state did to Damiens who in 1757 had tried unsuccessfully to assassinate the King.[2] They tortured him in public for three days before pulling him limb from limb. Foucault argued that the way of thinking in the Classical age was that the horrific nature of the crime committed – an attack on the body of the King – had to be responded to with a commensurate and appropriate attack on the body of the criminal.

Foucault argued that, if we want to understand the history of the West, then we should begin not with the mind and ideas but with the ways in which the body became subject to power. We should focus on the different technologies and strategies that were developed to create disciplined, docile, compliant bodies.

In the three hundred years since Damiens's demise, the torture and physical punishment of bodies has moved away from the public gaze to behind closed doors. Even there, it is strictly regulated and controlled and mostly associated with terrorists and others who have committed crimes against humanity. The practice of parents hitting their children has been the subject of public debate: many find it repulsive when it is done in public.[3]

Foucault argued that over the next two hundred years there was a general shift in punishment techniques. Instead of physical attacks on the body, softer, longer, more subtle, forms were developed that focused on reforming the soul rather than punishing the body, and revolved around confinement, surveillance, work, training and education. He was interested in how forms of correction, discipline and punishment became specialised technologies that were applied in schools to the wider population of children. It may be that what is different, if not unique, about the Irish was the forms of discipline and punishment that were developed in industrial and reformatory schools, in Magdalen laundries, and other special institutions for dealing with misfits, delinquents and those who did not conform to the dominant Catholic normative order.

Foucault emphasised how the creation and maintenance of social order was dependent on building a scientific knowledge of what bodies did and how they could be regulated. In his later work, he focused on sexuality. He argued that in the nineteenth century, rather than repressing sex, the Victorians became obsessed with it. Sex came under the microscope. This operated at two levels. At the level of power, there was a new emphasis on demographic studies, of accumulating scientific information through censuses and other studies, about who was living where, in what conditions and how many children were being produced by whom.

There was an obsession with discovering how sex operated, the pathologies and perversions to which it gave rise – hysterical women, masturbating children, and homosexual men. These studies eventually gave rise to new scientific disciplines such as psychiatry and psychology.[4]

At the level of the subject, individuals were sexualised. There were strategies of dividing and separating the sexes, of regulating and controlling desire. Adults and children were made aware of sex. They were educated in the art of confession, how to talk about sex, how to recognise the ways in which it infiltrated and penetrated their bodies. At the same time, there was a move towards making individuals regulate themselves through making them responsible for controlling their instincts, urges and desires.

It was through the regulation of bodies and strategies of sexualisation of self-monitoring and regulation that the modern self emerged. The modern individual is constituted within the move away from punitive regimes to systems and strategies of critical self-awareness. The self emerges through individual moral responsibility, particularly sexual responsibility. It may well be, then, that if there is a cultural difference about the Irish, it lies in the way this process took place in Ireland and how the Catholic Church developed a monopoly not just over schooling and the discipline and punishment of bodies, but over the discourse and practice of sexualising bodies.[5]

Dealing with deviant bodies

In his history of discipline and punishment, Foucault did not examine the emergence of specialised schools and institutions that were developed for children who were deemed not to be cared for, disciplined and controlled by their parents. These included orphanages, industrial and reformatory schools, asylums and Magdalen laundries. It may well be that what makes Ireland different is not just the proliferation of these specialised institutions but the techniques of discipline and punishment that were developed within them. It was not just the regimes of physical punishment but the strategies of denying sex, shaming, demeaning and demoralising those who did not conform to the normative, particularly sexual, Catholic social order.

The creation of industrial and reformatory schools was, then, part of the new order of schooling that developed in the nineteenth century. In these schools, over generations, wild, unruly, uncivilised children were coerced, trained and educated to become orderly, docile, compliant, productive and efficient bodies. Children were socialised into a sense of self that recognised and internalised systems of regulated time and space and how they, like everything and everyone, had to be in their proper time and place.

These transformations came about mainly through voluntary compliance that revolved around parents and children seeking honour and respect: there was an interest and desire to be self-regulated and civilised. In general, people wanted to become polite and well-mannered and to be able to regulate and control their own emotions. Children who did not go to ordinary school, whose parents were deemed to be unable to look after them, were incarcerated in special schools.

The forms of punishment that were employed in industrial and reformatory schools in Ireland during the twentieth century, as summarised by the Ryan Commission report at the beginning of this chapter, do not include the various forms of sexual assaults that were perpetrated on inmates. The Ryan report found that sexual abuse was endemic in these schools and followed definite patterns. It would seem that the abuse was a form of sadistic pleasure but also a way of exerting power and maintaining control over the inmates.

The question is to whether these forms of sexual abuse were pathological practices that bore little or no resemblance to what was happening outside of the schools, or to what extent it resembled forms of abuse, discipline and control that were exercised over a wide range of children in wider society. A detailed survey of Irish adults in 2001 found that three in ten women and one in four men reported some level of sexual abuse in childhood. Amongst the women, one in five reported some kind of physical contact sexual abuse: one in twenty women participants reported that the abuse involved penetrative sex. Amongst men, one in six reported contact physical abuse in childhood.[6]

One of the questions that the Ryan Report did not address is whether the pathological practices of the schools reveal what was normal in wider Irish society.[7] Was what happened in industrial and reformatory schools exceptional, or did it reflect a negative, harsh and often brutal attitude to the body and children that was normal in wider Irish society? There is no society that does not have mechanisms and strategies for disciplining and controlling children, some of them more brutal than others, but perhaps what makes the Irish different was the way in which children were seen, understood and treated, not just in industrial and reformatory schools but in wider society.

There is plenty of evidence to suggest that corporal punishment, including physical beatings with the use of hands, canes and leathers, was still common in Irish primary and secondary schools up until the early 1970s. Corporal punishment in schools was eventually banned in 1982 and its use was made a criminal offence in 1996. While there is no evidence to suggest that Ireland was different in abandoning the use of corporal punishment, what is not known is what forms of corporal punishment were used, when, where and by whom, and to what extent these were similar to or different from forms used in other Western societies.[8]

In her study of a Kerry community in the 1970s, the American anthropologist Scheper-Hughes claimed that corporal punishment of young school children was endemic in the local primary school and was defended as a right by teachers – who were supported by the local clergy and parents – for children who were considered to be the 'bold' ones. She also argued that the lack of concern about the corporal punishment of children, and its damaging effects, was part of a general lack of physical and emotional attachment that some mothers had for their children. She claimed that some mothers were forced to live the illusion and engage in the rhetoric of the honour of having large families, but deliberately used children-rearing strategies that prevented them from becoming too close or attached to some of their children, as they knew many of them would have to migrate and leave home. Scheper-Hughes referred, in particular, to the lack of physical affection between some of the mothers she studied and their children, especially the practice of wrapping babies in swaddling clothes and leaving them isolated and unattended.[9] We do not know much about how the dispositions and practices of these mothers were different from other mothers in Ireland and other parts of the West.

We do know, however, that there were many related strategies of power that were exercised over children and adults that involved secreting away, isolating, expelling and confining those who did not conform to the dominant norms and values. We know that women who became sexually deviant were taken away and confined against their will, often illegally, in Magdalen laundries and asylums – 10,015 between 1922 and 1996.[10] There was also a general propensity to confine people who did not conform to the norm in psychiatric hospitals. This reached a peak of 21,075 in 1958 the majority of whom were committed involuntarily and many of whom were men and women who were designated as 'feeble minded', some of whom were single women confined after childbirth or miscarriage.[11] We know that babies of many women who gave birth outside marriage were sent to America, often illegally, to be adopted: the estimated number between 1949 and 1973 was about 2,100.[12] What we do not know is to what extent the strategies that were exercised over deviant bodies in Ireland were exceptional, unique or even significantly different from what happened in the rest of Western society. And the question remains as to what extent this treatment of deviant bodies was part of a wider cultural disposition to sexuality, fertility and children.

Regulating sex

Through Foucault, then, we can begin to understand Irish difference in terms of sexuality and the harsh regimes of bodily discipline and control instituted over centuries. We might start, then, with the Irish monks and their development of penitential practices. Michael Carroll has suggested that there is an Irish form of body that has its roots in the penitential practices of the monks of the fifth and sixth centuries and which, as part of the process of differentiation from those who became Protestant after the Reformation, were adopted by the Irish who remained staunchly Catholic.[13] Analysing how this penitential approach to the body became infiltrated with the neo-Jansenistic teachings of the Catholic Church that became dominant in the nineteenth century, helps shine a light on Irish attitudes and practices in relation to desire, pleasure and sexuality. These bodily practices were central to the peculiar forms of Irish modernisation and the way in which the Irish continued to have high levels of fertility despite high levels of postponed marriage and permanent celibacy which, in each generation, necessitated continuing high levels of emigration.

The Church became central to attempts to modernise Irish farming and society. It was in and through the Church that many Irish people were able to bring rationalised order to family life, to control marriage, to develop a decent standard of living and to become emotionally self-disciplined and civilised like other Europeans. At the same time, becoming staunch, loyal, devoted Catholics meant that they were able to establish a separate identity from their colonial masters.[14] The strategies of controlling marriage had a profound effect on Irish social and cultural life that was to last for generations. As Lee put it:

> It was therefore crucial to maintain the economic dominance of the new order that all thoughts of marriage in Ireland should be banished from minds of the majority of Irish youth. Temptation must not be placed in their way. Sex, therefore, must be denounced as a satanic snare, in even what had been its most innocent pre-Famine manifestations. Sex posed a far more severe threat than the landlord to the security and status of the family. Boys and girls must be kept apart at all costs.[15]

Throughout the nineteenth century, sex became increasingly problematic. It had to be watched, supervised and suppressed. The economic strategy of a farmer intent on improving his standard of living could be ruined by the transgressive actions of his daughters. Consequently, girls from this class were continuously watched and gossiped about. This served as a primary mechanism of external sexual control.[16] It became inscribed as a problem in the minds and bodies of each new generation of boys and girls. The silencing, hiding and denial of sex, the confinement of talk about sex to the confessional, may have significantly influenced the way men and women read and understood the world. What we do not know is to what extent this form of sexualisation was significantly different from what happened elsewhere in the West.

What we do know is that, for a long time during the twentieth century, Ireland had quite different, if not exceptional, demographic patterns that revolved around low levels of marriage but, among those who did marry, high levels of birth. In 1961, the marital fertility rate was 195 per 1000 women married. This was 40 points higher than New Zealand (155) and more than twice as high as Sweden (87). This led to a pattern of large families. In 1955, three in ten of all births were fifth babies and in 1962 there were 2000 births to mothers with ten children or more. Given the restrictions on marriage, particularly in rural areas, the inheritance strategy of farms being passed on intact to one son and one daughter being given a dowry to enable her to marry, led, in successive generations, to high levels of emigration, postponed marriage and permanent celibacy. These bodily practices were inextricably woven into a particular way of being Catholic and forms of sexuality and repression of self and desire that were, in turn, part of economic modernisation.[17]

When we think of Irish cultural difference, it is also important to remember that Irish Catholics became devoted to the institutional Church and its rituals. Many family homes became Catholic spaces festooned with crucifixes, statues, pictures and other religious imagery. Daily life and the calendar year were marked by Catholic rituals and events. People knelt to pray. There was a litany of saints to which people made petitions. Many of the devotional practices were magical in orientation, with prayers being said, novenas being made and pilgrimages being undertaken in the hope that God, Jesus, Our Lady or one the saints would directly intervene in the penitents' lives.

It would be wrong, however, to see what happened within families as part of the same coercive regime that existed within industrial and reformatory schools. Married women were not forced into giving birth. To understand why Irish mothers continued to have so many children, we need to understand how they were symbolically dominated and controlled by a culture shaped by the Catholic Church. While the strategy of silencing and hiding sex and confining it to a religious and medical discourse, which was combined with a lack of availability, knowledge and information about contraception, may have been factors in the high birth rate, these factors were prevalent throughout the rest of Europe in the late nineteenth and early twentieth centuries when women began to want to limit and control their fertility. But evidence from 1988 indicates that, in comparison with other countries, Irish men and women still saw large families as ideal.[18]

This would suggest that most married women willingly subscribed to the concept of the ideal mother put forward by the Catholic Church. More importantly, it may be because mothers, who were confined to the home and were relatively powerless, were dependent on the Church for status, honour and respect. It may well be that, being born into a Catholic culture in which Catholicism was deeply imbued in society, in families and communities, women were coerced into embodying the Church's image of what it was to be a good woman and that they reinforced this image among each other. For many, being a good woman became linked to being a good mother and being a good mother became linked to having a large family. Examining the period 1946–61, Kennedy concluded not only that the desire to have larger families was stronger among Catholics but that the size of families increased as the value of farms increased: 'the better off a Catholic farmer was in Ireland, the better a Catholic he tried to be at least in terms of having a larger family'.[19]

It may well be, then, that, in successive generations from the late nineteenth century, mothers enforced the same strategies of sexual control on their children as had been enforced on them. They inculcated the same strategies of hiding and silencing sex, of sublimating and controlling pleasure and desire, and inculcated the same notions of self-mortification, denial and self-sacrifice, the same sense of shame, disdain and fear of the body. The question, prompted by Lee's description, is to what extent men and women talked about and negotiated family size and, if they did, what did they say to each other, what words did they use, and within what kind of language and discourse was it couched? Whatever happened, there is evidence to suggest that this language and discourse began to change. In a study of working-class mothers in Cork in the early 1970s, Hilliard found that women began to talk differently to their daughters and encouraged them not to embody the habitus and practice of good Catholic mothers as they had done. Whatever happened in homes, we do know that from the 1960s there was a steady decline both in marital fertility and in the number of women having large families. What was odd, as Fahey points out in Chapter 7 above, is that this decline had taken place much sooner elsewhere in Europe.

The question, however, is to what extent there is a connection between the level of communication between husbands and wives in relation to sex up to the 1970s and the level of communication in religious houses between nuns, priests and brothers – in particular, among those running specialised institutions – about sex, repressed desire, self-denial. In what way did the laity embody the *habitus* of the religious? In what way were the hiding, silencing and repression of sex, in Irish culture generally, linked to the way brothers, priests and nuns related to and treated children? What happened to children in industrial and reformatory schools and to women in Magdalen laundries, cannot be divorced from the separation of celibates from the rest of society and the task they had in regulating, controlling, disciplining and punishing those who did not comply to the normative Catholic order. Indeed the separation of celibates was part of a more general system of division and separation between males and females in Irish society.

When we think of Irish men and women negotiating fertility and family size in a Catholic culture, it is important to conceptualise the bodily division between men and women, between what women and men did in the home, the spaces they occupied, and then, outside the home, who went where and where they went together. Again, it is not to say that homes, churches, pubs, shops, schools, hospitals and many welfare homes were not gendered spaces in other parts of the West. It is to suggest that gendered spaces may have lasted longer and penetrated deeper into Irish social and cultural life than they did elsewhere.

There is plenty of ethnographic evidence to show that, for much of the twentieth century, pubs were primarily male spaces and attracted large numbers of bachelor men. There is also evidence to suggest that pubs were highly ritualised, embodied spaces, with men engaging in banter and repartee, teasing and joking with each other, often within the context of hard drinking and often within a 'round' system in which each member bought all other members of the group a drink. This culture produced a *habitus*, a taken-for-granted, second-nature way of being in the world that was, at the same time, flexible, dynamic and transposable. While there was a general cultural system, there were no strict rules. Being in the pub was a game in which participants were able to use the culture and its rituals to gain honour and respect. Finally, while there may have been local rules, the cultural system was similar in most pubs. It may well be that the more time men spent with each other in pubs and other predominantly male spaces, the more they developed an identity and sense of self through the ways of talking and being with other males, the more they had difficultly relating to women.[20]

A focus on the body helps us to think imaginatively when it comes to understanding Irish difference. Instead of examining the world of politics, institutions and elites – and the implicit notion that the Irish *habitus* trickles down from great minds – we should instead focus on bodies in spaces in everyday life, with the implicit notion of culture, imagination and creativity sprouting up from below.

It seems strange, for example, that in popular culture Ireland has an international reputation for the pub and particular forms of drinking, and yet the history of the Irish pub and drinking has largely remained unexamined. The stories of Ireland, the imagination, the humour and the sense of self, from which cultural creativity emerges, may have significant roots in what happened in homes and pubs. It also seems strange that, if one of the main differences about the Irish was a high birth rate, the history of what happened between men and women, particularly in relation to sex, has remained unexamined. Finally, it seems strange that for a culture characterised by Catholicism and high levels of religiosity, we know little about how being Catholic permeated the everyday lives of Irish people. Any understanding we have comes primarily through literature and films. It may well be that the absence of such knowledge is related not just to the narrow range of theories and concepts that are applied to exploring Irish difference but to the empirical sources that are examined and the methods that are used in the examination.

It may well be here, in and around Catholic time and space, rich with rituals and imagery, that we can make a connection between the body and the Irish mind. The ability to think outside the box of *either/or* and to see the world as *both/and* may be related to more Irish people spending more time in enchanted time and space in which things are never always what they seem, in which there is a dual logic in operation, that of the logical rational scientific world and that of the world of spirits and magical transformations. It may be that this spiritual and magical world is a rich source of creative imagination. It may well be that the origins of the Irish 'mind' lie less in the mental machinations of philosophers and more in the world of magic, fairies, miracles and in the tradition of kneeling and praying. It may be that such bodily practices help people to think differently and perhaps, as we saw throughout Ireland in 1985, see statues move.

Conclusion

Rather than asserting that there is something unique, different and perhaps even exceptional about the Irish, it might be better to start by arguing the opposite and claim that there is nothing different about the Irish. We would then have to decide what kind of evidence we were going to look at – it could be economic, political, social or cultural – and, within this realm, where we might find clues that might reveal a wider pattern.

I have argued that, when it comes to looking for difference, it is best to look within the realm of culture. When we think of Irish culture, particularly in terms of difference, we often think of the Irish language, the GAA, traditional music, Catholicism and a myriad of folk traditions. They are important elements in contributing to people's meaning and understanding of life and to how to live a good life. Irish people are, then, born into this evolving culture and, in their everyday lives, make use of it to create their own meaning and sense of self.

However, I would argue that, when it comes to looking for clues to Irish difference, it is analytically important to focus on the body. In doing so, I am arguing not that the body is primary to the mind – some sort of biological determinism – but rather that there is at least a symbiotic relationship between the two in which ways of being become habituated in bodily practices and that this is linked to and often generates ways of thinking. What is important in this is to recognise that there is not a mind that directs the body: it is not an either/or. Rather the mind and the body are both one and the same in being in the world. It may well be that the Irish are not significantly different in their bodily practices, particularly in relation to children, corporal punishment and sex, and it may well be that the forms of disciplining and controlling children and women were simply more extreme, but there is plenty of evidence to suggest that the Irish body demands more attention.

Notes

1 The Commission to Inquire into Child Abuse, *Commission to Inquire into Child Abuse Report*, vol. III (Dublin: The Stationery Office, 2009), p. 56.

2 Michel Foucault, *Discipline & Punish: The Birth of the Prison* (New York: Vintage Books, 1979), pp. 3–6.

3 Jennifer O'Connell, 'You Wouldn't Hit a Partner for Their Own Good, So Why Would You Hit a Child', *Irish Times*, 6 February 2013.

4 Michel Foucault, *The History of Sexuality*, Vol. 1 (New York: Vintage, 1980).

5 Tom Inglis, *Moral Monopoly: The Rise and Fall of the Catholic Church in Modern Ireland*, 2nd ed. (Dublin: University College Dublin Press, 1998), pp. 136–43.

6 Hannah McGee, Rebecca Garavan, Mairéad de Barra, Joanne Byrne and Ronán Conroy, 'The Savi Report: Sexual Abuse and Violence in Ireland'. (Dublin: Liffey Press and the Dublin Rape Crisis Centre, 2002).

7 The French sociologist Émile Durkheim argued that what we see as pathological, for example crime, reveals a good deal about the nature of the wider society. See Émile Durkheim, *The Rules of the Sociological Method* (New York: The Free Press, 1938), p. 75.

8 Mary Raftery and Eoin O'Sullivan, *Suffer the Little Children: The Inside Story of Ireland's Industrial Schools* (Dublin: New Island, 1999).

9 Nancy Scheper-Hughes, *Saints, Scholars, and Schizophrenics: Mental Illness in Rural Ireland*, 2nd ed. (Berkeley: University of California Press, 2001).

10 'Report of the Inter-Departmental Committee to Establish the Facts of State Involvement with the Magdalen Laundries' (Dublin: Department of Justice and Equality, 2013).

11 Ian O'Donnell and Eoin O'Sullivan, 'Introduction', in Eoin O'Sullivan and Ian O'Donnell (eds), *Coercive Confinement in Ireland: Patients, Prisoners and Penitents* (Manchester: Manchester University Press, 2012), pp. 12, 13, 26.

12 Mike Milotte, *Banished Babies: The Secret History of Ireland's Baby Export Business* (Dublin: New Island, 1997), p. 16.

13 Michael Carroll, *Irish Pilgrimage: Holy Wells and Popular Catholic Devotion* (Baltimore: John Hopkins University Press, 1999).

14 Eugene Hynes, 'The Great Hunger and Irish Catholicism', *Societas*, pp. VIII (1978), pp. 81–98.

15 Joseph Lee, 'Women and the Irish Church since the Famine', in Margaret McCurtain and Donnchadh Ó Corráin (eds), *Women in Irish Society* (Dublin: Arlen House, 1978), p. 39.

16 Dympna McLoughlin, 'Women and Sexuality in Nineteenth Century Ireland', *Irish Journal of Psychology*, 15:2–3 (1994), p. 273.

17 Tony Fahey and Helen Russell, *Family Formation in Ireland: Trends, Data Needs and Implications* (Dublin: Economic and Social Research Institute, 2001), pp. 34–5; Tom Inglis, *Lessons in Irish Sexuality* (Dublin: University College Dublin Press, 1998), pp. 30–2.

18 Results from the International Social Survey Programme showed that 51 per cent of Irish respondents thought that to have four or more children was ideal; this compared with 3.5 per cent from Britain, 4 per cent from Hungary, 5 per cent from West Germany, and 19 per

cent from the US. See Stephen Harding, 'Interim Report: The Changing Family', in Roger Jowell, Lindsay Brook and Sharon Witherspoon (eds), *British Social Attitudes: Special International Report* (Aldershot: Gower, 1989), p. 149.

19 Robert Kennedy Jr, *The Irish: Emigration, Marriage, and Fertility* (Berkeley: University of California Press, 1973), p. 189.

20 For a pioneering analysis of pubs as male spaces, see Patrick McNabb, *Limerick Rural Survey: Social Structure* (Tipperary: Muintir na Tire, 1962), pp. 6–9; 42–51.

10

Sexual abuse and the Catholic Church

Marie Keenan

The revelations of the Cloyne report have brought the Government, Irish Catholics and the Vatican to an unprecedented juncture. It's fair to say that after the Ryan and Murphy Reports Ireland is, perhaps, unshockable when it comes to the abuse of children. But Cloyne has proved to be of a different order. Because for the first time in Ireland, a report into child sexual-abuse exposes an attempt by the Holy See, to frustrate an Inquiry in a sovereign, democratic republic ... the Cloyne Report excavates the dysfunction, disconnection, elitism ... the narcissism ... that dominate the culture of the Vatican to this day. (Enda Kenny, Taoiseach, 20 July 2011)[1]

Some commentators – including Tom Doyle, an American priest who served for five years as a canon lawyer at the Vatican Embassy in Washington, DC – have argued that child sexual abuse by Catholic clergy is one of the greatest crises in the history of the Catholic Church. Whatever the validity of this argument, child sexual abuse by Catholic clergy has been reported on widely throughout the world as a scandal, a crisis and a betrayal. One of the major issues to emerge is that most cases occurred long before they were made known to the civil authorities, and the response of the Church is seen as having been ineffective at best and, at worst, a 'cover up'. Abusive clergy, some of whom were sent for psychiatric assessment and spiritual guidance, were moved from the site of 'temptation' to another parish or ministry, where some continued to abuse. The mind-set of the Catholic hierarchy was, and to some extent still is, that this was a problem of flawed individuals, rather than a problem that has significant organisational causative dimensions that became systematically embedded in Church thinking and practice.[2]

The sexual abuse of children by Catholic clergy has had a profound effect on Irish culture and society. In 1994, the Irish government collapsed when it emerged that the state had failed to extradite from the Republic a priest who had been found guilty of sex abuse charges to answer similar charges in Northern Ireland. This occurred at a time when the relationship between the Catholic Church and the Irish state was undergoing significant change. However, it was in 2011, following the publication of several government-appointed commission reports into sexual abuse by Catholic clergy, that the relational dynamics between the Catholic Church and the Irish state reached a new low, and this time it involved the Vatican.[3] In a radical break with his usually composed presentation, the Taoiseach, Enda Kenny, gave expression to an anger that had perhaps been brewing for generations. The failures of the Catholic Church in dealing with the abuse of children was the straw that would finally break the camel's back, and seriously undermine the power, authority and respect of the Catholic Church in Ireland.

The clergy abuse situation in Ireland is often seen as unique, in part because of the close relationship between the Irish Church and the new Irish state founded in 1922. It is also thought to be unique since the Irish surnames of the Irish diaspora, some of whom are priests and bishops in the United States, Canada and Australia, have been listed in abuse cases in those countries. This has raised questions about the oppressive power of the Catholic Church in Ireland and its influence on the Irish political process. Questions have been raised about the Irish 'culture of deference' and how this related to the abuse situation. Some wonder if the Church and state worked separately and together in covering up the sexual abuse of Irish children. Some also wonder if 'Irish' Catholicism has peculiar features, which, when exported throughout the world, contributed to the abuse of children by Catholic clergy. As a monocultural society, rendering Ireland 'the most Catholic country in the world' the Catholic Church, once considered the ultimate arbiter of morality has found itself on the margins of influence in Irish public life.[4]

However, it is at times when the public is most agitated by the perceived wrong-doings of one sector of society that statutory inquiries and a responsible media have to be seen to carry out their work in a calm, impartial and dispassionate manner. As an academic social scientist and a practising psychotherapist, I have had doubts and concerns about both statutory instruments of inquiry and the media reporting of the problem, in relation to sexual abuse generally, and to the Catholic Church in particular. My concerns relate to real questions as to whether victims are well served by the name and shame approach taken to the problem and whether restorative as well as criminal justice instruments might be more widely applied. I also have justice concerns in relation to how some of the clergy have been dealt with by the statutory instruments to inquire into abuse in the Church and into the subsequent media reporting of same.[5] For example a number of serious shortcomings are immediately apparent in several of the statutory Commissions of Investigation into the handling of abuse complaints by a number of Irish Catholic Dioceses: (1) the Reports are rarely based on any rigorous comparative work which would offer an analysis of the behaviour of the Catholic Church in the handling of abuse complaints in comparison to other organisations, (2) the Reports are in the main ahistorical and lacking in sociological or anthropological analysis, (3) Church 'witnesses' appearing before the Commissions appear to have become 'defendants' rather than witnesses, without their rights being protected either constitutionally or in natural justice and (4) some of the Commission Reports have taken a name and shame approach to the senior clerics which is beyond the remit of either the legislation framing the work of the Commissions of investigation or indeed their own terms of reference.[6] These shortcomings have been compounded by media representations of sexual abuse, best summarised as a hugely complex issue being told as a common singular story.[7] However, while holding firm to the horrific experiences of the children abused by Catholic clergy, I want to raise questions about how the story of abuse in the Catholic Church has been presented and to offer alternative perspectives. It is in nobody's interest that one injustice begets another, especially if it is in the name of justice.

In this chapter I argue that the abuse of children by Catholic clergy in Ireland and the responses of the Catholic hierarchy must be located within a historical and comparative context. I also argue that sexual abuse by Catholic clergy is best understood not as a problem of 'flawed' individuals but as a systemic problem that comprises individual, local organisational and global institutional dimensions. Finally, in a radical break with popular discourse, I wish to argue that, in the aftermath of the disclosures of abuse of countless children by Catholic clergy, we have not so much transcended as inherited a new state of fear and oppression in Ireland. This time it is not the Church hierarchy that is to be feared but rather a new state of fear has been born that is based on an approach to children, families and 'child protection' that, far from bringing forth a safer society for children or a new state of well-being for victims of abuse, has rendered all men as suspects and a generation of children denied the love of men.

Historical and comparative context

Sexual violence is a significant problem in Ireland. According to one major study 42 per cent of women and 28 per cent of men reported experiencing some form of sexual assault over their lifespan (30 per cent of women and 24 per cent of men experienced sexual abuse in childhood and 26 per cent of women and 12 per cent of men experienced sexual assault in adulthood).[8] Of those who are now adults, and who had been abused as children, Roman Catholic clergy were the perpetrators in 3.9 per cent of cases (5.8 per cent of all male victims and 1.4 per cent of all female victims). While the Irish rate of sexual abuse for females is in line with international trends, the rate of sexual abuse of young males in Ireland is at the higher end of international trends. When it comes to what percentage of the abuse is perpetrated by Catholic clergy, those data that are available suggest that between 4 and 8 per cent of Catholic clergy have been accused of the sexual abuse of minors, and this figure is regarded as reliable in Ireland as well as internationally, although one always needs to be cautious with data when there is a dearth of quantitative studies on which to base one's findings.⁹ For comparative purposes 6 per cent of the adult male population is thought to perpetrate sexual abuse against minors.¹⁰ However, apart from the sexual abuse of minors the Catholic Church in Ireland now faces a problem of professional misconduct by Catholic clergy who have had sexual relations with women and men and indeed religious sisters, all in the course of their ministries. How many Catholic clerics have engaged in such sexual 'boundary violation' of adults is unknown and neither is it known how many priests and religious in Ireland have fathered children in consensual relationships, although there is growing evidence as to the existence of this phenomenon. Whichever way it is understood, the Catholic Church in Ireland has a significant issue on its hands regarding the sexual behaviour of its Catholic clergy.

Much has been written about the failure of the Catholic Church in Ireland to adequately respond to the sexual abuse of children, and in particular its failure to report abuse allegations to the police, at least until the 1990s. Much less analysis has focused on the Irish state's response to the abuse of children, or on comparing Church and state responses across time. From my analysis, while the accusation of cover-up has been levelled at the Catholic Church, it may well be the case that cover-up was a feature of how Irish people and the Irish state responded to the abuse of children from the 1920s until the 1990s and that the neglect of children's plight was not a feature of the Catholic Church alone. And this state of affairs was in the main broken by the courage of victims and the determination of some investigative journalists who took up their cases and began to give voice to their hidden stories of abuse through the newspaper pages and through television documentaries. While a full comparative analysis of the historical and cultural context of the abuse of minors is beyond the scope of this chapter, I want to highlight three occurrences between the 1920s and the 1990s that I believe give a historical and social context to how the abuse of minors was seen in Irish society and by the Irish political class.

First, in 1930 the Government of Ireland established a committee to review the Criminal Law Amendment Acts (1880–85) relating to sexual crime in Ireland and to consider the situation of juvenile prostitution in the country.¹¹ William Carrigan KC was appointed to chair the Committee. The Report indicated a rise in sexual crime in general, and crimes against children in particular. It reported that fewer than 15 per cent of the cases concerning children were prosecuted because of the desire of parents to keep the abuse secret or because of their reluctance to have their child appear in court. The report noted the views of the Police Commissioner who argued that sentences for sexual offences were too lenient and that legislation did not provide sufficient punishment to act as a deterrent. Carrigan concluded that the law as it stood contributed to the frequency of assaults on children and made a number of recommendations. These included that the age of consent be raised from sixteen to eighteen, that the grounds for acquittal based on the belief that the girl was above the age of consent be abolished, and that the time allowed for commencing a prosecution under the Criminal Law Act be extended (it was six months at the time of the Carrigan Report).

When the Report was circulated in 1931, the Department of Justice decided that it would be unwise to publish it, warning that the allegations contained in it were damaging to the standard of morality in the country. A new government in 1932 was similarly critical of the Report, which it also felt should not be published. The Minister for Justice claimed that a rise in the age of consent would act as a mechanism whereby women could blackmail men and that there would be an increase in the amount of crime reported. Moreover, he was also reluctant to give any weight to the evidence of children, suggesting that one could not trust the evidence of a child 'with a vivid imagination'.[12] This historical detail just captures the *habitus* or mind-set of the Irish political class of the time.

In the history of child sexual abuse in Ireland many commentators see the suppression of the Carrigan Report as hugely significant. Kennedy argues that the recommendations of the Carrigan Committee, which had sought to tighten the law in relation to abuse of children, was seen as being too harsh on men and disbelieving of children. Raftery and O'Sullivan argue that failure to publish the Report meant that sexual abuse did not become an issue of public debate until the 1980s and the potential of the Report to increase public awareness of the issue was never realised. They argue that the existence of the Carrigan Report demonstrates that both the Irish police and the Department of Justice were aware in the early 1930s that adults could and did sexually abuse children.

Second, the criminal law is only one means of dealing with the sexual abuse of children. In many cases criminal proceedings are not instituted for a variety of reasons and in some cases it is often difficult to obtain the proof necessary to secure a criminal conviction 'beyond reasonable doubt'. However, the state can intervene in other ways to protect children who are being abused, and social policy during the relevant period gives clues as to how the state responded to the abuse of minors. My analysis suggests that policies on child abuse were practically non-existent in late nineteenth- and early twentieth-century Ireland. Until 1970 the Irish Society for the Prevention of Cruelty to Children investigated and processed most child cruelty cases coming before the courts. It worked under the provisions of the 1908 Children Act, which covered offences against and by children. In its first report, published in 1957, cases of assault of children, of incest and of neglect (the most frequent) were all recorded. Whilst the 1908 Act was amended several times, parts of the Children Act (1908) as amended formed the principal legislation for the protection and welfare of children until 1991. Two new pieces of legislation, the Child Care Act (1991) and, later, the Children Act (2001), heralded a new departure in relation to child welfare and child protection legislation. What is notable, however, is how long it took for the modern Irish state to enact suitable legislation for the protection and welfare of children and to decouple offences against children (Child Care Act, 1991) from offences by children

(Children Act, 2001). Again, this history gives glimpses to the *habitus* and thinking of the Irish people and the political class at the time.

In a third glimpse into Ireland's history of concern, or lack of it, for children, we see that, whilst several sets of guidelines on the identification and management of child abuse were issued by the state from the 1970s, it was in fact 1983 before the first mention was made of sexual abuse in official guidelines. It was not until 1987 that child sexual abuse was distinguished from other forms of abuse as requiring additional methods of identification and validation. The 1987 guidelines also used the term 'child abuse' rather than 'non-accidental injury' for the first time. Further, in statutory inquiries into the abuse of children in their family home, we learn that, despite the 1987 Health Board Guidelines, many were not being implemented and many professionals were not even aware of their existence.[13] In 1998, a team of experts who examined the abuse of children by their fathers over a twenty year period, concluded that a genuine incredulity of the possibility of sexual abuse existed, particularly at the beginning of the period, both at senior social work management level and among family doctors.[14]

So when we locate the story of alleged 'cover-up' by the Catholic Church in the context of the Irish mind of the time, what emerges is a story of cover-up on all sides and of the neglect of the welfare of children on the part of both the Irish state and the Church. This is not to deny or doubt the care that many children received in their families or in alternative care systems run by the religious orders on behalf of the Irish state. The perception of the state as opting out of child welfare and protection and handing it over to the religious and voluntary sector is also borne out by the historical data. And it also becomes clear that the state and its agents were aware from the 1930s onwards that adults can and do sexually abuse children, both inside and outside of the family. It is a sad fact of Irish history that the abuse of children was not given due attention by either Church or state. It reveals a culture of denial, and provides an insight into how children were seen and understood.

A systemic problem

It is a feature of many areas of academic study that certain perspectives, theories and methods dominate while others are neglected or excluded. This is certainly true in relation to the study of child sexual abuse within the Catholic Church. Much scholarly work focuses on the assumed psychopathology of the perpetrator and on failures of individuals who were in positions of authority in the Church in relation to their handling of abuse complaints. I suggest that there is a need to expand such individualistic perspectives and examine how cultural, theological, organisational and institutional Church influences were integrated and assimilated into and in turn influenced the Irish Church in creating a climate in which the abuse of children became possible. What needs to be examined is the way the Irish priest offender was moulded by the Catholic Church in creative dynamic relation with his individual and personal circumstances to influence his understanding of himself and his subsequent abuse of minors. What also needs to be examined is how the bishops or Church leaders were influenced by a variety of Church policies, practices, cultures and thought in dynamic interaction with their own personal history to bring forth their response to the problem. In doing so I suggest that there are vibrant and dynamic ways in which both individual abuse perpetrators and individual bishops and Church leaders were not just 'flawed' or 'erring' individuals but were part of the same culture. In both cases Church culture, combined with individual struggles to attain position within the Catholic Church, was to influence both the abuse perpetrators and the Church leaders at a structural level, as they continually reinvented their everyday lives and what it was to be a good clergyman or a good leader of the Catholic Church in Ireland. In undertaking this work I attempt to link structural issues with the micro-world of struggle of individuals to develop and maintain their identity and social position and how both structural and individual factors were to contribute to their resultant behaviour.

In adopting this micro–macro approach I am influenced by three key questions: What kind of an organisation could accommodate the scenario of abuse of children that we have seen to emerge in the Catholic Church? What would the rest of the organisation have to be like for its members to behave in the manner in which they did? And what would the whole story of the organisation and the institution have to be for the various steps that we have seen to occur in the Catholic Church in relation to the abuse of minors by clergy?[15] In answering these questions it is possible to identify a number of features of sexual abuse within the Catholic Church that have a role in giving rise not only to the abuse itself but also to the response of the bishops and Church leaders to the emerging problem.[16]

First, sexual abuse is best seen as part of a continuum of sexual behaviour of Catholic clergy. Although the abuse of children is often seen as aberrant because of the criminal parameters of the problem, my research suggests that child sexual abuse by Catholic clergy must be considered against the background of the literature on the sexual underworld of 'normal' clergy and not as an unrelated sphere of clergy sexual activity. There is substantial literature on the sexual lives and behaviour of 'normal' clergy who make a celibate commitment at ordination. The sexual underworld of 'normal' clergy and the unhealthy organisational culture, in which the problems of sexuality arise, are part of the context in which child sexual abuse by Catholic clergy becomes possible. This perspective raises the issue of celibacy as an important area for research in relation to this problem.

Second, an inadequate theology of sexuality and the absence of a relational sexual ethics for clergy is also part of the problem of sexual abuse of minors by Catholic clergy. My research suggests that Catholic clergy were so focused on control of 'the sex act' that they did not think about the consequences of the 'act' for the other person, or even of the full significance of the age of the other person, when that person was a child or minor. When disclosures of abuse of minors were made, Church leaders often sent the perpetrators to confession and therapy, while the child was largely ignored.

Third, the Church's theology of scandal also forms part of the context that enabled the abuse by clergy to continue. Church leaders believed that informing the laity of the truth was akin to giving scandal and this was to be avoided. The theology of scandal underpins much of the behaviour of senior Church clerics who believed that the laity must not be scandalised by the truth of human frailty.

Fourth, clericalism can also be identified as having played a significant role in the clergy sexual abuse problem – clericalism which was premised on the idea of clergy as an elite who were set apart from and above the laity. This thinking influenced both clergy and laity alike. For the Catholic laity, clericalism implied that Catholic clergy could do no wrong; thus children were not believed. For Catholic clergy it led to the belief that children would never tell and that families would not speak 'ill' of their clergy, giving some security to those abusive clergy that the stories would never be told.

Fifth, the interplay of power and powerlessness contributed to the genesis of the problem of sexual abuse for those clergy who became abuse perpetrators. It is also significant in explaining how the Church leaders responded to the abuse disclosures. In the public sphere, clergy appear independent in the exercise of their duties and powerful in the minds of the public. However, despite experiencing the trappings of such a dominant power position in the public realm, many clerical perpetrators revealed that they experienced personal powerlessness, lack of autonomy and frustration in the private sphere. This can be related to the power, authority and governance structures of the Catholic Church and to the nature of their relationships with superiors. Bishops also experienced powerlessness vis-à-vis the powerful Curia in Rome. Power within the Catholic Church was taught and seen to be in one direction only – upwards. Priests feared the bishops, and bishops feared Rome.

Finally, a moral education that is overly intellectualised and technical and focuses mainly or only on theoretical or abstract problems does not equip its students to make good moral judgements. As Arendt has observed, the precondition for the kind of judgement that is necessary to prevent wrongdoing is not a highly developed intelligence or sophistication in moral matters. Rather, good judgement requires wisdom, skill and disposition to engage in an ongoing silent dialogue with oneself, especially about the consequences of one's potential actions for another.[17] Judgement needs the special presence of others 'in whose place' we must imagine ourselves in emotion and thought and ultimately whose perspectives we must take into consideration before we act. What was absent from the education of Catholic clergy was such a relational approach to morality and judgement. Instead the morality taught in Irish Catholic seminaries was based on a rule book that relied on moral absolutes and theoretical understandings. Rule-book morality failed to equip the Catholic clergy and the Church leaders for the challenges they would face in their complex ministries. Rule-book morality was also easy to bargain with and confession could be used to clear the conscience.

New states of fear and oppression

In order to understand the consequences of playing rhetorical or political games with a problem as important and tragic as child sexual abuse it is useful to employ a critical analysis to the current state of childhood in Ireland in the aftermath of sexual abuse disclosures by so many and to ask if childhood is now better for Irish children. Aside from the general good that has been reported by adult victim-survivors of childhood sexual abuse because of the public support they received and the public vindication that followed the telling of their stories, what I wish to argue is that we have not so much transcended as inherited a new state of fear and oppression in Ireland, in which many if not most men are potential suspects. The unintended consequence of this is that a generation of children may be denied the love of men and a new silence is being imposed on the public discourse of childhood. What is most striking about this situation is that ultimately children stand to lose. The newly established super structures of surveillance that have become the political if highly questionable means to resolve the crisis of child sexual abuse in Ireland have not been accompanied by reasoned scholarship making its mark on these highly sensitive political processes.

Data mined from the Growing Up in Ireland survey of over twenty thousand children and presented in 2013 show that poor children are over three times as likely to be obese at age three compared to better-off children, and similar patterns have been identified for mental health. A child's psychological well-being is worse in lower-income families than in higher socio-economic groups. The risk of serious emotional and behavioural problems at age nine is also twice as high in the bottom half of income distribution. Health problems persist into adulthood, and the risk of cardiovascular disease in later life is over a fifth higher among people who grew up in poor households. Overall, some 3.5 per cent of children experienced drug taking or alcoholism or mental disorder in their family.

In separate research, which looked at the experience of adults aged fifty years or older it was found that 7.1 per cent of respondents had been physically abused in childhood and 6.2 per cent had experienced sexual abuse as children. Some 8.6 per cent reported drink or drug use by parents when they were under eighteen years. There was strong evidence of the lasting physical and psychological effects of these adverse effects. Children who were abused were over 30 per cent more likely to suffer heart disease as adults and they were also over three times more likely to have psychiatric problems. In light of the evolving evidence it would be wrong then to think that, just because clerical child sex abuse has been identified and analysed, the problems of children are over and that none of them suffer abuse, either sexual or physical, or neglect. Much remains to be done.

In returning specifically to the issue of sexual abuse, cultural narratives can prevent critical issues from being addressed, as some theorists such as Kincaid argue.[18] For example, when one thinks about how Western culture has 'enthusiastically sexualised the child while denying just as enthusiastically that it was doing any such thing' one begins to see how the dynamics of this particular problem can play out. Clearly, a society that regards children as erotic (such as in representations used to sell products and in some sections of the pop industry), but also regards an erotic response to children as criminally unimaginable, has a significant problem on its hands. From this perspective, the extent of the abuse of children is still denied because the complexities involved in the interplay of childhood, sexuality and adulthood are also denied. It must thus become clear that a society that wants to protect children from sexual abuse, and understand how the problem is constituted, must change the dominant discourse to one that includes a better understanding of the complexities of adult and childhood sexuality and is less marginalising of men. In the current situation, many children suffer: those children who are sexually abused and those who are denied a nurturing relationship with men.

Conclusion

We know that conceptual models, or frames, are more than simply angles or approaches to a problem. Each comprises theories, assumptions and categories that influence where we look and what we find. Frames shape how questions are asked, what is taken as evidence, the conclusions drawn and the subsequent actions taken. In this we need to keep alert to all that is being said if we are to truly understand the root social causes of the child abuse problem in the Catholic Church and in Irish society and the policy recommendations that should follow. However, it is in this very context that academics must ask the right questions and question taken-for-granted knowledge that seems to be increasingly a new part of the current problem in Ireland.

Notes

1   Department of Taoiseach, 2011, statement by the Taoiseach of Ireland (Prime Minister) in the Irish Dáil (Parliament) on 20 July in responding to a motion on the report of the Commission of Investigation into the Catholic Diocese of Cloyne (2011).

2   For fuller discussion of all issues relating to child sexual abuse and the Catholic Church see Marie Keenan, *Child Sexual Abuse and the Catholic Church: Gender, Power and Organisational Culture* (New York: Oxford University Press, 2012), and Pat Claffey, Joe Egan and Marie Keenan (eds), *Broken Faith, Why Hope Matters* (London: Lang Publishers, 2013).

3   Department of Taoiseach, 2011, statement by the Taoiseach of Ireland (Prime Minister) in

the Irish Dáil (Parliament) on 20 July in responding to a motion on the report of the Commission of Investigation into the Catholic Diocese of Cloyne (2011).

4 Paul Blanshard, *The Irish and Catholic Power* (London: Derek Verschoyle, 1954), p 17.

5 The Commission of Investigation into the Catholic Archdiocese of Dublin, *Report of The Commission of Investigation into the Catholic Archdiocese of Dublin* (Dublin: Government Stationery Office, 2009; Chapter 1.24) states 'Some priests were aware that particular instances of abuse had occurred. A few were courageous and brought complaints to the attention of their superiors. The vast majority simply chose to turn a blind eye.' A careful reading shows us that this 'vast majority' is a majority of that unspecified cohort, 'some priests who were aware'. However, it too easy to take an entirely different impression from such a passage and indeed in the rush by journalists into print after the publication of the Murphy Report this passage had morphed into the shorthand media impression, also heard on other media, that the Murphy Commission had found that the vast majority of priests in the Dublin diocese were in fact aware of instances of child sexual abuse, but they simply chose to turn a blind eye.

6 See details of The Commissions of Investigation Act (2004) and, in particular, The Commission of Investigation into the Catholic Archdiocese of Dublin, *Report of The Commission of Investigation into the Catholic Archdiocese of Dublin* (Dublin: Government Stationery Office, 2009).

7 See Keenan, *Child Sexual Abuse and the Catholic Church*, pp. 108–9.

8 Hannah McGee, Rebecca Garavan, Mairéad de Barra, Joanne Byrne and Ronán Conroy, *The SAVI Report: Sexual Abuse and Violence in Ireland. A National Study of Irish Experiences, Beliefs and Attitudes Concerning Sexual Violence* (Dublin: The Liffey Press, 2002), pp. xxxiii, 88.

9 See John Jay College of Criminal Justice, *The Causes and Context of Sexual Abuse of Minors by Catholic Priests in the United States, 1950–2010* (Washington, DC: United States Conference of Catholic Bishops, 2011), David Quinn, '241 Clerics Accused of Sex Abuse over Four Decades', *Irish Independent*, 28 October 2005, pp. 26–7.

10 P. Marshall, 'The Prevalence of Convictions for Sexual Offending', *Research Findings*, no. 55 (Croydon: Home Office Research and Statistics Directorate, 1997).

11. For much that is contained in the next section on the Carrigan Report see Finola Kennedy, 'The Suppression of the Carrigan Report: A Historical Perspective on Child Abuse', *Studies*, 89 (2000), pp. 354–63; and Mary Raftery and Eoin O'Sullivan, *Suffer the Little Children* (Dublin: New Island, 1999).

12 See Kennedy, 'Suppression of Carrigan', p. 356.

13 Catherine McGuinness, *Report of the Kilkenny Incest Investigation* (Dublin: Government Stationery Office, 1993).

14 North Western Health Board Review Group, *West of Ireland Farmer Case: Report of the Review Group* (Dublin: Government Stationery Office, 1998).

15 These questions are based on questions that were offered first in Charles Ragin and Howard Becker, *What Is a Case? Exploring the Foundations of Social Inquiry* (Cambridge: Cambridge University Press, 1992), p. 231.

16 For fuller elaboration of issues involved here see Keenan, *Child Sexual Abuse*.

17 Hannah Arendt, *The Portable Hannah Arendt* (New York: Penguin Classics, 2000).

18 James Kincaid, *Erotic Innocence: The Culture of Child Molesting* (Durham and London: Duke University Press, 1998), pp. 8, 13, 20.

11

The difference between Irish and American Catholicism

Michele Dillon

When, during the historic papal visit in 1979, Pope John Paul II and the arch-bishop of Dublin Dr Dermot Ryan – a tall, lean man of aloof bearing – were riding down O'Connell Street, Dublin, atop the then novel Popemobile, the story goes that an unabashedly direct Moore Street trader woman shouted to Ryan, 'Sit down lanky. It's not you we've come to see.' This heckle was recounted repeatedly, prompted by mirth at the woman's boldness and envy that she was able to get away with it. It was not customary in Ireland in those days to speak so irreverently to a priest, never mind a bishop; 'Yes Father, no Father', 'Yes my Lord Bishop, no my Lord Bishop' were the more typical expressions. The Catholic Church in Ireland long enjoyed a powerful and uncontested moral monopoly over the minds, heart and bodies of all Irish Catholics, a dominance further consolidated by the Church's organisational control in the fields of education and health and its unquestioned influence in Irish media, politics and law.[1]

The Pope's visit was a major event in Ireland, the main topic of news for many months in advance, and, as the visit unfolded, a source of collective self-congratu-lations that the Irish could organise such a phenomenally successful event. Record numbers turned out to all of the Pope's Masses and record numbers cheered as his motorcade – and even his aeroplane – traversed to and from various venues. His Irish visit concluded, John Paul travelled via Aer Lingus on the aptly named *St Patrick* to Boston, the first destination of his first visit to the United States. As in Ireland, the Pope was greeted by a host of Church and state dignitaries and by tremendously large crowds – many of Irish ancestry but many too from Italy, Poland, Brazil, Central America and Vietnam, among other places of origin. As a large-scale and highly visible public event, the Pope's American visit was no less a success than his trip to Ireland. Catholics on both sides of the Atlantic rejoiced in their Catholicism, aglow in the physical and charismatic presence of the universal Church's leader, essentially the first to bring the trans-national presence of the Church right into the cathedrals, streets, neighbourhoods and iconic secular spaces – the Phoenix Park in Dublin and Boston Common – of cities across the globe.

For a few days in September 1979, the universality of Catholic identity seemed to trump the particularity of ancestry and national context, notwithstanding the fact that the Catholic Church in the US occupied a much different place in America and in American Catholics' lives than was the case in Ireland. Unlike the institutional and cultural monopoly of the Irish Church, the Catholic Church in America is, historically, a cultural outsider in a multi-denominational Protestant land where the spirit of religious pluralism fosters competition rather than the taken-for-granted dominance of any one religious authority structure. Thus, denominational pluralism fostered, on the one hand, an ethos of individual choice across religions and, on the other, the establishment of religion as a stable structural and cultural phenomenon. To identify as Protestant, Catholic or Jew, while voluntary, became part and parcel of being American; a social identity both anchored and telegraphed by religious affiliation, and, invariably too, bound with ethnic ancestry.[2] Therefore, although there has been an almost threefold increase since the mid-1990s in the proportion of Americans who express no religious affiliation, from 7 per cent to 20 per cent, at the same time the social presence and relevance of religion – and of Catholicism in particular – have remained remarkably stable.[3] In Ireland, by contrast, although the vast majority still identify as Catholic, there has been a precipitous decrease in the proportion attending weekly Mass, from approximately 85 per cent in the late 1980s to 43 per cent today.[4] We are thus prompted to ask why Irish Catholicism appears to be more vulnerable than American Catholicism to external threats. The forces of modernisation, secularism and individualisation and the priest sex abuse crisis impinge in both societies, yet American Catholicism seems more resilient than Irish Catholicism in the current moment. This chapter probes the commonalities and divergences apparent in a cross-national comparison of Irish and US Catholicism, and assesses how and why national context influences the particularised expression of a universal Catholicism.

Irish public Catholicism in the 1980s

The shared public enthusiasm of Catholics on both sides of the Atlantic during John Paul's 1979 tour suggested a shared Catholic reality that was largely independent of societal context. The ensuing decade, however, gave lie to this assumption with the forceful emergence of contrasting expressions of public Catholicism. In Ireland, the 1980s emerged as an era of public moral conflict and debate.[5] Abortion and divorce were thrust on the public agenda and stimulated over ten years of unprecedented and intense discussion. The questions at issue were complex and wide-ranging, encompassing individual rights, family structure, support and protection, the role of the Church, the duties of the state and the character of Irish society. Legislation enacted in 1979 made contraceptives available but only for married couples and only for *bona fide* family planning purposes – dubbed in an appeal to Irish distinctiveness by the then Health Minister Charles Haughey as 'an Irish solution to an Irish problem'. The same act also affirmed the criminal status of abortion dating to a pre-Independence 1861 law.

Abortion, none the less, soon became a highly contested issue propelled on to the public agenda as a result of the establishment of a Right-to-Life Movement in Ireland in 1980. Galvanised in part by John Paul's visit and his emphasis on the sacredness of human life, the movement's Pro Life Amendment Campaign (PLAC) saw the Irish embark on a divisive debate in 1983 about whether and how the Constitution should explicitly prohibit abortion. Though two-thirds of the electorate voted in favour of constitutional protection for the unborn, the provision did little to clarify the right to life of pregnant women experiencing ill-health. Additional public referendums resulted in the expansion of some abortion rights such as, for example, the right of Irish women to information about abortion and to travel abroad for an abortion. Most recently, in July 2013, after a contentious debate and despite opposition from the Catholic bishops, the Irish parliament voted in favour of new legislation recognising the right to an abortion in cases where the pregnant woman's life is threatened by ill-health or suicide ideation.

Back in the 1980s, however, PLAC's success affirmed the continuing moral authority of the Catholic bishops and of Catholic moral teaching notwithstanding the occasional flashes of secularism that alighted amid Ireland's expanding economic and social modernisation. The subsequent defeat of a pro-divorce amendment in 1986 offered further vindication of the moral authority of the bishops. Notwithstanding the increased visibility of marital breakdown in Ireland, and opinion poll trends demonstrating a consistent pattern of steady increase in the public's support for some form of legal divorce, the Irish deferred to the status quo. After a vigorous nine weeks of campaigning on both sides of the issue, the pro-divorce amendment was defeated by a two-to-one majority.[6] Within another decade, the Irish had changed their minds: in 1996, a majority voted in favour of a new divorce proposal that was in many respects similar to the 1986 proposal.[7] But in 1986, at the end of an intense and highly contested debate in which the bishops had insisted that, while they would not be campaigning per se, they would be using their rightful moral authority and the authority of the pulpit to emphasise that divorce was contrary to Catholic moral teaching, the rejection of divorce presented the bishops with a clear victory. For the first time in the history of the state, the Irish people themselves, confronted with the practical consequences of marital breakdown and given the choice of whether they wanted to support a legislative initiative that would sever the long institutionalised and deeply felt cultural synchrony between Catholic moral teaching and civil law, chose to maintain that synchrony. In essence, they deferred to the moral authority of the bishops. It thus seemed at the end of the 1980s that despite its increased modernisation and urbanisation, Ireland was indeed, as Eamon de Valera had declared fifty years earlier, 'a Catholic nation' and intended to remain as such.

American public Catholicism in the 1980s

By contrast to the defensively triumphant expression of Catholicism in Ireland in the 1980s, the Catholic Church in the US during that same decade was proactively engaged in articulating a public moral voice for the nation as a whole. The American bishops were relatively passive in response to American Catholics' disregard of *Humanae Vitae*'s (1968) ban on artificial contraception, and they maintained a low profile during the social movement and civil rights activism of the late 1960s and 1970s.[8] In the 1980s, however, they unfolded a fully fledged public Catholicism. Their full-court foray into the public sphere coincided with the increased establishment of Catholics as part of the well-educated and suburbanised middle and upper-middle classes, cohorts who were as comfortable with American economic and social liberalism as earlier generations of immigrant Catholics had been discomfited by it. Although the US Catholic bishops had been in the vanguard of political activism against abortion since the early 1970s, and especially so following the US Supreme Court's ruling in favour of legal abortion in 1973 (*Roe v Wade*), the 1980s saw them encompass other issues: most notably, moving beyond abortion – an issue that was widely seen as a narrow Catholic preoccupation despite the bishops' persistent framing of it as a human rights issue transcending religious belief – the US bishops directed their attention to economic justice and nuclear war.

Papal encyclicals and bishops' statements since the end of the nineteenth century had long criticised the individualistic excesses of free market capitalism, and church documents had also outlined the high moral threshold that would need to be met in order to justify acts of war. But when the US bishops issued their 1983 pastoral letter on nuclear war, *The Challenge of Peace*, and three years later their pastoral letter *Economic Justice for All*, these public interventions marked a new departure for the American Catholic Church. Specifically, the letters offered trenchant and lengthy critiques of 'the ethical underpinnings of nuclear defence policies and American economic life' and drew extensively not only on Catholic teaching but also on secular scholarship.[9] The pastoral letters waded into – and made no apology for wading into – a moral and policy domain that many Catholics and non-Catholics alike deemed as being outside of the bishops' authority. Contrary to that view, the bishops presented a compelling articulation of a publicly relevant Catholicism, and their respective critiques of American economic culture and defence policy received extensive national media coverage. Although many Americans, including many Catholics, did not actually read or discuss the content of the letters, their publication made a positive impact among US elites and served as a marker to the public at large that the US bishops were committed to articulating a legitimate public voice on socio-political issues that had wide import for Americans as a whole.

Place matters

The defensive Catholicism of the Irish bishops in contrast to the proactive socio-political engagement of the US bishops points to the relevance of societal context – and of a country's specific history and culture – in shaping how Catholic teaching is articulated and used to maintain the public presence of a universal Church. Catholicism in the US, unlike in Ireland, is a minority and immigrant church, and it is embedded in a pluralistic denominational society rather than, as in Ireland, a Catholic nation. The differentiated nature of the religious landscape in the US facilitated the Catholic Church's competitive push not only to distinguish itself from other denominations but also to proactively achieve and maintain a religious, moral and institutional relevance. The Church managed to accomplish an impressive history of institution-building (churches, schools and colleges, community centres, hospitals, social services) and it was quick to achieve, and consistent in maintaining, a well-developed and highly visible physical and symbolic presence. In the absence of a monopoly Church, Catholics were not obliged to be Catholics or to participate in church structures – they had many alternatives available to them, and indeed some chose to disaffiliate while many others remained (or became) Catholic. As has long been true of religious affiliation in the US more generally, the lived experience of being Catholic entailed a certain amount of individual interpretative autonomy.

Interpretative autonomy became more real for Catholics as a result of Vatican II (1962–65) and its emphasis on personal conscience, religious freedom and the relevance of secular expertise and lived experience in the interpretation of doctrine. By the 1980s, American Catholics had achieved upward mobility and an impressively high level of socio-economic status. And coincidentally, mainline churches were losing some of their historically impressive numerical and political strength. In this context, the Catholic bishops, emboldened by Vatican II's emphasis on a publicly engaged Catholicism, were ready to step up, engage with and critique core economic ideas (e.g. unfettered free markets) and cultural ideas (e.g. individualism) in American society.

The Irish bishops, by contrast, were in a more awkward contextual situation during this same decade. Having long enjoyed hegemony as the singular, unilateral and unquestioned moral authority in Irish society, the liberalising impact of Ireland's economic and social modernisation processes set in motion in the 1960s and 1970s (e.g. increased urbanisation and increased access to secondary and tertiary education) was beginning to crack the bishops' moral monopoly. Despite Vatican II's recognition of the legitimate differentiation of Church and state, and notwithstanding the Irish bishops' invocation of a language of Church–state differentiation, they ultimately looked to civil law as a way to reinforce Catholic moral teaching and to stem the tides of secularism. Hence the bishops' adoption of a defensive posture that sought to realign Irishness with Catholicism and their systematic push back against initiatives (e.g. divorce) that undermine the construct of Ireland as a Catholic nation.

Convergence in Public Catholicism

When we turn our gaze from the 1980s to today, we see a relative convergence in public Catholicism. Today, the economic justice strand of the US bishops' public Catholicism is largely muted. It is displaced by their focus on abortion, same-sex issues and the previously moot issue of contraception, now invigorated by the bishops' public and legal campaign arguing that religious liberty is infringed by government health insurance mandates requiring Catholic institutional employers to pay employee contraception insurance costs. Similarly, while Irish bishops offer some commentary on the need to protect marginalised socio-economic groups during Ireland's current economic austerity as it deals with the fallout from the collapse of the Celtic Tiger, they too are preoccupied with same-sex rights and again the status of abortion.

This post-1980s convergence is prompted by two separate factors. Pope John Paul II exuded a joyful charisma as he travelled the world. But he also reinstituted a pre-Vatican II defensiveness that emphasised a highly conservative stand on sexual morality and women's issues and combined it with an authoritarian rather than a collegial ruling style. Ironically, in the wake of Pope Benedict XVI's resignation in February 2013, many media commentators disparagingly contrasted the aloof intellectualism and conservatism of Benedict with the popularity of his predecessor. Lost in this comparison, however, was the recognition that John Paul's moral and political conservatism was the framework Benedict inherited.

While Benedict indeed executed and contributed to John Paul's dogmaticism as head of the Congregation for the Doctrine of the Faith during John Paul's papacy, it was none the less John Paul's doctrinal agenda that reoriented the Church over a twenty-eight-year reign (1978–2005). Thus the latter consistently gave dogmatic emphasis to the Church's opposition to abortion and contraception, formally denounced the grave immorality of same-sex sexual behaviour and reaffirmed the Church's opposition to the ordination of women as well as declaring that discussion of the issue was itself an act in contradiction with Catholicism. More generally, John Paul appointed doctrinally conservative bishops, reined in public theological discussion as a whole and restricted Catholic academic freedom and independent lay thinking. The doctrinal environment that he fostered dampened the dialogical vibrancy of a public Catholicism attentive to pressing social and economic justice issues and, instead, favoured public articulation of the Church's teachings on sex and gender.

National bishops' conferences more or less capitulated to the Vatican's re-energised moral conservatism and, as the years progressed and John Paul appointed bishops and cardinals who were in tune with his views, the bishops needed little prodding with respect to Church priorities. Moreover, the church's sex abuse scandal erupted, first in Boston in 2001, then enveloping other US dioceses, Ireland and other countries. Consequently, the US bishops were comparatively mute on social and economic issues for a decade or so while they focused on devising and implementing procedural changes in response to legal penalties and public outrage over their protection of child sex-abusive priests.

Ireland experienced its own protracted share of child and other sex-related scandals that implicated prominent bishops and priests. Starting in the mid-1990s, these stories were extensively covered by the Irish news media and their shock reverberated among faithful Catholics more used to defending than criticising priests and bishops. Even so, when the details of the various abuses and of the church hierarchy's pattern of covering-up such actions were documented in government-commissioned independent inquiries, their publication in 2009–11 further cemented the Irish Church hierarchy's loss of credibility. Thus in Ireland, as in the US, the sex abuse scandal seriously undermined the ability of Church leaders to speak out on social and political issues and it, along with John Paul's directives, contributed to a muted public Catholicism on both sides of the Atlantic.

This decade or so of relative quietude abruptly ended in the US in late 2011 when the US bishops embarked on a public campaign against contraception insurance coverage. In Ireland, the renewed presence of bishops' voices in the public domain coincides with the effort to liberalise same-sex marriage and a renewed attempt to clarify the legislative situation regarding abortion. Thus the convergence in the character of post-1980s public Catholicism in the US and Ireland was driven by similar Catholic forces – Pope John Paul's anti-dialogical papacy and the Church's sex abuse scandals. And by the same token, the current resurgence of public Catholicism is driven both in Ireland and the US by what church officials see as secular threats undermining Catholic teaching in the domain of sexuality.

Divergence in the lay practice of Catholicism

Notwithstanding the Irish and American convergence currently observable in public Catholicism, the lay practice of Irish and American Catholicism is substantially different. At the end of the 1980s, approximately eight in ten Irish adults (85 per cent) were attending weekly Mass whereas approximately four in ten of

American Catholics (44 per cent) were doing so.[10] Thus while both Irish and American Catholics joyfully greeted Pope John Paul in 1979, American Catholics were less likely than their Irish co-religionists to go to Mass the following weekend. Even in the early decades of the twentieth century, weekly Mass attendance was not perceived by American Catholics as the absolutely strict obligation it was in Ireland, and the relative autonomy around it substantially increased in the wake of *Humanae Vitae*. The various deliberations of Vatican II with respect to the rightful moral and interpretative authority of lay Catholics, the importance of personal conscience, the exercise of religious freedom and the obligation of Church officials and lay Catholics alike to be open to developments in knowledge and science led many Catholics to anticipate that Paul VI would acknowledge the contextual morality of contraception. When instead he denounced it, many American Catholics, already using some form of birth control, stopped going to Mass and Communion. Many priests and bishops remained quiet on the issue and it was widely reported that the use of contraception was not a source of condemnation in confession.

After an interval of a few years, many American Catholics resumed Mass attendance and did so while continuing to use contraception. Henceforth, they would be Catholic on their own terms.[11] Thus began the crafting of a Catholic identity that saw Catholics assert their own individual autonomy vis-à-vis the church hierarchy; they would decide for themselves what is entailed in being a good Catholic and, in particular, would make up their own minds about personal sexual morality. Thus, two-thirds of American Catholics in the 1980s – and over three-quarters (78 per cent) in 2011 – expressed the view that a person can be a good Catholic without going to Mass every Sunday, and without obeying the Church's teaching on birth control.[12] By contrast, Irish Catholicism in the 1970s and 1980s was seen as dogmatic and legalistic, meaning that Catholics were quite literal and inflexible in their interpretation of the rules of the Church.[13] In this view, the obligation of Sunday Mass required Sunday Mass attendance irrespective of pressing personal or family circumstances. And even if one conceded recognition of the legitimacy of Church-state separation, the Catholic consensual view nonetheless was that contraception, sex outside marriage and divorce were mortal sins. The idea that Catholics might have a personal morality that was independent of official Church teaching was slow to intrude on the Irish mind.

Much has happened in the US and Ireland over the last three decades and with those changes there has been considerable change in religious attitudes and practices. None the less, a survey snapshot of US Catholics today shows that they are as committed to the church as were US Catholics in the 1980s.[14] As befits a Church that emphasises balance among an individual's various commitments – to family, work, church, and civic life – this is a moderate level of commitment, and its contours have remained remarkably stable over the last three decades. There has been a decline in the frequency of Mass attendance, especially among women, and monthly rather than weekly attendance is the current norm. Similarly, too, there has been a continuing increase in the proportions who express a relatively autonomous view of what it means to be a good Catholic, and who believe that personal conscience rather than Church rules should determine an individual Catholic's behaviour in regard to contraception, same-sex relationships and divorce and remarriage. Taken as a whole, the data suggest that American Catholics are quite autonomous in their interpretation and practice of Catholicism. Their sense of Catholicism is variously shaped by secular forces and, as noted earlier, a Protestant culture of individual freedom. However, in the US, an emphasis on individual freedom, as Alexis de Tocqueville long ago observed, has correlated with the freedom to positively choose to go to church and to determine how to be religious. Catholics' autonomy also finds support in the understanding of Catholicism articulated by Vatican II – its emphases on personal conscience and the relevance of individual interpretive authority and lived experience. These are all forceful strands that facilitate both American Catholics' individualised independence from Rome and their simultaneously strong personal sense of Catholic identity and attachment to many elements of the Catholic tradition.

The bottom line is that American Catholics understand and practise Catholicism today in much the same way as American Catholics did in the 1980s. The same cannot be said of Irish Catholics. Rather than showing stability, their involvement in the Church has precipitously diminished. This decline was driven in part by the angry response in Ireland to the high-profile accounts of priest sex abuse and its institutional cover-up, an exposure that toppled Church officials off their lofty pedestal. It was also driven by the impact of the Celtic Tiger, the economic transformation that took hold in Ireland between approximately 1993 and 2007. Ireland's phenomenal economic prosperity during that fifteen-year interval was recorded in its exceptionally high levels of per annum Gross Domestic Product (GDP), exceptionally high levels of personal disposable income and consumer spending, and exceptionally low unemployment rates (e.g. less than five per cent).

The sweeping economic and social impact of the Celtic Tiger might well be expected in and of itself to have had a major impact on the religious habits of the Irish people. Just one aspect of this transformation, such as increased consumer spending on foreign vacations and foreign holiday homes, for example, opens up a way of thinking and being that was an alternative to the norm in Ireland even in the 1980s. Taken together, the socio-economic changes in Irish lived experience, coupled with the ongoing exposure of abuses by the Church, have pushed the previously imposing Church out of the consciousness of many Irish Catholics. Most notably, almost half as many adults (43 per cent) were reporting weekly Mass attendance in late 2007 and early 2008 as were doing so twenty years earlier (85 per cent). By contrast, the initial trend of decline in the twenty years prior to 1990 was more gradual, recording a drop of 6 per cent (down from 91 per cent in 1974 to 85 per cent in 1988–89).[15] From a comparative perspective, weekly Mass attendance in Ireland is still relatively high; it is higher than the 31 per cent of US Catholics who attend Mass weekly, and far higher than the numbers observed in the UK and Western Europe over the past four decades.[16]

The Irish have certainly not disavowed their Catholic identity. In the April 2011 Census, 84 per cent identified as Catholic; and large proportions continue to believe in God and the sacraments, and find personal support in their faith.[17] Their increased absence from Mass, however – a trend that is especially evident among the majority urban population and among younger cohorts – may signal a larger rupture in communal regard for the Church. In the US too, younger cohorts, especially white women in their twenties and thirties, are significantly more indifferent towards Catholicism than their parents and grandparents.[18] This cross-national generational shift may not reverse itself as these younger cohorts move through the life-course, unlike the earlier pattern in the US when the life-course effects of marriage, work and parenting motivated individuals to return to Church.

Notwithstanding some generational commonalities among young Irish and American Catholics, the distinctiveness of Irish Catholicism today may lie in its newly emerging disenchantment with the Church. Irish Catholics are no longer deferential to the moral prohibitions of the bishops – only 25 per cent of Irish Catholics say, for example, that same-gender sexual relationships are always wrong, down from 47 per cent who said so in 1998 – and they no longer feel the obligatory communal force of weekly Mass attendance.[19] It seems as if they are developing a distaste toward Catholicism, as if the sins of Church officials have contaminated the mosaic of the Catholic tradition as a whole. This may change. But unlike American Catholics they do not seem to be able, at least in the present moment, to balance criticism of, with loyalty to, the Church and Catholicism.[20] Although Vatican II impacted Irish Catholicism, a significant element of Vatican II theology – the idea of the Church as the 'People of God' – did not secure a foothold in Irish Catholicism. The laity in Ireland have long been active providers of unpaid labour in and for the Church. But they have never claimed the Church as their own, unlike American Catholics, for different historical and contextual reasons (for example, the structure and culture of denominational pluralism, freedom and identity). Instead, a dominant view in Ireland is that the Church is the Church hierarchy and it, not the laity, owns and controls the institution and the larger Catholic tradition.

Thus with the impact of the sex abuse crisis, coupled with the increased individualism and consumerism prompted by the Celtic Tiger – and now faced with austerity resulting from its failure – the Irish are not emboldened by their Catholic identity.[21] Increased individualisation and secularisation distance Irish Catholics from the Church, unlike in the US where the forces of secularism and individualism have long accommodated and indeed bolstered religion (though not without tension). Today, the Irish are beginning to look not like their American counterparts but more like their peers in Europe, where too the historical monopoly of the

Catholic Church – in France, Italy, Spain and Poland – has not been sufficient to stem the reach of religious indifference in the face of secular forces.

Notes

1 Tom Inglis, *Moral Monopoly: Catholic Church in Modern Irish Society* (Dublin: Gill and Macmillan, 1987).
2 Will Herberg, *Protestant-Catholic-Jew* (New York: Doubleday, 1955).
3 William D'Antonio, Michele Dillon and Mary Gautier, *American Catholics in Transition* (Lanham, MD: Rowman and Littlefield, 2013).
4 M. Nic Ghiolla Phádraig 'Religion in Ireland: No longer an exception?' ARK (Access Research Knowledge): Research Update 64, 2009. www.ark.ac.uk.
5 Michele Dillon, *Debating Divorce: Moral Conflict in Ireland* (Lexington: University Press of Kentucky, 1993).
6 Dillon, *Debating Divorce*, p. 2.
7 Tony Fahey and Richard Layte, 'Family and Sexuality', in Tony Fahey (ed.), *Quality of Life in Ireland* (New York: Springer, 2008).
8 *Humanae Vitae: Encyclical Letter of His Holiness Pope Paul VI* (San Francisco: Ignatius Press, 1968/1983).
9 Gene Burns, *The Frontiers of Catholicism: The Politics of Ideology in a Liberal World* (Berkeley, CA: University of California Press, 1992), p. 110.
10 See Nic Ghiolla Phádraig, 'Religion in Ireland' for Irish Mass attendance; and D'Antonio, Dillon and Gautier, *American Catholics in Transition*, p. 109, for US Catholics' Mass attendance.
11 Andrew Greeley, *American Catholics since the Council* (Chicago: Thomas More Press, 1985).
12 William D'Antonio, James Davidson, Dean Hoge and Ruth Wallace, *American Catholic Laity in a Changing Church* (Kansas City, MO: Sheed and Ward, 1989), p. 57; D'Antonio, Dillon and Gautier, *American Catholics in Transition*, p. 50.
13 Inglis, *Moral Monopoly: Catholic Church in Modern Irish Society*.
14 D'Antonio, Dillon and Gautier, *American Catholics in Transition*.
15 Mac Gréil, *The Challenge of Indifference*.
16 D'Antonio, Dillon and Gautier, *American Catholics in Transition*, p. 109; Andrew Greeley, *Religion in Europe at the End of the Second Millennium* (New Brunswick, NJ: Transaction, 2003), p. 70.
17 Mac Gréil, *The Challenge of Indifference*.
18 D'Antonio, Dillon and Gautier, *American Catholics in Transition*, pp. 139–50.
19 Author's own analysis of Irish Catholics' responses in the cross-national International Social Survey Program (ISSP) 1998 and 2008 modules.
20 Michele Dillon, *Catholic Identity: Balancing Reason, Faith, and Power* (New York: Cambridge University Press, 1999).
21 Tom Inglis, 'Individualisation and Secularisation in Catholic Ireland', in Sara O'Sullivan (ed.), *Contemporary Ireland: A Sociological Map* (Dublin: University College Dublin Press, 2007).

12

Postcolonial legacies and the Irish psyche

Geraldine Moane

A notable feature of discussions since 2008 about the collapse of the Celtic Tiger has been the emergence of a dominant discourse of 'we all'. Phrases such as 'we all partied', 'the Irish people borrowed more than anyone else' invoke an undifferentiated collective who are responsible for the economic collapse. Perhaps the most dramatic example of such a discourse is provided in comments made by the current Taoiseach (Enda Kenny) at a meeting of the World Economic Forum in Davos on 26 January 2012. Kenny is quoted as saying: 'What happened in our country was that people simply went mad borrowing'.[1] This comment is notable not only for the use of the generic 'people' but also for the term 'mad'. I would argue that the willingness of a national leader to use this phrase about his or her people at a global economic forum is itself symptomatic of a postcolonial mentality, one that can use a dominator discourse of madness, echoing colonial stereotypes.

This is just one instance of what can seem like a chorus of commentaries in print media and elsewhere on the characteristics of the Irish or of the Irish psyche. Another example is provided by Michael Casey, a former member of the board of the International Monetary Fund (IMF). Writing in the *The Irish Times*, Casey argues that 'characteristics of the Irish psyche must be taken into account in any economic analysis of how we got here and where we want to go'. In this article (and in a book) he writes of the Irish 'obsession' with 'owning bricks and mortar', 'bureaucratic inertia and reluctance to take responsibility', 'people pleasing' and a 'lurch' from mania to despair, linking these to our colonial past, which is also linked to 'diffidence and deference'. Another element of this discourse is a commonly asked question – why are 'the Irish' not out on the streets like 'the Greeks', a comment on the contrast between on-street demonstrations in Athens and the lack thereof in Dublin. The usual answer refers to the passivity and compliance of 'the Irish'.[2]

These examples illustrate the trend in public discussion to focus on what is wrong with us as a people, often accompanied by disturbing levels of contempt and self-hatred. This may be contrasted with the focus on the creativity, perseverance and courage of the Irish people articulated in the statements of the current President Michael D. Higgins, or the emphasis of psychologist Maureen Gaffney on resilience. It is as if our public discussions of the Irish are themselves polarised in the dualistic worldview ('good' versus 'bad') described by Frantz Fanon as the Manichean worldview of colonialism. One of Fanon's arguments, taken up by many in postcolonial and liberation psychologies, is the need to transcend the dualistic thinking that permeates and perpetrates domination.[3]

In this chapter I hope to illustrate the importance, and indeed the need for, a postcolonial analysis of the Irish context. I will draw particularly on postcolonial psychology as a perspective that can offer rich understandings and possibilities for transformation. Before proceeding with a discussion of what is a highly complex topic I would like to set out some of my starting points.[4] The first is that Ireland has a history of colonisation, albeit with distinctive features. Systematic plantations and military invasions were well established by Elizabethan times (late sixteenth century) and the country was under colonial domination until 1921. This history includes suppression of culture and language, religious control, slaughter, rape, famine and mass migrations and emigrations of people.

The second starting point is that postcolonial legacies continue to influence the Irish economy, culture, politics and society. In contrast to the humanities and Irish studies, I would argue that the human sciences in Ireland are noteworthy for the *lack* of attention to colonisation and its legacies.[5] Yet when viewed from a postcolonial perspective there are numerous examples of legacies of colonisation. Here I will provide ten examples of where the Republic of Ireland is still postcolonial, that is, where legacies of colonisation continue to be manifest. These examples focus specifically on socio-political issues (leaving aside cultural and economic issues). To begin, the name of country (Eire, Ireland, Republic of Ireland), the map of the country (the island, not the twenty-six counties), the flag of the country and partition all reflect divisions that are legacies of colonisation. Other examples are: the national anthem (content and lack of familiarity with the words); the official language (Irish, spoken by a small percentage); the dominance of the Catholic Church (established during colonisation); population trends (legacy of famine and emigration); the dominance of a single party in government (Fianna Fáil, in power for over sixty years); and the dominance within the political system of two major parties divided by legacies of the civil war (Fianna Fáil and Fine Gael).

A third starting point is the acknowledgement of complexities within Irish society, and in the relationship between Ireland and Britain. As many writers on colonisation have argued, colonisation is a complex process of collusion as well as domination. It involves societies that are themselves stratified into systems of domination, with elites often co-operating for their own benefit. Furthermore, in a postcolonial society elites often exploit the legacies of colonisation for their own benefits, as some argue, stepping into the shoes of the colonizers. And of course colonisation has been accompanied by many forms of resistance.

These starting points are necessary before proceeding to a consideration of the Irish psyche, a term often used to refer to psychological patterns associated with being Irish. The different meanings and understanding of this term, how it has been and can be understood, is the topic of the following discussion. I will first outline some assumptions of postcolonial psychology. I will then consider the ways in which (mostly) psychologists have described the Irish psyche, particularly through assigning attributes. I will then present alternative approaches that focus on developing discourses and understandings aimed at transformation.

Postcolonial theory and postcolonial psychology

Postcolonial psychology engages with contexts and concepts related to historical processes of colonisation, postcolonial development and decolonisation. It draws on early writings on the psychology of colonisation, notably those of Frantz Fanon and Albert Memmi, and on postcolonial theory. Postcolonial theory has developed primarily as an interdisciplinary approach to literature and culture. It elaborates concepts that are of interest to psychologists, such as culture, discourse, identity and consciousness. Postcolonial psychology and postcolonial theory do not assume that colonisation has ended; the term 'postcolonial' is used to refer to theory and research written during or after the second half of the twentieth century that explicitly engages with colonisation and related terms. Such theory and research aim to develop understandings of how legacies of colonisation influence psychological and social patterns, possibly in ways that can be damaging. Such understandings can then play a role in helping to change or transform these negative patterns. They can also aid contemporary analysis of legacies of colonisation such as global poverty and inequalities, migration and the marginalisation of indigenous people.

The writings of Frantz Fanon (Martinique/Algeria) and Albert Memmi (Tunisia) are key historical influences in the development of postcolonial psychology. Both wrote of the dynamic relationship and even interdependency between colonisers and colonised whereby both influenced each other, albeit unequally. They argued that both groups developed distinctive psychological patterns that reflected their respective roles as dominator (coloniser) or as subjugated (colonised). Their examples of coloniser attributes that could facilitate domination include a sense of superiority, dehumanisation and aggression. Patterns attributed to the colonised (developed in response to domination) include sense of inferiority, helplessness, irresponsibility, alcohol abuse, self-hatred, ambivalence and restricted identity. They saw racism as intrinsic to colonisation. The Indian psychologist Ashis Nandy echoed some of these themes and also explored the gendered dynamic of colonisation, whereby the superior attributes of the colonizer are judged to be masculine in contrast with the inferior attributes of the colonised, judged as feminine. Colonisation is thus associated with sexism and the valuing of hypermasculinity.[6]

These writers clearly linked psychological attributes to patterns of colonisation including violence, political exclusion, economic exploitation and control of culture. For example, abuses of alcohol were linked to the oppression and restrictions of colonisation. They also acknowledged strengths associated with oppression such as courage, perseverance and generosity. Fanon and Memmi both argued that colonisation involved both social and psychological domination. In their view, even if economic and political domination ended, psychological patterns would remain. The concept of internalised oppression or internalised colonisation then developed to refer to the ways in which oppressed groups in particular came to believe that patterns related to colonisation were an intrinsic part of their own psyche, believing in their own inferiority. Decolonisation thus requires both psychological and political transformation.

Further developments in postcolonial psychology moved away from assignment of attributes to a critical analysis of how the assignment of attributes may be used as a form of oppression, especially if they reinforce a sense of inferiority. The assignment of attributes itself can be seen as an assertion of power, as generating a discourse of inferiority which can shape the subjectivity of those so described. Rather than aiming to provide an accurate description of psychological patterns, this approach sees the assignment of psychological patterns as a discourse that can be critically analysed – what we and others say about ourselves (discourses) shapes how we and others view us and also shapes our behaviours. Decolonisation, that is transformation of legacies of colonisation, can come about by critically examining our discourses, and also by constructing new ways of talking about and perceiving ourselves.

Postcolonial psychology has been applied in many contexts globally – Algeria, Tunisia and India have already been mentioned. Other contexts where there is published work include Puerto Rico, Australia and New Zealand, the Philippines, Hawaii and South Africa. In the North American context, Hussein Bulhan developed Fanon's work to call for a psychology of liberation for African Americans, but with relevance to those in other contexts with colonial histories. Eduardo and Bonnie Duran set out to develop a postcolonial Native American psychology that would draw on the cultural resources and practices that had been erased or suppressed by colonisation.[7] While these are obviously very different contexts and histories, there are commonalities of theory and practice and many insights of relevance to the Irish context.

Often these international examples combine what I will call the attributional approach (what are the characteristics of colonised people and how can we change them?) with the discursive approach (how do we talk about colonised people and how can we develop new discourses?). Both approaches share the aim of transforming psychological and cultural practices associated with colonisation, especially those that can inhibit or damage those who have been colonised. They are part of a bigger trend in psychology to recognise oppression and liberation at a socio-political as well as at an individual level. This trend towards liberation involves a shift away from an emphasis on oppression, loss and trauma to an interest in liberation, transformation and recovery. I agree with this double-edged focus. Those who have been oppressed are seen no longer as passive victims of oppression but rather as agents negotiating and making choices, creating contexts which offer some scope, however limited, for resistance, pride, creativity and joy.

Postcolonial patterns and the Irish psyche

Psychologists (and psychiatrists) have written about characteristics of 'the Irish' in several contexts. As is typical of psychology, most of this analysis has been based on clinical or empirical evidence, and is written with the aim of enhancing psychological understanding and practice. A notable example in psychology was a Special Issue of *The Irish Journal of Psychology*, published in 1994, in which contributors addressed the theme of the Irish psyche. Here and elsewhere there has been acknowledgement that the Irish psyche is not an essentialist or unitary entity, but is rather complex and fluid, shaped by multiple historical and social factors.[8] Many contributors to this volume emphasised strengths (such as imagination) as well as negative patterns (such as inferiority). Elsewhere, many discussions refer to 'the Irish' as an undifferentiated whole, and often focus on negative attributes. However, there has been little systematic critical or empirical analysis of such writings. Here I will focus on discussions that make explicit links to our history of colonisation.

Perhaps one of the best known writers in this area has been Monica McGoldrick, an Irish American family systems therapist, who began writing about Irish American families in the 1980s. Along with Nancy Scheper-Hughes, McGoldrick has been highly influential in both American and Irish writings. Her description of the Irish has been used at length in many different contexts; indeed virtually all discussions of Irish Americans knowingly or unknowingly use her phrases. Writing for family therapists and aiming to identify distinctive cultural patterns McGoldrick discusses the impact on family relations of diaspora, the Church, communication and conflict, humour, alcohol use, suffering, shame and guilt. She writes:

> The Irish are a people of many paradoxes. While having a tremendous flair for bravado, they may inwardly assume that anything that goes wrong is the result of their sins. They are dreamers but also pragmatic hard workers. ... they are good humored, charming, hospitable, and gregarious, but often avoid intimacy. They love

a good time, which includes teasing, verbal word play and sparring, yet are drawn to tragedy. Although they are known for fighting against all odds, the Irish have also had a strong sense of human powerlessness.[9]

Returning to the Irish context, several discussions have made explicit links to colonisation. Writing in 1985, Vincent Kenny drew on a constructivist perspective. He presented a theoretical analysis of the impact of subordination (colonisation), associating it with various patterns of constriction. Secrecy, superficial compliance, indirect communication, limited self-revelation, use of fantasy, magical thinking and superstition, helplessness, passivity, shame, self-hatred and sense of worthlessness are among the many patterns he identifies. Anthony Clare, writing in 1994, commented on the high rates of mood disorders in Ireland: 'The most compelling cultural explanation has been that which points to the impact of centuries of foreign political and psychological domination on the Irish mind, a mind enveloped and to an extent suffocated in an English mental embrace'. Several papers in the above-mentioned Special Issue (including my own) identified attributes of the Irish psyche.[10]

Trisha McDonnell undertook an empirical study of internal colonisation through in-depth qualitative interviews with sixteen people. Twelve of these were considered elite in the sense of being trained mental health practitioners or public commentators, and four were non-elites, with eight females and eight males in the sample. Her thematic analysis identified over thirty attributes that interviewees attributed to the Irish psyche. At least half of the sample (over 50 per cent) identified the following themes, which also recur in popular culture and in theoretical writings: obtuse (unclear) communication; identity issues; religion and spirituality; imagination and avoidance; ambivalent attitudes towards authority; focus on survival; horizontal hostility (begrudgery); identification with the Other (rather than with Self).[11]

In my informal engagements with the topic of postcolonial legacies and the Irish psyche, in presentations, workshops and discussions, I have found that there is a keen interest in the topic, but also a readiness to assign mostly negative attributes to the Irish. Psychologists and psychotherapists in particular could identify recurring patterns in clinical contexts that they felt could be linked to culture and our history of colonisation. In classes and workshops, participants often react to examples such as McGoldrick above first with laughter but then with a sense of recognition, sometimes silenced by the sense of something familiar yet not fully articulated. There is a need for more complex discussion of these issues that can move beyond describing characteristics of the Irish.

In aiming to draw conclusions myself, I initially took the view that extensive empirical studies would be needed comparing attributes of the Irish with those of people from other countries (allowing for variations by class, age, gender, sexual orientation and other dimensions of inequality and oppression). In an analysis published in 2002, I argued that our history of colonisation rendered us culturally more vulnerable to new forces of globalisation, and psychologically more vulnerable to exploitation. I identified five patterns that I called 'cultural pathologies'. I argued that these patterns were well supported by empirical evidence, could be systematically linked to our history of colonisation and were identified in other postcolonial contexts. I labelled them: alcohol and drug abuse; denial and doublethink (Irish solution to an Irish problem); distortions of sexuality; horizontal hostility (begrudgery); and social irresponsibility. Adopting a liberation psychology perspective that also highlights strengths from oppression, I identified three strengths that I suggested were resources for resistance and transformation, namely community, creativity and spirituality. These patterns can be seen as psychosocial patterns, operating at both the sociological and psychological levels.[12]

In a further attempt to mobilise empirical evidence, I focused on the topic of alcohol consumption as a single example to pursue in detail. The view of the Irish as heavy drinkers, as alcoholic, as dysfunctional in regard to alcohol, is one of the most recurring in popular culture and in the literature. A detailed comparison of alcohol consumption figures across cultures provides clear evidence that Irish consumption is almost always at or near the top of the list in terms of, for example, numbers of binge drinkers; amount consumed by regular heavy drinkers; amount consumed by regular moderate drinkers. The country next most likely to be at or near the top of the list is Britain. Both countries share similar patterns of alcohol consumption. Yet the Irish are far more likely to be labelled as 'heavy' drinkers. Further qualitative research on this topic revealed the extent to which the discourse about the Irish as drinkers has been internalised, in this instance by a student sample. In interviews with twelve students who were moderate to heavy drinkers, Sinéad Ní Chaoláin found a consistent theme of feeling the need to drink in order to perform socially, epitomised in the following: 'I felt . . . I couldn't go out if I wasn't tanked up, like we were supposed to have the craic'. Phrases linking Irishness to drink recurred – 'we're Irish, we drink'. Open-ended responses in a survey of 312 students provided an overall sense not only of permission but of pressure in Irish culture to drink. Thus 'the Irish as drinkers' operates as a perception by others, as an identity or internalised self-perception, and as behavioural and cultural patterns, creating a self-perpetuating cycle.[13]

The example of alcohol offers empirical evidence for practitioners and commentators, and along with other research in the Irish context provides some insights relating to actual alcohol consumption patterns in the Irish context. It also raises the more discursive questions of postcolonial psychology – why is the discourse of alcoholism invoked so readily and persistently in the case of 'the Irish', but not in the case of 'the British'? Who invokes this discourse, in what contexts, and for what purposes? What form of discourse about alcohol is invoked? This approach points to the need for new approaches that have the potential for disrupting existing perspectives and offer new approaches to transformation. The indigenous psychology stream in postcolonial psychology offers examples of new approaches.

Indigenous and transpersonal approaches to transforming the Irish psyche

A recurring theme in more recent postcolonial psychology concerns the loss or suppression of indigenous psychologies and healing practices as a result of colonisation. A postcolonial pattern has been the importation of Western psychological practice and the displacement of traditional healers. As indigenous people, particularly in Australia and North America, developed their analysis, the field of indigenous psychology emerged with the aim of developing theory and practice that would draw on cultural, linguistic and spiritual traditions that had been displaced or destroyed by colonial processes. A common aim in countries ranging from India to South Africa to the Americas has been to combine indigenous and established Western psychological practices.

Indigenous psychology seeks new language and meanings that provide a link to traditional practices and that can draw on collective memory and consciousness. Eduardo and Bonnie Duran, early exponents of a postcolonial Native American psychology, argue that key themes are firstly knowledge of historical processes. Psychological and cultural patterns must be placed in historical context, in particular the experiences of collective trauma, loss and dispossession. A second theme involves practices that draw on existing cultural myths, symbols, stories and narratives. A third is familiarity with traditional cultural practices related to ancestors and the land. Eduardo Duran also argues for the placing of spirituality as a central component in practice. He views the imposition of religion as key to colonisation, arguing that the loss of spirituality, or soul loss, shapes the collective consciousness of indigenous people. Duran calls on counsellors to practise 'epistemological hybridity', to draw both on Native American traditions regarding Spirit and Soul and also on more individualised and symptom-oriented Western practices: 'the intention is to provide a bridge between Western and Traditional Native healing worlds and in this manner bring healing to the historical trauma that all people have suffered at one time in their history'.[14]

While the Irish context is not comparable to the Native American (although connections have been made by both groups), the particular colonial experience in the Irish context played a destructive role in relation to language, culture and healing traditions over centuries. The Irish psychologist Eunice McCarthy was one of the first to argue for distinctive cultural practices of myth and storytelling that could be integrated with new psychological practice. As someone whose life was embedded in Celtic traditions and who also witnessed the establishment of the discipline of psychology in the Republic of Ireland in the 1950s, she saw the value of both approaches. In her contribution to the 1994 Special Issue of *The Irish Journal of Psychology*, she argued that there was a deep unconscious that could be a resource for modern psychology. She developed this theme further in a recent interview, suggesting that stories and myths provided what might now be called narrative therapy: 'We're only talking decades against thousands of years so of course people were always coping and they all had models of reality . . . people were able to analyse their own situation. They had this richness of storytelling, stories over the centuries . . . they could immediately zone in.'[15]

An approach explicitly drawing on Irish mythology and language is that of Fifth Province Associates, a group of psychotherapists who developed their practice through working with theme of the Fifth Province in Irish mythology. The Fifth Province was proposed by Richard Kearney and Mark Hederman as an impetus for a new discourse and imagination where there could be deconstruction and reconstruction. Echoing themes of postcolonial psychology, Imelda McCarthy writes: 'Today I see what I call a fifth province co-creative therapy as facilitating conversations and contexts of transformation which bring us beyond the enthralment and/or dilemmas of a dualistic world view'. By engaging in a dialogical process involving dreams, connections with land and ancestors, and reference to sacred space, McCarthy describes how for her (and her colleagues Philip Kearney and Noirín Byrne) therapy becomes a transcendent or transpersonal space in which healing and spirituality are present: 'In this process, it is as if the participants merge together in what we might term a larger field'.[16]

There are also emerging approaches in which I have participated such as shamanic practices and neo-pagan spirituality. These draw on traditions of Irish Celtic spirituality and mythology, on the Irish language and on folk traditions. Irish mythology evokes Otherworlds and other ways of being; it is imbued with shape-shifting, magic and understandings of time as multidimensional. The Irish language with its own semantics and grammatical structure offers a vehicle for different concepts and forms of communication. Many reach back further to ancient landscapes and prehistoric sites such as the mysteries of Newgrange. Such neolithic stone structures and art hint at advanced knowledge and culture. These can be viewed as rich resources for exploring and developing alternative forms of consciousness and practice.

Rather than relying on imported forms of shamanism and paganism, emerging healing and spiritual practices aim to draw on these Irish resources to reclaim and renew a connection with ancestral traditions. They share the common aim of integrating Irish traditions and culture with modern evidence-based practice, with a view to transforming or healing individual, group and collective trauma. These approaches are related to emerging understandings of consciousness that are linked to transpersonal psychology, neuroscience and philosophy. They clearly position themselves as distinctively Irish, aiming to draw on specifically Irish traditions to develop new practices. These practices are seen not as revivals of traditions lost through colonisation and modernisation but rather as new practices that can echo and incorporate the remaining fragments of tradition and forge a sense of continuity over time.[17]

Conclusion

This chapter has addressed the question 'are the Irish different?' through the lenses of postcolonial psychology. It began by considering several examples of negative attributes assigned to the Irish psyche in the context of the current economic collapse. These attributes were used in a manner that seemed to hold the Irish responsible for the economic collapse because of intrinsic psychological weaknesses. Postcolonial psychology disputes the assignment of attributes, particularly where they are seen as intrinsic to a people or group. It draws attention to power dynamics, where attributes can be used to place blame, often by those in positions of power. Postcolonial psychology argues instead that attributes or behaviour patterns are shaped and maintained by social conditions, which are historically based and continue to evolve. It makes the connections between psychological patterns and culture and society: how we behave, how we see ourselves and how others see us create a self-perpetrating cycle. The example of alcohol illustrates this point: alcohol can be seen as having longstanding roots in our history of colonisation; it has permeated our identity and social mores; it is key in the perception of us by others. This more complex view suggests that transforming alcohol consumption (and other) patterns will require making links to deeper psychosocial and cultural roots, and critical engagement with how these patterns are discussed publicly. Rather than engaging in blame, postcolonial psychology seeks understandings that can facilitate transformation.

Such an approach to transformation would utilise both traditional psychological practices and emerging indigenous or transpersonal practices. It would also involve more collective practices, drawing on our strengths in culture, imagination and social solidarity which themselves can be seen as legacies of our history. In effect, by combining the human science and the humanities we can forge new ways of talking and thinking about ourselves. This can further enable decolonisation, a creative process in which psyche and society mutually construct a context where the human potential for co-operation, creativity, love and imagination can flourish.

Notes

1 Derek Scally and Elizabeth Burke Kennedy, 'Taoiseach Blames Crash on "Mad Borrowing" Frenzy', *Irish Times*, 26 January 2012.

2 Michael Casey, 'We Need to Look at Irish Culture', *Irish Times*, 9 October 2009. Michael Casey, *Ireland's Malaise: The Troubled Personality of the Irish Economy* (Dublin: The Liffey Press, 2009); Fintan O'Toole, 'Irish Society Is Colluding in Its Own Destruction', *Irish Times* 23 October 2012.

3 Maureen Gaffney, *Flourishing* (London: Penguin, 2011); Frantz Fanon, *The Wretched of the Earth* (Ringwood, Australia: Penguin, 1967).

4 Geraldine Moane, 'A Psychological Analysis of Colonialism in an Irish Context', *Irish Journal of Psychology*, 15 (1994), pp. 250–65; Geraldine Moane, 'Legacies of Colonialism for Irish

Women: Oppressive or Empowering?', *Irish Journal of Feminist Studies*, 1 (1996), pp. 100–18; Geraldine Moane, 'Legacies of History and the Quest for Vision: Colonialism and the Celtic Tiger', in Peadar Kirby, Luke Gibbons and Michael Cronin (eds), *Reinventing Ireland* (London: Pluto Press, 2002), pp. 109–23. Geraldine Moane, *Gender and Colonialism: A Psychological Analysis of Oppression and Liberation* (Basingstoke: Palgrave Macmillan, 2011).

5 Examples of discussions of colonialism by those in politics and sociology are provided in Claire Carroll and Patricia King (eds), *Ireland and Postcolonial Theory* (Bloomington: University of Notre Dame Press, 2003). See also social psychologist Michael O'Connell, *Changed Utterly: Ireland and the New Irish Psyche* (Dublin, Liffey Press, 2001).

6 Fanon, *The Wretched of the Earth*. Albert Memmi, *The Colonizer and the Colonised* (Boston: Beacon Press, 1967); Ashis Nandy, *The Intimate Enemy: Loss and Recovery of Self under Colonialism* (Delhi: Oxford University Press, 1983).

7 Eduardo Duran and Bonnie Duran, *Native American Postcolonial Psychology* (New York: New York University Press, 1985). Virgilio Enriquez, *From Colonial to Liberation Psychology* (Manila: De La Salle University Press, 1995). Philip Culbertson, Margaret Agee and Cabrini Makasiale (eds), *Penina Uliuli: Contemporary Challenges in Mental Health for Pacific Peoples* (Honolulu: University of Hawaii Press, 2007). Raol Rosado, *Consciousness-in-action: Towards an Integral Psychology of Liberation and Transformation* (Cagnas, Puerto Rico: Ile Publications, 2007).

8 Anne Halliday and Kevin Coyle (eds), *The Irish Psyche*, Special Issue of *The Irish Journal of Psychology*, 15:2–3 (1994).

9 Monica McGoldrick, 'Irish Families', in Monica McGoldrick, Jon Pearce and Janice Giordano (eds), *Ethnicity and Family Therapy* (New York: Guildford Press, 1982). See also the most recent version: Monica McGoldrick, 'Irish Families', in Monica McGoldrick and Janice Giordano (eds), *Ethnicity and Family Therapy* (New York: The Guilford Press, 2005), pp. 595–615. Nancy Scheper-Hughes, *Saints, Scholars, and Schizophrenics: Mental Illness in Rural Ireland* (Berkeley: University of California Press, 1979).

10 Vincent Kenny, 'The Post-colonial Mind', *The Crane Bag*, 9:1 (1985), pp. 70–8. Anthony Clare, 'The Mad Irish?' in Colm Keane (ed.), *Mental Illness in Ireland* (Dublin: Gill & Macmillan, 1991), pp. 121–32. Anne Halliday and Kevin Coyle (eds), *The Irish Psyche*, Special Issue of *The Irish Journal of Psychology*, 15:2–3 (1994). Garrett O'Connor 'Recognizing and Healing Malignant Shame: A Statement About the Urgent Need for Psychological and Spiritual Recovery from the Effects of Colonialism in Ireland', in Grisha Ziff, Lucy Lippard and Perez Pilar (eds), *Distant Relations* (Santa Monica, CA: Smart Arts Press, 1995), pp. 120–61. Sean Ruth, 'Understanding Oppression and Liberation', *Studies*, 7 (1988), pp. 434–43.

11 Anne P. McDonnell, 'Internalized Colonisation, Ireland and Irish Culture: A Psychological Inquiry', Doctoral Thesis, San Francisco, American School of Professional Psychology, 2001. McDonnell's presentation, along with Elaine Martin's paper 'Narcissistic Personality and the Irish', received considerable interest at the Annual Conference, Psychological Society of Ireland (Cork, November 2012).

12 Geraldine Moane, 'Legacies of History and the Quest for Vision: Colonialism and the Celtic Tiger'.

13 Sinéad Ní Chaoláin, '"Just having the craic" – Irish Students' Patterns of Alcohol Consumption', PhD thesis, Dublin: University College Dublin, 2014.

14 Pat Dudgeon and Jo Fielder, 'Third Spaces within Tertiary Places: Indigenous Australian Studies', *Journal of Community and Applied Social Psychology*, 16 (2006), pp. 396–409.

Eduardo Duran, *Healing the Soul Wound, Counseling with American Indians and Other Native People* (New York: Teachers College Press, 2006).

15 Eunice McCarthy, 'Work and Mind: Searching for Our Celtic Legacy', *Irish Journal of Psychology*, 15:2:3 (1994), pp. 372–89; Geraldine Moane, 'The Establishment of the Higher Diploma in Psychology: An Interview with Eunice McCarthy', *Irish Psychologist*, 35:14 (2009), pp. 363–6.

16 Phillip Kearney, Noreen Byrne and Imelda McCarthy, 'Just Metaphors: Marginal Illuminations in a Colonial Retreat', *Family Therapy Case Studies*, 4 (1989), pp. 17–31. Imelda McCarthy, 'The Fifth Province: Imagining a Space of Dialogical Co-Creations!', *Context*, December 2010, pp. 21–4.

17 Dolores Whelan, *Ever Ancient Ever New: Celtic Spirituality in the Twenty First Century*, 2nd ed. (Dublin: Original Writing, 2011); Geraldine Moane, 'The Development of Shamanism in Ireland', conference paper, Ireland's New Religious Movements (National University of Ireland Maynooth, September 2010); Olivia Cosgrove, Laurence Cox, Carmel Kuhling and Peter Mulholland (eds), *Ireland's New Religious Movements* (Newcastle-upon-Tyne: Cambridge Scholars Publishing, 2011). See particularly the chapter by June Butler, 'Irish Neo-Paganism: Worldview and Identity', pp. 149–66.

13

Thinking about Ireland and the Irish diaspora

Mary J. Hickman

Emigration has been a defining feature of Irish history and is a key motif of the current social and economic crisis. And yet is relatively understudied in Ireland. The Great Famine has had enormous attention, in terms of its impact both in Ireland and on the massive emigrations that followed. But the impact of the two major phases of emigration in the twentieth century – the 1950s and 1980s – have been less integrated into the national story. Why is this? Is it because these evacuations cannot be blamed on a colonial relationship with Britain? Is it because the main destination for these emigrants was Britain rather than the United States of America? Or is it because the narrative about emigration has been rewritten and, instead of being seen as forced exile, is now cast in terms of opportunities for entrepreneurship?

A fully developed interdisciplinary Irish studies would rectify this omission. This is essential because contact and exchanges between the 'homeland' (Ireland) and the various spaces and places of the diaspora have been and continue to be mutually influential. Also it is impossible to consider what constitutes 'Irishness' today without acknowledging its contested character and recognising that one pivot of this debate is the diaspora. In other words, as Fintan O'Toole put it, 'a map of Ireland that does not include its elsewheres is not worth even glancing at, for it leaves out the places where Ireland is always landing and returning from'.[1]

Because of the specific history of Ireland, of which emigration and partition are two emblematic features, understanding Irishness cannot be limited to the boundaries of the nation-state. Thinking about the Irish diaspora and its multiplicity should therefore be a central aspect of Irish studies. To the extent that Irish studies flourishes in various diasporic locations, study of the diaspora, at least in relation to the immediate locale, is usually included in the curriculum. It is in Ireland where study of the diaspora is more often absent. Irish studies in Ireland, let alone social science in Ireland, does not address the Irish diaspora and emigration sufficiently.

This is strange given that interest in Irish studies, and the ever-increasing market for it, has been generated by external interest, much of it from people of Irish descent across the globe.

The Irish state and diaspora

It appears, at least in official discourses, that Ireland's relationship with the Irish diaspora is primarily perceived as a basis for the commodification of Irishness. This is obviously not, necessarily, the case at the level of the families and local communities that people have left. The interest of various institutions (universities, Tourism Ireland) and the government is largely centred on making either money or cultural capital out of the diaspora. The new Irish Ambassador to London, Dan Mulhall, speaking in 2012, described the development of the policy initiative of The Gathering in 2013 (the state-sponsored scheme to bring tourists and members of the diaspora to Ireland) as an example of 'using our international diaspora to benefit Ireland at a time of economic difficulty'. This was a result of the government coming to realise as it sought to 'develop our national brand' that 'our Irish communities abroad are a very significant source of influence and impact'.[2]

In this assessment, the Irish government views the diaspora as part of the 'wealth' of Ireland. The diaspora offers the opportunity for the commodification of the relationship between Ireland and its diaspora (realised through The Gathering) and the diaspora also offers esteem value. The diaspora as a source of influence and impact lends Ireland esteem because, as the Ambassador pointed out in his speech, more American Presidents had visited Ireland in the twentieth century than had visited Russia or the Soviet Union. In his emphasis on the development of the national brand of Ireland, and the utility of the diaspora for this marketing exercise, the Ambassador was indicating that visiting Ireland is for many customers worth paying for compared with other national brands. He said this was because they want to 'wear the name' (to use a clothing retail analogy) and they feel Ireland gives them status that other brands do not.

The traffic is not all one way. In 2001 the Irish government set up a Task Force on Policy Regarding Emigrants. The recommendations of the Task Force Report led to the establishment of the Irish Abroad Unit in the Department of Foreign Affairs in 2004 and, through the Emigrant Support Programme, to a significant increase in funds to assist vulnerable Irish people abroad.[3] The significance of the Task Force is that it named emigrants and their descendants as 'the Irish Abroad' and identified them as a constituency whose welfare, cultural and other integration needs should be considered, and in some cases responded to, by the Irish government.[4] The Emigrant Support programme appears to be state recognition of the 'safety valve' that emigration has always offered the Irish economy.

The launch of the Task Force was in line with the changes to the Irish Constitu-

tion that had occurred after the signing of the Good Friday Agreement. Article 2 of
the Constitution was amended after a Referendum in 1998. It provides that:

> It is the entitlement and birthright of every person born in the island of Ireland,
> which includes its islands and seas, to be part of the Irish Nation. That is also the enti-
> tlement of all persons otherwise qualified in accordance with law to be citizens of
> Ireland. Furthermore, the Irish nation cherishes its special affinity with people of
> Irish ancestry living abroad who share its cultural identity and heritage.

Anyone born outside Ireland who has a parent who is an Irish citizen and was born
in Ireland is therefore viewed as part of the Irish nation as enshrined in Article 2 of
the Constitution. However, full citizenship rights apply only if the citizen is
resident in Ireland (unless a member of the diplomatic corps or armed forces). In
this practice Ireland stands out as different to most of the European Union and
many other countries in the world (about which more below).

   While the Task Force was instructed to concentrate on the ways the Irish
government could support both the vulnerable Irish abroad and Irish culture in the
diaspora, it could have been given a different and/or wider remit. Recognising that
diaspora strategies are being prioritised worldwide, the Task Force had an opportunity to promote a more holistic relationship between Ireland and its diaspora.
Some commentators in Ireland have advised that any strategy must extend well
beyond the notion of using the diaspora for economic gain.[5] Nevertheless a recent
'outreach' to the diaspora had such an agenda. With the rapid onset of recession
and demise of the Celtic Tiger economy, a Global Irish Economic Forum
(September 2009) was set up and funded by the Irish government to bring
members of the diaspora to Dublin for consultation on ways forward for Ireland.
This initiative, while very understandable in the context of the financial crisis, was
also signalled as 'taking an important step toward establishing a new, more
dynamic relationship between Ireland and its diaspora.'[6] It did not seem new, rather
it was in keeping with what have been the two elements of the Irish state's diaspora
strategy to date. This hinges on maximising the knowledge and connections of the
diaspora for Ireland's benefit and extending support to particular categories of Irish
people abroad in implicit acknowledgement that the official story about Irish
emigration and success is by no means a comprehensive account.

Irish stereotypes of the diaspora

The success of modern Ireland is generally measured by those who do not
emigrate. The measurement does not include the experiences and social, cultural
and economic remittances of those who left. Apart from the Task Force and the
occasional investigation into emigration there has never been a great effort
invested in getting 'to know' the Irish diaspora. Consequently what has flourished
is a set of stereotypes. Irish emigration, until recently, was largely viewed as 'going

to America'. Despite much larger numbers of the Irish-born residing in Britain, the
quintessential Irish migrant always appeared to be someone who left for the United
States in the nineteenth century. The relative silence about the Irish in Britain is in
part due to movement to England barely being seen as emigration. There is also
perhaps a stigma of failure that is not associated with going to the United States. So
the stereotype of the Irish immigrant in Britain as a down-on-his-luck Irish
labourer (the 'forgotten Irish') is pitched against one of a rich (compared to
Ireland) and ignorant (of contemporary Ireland) Irish American. A third stereotype quite *au courant* is that of the emigrant as entrepreneurial adventurer or
experience-seeking professional away for a few years before returning to enrich
Ireland. While stereotypes can be matched and defied by various anecdotes or
evidence, they often reveal most about those doing the stereotyping. For example,
why is the historic stereotype of an Irish American not that of a second-generation
woman teaching in a public school, and why is the image of the contemporary Irish
in Britain not that of a worker in the voluntary sector or the City? The notion of
alternative images or stereotypes can be developed further. Is there room in
Ireland's pictures of the Irish diaspora for the young drug taker in Birmingham
from an Irish town or city, or the young woman who left seeking an abortion, or the
young person leaving because of physical or sexual abuse, or because they could
not be openly gay or lesbian? The Irish diaspora includes many 'hidden histories'
of Ireland that the traditional stereotypes mask.

Are these stereotypes – of the successful Irish American businessman and the
retired and impoverished Irish construction worker in Britain (both male) – a way
of 'not knowing' the diaspora and therefore avoiding the momentous implications
that emigration has had in Ireland's formation? Irish society is a highly porous
entity, as current emigration and recent immigration bear witness. Emigration
represents the dispatching of 'problems', not having to face what the phenomenon
fully signifies. On the other hand, the flow of immigrants into Ireland from the
1990s created resentment and social distance, more so since the crash of the Celtic
Tiger. I do not want to paint a homogenous picture of Irish attitudes to emigrants
or immigrants. There is evidence of generational and class differences on these
issues. But what does seem to be clear is that a form of twenty-six-county nationalism, or to put it another way a 'bonding of Irishness to the Republic of Ireland', has
taken place over the recent past and younger generations seem to buy into this as
much as any other. Or so research undertaken during the Celtic Tiger years seems
to indicate.[7] Now that emigration has reasserted itself and is running at a high level
there is also evidence that young emigrants are rethinking their relationship with
Ireland. Some are proclaiming that they should not lose their citizenship rights on
leaving Ireland and would like votes for citizens abroad.

What is required, then, is greater recognition in national narratives of emigration and its impact and of the influence of the diaspora. There is also a need for a
greater emphasis on what have been the continuous contacts and exchanges that

characterise a dynamic maritime culture. Exploring these questions entails acknowledging and reviewing the historical integration and positioning of Ireland in the global economic system. We need to re-examine Irish history as a place of mobile economic and cultural flows – be they remittances, capital, letters, literature, or emigrants, returning migrants or refugees – all the ways in the centuries prior to the 1990s that Ireland was part of modernity. Taking this perspective challenges the notion of Ireland as a monocultural nation prior to recent immigration and enables contemporary migrants, of whom inevitably a sizeable proportion will settle in Ireland, a potential place in the nation. It refigures Ireland as a place of mobile cultural and economic flows rather than the site of cultural purity and authenticity threatened by external forces.[8] Some of this work is well under way, but does it integrate the significance of emigration or diaspora sufficiently, and their impact in Ireland on families and communities?

I want to explore the implication of these comments more fully in two ways. First by examining the complexity and hybridity of different diaspora spaces to which the Irish have emigrated. Greater understanding of Ireland and Irishness involves greater knowledge of the complexity of the diaspora. This complexity in part is due to the different contexts of national formation in which settlement has taken place. Second, I want to look at who is taken as belonging in Ireland and how traditional views on this are being challenged. In particular, I focus on the exclusion of Irish citizens abroad from full political participation in the life of the nation.

Complexity of the Irish diaspora

The very different imaginings of being 'Irish' or 'of Irish descent' that come to be meaningful for members of the Irish diaspora in different places of arrival are part of its social formation. It is this very hybridity that constitutes the diasporic. This has happened in different ways. Irish migrants have had an important impact on the (re)formation of the national spaces and national imaginaries of their main settlement destinations. They are not just *of* Ireland, but *of* their new place. Instead of assessing the push/pull of processes of transnationalism and assimilation, our understanding of the Irish diaspora is widened by considering how individuals and social groups in the diaspora are *between* and *of* the two processes simultaneously. What therefore can examining the Irish diaspora tell us about the making of a variety of national populations? This approach also means challenging the dominance of the Ireland/US binary when discussing diaspora. A conversation between other locations of the Irish diaspora and the US can facilitate more comparative work. It can bring into view the complexity and heterogeneity of Irish diasporic experiences and enable greater integration into the wider debates about the history of national formation in societies constituting themselves as multicultural, including Ireland.

We need a reformulation of the concept of society in order to rethink the boundaries of social life. We need to imagine there being no contradiction for migrants between the incorporation of individuals into nation states (places of settlement) and the maintenance of transnational connections (with the 'homeland' and across the diaspora). Diasporas are historical formations in process. They change over time as part of the political, social and economic developments in and between various places of settlement (including 'the homeland').

One aspect of their hybridity is that new social relations are produced and lived in diasporic space. By diaspora space is meant the places of encounter between immigrants and long-term settled populations. The point about diaspora space is that all who inhabit it are subject to transformation, including the long-term settled population.[9] The lens of diaspora space focuses on the creation of new social relations and identifications resulting from the specificities of encounters. In this view, the origins and identities of all who are party to encounters in diasporic spaces constitutes national formation 'from below'.

The two main destinations for Irish emigrants, Britain and the US, represent different ethno-racial regimes and different ways of telling the national story. Although, for example, the US understands itself as a country of immigration, this story includes many silences not only of race and indigenous people but also of ethnicity. The literature on 'how the Irish became white' has enabled us to recover some of these absences. With a focus on diaspora space we can more fully understand the heterogeneity of Irish experiences and trajectories in the diaspora spaces that have constituted American society in formation at different times. The advantage is that it provides an alternative approach to the teleological trajectory of assimilation and points to the value of examining the variously weighted encounters of different groupings in different places, at different junctures, across the intercutting cleavages of race, ethnicity, gender and class.

In Britain, the notion that diaspora space was constitutive for British national formation prior to the 1950s is not widely accepted, either in official or in academic discourses. This reflects the investment there was in drawing a 'colour line' in the 1950s and portraying Britain as culturally homogenous prior to the immigrations from the Caribbean and the Indian sub-continent. For Britain the advantage of using the concept of diaspora space is that it directs attention to the heterogeneities and hybridities in the domestic realm prior to 1950, when Irish people formed the main source of immigrant labour.

One of the ways in which the specificity of the experiences of the Irish in Britain and those of the Irish in the US is calibrated is in terms of the contrasting availability and non-availability of identity terms which everyone recognises and understands. For example, the Irish American is an almost mythical figure and no such equivalent term exists to represent the Irish in Britain. The encounters and contestations in the diaspora spaces of mid-nineteenth-century America were critical for creating and reproducing social divisions in a fast industrialising society, and this included the creation of an Irish (Catholic) ethnic identity in the United States.

It was a period characterised by a rhetoric that excluded new Irish immigrants from the American Dream as the most reviled of foreign immigrants (compared especially with German immigrants of the same era). However, Irish immigrants were arriving at a time when the US was in the midst of struggles that would move it towards becoming a post-slavery society. This was also a period in which an ethnic hierarchy was established which classified categories of white immigrant labour in terms of their qualifications to belong to the republic. The change in the positioning of 'the Irish', from ambiguous racial group and reviled ethno-religious group, is directly related to the changes wrought by the processes of re-racialisation that resulted after the civil war and emancipation. Groups such as 'the Irish' of previously ambiguous status were consolidated as 'white' by virtue of being classified as 'ethnic'. Simultaneously this process opened a route to Americanisation, although this was far from a straightforward process.

National reformations are constructed and reconstructed on the terrain of diaspora spaces and involve both the long-term settled and the immigrant populations in new social relations. In the US, the moment of (re)formation discussed in the second half of the nineteenth century produced a bifurcated hierarchy of 'race' and 'ethnicity': Race/African American and Ethnicity/White immigrants (needless to say Anglo-Americans did not figure in these reformulations).[10] This is how the racial differentiations cleaving America were reconfigured after the civil war and set 'Irish America' on a path towards being celebrated as eventually 'coming into clover'.[11]

In Britain, one moment of national reformation was the 1950–60s. In this period, in contradistinction to the processes under way a century previously in the US, 'race' and ethnicity were conflated and whiteness (also of course a racialised term) came to represent the absence of ethnicity, instead of being synonymous with the attribution as in the US. Despite the largest number of immigrants of the period being from Ireland, the immigrant as a category became firmly welded to the representation of the sudden arrival of so-called 'coloured immigrants' in the 1940s and 1950s. Official discourses portrayed a homogenous national identity and culture prior to the arrival of these 'immigrants'. The myth of white homogeneity across 'the British Isles' that developed in official discourses (of politicians, in the media) at that time assumed that all people who were white were able to smoothly assimilate into the 'British way of life'. It was assumed that 'the problems' all resided with those who migrated and possessed a different skin colour, which was directly linked to different cultures and identities. It subsumed differences between whites in Britain into a common 'us', who all worried about the 'colour problem'.

The nation was therefore defined against the figure of the black immigrant, and whiteness was a factor in the repositioning and re-racialising of the Irish in that period. When the 1962 Commonwealth Immigration Act was debated in Parliament, the Irish were the most reviled immigrant group even though it was agreed that they should be exempt from most (though not all) of the controls on immigration that the legislation introduced. The 'we' of whiteness masked suppressed ethnicities, hidden racialisations and pre-existing hierarchies and set the Irish in Britain on a path of relative invisibility. This lasted until Irish community and welfare groups demanded and won an Irish category in the England and Wales Census in 2001. In the US Census the category 'Irish American' is included and those for whom it is meaningful can select this as their ethnicity; whereas in the England and Wales census the choice is a dichotomised one of 'White British' or 'White Irish' and therefore the hybridities of those of Irish descent remain invisible.

The national spaces of Britain and the US are both deeply racialised and have produced distinctive ethno-racial regimes. I have been able to deal only with one aspect of the processes that generated such regimes here.[12] In each case the presence of Irish immigrations has been a significant factor in national reconfigurations, be it at time of civil war or when a threat was perceived in mass immigration of 'coloured immigrants'. In the US, Irish Americans became almost an emblematic (white) ethnicity; while in Britain the failure to recognise that ethnicity is 'colour blind' has meant that any distinctiveness in Irish experiences has been consistently ignored. These are complicated scenarios which Irish immigrants and those of Irish descent 'learn', subliminally or otherwise, and come to effect in a variety of ways. This explains why there are very different imaginings of being 'Irish' or 'of Irish descent' held by members of the Irish diaspora in different places of settlement. These patterns to settlement in different national contexts are what has to be understood 'to know' the Irish diaspora. Ironically, to develop a fuller knowledge of Ireland and its diaspora it is necessary to acquire a deeper knowledge of other national contexts.

Who belongs in Ireland?

The Irish national imaginary has not only been challenged by Northern Ireland and the diaspora; since the mid-1990s it has also been challenged by the arrival of a variety of immigrant streams from Europe, Africa, South East Asia and Latin America. The idea of who belongs in Ireland is under continual contestation as newly settled people put down roots while they simultaneously create diasporic organisations. They, and all those they encounter in the diaspora spaces of Ireland, also create new cultural forms and practices. Nevertheless there is a language of differentiation between 'nationals' and 'non-nationals' permeating both official parlance and everyday vocabulary in Ireland, although an alternative 'New Irish' is also in circulation. A further referendum in 2004 led to a limiting of the opening declaration in Article 2 of the Constitution by the insertion of a new Article 9.2.1 which provided that:

Notwithstanding any other provision of this Constitution, a person born in the island of Ireland, which includes its islands and seas, who does not have, at the time of the birth of that person, at least one parent who is an Irish citizen or entitled to be an Irish citizen is not entitled to Irish citizenship or nationality, unless provided for by law.

Northern Ireland, the Irish diaspora and multinational immigration all pose challenges for the traditional definitions of the Irish nation and of who is accepted as Irish. At the same time contemporary politics and practices of governance in Ireland suggest that many of those traditional ideas remain in play. The identification of Ireland with its territory remains predominant, but is now reinforced by an insistence on blood lineage as the only automatic guarantor of the right to be an Irish citizen. This had always been the case prior to this period (the terms upon which those of Irish descent can claim citizenship demonstrates this), but the 2004 referendum made it more explicit and for the first time excluded certain categories of person born in Ireland. Ireland's historical imagination about itself since Independence assumed that various 'Others' (Jews, Protestants, Travellers) did not offer a serious threat to the form of twenty-six-county nationalism that had developed. Overwhelming support for the Good Friday Agreement, which includes a provision for a democratic route to a United Ireland, did not dilute this nationalism as the continuing lukewarm response to the idea of reunification emphasises.

Many Irish citizens experience a shock of 'not belonging' any more when they emigrate, the vast majority with a firm intention to return. They discover they are disenfranchised, and this is a source of anger and frustration for many. Ireland is different from much of the rest of the EU and many other countries round the world in not giving its citizens abroad the vote. Given the current state of the economy, and of the finances of individuals and families, the high numbers of Irish citizens emigrating each year (63,000 in the year to April 2013) are likely to continue. These repetitive cycles of emigration amount to a haemorrhaging of talent, a waste of educational investment, great sadness and difficulties due to split families, and periods of uncertainty and dislocation for the majority of emigrants. Irish citizens who have had to leave have no say about the direction the country should take in the twenty-first century. At this time of national economic crisis for Ireland, there have been many calls for changes in the political system and culture. One indication that such changes were under way would be if Ireland were to extend the franchise to include emigrant citizens living abroad.

Most Irish emigrants maintain strong ties with Ireland through their connections with family and friends and by using a variety of communications media to stay in touch with news from Ireland. These connections have never been easier to sustain owing to the proliferation of social media. Irish citizens abroad also remain connected to Ireland in that they remain subject to some laws and government decisions: the removal of the franchise is an obvious example. They are, in other words, lifelong stakeholders in the sense that, if born and brought up in Ireland, they are 'biographically subjected' to the state through their prior formative residence.[13] In addition most emigrants have a 'project of return', and whether this is realisable depends to a large measure on the management of the Irish economy. These significant ties and future-orientated interests make first-generation citizens abroad genuine stakeholders.[14] In these ways, therefore, Irish citizens abroad remain stakeholders in Ireland and for many their life circumstances link their individual well-being to the common good of the political community that is Ireland.

There is a contradiction in the close relationship Ireland has with all the nations that are the main destinations of Irish emigrants: in particular Britain, the US, Australia and Canada. Irish emigrants working and generating wealth in these economies are disenfranchised from their 'homeland', while US, Canadian, Australian and British citizens residing in Ireland, along with many newer immigrants to Ireland, like Polish citizens, not only have the right to vote 'back home' but are encouraged to do so.

Since the financial crash in 2008 the Irish government, on a number of occasions, has called upon the diaspora to help Ireland – setting up events like the Global Irish Forum – to which there has been a good response. Simultaneously, though, there has been a heightening of awareness of the democratic deficit in the relationship. Extending the franchise to enable Irish citizens abroad to vote in general elections would not only make good this democratic deficit, but would also cement the relationship between Ireland and its diaspora for the future in an increasingly globalised, competitive and fluid world.

For a country with such a significant history of emigration it is disturbing that Ireland is part of a very small minority in the European Union (twenty-four out of twenty-eight member states give citizens abroad the vote in parliamentary elections), and out of step with much of the rest of the world, in stripping its citizens of their ability to exercise rights linked to their citizenship. All these countries are responding to the realities of globalisation, increased migration (often circular) and the growth in dual citizenship. It appears that Ireland wants emigrants to go on contributing through a variety of ways, including economic, social and cultural remittances, but does not want them to have any say in the future political direction of the country to which many of them hope to return. In order to sustain the relationship between Ireland and its diaspora in a globalised world this viewpoint may have to change.

Conclusion

Although there is no residency qualification mentioned in the Constitution, the key to belonging in Ireland is to be a citizen who is *resident* in the Republic of Ireland. Only then can an individual citizen exercise their full rights. The right to vote is recognised globally as accompanying citizenship, but this is denied Irish citizens who leave Ireland, however forced their emigration may be. We need to place under an investigative spotlight the exceptionalism implied in Ireland's refusal to allow citizens abroad to vote in parliamentary elections. What role does this arrangement play in maintaining the political status quo in Ireland? Relations with the diaspora are therefore central to salient discussions of the need for change in the Irish political system. Sustaining Ireland's connection with its diaspora does not just hinge on granting votes to emigrants. It also depends on getting 'to know' the Irish diaspora in all its variety, and consigning traditional stereotypes to the graveyard of redundant ideas. The complexity of the diaspora helps us understand and appreciate the multiple ways of being Irish, and of imaginings of Irishness in the world. We might then recognize that the diasporic imaginations and ways of being Irish are all as valid as any expressed in Ireland.

Notes

1   Fintan O'Toole, *Black Hole, Green Card* (Dublin: New Island Books, 1994), p. 19.
2   Dan Mulhall, Lecture to the Institute for Cultural Diplomacy (Berlin, Germany: 15 March 2012). Available at:www.youtube.com/watch?v=woecLfsQBYo.
3   Task Force on Policy regarding Emigrants, *Ireland and the Irish Abroad* (Dublin: Department of Foreign Affairs, 2002).
4   Breda Gray, 'Migrant Integration Policy: A Nationalist Fantasy of Management and Control?', *Tranlocations: The Irish Migration, Race and Social Transformation Review*, 1:1 (2006), p. 2.
5   Mark Boyle and Rob Kitchen (eds), 'Towards an Irish Diaspora Strategy: A Position Paper', National Institute for Regional and Spatial Analysis, NUI Maynooth, Working Paper No. 37 (2008), p. 14.
6   Minster for Foreign Affairs, Michael Martin, quoted in Noreen Bowden, 'High Profile Members of the Diaspora Asked for Advice', *The Irish Emigrant* (2009), p. 1 at: www.emigrant.ie/index2.php?option=com_content&task+view&id+74069&pop+1&page+0.
7   Joseph Moffatt, 'Paradigms of Irishness for Young People in Dublin', PhD thesis, National University of Ireland Maynooth, 2011.
8   See discussion by Catherine Nash, *Of Irish Descent: Origin Stories, Genealogy & the Politics of Belonging* (Syracuse: Syracuse University Press, 2008).
9   Avtar Brah, *Cartographies of Diaspora, Contesting Identities* (London and New York: Routledge, 1996).
10 Banton's thesis on minus-one ethnicity, Michael Banton, *Racial Theories* (Cambridge: Polity Press, 1998).
11 Maureen Dezell, *Coming into Clover* (New York: Doubleday, Random House, 2002).
12 For a more detailed discussion of these points see Mary J. Hickman, 'Diaspora Spaces and National (Re)Formations', *Eire-Ireland*, 47:1 (2012), pp. 19–44.
13 Reiner Baubock, 'The Rights and Duties of External Citizenship', *Citizenship Studies*, 13:5 (2009), pp. 475–99.
14 Iseult Honohan, 'Should Irish Emigrants Have Votes? External Voting in Ireland', *Irish Political Studies*, 26:4 (2011), pp. 545–61.

14

Being Irish and male in Britain

Mairtin Mac an Ghaill and Chris Haywood

This chapter is written at a time when Ireland appears to have returned to a nothing but the same old emigrant story. According to the Office of National Statistics, although the numbers of emigrants and skilled and professional workers from Ireland travelling to the UK appear to be falling, the number of temporary workers continues to rise.[1] At the same time, across British cities, Muslims have displaced the Irish as the nation's major folk devils. Until recently, the Irish were portrayed as being obsessed with living in the past; that is, that 'the Irish can't forget'. In response to the British, the Irish claimed that the 'British can't remember'. It may be that this couplet of cultural remembering and forgetting provides a lens to explore the complexity of how we make sense of the British denial and the Irish affirmation of national and ethnic difference. The chapter sets out to explore the question of being Irish in Britain, in relation to the general theme of the book, are the Irish different? Like other diasporian groups, the Irish are conscious of a long history of the British state, public institutions, civil society, popular culture and the media projecting negative stereotypes about them. A difficulty in writing this chapter is that the book's general theme, addressing national or ethnic difference, may result in producing simplistic positive stereotypes of the Irish. Therefore, this chapter attempts to unpack the meanings that underpin notions of (Irish) difference.

The first section maps the shifting images of Irish men and masculinities within a British context of local and global change. Different generations of Irish men going to Britain include those of the Famine, the post-Second World War, the 1980s 'Ryanair' migrants and the current post-Celtic Tiger, transnational genera-tion of Skype/Facebook users.[2] The second section explores changing self-representations, social practices and cultural journeys among Irish men. We draw upon narratives of different generations that we have collected across different cities that include stories about workplace identities, friendship, cultural belonging, religious affiliation, memory, loss and home.

Global and local change and shifting images of the Irish

The interplay between global and local change and shifting images of Irish men as *different* can be identified in different periods. It can be seen in the nineteenth century, during what Kumar has called *The Great Transformation*.[3] The rapid changes brought about by Britain's industrialisation and urbanisation were linked to its imperialist project, and to wider transformations in the world economy which fuelled demand for migrant labour. Irish labour migrants represented strategic *economic* and *cultural* elements of this project. *Economically*, Ireland as the emigrant nursery to the world economy provided cheap and flexible labour for British capitalism.[4] Indeed, the Irish are the largest and oldest labour migrant group in Britain who have functioned at different historical periods as a key reserve army of labour. In so doing, they have played a vital role in developing Britain's infrastructure, working as navigators, coal miners, and road and house builders. Large numbers of both men and women worked in the cotton mills and factories and women also filled roles in agriculture and domestic work. *Culturally*, the Irish were perceived as 'colonial others', within the context of a 'shared life' between migrants and the 'host' society at the imperial centre.[5] This was an important moment for the British, in the reproduction of their collective self-identity as a 'superior race', who actively 'disidentified' with the Irish as an 'inferior race'.

In British race and ethnic relations literature, Irish immigrants in the late nineteenth and early twentieth centuries are represented as one of the main recipients of British colonial exploitation.[6] In these historical accounts the themes that emerge to explore the racialisation of Irish male immigrants, popularly referred to as *navvies*, focus upon issues of British imperialism and discrimination. A wide range of cultural markers of difference juxtaposed the dirtiness, drunkenness, laziness and violence of the Irish with the purity, industriousness and civilisation of the settled English. What was underreported at this time was their resistance to colonial exploitation.

With reference to the notion of difference, the *cultural visibility* of the Irish in the nineteenth century can be contrasted with the *cultural invisibility* of the post-1945 generation of immigrants, when the British economy was in the process of expansion. Known as the 'second wave' of emigration, it is this period – the 1950s to early 1960s – which established the reputation of male and female Irish immigrants as low-skilled, manual workers. At this time the demand for labour included construction work, transport and nursing. Hazelkorn in her essay 'British Capital and Irish Labour', suggests that between 1951 and 1956 on average 39,000 Irish people emigrated to England each year and from 1956 to 1961 this rose to 42,000 a year.[7] As the British welfare state expanded, Irish women in particular moved into new sectors of lower middle-class employment such as clerical work, nursing and teaching. By the 1970s, the Irish were made culturally invisible as a result of the adoption of an American model of race-relations that argued that colour was the key defining characteristic of racism in Britain. This reductive model, that of the black–white dualism, saw a collusion between British politicians, academics and policy makers in denying the ethnic difference of the Irish in Britain and the denial of the racial discrimination that they experienced. In response, Irish community workers and academics established the Irish on the ethnic and racial map.[8] However, an unintended effect of this stage of political mobilisation was that, in addressing the community's shared racialised experiences as a minority, this resulted in underplaying the different experiences of their migration and settlement.

During the early 1980s there was a shift away from a low cultural profile to one of the Irish community demanding public recognition and affirmation of their difference with the emergence of campaigning community organisations, including the Action Group for Irish Youth, alongside the FIS (Federation of Irish Societies). Of key importance in understanding this shift was the changing political transformations within and between Britain, the Republic of Ireland and Northern Ireland. McVeigh captures these political conditions, arguing that the concept of anti-Irish racism was born out of struggle. He notes: 'the definitive moment for anti-Irish racism came with the radicalisation and ethnicisation of politics in Britain in the early 1980s. For the Irish in Britain this combined with the politicisation around the Hunger Strikes and the rise of organisations like the IBRG (Irish in Britain Representation Group) which focused upon anti-Irish racism as one of its key organising principles.'[9]

Simultaneously, the early 1980s saw a new generation of emigrants from the Republic of Ireland, 'the Ryanair generation', who appear more as commuters compared to the earlier generation who arrived by boat.[10] Unlike the mainly rural, working-class population who arrived during the 1940s to 1960s, the 1980s emigrants were significantly different, with a high proportion of highly qualified middle-class people from urban areas. They worked in professional hi-tech jobs, in finance, banking and the media, and were located mainly in London. They performed a different sense of being Irish in Britain than earlier generations. For example, they emphasised their own authenticity as 'real Irish' by referring to second-generation Irish as 'plastic Paddies' and distanced themselves from the established (working-class) Irish community. This occurred just as the settled Irish community became increasingly aware of its own internal cultural diversity beyond the traditional concerns of nationalism, (Catholic) religion and rural values of an earlier generation. There was increasing awareness of gender and sexual differences, and increased awareness of the experiences of Protestants, Travellers and the second generation. Particularly significant was the question of gender, including the fact that Irish-born women outnumber Irish-born men in Britain since the 1920s. Feminist work challenged the assumption that migration was exclusively a political-economic phenomenon. As Walter argued:

It is often assumed that ethnicity, racism and nationalism are monolithic structures which have the same meaning for, and impact on whole collectivities. However, not only are representations of Irishness and Britishness highly gendered constructions, but the material experiences of being a woman or a man within the Irish community and an Irish woman or Irish man within British society are very different.[11]

In contrast to the social sciences, literary and cultural studies have explored the gendering during the nineteenth and twentieth centuries of Irishness which was seen by the British as an essentially feminine race.[12]

The Irish community's cultural invisibility and denial of difference were not simply an effect of what the British 'have done to them'. The Irish were active in making themselves invisible, by 'keeping their heads down' and 'not opening their mouths in public'. This notion of a projected sameness was a key strategy of survival, in response to the British state's pathologisation and criminalisation of Irish migrants. Also, the political situation in the North of Ireland between the 1970s and 1990s had a major impact in driving public expressions of Irish identity underground.

Against this background, Mary Robinson came to signify a new confident Ireland at the centre of Europe, marked by a cultural politics of inclusivity, that was of strategic significance to the changing cultural formation of the Irish diaspora in Britain. Also, the development of the Good Friday Agreement (10 April 1998) was highly significant in opening up the way for a new political settlement between the North and South of Ireland and Britain. Within these changing conditions, an increasingly confident community rediscovered the primary importance of cultural forms of resistance, thus emphasising their Irishness. As Hall suggests, migrant groups bear the traces of what they bring with them from their countries of origin.[13] This cultural response constituted an ethnic revival of self-affirmation of difference among the Irish diaspora – including public displays of ethnic pride, such as St Patrick's Day celebrations, the establishment of Irish studies centres, the revival of Irish language teaching and increasing interest in the national literature, traditional dance and national sports.

A final aspect of understanding difference in remaking the lives of the Irish diaspora during the 1990s was the changing British media representation of Ireland and Irish people. In shifting from a labour history tradition to one of semiotics – from race to ethnicity – Irishness is represented as a highly seductive culture.[14] Currently, within British popular culture the Irish are projected as a high-status cultural icon, with Irishness translated into a notion of cool, as illustrated by the pervasiveness of Irish theme bars and indigenous British parents naming their children Callum, Sean etc.

Focusing on the issue of difference, the above section maps out diverse and complex images of different generations of Irish men in response to global and local socio-economic and political changes. It is important to emphasise that this difference about Irish migration and settlement in Britain is historically and geographically specific. The next section explores changing-self-representations, social practices and cultural trajectories among Irish men and the specific meanings for how men perform Irish difference.

Settled immigrants: making ethnic difference

Over the years we have carried out research with the Irish diaspora, with a particular focus on Birmingham.[15] The city of Birmingham became a major destination for Irish emigrants after the Second World War when the British economy was in the process of expanding. The demand for a cheap and mobile reserve army of labour to fill the gaps in the UK's labour market, as referred to above, was met by, amongst others, the Irish, Caribbeans, Pakistanis, Bangladeshis and Indians. Each community experienced a specific process of migration, settlement and living out of ethnic difference Although there were those who arrived with qualifications, and who took up professional positions in the local economy, the majority of the Irish performed low-skilled work. However, the postwar generation of Irish immigrant men (and women) produced multilayered survival stories. These stories were marked by forced economic exile, occupational exploitation (by Irish and British employers) and racial discrimination. Alongside these barriers, there was also evidence of positive values of religious observance, family commitment, community support and male friendship. Among the men a range of occupational and domestic trajectories developed with some 'making it in a big way', becoming self-employed – many as building contractors – and owning several houses, while many of the men continued in the low-status world of casualised manual work and others, as explored below, became part of an occupational 'under class'.

The primary identity of the men in our study as economic immigrants was that of work. Most of them worked, or had formerly worked, in manufacturing and construction. Typically these men were involved in subcontracted work and were often 'hired and fired' at will. As a result of the casualised, deregulated and relatively non-unionised nature of the construction industry, many of its workers lacked security of employment as well as having no sick, holiday or redundancy pay. Hence, the workplace helped to produce a category of men who worked in dangerous conditions that resulted in high rates of injury and early death.

Much of their world was within all-male environments, with versions of masculinity shaped and lived out within male workplaces, community pubs and clubs and at Gaelic games. A specific diasporian gendered way of life was constructed based on a male-dominated hierarchical Catholic Church and an Irish nationalist politics. This was marked by the playing of the national anthem at public gatherings and the obligatory response in terms of a military-style stance, the high visibility of the Irish flag, the tricolour, at social events, the consumption of traditional Irish music, recalling the blood sacrifices of male Irish heroes and the celebration of Irish literary figures. Women and femininity tended to be written out of this hyper-masculine fantasy narrative.

Another key element that impacted on these men was the British state's criminalisation of the Irish community that had specific implications for Irish men within different regional areas. As indicated above, the study was carried out in the city of Birmingham, at a critical moment in the politics of Northern Ireland. In the British popular geographical imagination these two places are historically linked and fixed through the event of the 1974 Birmingham pub bombings. This event tends to have different cultural meanings for Irish and British people. For the British, there is an exclusive concern with the bombing itself as an act of terrorism. For the Irish, and most specifically those resident in Birmingham, there are also memories that the bombing claimed the lives of a number of Irish as well as indigenous Birmingham people. Also, the Irish have had to contend with the immediate backlash by the state against them and the criminalisation of their community, exemplified in the Prevention of Terrorism Act, which was set up initially as a temporary measure following the pub bombings. The immediate effect was a high-profile anti-Irish campaign led by the local media and political representatives that drove Irish ethnicity underground. The legacy of these attacks continues to emerge in the city whenever the Irish community makes public claims of cultural difference.

One of the major effects of the dominant black–white model of ethnic relations was that it did not help to understand the high levels of disadvantage experienced by sectors of the Irish community.[16] It was against the background of the official erasure of Irish difference that these Irish men challenged their cultural invisibility, thus constructing a protest form of masculinity. The political and cultural response of Irish men and women to their experiences of living in Birmingham included the search for ethnic minority status in the *national* Census and local monitoring of services, as well as the right to celebrate their national identity publicly. Within the context of intense local hostility, they were successful in their political mobilisation. For example, in 1986, the Irish community gained ethnic recognition from Birmingham city council and in 1998 were successful in establishing the St Patrick's Day Parade, which had not taken place for over twenty years. Thus they created an ethnic revivalism within the local community. Their protest helped them shift from a marginalised status ascribed to economic emigrants to that of a settled diasporian group with citizens' rights and recognition of their cultural difference within the local state.

Emigrants: social care and health needs as difference

A second study with which we were involved focused on the health, accommodation and social care needs of older Irish men in the city of Birmingham. 'Old' did not refer to their chronological age but rather to the range of social deprivations that resulted cumulatively in these men acquiring a lifestyle associated with the vulnerabilities of marginalised older citizens. Indeed, people born in Ireland have suffered disproportionately from accidents, illness and suicide, and Irish men have been shown to die younger in Britain than in Ireland, with overall health standards being lower. While the term 'diasporian status' would apply generally to the Irish community in Britain, for these older Irish men it was more appropriate to see them as part of an earlier social category of *emigrants*, whose masculinity was shaped by a double exclusion from citizenship, living on the margins of both the British indigenous and the Irish communities, while at the same time feeling unable to return home. For these men, migration was institutionalised in their youth in the local areas of Kerry, Monaghan, Clare etc., becoming a rite of passage to an adult masculinity that would be lived out on the margins.

The older Irish men were born into a national exclusion that has continued throughout their lives as part of a generation whom the island of Ireland was not big enough to accommodate. Many of the older Irish men experienced dual processes of proletarianisation as former rural workers and racialisation. Most did not intend to stay in Britain and so never fully integrated as citizens with a sense of welfare or civil rights. They were overrepresented in low-skilled, manual work in a disappearing world of 'navvying', 'gangermen' and 'gaffers'.

The cumulative effects of the globalisation of capital led to new patterns in the international division of labour, new labour processes and new technologies. This was accompanied by the changing nature of the nation-state and a crisis in Anglo-ethnicity which created new conditions for a deindustrialising post-imperial Britain. These occupational changes increased social and economic polarisation between professional elites, multi-skilled workers, a class of service workers employed in low-paid, part-time, non-unionised jobs and an 'underclass' of which the older Irish men in this study belong. By the late 1990s, their isolation had intensified with the extreme effects of the internal changes in the Irish community that fragmented in the 1980s. The socially mobile moved to the suburbs, leaving behind these older Irish men, many of whom were divorced or separated or had never married and who had limited social support networks and limited contact with families in Ireland. A large percentage of the older Irish men were homeless and sleeping rough. Legislation at this time encouraging 'care in the community' resulted in an increased number of them – typically overrepresented in psychiatric institutions – leaving institutions and becoming homeless.

In short, within the local hierarchy of ethnic minority masculinities, including Caribbeans and South Asians, these older Irish men were located at the bottom – without nation, family or status. Institutionally, they experienced a wide range of systematic discrimination and social exclusion. Spending more time in public spaces – 'on the streets' – than other Irish men increased their visibility and made them more vulnerable to verbal and physical abuse. In response to institutionalised surveillance and interrogation, they developed strategies of contestation and survival.

Sexual migration: the new diaspora

A third area with which we were involved was a two-year qualitative study involving over thirty Irish-born gay men, aged sixteen to twenty-seven, all of whom were situated in London. This study is important in challenging the dominant explanation of Irish migration to Britain in terms of nation, ethnicity and national difference. These young men, as part of a self-conscious and visible diaspora, were in the process of producing new ways of being a (post) modern Irish man. They spoke of how anti-Irish racism and homophobia affected their lives as migrants, describing their own experiences of the British state criminalisation of the Irish and gay men. They linked the Prevention of Terrorism Act, Section 28 (which barred local authorities from 'promoting' homosexuality) and the discriminatory age of consent for gay men (twenty-one at the time of interviewing) as attempts to enforce and codify a way of life. The young men provided an interesting contrast between the Catholic Church's overt religious instruments of sexual control – for example, the confessional – that circumscribed their childhoods, and experiences of the sexually repressive technologies of the modern, secular state in Britain – making the confessional 'coming out' more difficult for young Irish gay men.

As explored below, the research unexpectedly highlighted diverse class-cultural affiliations among the young men that were of key importance in the development of their sex/gender identity. For example, working-class young men provided accounts of their institutional marginalisation in Britain, emphasising their employment experiences, which were located within low-paid service sector jobs and a rapidly declining construction industry. The labour market continues to be a key site for Irish working-class young men, both materially and culturally. However, in response to structural discrimination in their workplaces which denied them the privileges ascribed to English masculinity, they appeared not to have adopted predictable sex/gendered forms of contestation and resistance common among British gay young men. Rather, similar to other diasporian groups, their response was lived out in terms of an increased sense of difference around their national affiliation. Irishness, as a unifying fiction, appeared to operate as a collective strategy that served to contest their lack of masculine power in English public spaces. It was played out and developed in unofficially segregated subordinated workplaces that often had an Irish majority workforce and separated settlement patterns that included overrepresentation in low-status multiple occupied residences and hostels. Their sense of social dislocation and institutional masculine subordination was eased within cultural spaces provided by Irish pubs, clubs and leisure arenas, such as Gaelic games. The young men's accounts illustrate the complexity of living with multiple socially marginalised identities. At this time in London, their experience of strong anti-Irish discrimination in public spaces resulted in their 'feeling at home' among the established Irish working class, while not exhibiting their gay identity.

One reading of these young men's responses to their masculine subordination is to assume that national belonging was more important than sex/gender relations as an explanation of how these young men constructed their lives as different. An alternative reading is to see Irish nationalism as a form of sexual politics which has specific implications for the construction of young Irish masculinities. As indicated above, the masculinity of Irish nationalist politics is displayed by a wide range of cultural signifiers, including that of militarisation, encapsulated in the Irish Republic's national anthem (translated as *The Soldier's Song*), which serves to maintain symbolically a public collective consciousness of what it means to be a 'proper man'. It should be noted that this version of Irish nationalist politics, from a revisionist standpoint, which is in the ascendancy in the Republic of Ireland, may be read as adopting a rather atavistic stance. Nevertheless, it is also a potentially powerful political mobilising force in a nation for whom a normal mode of citizenship is that of immigrant status, social exclusion and heterosexual masculinity.

The significance of class-cultural affiliations was made explicit in the young Irish middle-class gays' accounts of life in Britain. In contrast to the working-class young men's sexual identity that could be seen to coalesce around nationality and nationalism, middle-class Irish young gay men's experiences as sexual migrants appeared to take a more expected form. For example, although the latter were critical of the English gay scene, they claimed that they 'felt at home' there. The anti-Irish racism that they experienced among British gay men was less of a problem for them than the homophobia of the Irish community in Britain. The young men developed their explanations of the diverse class-cultural affiliations of more recent Irish immigrants and the range of masculine subject positions that are made available to them. Most significantly, they pointed to their involvement in the English gay scene as part of a broader contemporary identity politics based on middle-class values of individualisation, consumption patterns and cultural lifestyles. In contrast, working-class gays seemed to identify more easily with traditional Irish nationalist and republican politics in Britain based on working-class values around manual labour, community and collectivism. In short, the middle-class gay young men illustrated their inclusion in a public space as part of a broader transnational trajectory, while the working-class gay men exemplified the potential danger of not belonging anywhere, among either the traditional Irish community in Britain or the British gay community. These differences are important to hold on to at a time when postmodernist accounts of migration emphasise contemporary discontinuities with the past, while repressing social continuities. In other words it is an open question as to whether the young working-class gay men have more in common with older emigrants in terms of difference – as cultural outsiders – than they do with their middle-class gay peers.

Conclusion

In modern 'mediaspeak' Muslims in Britain are the new Irish. Currently, we are working with young Muslim men in the city of Birmingham and arrange for these young men to meet with older Irish men. As outlined above, the latter's experience of being represented as postcolonial folk devils marks the young Muslim men's current experiences. Most interestingly, in this inter-generational conversation, the older men make clear that difference does not simply emerge from what Britain does to diasporian groups, for example, Irish Catholics or Pakistani Muslims. This has led to each group of men telling stories of adopting diverse social trajectories, cultural lifestyles and individual identities in forging their urban lives.

We opened this chapter warning against the danger of exchanging positive stereotypes for negatives ones. Until recently, there have been two major representations in British academic, political and popular accounts of Irish masculinity. Firstly, that of low-status manual workers living in segregated ethnic occupational enclaves. The second major representation has been the criminalisation of Irish masculinity, with pervasive images of Irish men as of low intelligence, feckless, drunkards and bombers. As indicated above, by the 1990s, in Britain, it was cool to be Irish. Irish men have served a long apprenticeship within Britain's economy of signs. The Irish, or more specifically Irish masculinity, can be read as providing a diverse range of cultural archetypes within changing global and local changes. Irish men have been constructed as the 'significant other' for centuries, the longest-standing representation of what British masculinity is not and cannot be. Historically, the main cultural shift has been from a racialised masculinity with a focus on working *with* the body (for example the navvy) to a diasporian masculinity of working *on* the body (for example, the dancer). This shift can be read as an effect of a broader movement from work or production to consumption, as a key dynamic in defining difference. And so an archaeology of difference of the recent past might reveal: Paddy the exile, Paddy the lumpenproletariat, Paddy the socially excluded, Paddy the urban terrorist, Paddy the hybrid (the insider/outsider) and Paddy the transnational hi-tech networked user. More recently, the emergence of images of 'terrorist' Muslim men has accompanied Irish men joining black men and gay men at the postcolonial periphery as objects of desire of English heterosexuality. These changes are part of a wider crisis in the Anglo-ethnic majority's sense of post-imperial loss and disenchantment. However, as a cultural minority, like all minorities, the Irish must carry the anxieties of the social majority that are transferred to them. [17] Nevertheless, returning to our opening comment, Irish men's experience in Britain is not a nothing but the same old emigrant story. Rather, as illustrated above, it is a multilayered story of continuities and changes driven by global change. [18]

Notes

1 Home Office, UK Immigration Statistics January to March 2013.

2 See the *Irish Times* Generation Emigration blog.

3 Krishan Kumar, *Prophesy and Progress* (Harmondsworth: Penguin Books, 1978).

4 See Jim Mac Laughlin, *Ireland: The Immigrant Nursery and the World Economy* (Cork: Cork University Press, 1994).

5 John A. Jackson, *The Irish in Britain* (London: Routledge and Kegan Paul, 1963).

6 Lewis P. Curtis, *Anglo-Saxons and Celts* (Connecticut: University of Bridgeport, 1968), p. 84.

7 Ellen Hazelkorn, 'British Capital and Irish Labour Evidence: from the 1980s', in *The Emigrant Experience* (Galway Labour History Group, Galway, 1991), pp. 124–41.

8 Chris Haywood and Mairtin Mac an Ghaill, 'Young (Male) Irelanders: Postcolonial Ethnicities – Expanding the Nation and the Irish', *European Journal of Cultural Studies*, 6:3 (2003), pp. 386–403.

9 Robbie McVeigh, 'Nick, Nack, Paddywhack: Anti-Irish Racism and the Racialisation of Irishness', in Ronit Lentin and Robbie McVeigh (eds), *Racism and Anti-Racism in Ireland* (Belfast: Beyond the Pale, 2002), p. 146; see also Liz Curtis, *Nothing But the Same Old Story* (London: Information on Ireland Press, 1984).

10 Dermot Bolger (ed.), *Ireland in Exile: Irish Writers Abroad* (Dublin: New Ireland, 1993).

11 Bronwen Walter, 'Irishness, Gender and Space', *Society and Space*, 13 (1995), pp. 35–50.

12 Catherine Nash, Remapping and renaming: New Cartologies of Identity, Gender and Landscape in Ireland', *Feminist Review*, 44 (1993), pp. 39–57.

13 Stuart Hall, 'Old and New Ethnicities', in Anthony King (ed.), *Culture, Globalisation and the World System* (London: Macmillan, 1991).

14 John O'Sullivan, 'If You're Hip You Must Be Irish', *The Independent*, 1 July 1996.

15 Chris Haywood and Mairtin Mac an Ghaill, 'Young (Male) Irelanders: Postcolonial Ethnicities – Expanding the Nation and the Irish', *European Journal of Cultural Studies*, 6:3 (2003), pp. 386–403; Liviu Popoviciu, Chris Haywood and Mairtin Mac an Ghaill, 'Migrating Masculinities: The Irish Diaspora in Britain', *Irish Studies Review*, 14:2 (2006), pp. 169–87; Mairtin Mac an Ghaill and Chris Haywood, '"Nothing to write home about": Troubling Concepts of Home, Racialization and Self in Theories of Irish Male (E)migration', *Cultural Sociology*, 5:3 (2011), pp. 385–402; Iestyn Williams and Mairtin Mac an Ghaill, *Health, Accommodation and Social Care Needs of Older Irish Men in Birmingham* (Birmingham: Irish Government and Birmingham Irish Community Forum Ltd, 1998); Mairtin Mac an Ghaill, 'Irish Masculinities and Sexualities in England' in L. Adkins, J. Holland, V. Merchant and J. Weeks (eds), *Power and Organisation of Sexuality* (London: Macmillan, 1996), pp. 122–44.

16 See Mary J. Hickman and Bronwen Walter, *Discrimination and the Irish Community in Britain.* (London: Commission for Racial Equality, 1997); and Mac an Ghaill and Haywood, '"Nothing to write home about".

17 Edward Said, *Orientalism* (Harmondsworth: Penguin, 1985).

18 Tom Inglis, *Global Ireland Same Difference* (London: Routledge, 2008).

15

The new Irish and the Irish nation

Bryan Fanning

In James Joyce's *Ulysses* set in Dublin in 1904 the fictional Irish Jew Leopold Bloom is confronted by the citizen, a public house bully, who asks him: 'What is your nation?' The citizen was modelled on Michael Cusack, the founder of the Gaelic Athletic Association. 'Ireland,' Bloom replies, 'I was born here. Ireland.' Bloom then refers to his Jewishness, saying that he belonged also to a race that was hated and persecuted. Near the end of Neil Jordan's 1982 film *Angel* a policeman named Bloom played by Ray McAnally tells the Catholic protagonist Danny played by Steven Rea that he is Jewish. Are you, Danny asks, a Protestant Jew or a Catholic Jew? In Clare Boylan's 1988 novel *Black Baby* an aged Irish spinster who, as a child, had donated her first communion money to the missions is visited by an African woman. The title of the book refers to a once-common catchphrase 'a penny for the black baby' used in appeals for donations to support Catholic missions. Irish missionaries were viewed as heroic figures. Through them Ireland acquired a spiritual empire and a sense of playing an important role in the world. In Roddy Doyle's 1988 novel *The Commitments* Jimmy Rabbitte, the manager of the eponymous band, describes the Irish as the niggers of Europe and exhorts its members to be black and proud. In a 1998 episode of *Father Ted*, Craggy Island's Chinese community are repeatedly offended by Ted's blunders as he digs himself into an ever deeper hole trying to prove that he is not a racist. The comedy or drama of each of these encounters turned on narcissistic conceptions of Irishness and bemusement at the very idea of an ethnically or religiously diverse Ireland.

Such fictive encounters gave way to real ones when the Republic of Ireland (hereafter 'Ireland') experienced large-scale immigration. This chapter examines some of these. The focus is upon experiences of immigrants as part of Irish society but also, crucially, on their relationship with the twenty-first-century Irish nation. Politicians and media sometimes refer to immigrants as the new Irish, but it is not as simple as that. Non-Irish nationals (544,357) according to the 2011 Census made up more than eleven per cent of the population of the Republic of Ireland.[1] But immigrants constituted only about one half of one per cent of Irish citizens living in the Republic. The vast majority of Irish citizens are drawn from the same ethnic group. In this context Irishness still seems to be heavily associated with the majority ethnic identity. The place of naturalised immigrants within this Irish nation remains somewhat ambiguous.

Old guests of the nation

Leopold Bloom never existed, but Ireland by 1904 did have a community of Irish-born Jews, many of whom fled Lithuanian villages in the years after 1881 when the assassination of the Tsar triggered pogroms across Russia. By 1904 there were more than two thousand Jews living in Dublin and a few hundred elsewhere in the country. Over half of these had arrived since 1891.[2] Their position within an increasingly nationalistic Irish society was somewhat precarious. Cormac O'Grada in *Jewish Ireland in the Age of Joyce* has described an economically vibrant but clannish community, steeped in what sociologists call social capital, of which Leopold Bloom would have been a most unlikely member, the son of a Hungarian-Jewish father (when most of Dublin's Jews were Litvaks) and a Protestant Irish mother (when it would have been almost unimaginable for an Irish Jew to 'marry out').[3] Leopold Bloom was a multicultural creation invented in part to make points about Irish nationalism and about Dublin, and to reflect on Joyce's own cosmopolitan identity.

In 1904 the nationalist newspaper *The Leader* carried an advertisement on behalf of trade-unionised Irish tailors urging Irishmen to help 'stamp out Sweated, Jewish Labour in the Tailoring Trade in Dublin' – there were about seventy Jewish tailors in the city at the time.[4] That same year a small Jewish community consisting of about twenty-five families was driven out of Limerick city following a campaign led by a Redemptorist priest who depicted them as enemies of the Irish nation. Fr Creagh was the spiritual director of the Arch-Confraternity of the Holy Family, which had a membership of about six thousand Limerick lay-Catholics. In one of his sermons Fr Creagh called for the Jews to be turned out of Ireland as they had been turned out of other nations.[5] In another he depicted the Jews as enslavers of the Irish people worse than Cromwell. He urged his congregation 'not to be false to Ireland, false to your country and false to your religion, by continuing to deal with the Jews'. He instructed Limerick customers of Jewish traders not to pay their debts and suppliers of milk not to sell to the Jewish community. The resultant 'boycott' led to Limerick's Jewish community being permanently forced from the city.[6] The practice took its name from the shunning of Captain Boycott, a landlord's agent in Mayo who had sent eviction notices to tenants who had petitioned for fair rents. Boycotting was employed against landlords by the Land League in an attempt to protect vulnerable peasants from losing their homes and means of living. However the boycott against the Jews in Limerick aimed to deprive the Jews of their homes and livelihoods. An editorial in the *United Irishman* in 1904 by Arthur Griffith also identified the Jews as enemies of the nation:

> No thoughtful Irishman or woman can view without apprehension the continuous influx of Jews into Ireland ... strange people, alien to us in thought, alien to us in sympathy, from Russia, Poland, Germany and Austria – people who come to live amongst us, but who never become of us ... Our sympathy – insular as it may be – goes wholly to our countryman the artisan whom the Jew deprives of the means of livelihood, to our countryman the trader whom he ruins in business by unscrupulous methods, to our countryman the farmer whom he draws into his usurer's toils and drives to the workhouse across the water.[7]

The place of Irish Jews within a narrowly imagined 'Irish' society remained as precarious following Independence as Joyce had depicted it in *Ulysses*. Notwithstanding the prominence of some Irish Jews in the main political parties, the Irish state was explicitly anti-Semetic in its responses to Jewish refugees before, during and after the Holocaust. Until the late 1950s Department of Justice documents stated that it was departmental policy not to admit Jews into Ireland.[8] Official anti-Semitism abated around the time that Ireland joined the United Nations in 1956, but for some Irish Jews feelings persisted that their place within the Irish nation remained ambiguous – as put by Louis Lentin in a 2008 article based on an earlier television documentary about the history of Irish Jews who were descended from refugees who had fled the 1880s Russian pogroms:

> I joined the fledgling RTE where I produced and directed drama, most of the subjects deeply Irish. Yet it was there that a senior colleague shocked me by saying *'how can you possibly understand that, you're not Irish, you're Jewish?'.* Far from being the anti-Semitic ravings of an anonymous nutter and emphatically not quoted here as an indictment of RTE, this was a blunt statement from a respected friend, stating that as I was not a member of the parish ... So possibly for the first time I was forced to confront the perpetual dilemma of the Jew in the diaspora. Was it *possible* to be accepted as Irish and not be *of* Ireland? Where did that leave my work? More to the point, where did it leave me as a hyphenated Irish-Jew?[9]

Neil Jordan's 1982 film *Angel* touches on similar bewilderment amongst the real Irish that Jews born in Ireland, standing outside the dominant tribe, could really be Irish. Bloomsday is now prominent in Dublin's annual calendar of festivals: a St Patrick's Day for those who read lots of books and sometimes drink beer rather than the other way around. The non-existent Leopold Bloom like St Patrick (who might also not have existed or have been one of several people) has become (in Dublin at least) a patron saint of Irishness. He is not an icon of some multicultural Irishness but emblematic of a still-prevalent solipsistic sense of national identity, a figure who demonstrates that the Irish are important, like those American Presidential candidates who discover Irish roots before elections, but are celebrated for this in Ireland – if they win – as honorary Irish, a bit like Bloom, but not really Irish.

A hundred years after the first Bloomsday, eighty per cent of voters in the 2004 Referendum on Citizenship, true to the kind of nationalism professed by the Citizen in *Ulysses*, voted to remove from the Constitution the birth right to Irish citizenship from the Irish-born children of immigrants. The 2011 Census recorded a Jewish population of 1984, a little more than half of what it had been at the time Ireland became an independent nation-state.

The new black Irish and the Irish nation

Former missionaries and development workers played a leading role from the late 1990s in developing services for asylum seekers, some of whom described their first encounters with Ireland as through Irish priests and nuns – as recalled by Theophilis Ejorh, a sociologist who came to Ireland from Nigeria in 2002:

> I mused over the mirthful stories to us children by Father O'Leary, the Irish priest in my village, about the congeniality of the Irish, their kind-heartedness and warmth. Times and times, images tumbled on my mind, as I imagined myself walking the cobbled streets of Ireland and beholding the warm affable faces that bore the happy indications of the life I craved.
>
> I took up residence in Waterford, Ireland's oldest city, celebrated for its crystals. Two days after my arrival, I went window-shopping at the city centre, in the company of two African friends whom I met a fortnight earlier. While there, a White Irish woman who looked rather dishevelled and reeked of stale liquor advanced towards us, waving a hand menacingly and yelling with umbrage; 'You f**king niggers! Who bought ya here? Go back to ya f**king jungle!' We were astonished by this unprovoked outrage, but soon learned that this incident was only a foretaste of the wider xenophobia and racism in Ireland.[11]

The 2006 Census identified a black or black African population of 53,318, of which Nigerians were the numerically largest group; the census recorded 16,677 Nigerian-born living in Ireland rising to 19,780 in the 2011 Census. By 2011 the overall African-born population had risen to 54,419. A significant proportion of these are former asylum seekers with Irish-born children. The 2006 Census found that 41 per cent of Nigerian-born migrants were educated to degree level or higher compared to just over one-quarter of Poles, 17 per cent of Lithuanians and 28 per cent of Chinese.[11] Yet, Africans experienced disproportionately high levels of unemployment during the Celtic Tiger boom years. The reasons for this included state-fostered exclusions (asylum seekers were prevented from working or under-taking state-funded employment training during the years they waited for their cases to be determined) and racism. A 2008 report founded that unemployment rates were nine times higher amongst black respondents than for the population as a whole. This drew on 2004 and 2005 data but when the research was repeated in 2012 the gap had not closed.[12] A 2005 survey found that black Africans were more likely than any other respondents to experience harassment on the street, on public transport and in public places. Africans also reported higher levels of discrimination in the workplace than other respondents.[13] A 2009 EU-wide survey found that 73 per cent of black African respondents in Ireland believed that discrimination was widespread in the country. Ireland was found to be amongst the worst five amongst the twenty-seven EU member states for experiences of racist assaults or harassment. All African interviewees in the Irish case lived in the Dublin metropolitan area.[14] A black African respondent in a 2011 study of racist violence, harassment and anti-social behaviour in the Dublin area, described his experience as follows:

> I experience racism every day. Just today, for example, on my way to this meeting, I asked a man for a ticket and he replied: 'Fuck off nigger.' I told him to get off the tram, which he did. Sometimes passengers say: 'Go back to you country, black monkey, you're thieves stealing our jobs'.
>
> At the Red Cow stop last week I passed a man in his late 20s who was with his three-year-old child. The man asked his child: Do you want to see a monkey now? A black monkey is coming now. Can you make the sound of a monkey?[15]

Jimmy Rabbitte's 1988 description of the Irish as the niggers of Europe has dated poorly. More recently Doyle has written stories that address Irish responses to immigration and ones told from the perspectives of African immigrants. The titular story of his 2007 short story collection *The Deportees* revisited a now thirty-six-year-old Jimmy Rabbitte managing a band comprised of immigrants. In his preface Doyle described an Ireland radically different from the one portrayed in *The Commitments*, and very different from the Ireland of the second decade of the twenty-first century:

> In 1994 and 1995, I wrote *The Woman Who Walked Into Doors*. It was narrated by a woman called Paula Spenser, who earned her money by cleaning offices. She went to work with other working-class women like herself. Ten years later, I wrote *Paula Spenser*. Paula was still cleaning offices but now she went to work alone and the other cleaners were men from Romania and Nigeria. In 1986, I wrote *The Commitments*. In that book, the main character, a young man called Jimmy Rabbitte, delivers a line that became quite famous: – The Irish are the niggers of Europe. Twenty years on, there are thousands of Africans living in Ireland and, if I was writing that book today, I wouldn't use that line. It wouldn't actually occur to me, because Ireland has become one of the wealthiest countries in Europe and the line would make no sense.[16]

The stories in *The Deporteess* were first serialised in *Metro Éireann*, a newspaper with a distinctly Irish name founded by two Nigerian journalists, Chinedu Onyejelem and Abel Ugba. It is targeted at Ireland's new immigrant communities.

Doyle went on to publish further serials in *Metro Éireann*. One month before the June 2009 election *Metro Éireann* began its serialisation of 'Local', Doyle's tale of Chidimma Agu, a fictional Fianna Fáil candidate standing in Mulhuddart in Dublin 15. The front cover of the same issue of *Metro Éireann* carried four advertisement for actual African candidates standing in the election, though, by some curious symmetry, none for the real Fianna Fáil candidate, Idowu Olafimiham, who stood for election in Mulhuddart. An article on page seven reported that Brian Lenihan, the Minister of Finance and TD for the area, had taken time out from dealing with the banking crisis to address Olafimiham's supporters.

In 2004 two Nigerian former asylum seekers had been elected as town councillors, Tawio Matthews in Ennis, County Clare, and Rotimi Adebari in Portlaoise. Adabari became Ireland's first black mayor and was re-elected by a predominantly non-immigrant electorate in the 2009 local government election. Inspired by Adebari, several African candidates stood on behalf of Fianna Fáil, Fine Gael and the Green Party or as independents. They ran high-profile campaigns in Dundalk and Drogheda as well in Dublin and Portlaoise. In all some forty immigrant candidates stood for local elections in 2009. About half of these were African, about half from Eastern Europe. Residency rather than citizenship criteria determines who is entitled to vote in Irish local government elections. In Mulhuddart in 2009 three African candidates stood against one another and none was elected. Those who fared best around the country (as measured in terms of votes and transfers) had successfully become identified within their electoral areas as locals. Nevertheless many African candidates in the 2009 elections identified racism as a problem.[17]

New maps of Ireland

Craggy Island is not a real place. Rural Ireland has no Chinatowns. The very idea of one in 1990s rural Ireland was the stuff of whimsical comedy. But not all of rural Ireland was homogenous. The small County Mayo town of Ballyhaunis has a long-standing Muslim population dating back to the 1970s when a Pakistani entrepreneur purchased a local meat processing plant in order to export halal products. The first purpose-built mosque in Ireland was opened there in 1987. There are two purpose-built mosques in Dublin. Others in cities such as Cork, Limerick, Galway, Waterford and Wexford and towns such as Tralee, Ennis, Cavan, Tuam, Kilkenny and Naas have makeshift facilities in warehouses, flats and houses.[18] By the 1990s the Muslim community in Ballyhaunis had grown to thirty families of Pakistani and Middle Eastern origin. A 250-person asylum seeker hostel was established in the town centre in 2001. Many of the asylum seekers accommodated in Ballyhaunis were Muslims from the Middle-East, Asia and Africa.[19] The 2006 Census found that almost twenty per cent of the population of the town were Muslim. They variously spoke Urdu, Punjabi and Arabic in their homes. The 2002 Census identified 19,147 Muslims in Ireland. By 2006 the total had risen to 32,529.

By 2006 some 9761 Muslims held Irish citizenship; of these 7504 were born in Ireland. Until the 1990s the community was mostly composed of educated professionals. Later the Shia population expanded with the arrival of asylum seekers, particularly from Iraq, and labour migrants, particularly from Pakistan.[20] By 2012 there were a total of 49,204 Muslims living in Ireland More than 90 per cent of these were Shia.

A 2012 article in *The Mayo News* proclaimed Ballyhaunis as Ireland's most 'cosmopolitan' town.[21] The 2011 Census identified Ballyhaunis as the most diverse town in Ireland, with some 2299 non-Irish nationals comprising 42 per cent of the population. Since the 2006 Census it had overtaken Gort in County Galway which was found to have a non-Irish national population of 40.7 per cent. Both these towns contain a higher percentage of immigrants than urban areas such as Mulhuddart in Dublin 15. In 2006, 36 per cent of migrants lived in Dublin city and county, 10.5 per cent in Cork city and county, 5.8 per cent in Galway city and county and 3.5 per cent in Limerick city and county; the remaining 44.2 per cent were distributed throughout the remaining twenty-two counties. All parts of Ireland have experienced immigration. But immigrant experiences and encounters with host communities have by no means been the same in different places.

Nine out of the seventeen teenage girls who participated in a 2007–11 study by Orla McGarry of Muslim teenagers in Ballyhaunis wore headscarves to school; three of these were Irish-born. One consequence of the rule of female modesty was that they did not participate in extra-curricular activities with non-Muslim school friends. McGarry's recommendations to counter the social isolation experienced by many female Muslims in Ballyhaunis include female-only leisure activities that allow for the wearing of modest clothing and the provision of a supervised public space, such as a youth café where they could socialise with parental permission outside of school hours. Boys were less likely to have Irish friends, though some played hurling with the local GAA team and for the Ballyhaunis Community School team and got on well on the pitch with non-Muslim teammates.

One Muslim hurler on the school team was given the nickname Setanta. The original Setanta, also called Cuchulainn in Gaelic myth, had been a hurler of supernatural prowess. The nickname was perhaps also a reference to Setanta Ó'Hailpin, a hurling star of Irish-Fijian origin who had played for County Cork.[22] The Ballyhaunis 'Setanta' spoke Urdu on the pitch during games with another defender and the goalkeeper. Off the pitch, Muslim teenage boys always socialised with one another according to one female interviewee. 'Setanta' had been especially friendly with non-Mulsim children at primary school but now hung out mostly with fellow Pakistanis at Ballyhaunis Community School and spoke mostly Urdu and Punjabi with them. Muslim teenagers felt that an increasingly reduced social interaction with non-Muslims was party due to the growing size of the Muslim population and the peer pressures that boys in particular placed upon one another. Girls, kept under strict parental control, did not have the opportunity to socialise with Irish friends outside of school. But Ballyhaunis Muslim teenagers were hardly a homogenous group. Urdu-speaking asylum seeker teenage boys including 'Setanta' described being marginalised by members of the longer-established Punjabi-speaking (Pakistani) group.

In 1998 the owner of a Gort meat processing plant recruited some workers from the small town of Via Fabril in Brazil. This initial cohort was joined by family members and neighbours in a classic pattern of chain migration which thereafter linked both localities. Over time they branched out into the retail, catering, construction and transport sectors.[23] The arrival of the Brazilians in Gort reversed generations of population decline and injected, according to several newspaper articles, a new vibrancy into the social life of the town. One article from 2004 described how, each year, hundreds of Brazilians gathered in the town's square to celebrate the carnival season. As described by an Irish interviewee, 'They all dressed in their costumes and danced from twelve in the morning till twelve at night. It's like Dirty Dancing here.' The article noted that Western Union had set up a branch in Gort because the Brazilians sent a substantial volume of money back home each week. The principal of the Convent of Mercy primary school reported that there were more than thirty children from Brazil attending the school. The school had recruited two language-support teachers to help the newcomers with English. The children, she said, fitted in well. The Brazilians were 'lovely people and very polite and refined'.[24]

Research on Gort's Brazilian community undertaken between 2004 and 2007 revealed some underlying complexities. It consisted of Pentecostals, Mormons and Catholics. The Pentecostal congregation, Assembléia de Deus, has set up a church in the area and was responsible for the annual summer carnival; it catered for 'approximately 150 attendees on any given night'. The Brazilian Catholic community was ministered to by a Limerick-based priest who had worked for twenty years in Brazil; he said Mass in Portuguese every Sunday in the local Catholic church. Some of the Brazilians benefited from close-knit family and community networks when it came to settling into life in County Galway. Some others without such networks were vulnerable to exploitation. It seemed to be an accepted practice for fellow Brazilians and even relatives to charge new arrivals for almost any type of help. This might include basic accommodation, such as sleeping on a sofa, help in interpreting forms, paying to translate with medical professionals or even for making phone calls to the Electricity Supply Board. As numerous studies amongst immigrant communities around the world have found, the practice of 'selling' jobs was hardly uncommon. One of the Gort study interviewees described how another Brazilian woman proposed to charge her €400 for a cleaning job. As she put it: 'I had no language and they knew the lay of the land a little bit so I had to go through them to get work'. Another described paying €500 for a job that lasted only four months; he was paid €350 a week. In effect the broker took just under 20 per cent of his earnings for that period.

Immigrants sometimes lead different kinds of lives from those of others in the localities where they settle, sometimes as a result of cultural, religious or linguistic differences, sometimes as a result of workplace exploitation (as a number of studies by the Migrant Rights Centre Ireland have documented) or because of racism.[25] However, many immigrants possess comparatively high levels of human capital. Analysis of the 2006 Census revealed that in all electoral areas in Dublin migrants were better educated on average than Irish nationals.[26] For example, in the Liberties, an economically disadvantaged inner-city area in Dublin where immigrants constituted 30 per cent of the population, research has identified immigrant families with middle-class norms and relatively high levels of education. These immigrants were mostly Eastern Europeans. Many lived in new apartment blocks built to regenerate the area. Although immigrant adults possessed more human capital than the long-standing population and had higher levels of economic participation, many led lives that kept them isolated from the wider community. In many cases their economic well-being did not translate into psychological well-being. Although Irish citizen locals lacked human capital by comparison to immigrants, they possessed more social capital measured in terms of trust and reciprocity with others in their community.[27] These findings reflected concerns about anomie and social isolation articulated by various Polish candidates interviewed before the 2009 local elections.[28]

Yet immigrant children living in the Liberties exhibited better psychological well-being than Irish citizen children in the neighbourhood. They were less likely than Irish citizen children to exhibit difficulties with peer relationships, emotional well-being and anti-social behaviour. They were better placed to do well in school. Compared to Irish citizens' children, they processed higher levels of cultural capital, in essence middle-class values that were responded positively by teachers. No great claim can be made arising from such findings except to note that, as in Ballyhaunis, Gort and Dublin 15, immigration has altered the dynamics of all such localities, that the new emerging communities are all likely to be somewhat different from one another and that all this change has yet to be acknowledged by the Irish nation-state.

The new communities and the nation-state

The most successful Irish movie in recent years, *Once* (2006), tells the story of a romance between a Czech musician played by Markéta Irgová and an Irish one played by Glen Hansard who also starred in the 1991 film of *The Commitments*. At the end of the film he emigrates to London and she stays in Dublin. Notwithstanding expectations that many immigrants would return to their home countries after the boom, the 2011 Census revealed a growth in Ireland's immigrant population since 2006. Census data identified a rise in the non-Irish citizen population from 419,733 in 2006 to 544,357 in 2011. The 2011 Census identified 122,585 Poles living in Ireland. Ireland's Polish community had more than doubled since 2006 and Polish had overtaken Irish as the second most commonly spoken language in the state.[29]

There is now a huge disjuncture between official Ireland and the diversity of Irish society. Only a tiny minority of immigrants are Irish citizens, and the Irish nation, for the most part, persists as the monoethnic entity envisaged by early twentieth-century cultural nationalists. Immigration has received little attention from Irish politicians and policy makers since the 2004 Referendum which removed a constitutional right to citizenship from Irish-born children whose fore-bearers were not Irish. Ireland's main response to immigration was to retreat into a *ius sanguine* definition of Irishness: an Irish race defined by bloodlines. Before 2004 the Irish nation was constitutionally defined in *ius soli* terms as potentially including all those who lived within the borders of the Irish nation-state. Now even children of immigrant origin born in Ireland get to be defined as Irish only if their parents naturalise. Those seeking to do so are predominantly migrants from outside the European Union. Migrants from within the EU tend not to naturalise when they move from one member state to another. They do not need to do so to ensure a right to live and work in another member state. New Irish citizens have predominantly come from non-EU countries. Those eligible to naturalise in any given year will have arrived in Ireland several years previous. The majority of immigrants who became Irish citizens from 2000 to 2004 were Pakistanis and other Muslims who had arrived in Ireland several years earlier, just as most of those who have more recently become Irish citizens were immigrants from Africa and Aisa. Arguably insufficient numbers have naturalised to shift how the Irish think of themselves. Most immigrants lie empirically outside the Irish nation as this is insti-tutionalised though citizenship. They remain, as the commonly used term puts it, 'non-nationals'. They do not have the right to vote in parliamentary elections. However, they are entitled to vote or stand in local elections, hence the focus by researchers and NGOs on the opportunities such candidates and voters have to redefine what it is to be Irish at a community level. Localism within politics and community life has the potential to offer wider definitions of what it is to be Irish than those institutionalised within the nation-state. The converse also holds. In this context it is crucial to understand how migrants are coming to be accepted as being from Portloaise, Ballyhaunis, Drogheda, Dundalk or Gort and the obstacles to integration they face in such specific communities.

Notes

1 www.cso.ie.

2 Dermot Keogh, *Jews in Twentieth-century Ireland* (Cork: Cork University Press, 1998), p. 9.

3 Cormac O'Grada, *Jewish Ireland in the Age of Joyce: A Socioeconomic History* (Princeton: Princeton University Press, 2006).

4   Keogh, *Jews in Twentieth-century Ireland*, p. 54.

5   Keogh, *Jews in Twentieth-century Ireland*, p. 28.

6   Des Ryan, 'The Jews of Limerick: Part Two', *The Old Limerick Journal*, 18 (1985), pp. 36–40.

7   Arthur Griffith, 'Editorial', *United Irishman*, 13 January 1904.

8   Bryan Fanning, *Racism and Social Change in the Republic of Ireland* (Manchester: Manchester University Press, 2012), p. 77.

9   Louis Lentin, 'Grandpa ... Speak to Me in Russian', *Translocations*, 3:1 (2008), pp. 153–63.

10 Theophilis Ejorh, 'African Immigrant Experiences of Racism, Adaptation and Belonging', in Bryan Fanning and Ronaldo Munck (eds), *Globalisation, Migration and Social Transformation: Ireland, Europe and the World* (London Ashgate, 2011), p. 148.

11 www.cso.ie.

12 Philip J. O'Connell and Frances McGinnity, *Immigrants at Work: Ethnicity and Nationality in the Irish Labour Market* (Dublin: Economic and Social Research Institute, 2008), p. ix.

13 Frances McGinnity, Philip O'Connell, Emma Quinn and James Williams, *Migrants' Experience or Racism and Discrimination in Ireland: Survey Report'*, (Dublin: Economic and Social Research Institute, 2006).

14 European Union Agency for Fundamental Rights, *European Union Minorities and Discrimination Survey: Main Results Report* (December 2009).

15 Bryan Fanning, Brian Killoran and Saorlaith Ní Bhroin, *Taking Racism Seriously: Migrants' Experiences of Violence, Harassment and Anti-Social Behaviour in the Dublin Area* (Dublin: Immigrant Council of Ireland, 2011), p. 21.

16 Roddy Doyle, *The Deporteess and Other Stories* (London: Jonathan Cape, 2007), p. xii.

17 Bryan Fanning, Kevin Howard and Neil O'Boyle, 'Immigrant Candidates and Politics in the Republic of Ireland: Racialization, Ethnic Nepotism or Localism?', *Nationalism and Ethnic Politics*, 16:3 (2011), p. 431.

18 Oliver Scharbrodt and Tuala Sakaranaho, 'Islam and Muslims in the Republic of Ireland: An Introduction to the Special Issue', *Journal of Muslim Minority Affairs*, 31:4 (2001), p. 476.

19 Orla McGarry, 'Identity Formation among Teenaged Members of the Muslim Population of Ballyhaunis, Co. Mayo', PhD, National University of Ireland, Galway, 2012.

20 Oliver Scharbrodt, 'Shaping the Public Image of Islam: The Shiis of Ireland as "Moderate" Muslims', *Journal of Muslim Minority Affairs*, 3:1 (2011), pp. 518–33.

21 Edwin McGreal, 'Ballyhaunis Ireland's Most "Cosmopolitan" Town', *Mayo News*, 8 October 2012.

22 McGarry, 'Identity Formation', p. 237.

23 Claire Healy, 'Carnaval Do Galway: The Brazilian Community in Gort, 1999–2006', *Irish Migration Studies in Latin America*, 4:3 (2006), pp. 150–3.

24 *Independent on Sunday*, 10 October 2004.

25 For case studies of migrant worker exploitation see www.mrci.ie.

26 Tony Fahey and Bryan Fanning, 'Immigration and Socio-spatial Segregation in Dublin, 1996–2006', *Urban Studies*, 47:8 (2010), pp. 1625–42.

27 Bryan Fanning, Trutz Haase and Neil O'Boyle, 'Well-being, Cultural Capital and Social Inclusion: Immigrants in the Republic of Ireland', *Journal of International Migration and Integration*, 12:1 (2011), pp. 1–24.

28 Bryan Fanning and Neil O'Boyle, 'Immigrants in Irish Politics: African and East European Candidates in the 2009 Local Government Elections', *Irish Political Studies*, 25 (2010), p. 425.

29 www.cso.ie.

16

Conflict and reconciliation in Northern Ireland

Joseph Ruane

On 2 December 2012 Belfast City Council decided by majority vote to cease flying the Union Jack over City Hall every day of the year and to fly it on just eighteen, designated days. The pressure for change came from the nationalist parties on the council, Sinn Fein and the Social Democratic and Labour Party (SDLP), who had not wanted it flown at all. The agreement to fly it on designated days only was a compromise to secure the support of the middle-ground Alliance Party. The proposal to change the practice was opposed by the unionist parties on the council, the Democratic Unionist Party (DUP) and Ulster Unionist Party (UUP). The change triggered the most serious loyalist protests since the Good Friday Agreement (GFA) of 1998. They lasted almost three months and involved thousands of protesters. There were nightly riots, roads were blocked, cars were burned, and police were attacked using bricks and petrol bombs. The police responded with water cannon and plastic bullets and over two hundred arrests. Members of the Alliance Party were targeted with death threats and attacks on their homes and offices. The unionist parties initially encouraged protest, but then distanced themselves while continuing to condemn the decision of the council. By February the impetus was fading and protests were on a decreasing scale. Violence returned during the summer of 2013, this time about the banning or rerouting of marches.[1]

The intensity of the protests shocked local observers and there was much comment about the politics of working-class loyalists and the tensions created by the 'nationalist equality agenda'. The protests also surprised external observers (had this conflict not been resolved?) and renewed their perception of Ireland's distinctiveness, as least as far as religion was concerned. From the outset of the Troubles their question had been: how was it possible that Catholics and Protestants were still killing each other in any part of Europe today? The response that the differences were ethnic and political rather than religious rarely changed their view that this was a conflict out of its time that made little sense. It may be a conflict out of its time but, as will become clear, it makes a lot of sense to those who have no choice but to deal with the legacies of history.

The disturbances shocked because they called into question the assumption that the GFA had addressed the root cause of the conflict and that reconciliation was now under way. It was possible to downplay their significance by pointing out, for example, the manipulative role of the DUP seeking to reclaim a parliamentary seat it had lost to the Alliance Party, or the socially marginal background of the protestors. But it was also possible to see the events as an indication of just how fragile the peace was. The more optimistic could point to the declining incidence of personal violence, the increased Catholic support of the police, the growth in inter-school programmes, the advanced level of integration of workplaces. The more pessimistic could point to the continuing (and perhaps increasing) tendency for the communities to live apart, the increase in the numbers of peace walls, conflicts about parades, disputes about housing and the lack of progress in dealing with the past.[2] The pessimistic view was reinforced when the Haass Talks, convened in September 2013 to resolve remaining difference on flags, marches and the past ended in December without agreement.

In 1998 the Good Friday Agreement was presented as a historic breakthrough, one that would bring to an end centuries of conflict between Britain and Ireland and between Protestants and Catholics in Ireland. Few expected it to do all of that, but it generated considerable optimism. It accomplished a lot: it gave permanence to the loyalist and republican ceasefires, brought Sinn Fein fully into the political process and provided the two communities with a set of principles and an institutional framework to regulate their affairs. But it did not end the conflict, and now disagreement about what the Agreement implies, particularly in the matter of equality, is itself producing conflict.

A long history of conflict

To understand what the GFA achieved and why it did not achieve more, it is necessary to go back to the origins of the conflict because it was then that the conflict took a shape that it has retained until very recently. The goal of the Crown during the sixteenth and seventeenth centuries was to reconstruct Ireland politically, economically and religiously.[3] From the 1570s colonisation was used as a policy instrument. In the century that followed, ownership of the land and control of the institutions of state were transferred to English and Scottish Protestant settlers; formal plantation was reinforced by immigration; and towns and villages were established to act as nodes from which assimilatory influences would spread outwards. The extent of native displacement varied. In most areas it affected

primarily the higher classes, but in Ulster it took place at all levels.[4] The original
goals were largely achieved: state structures were established, the economy was
opened up, a coherent land system was put in place, Anglicanism became the
established religion and English the dominant language. The manner in which this
was done carried a price, however: permanent ethno-religious division and a
crisis-prone social and political order.

A key component of the new political order was a triangular set of geopolitical
relationships: Britain controlled Ireland through the loyal Protestant minority
whose privileges it underwrote; in return they kept the disloyal Catholic majority
in check.[5] On the ground this meant ethnically and religiously distinct communities living side by side with differential access to power and resources. The quality
of local relationships varied but the risk of conflict increased at times of competition for resources and of heightened political or religious tension. The religious
dimension was intertwined with the colonial one: Catholics saw Protestants as
heretics, interlopers and usurpers; Protestants remained conscious of their
different ancestry and what their fate would be if the Catholic majority ever got the
upper hand. The British government was mindful of the danger of Catholic disaf-
fection, but for a time the threat seemed minimal: with their military capacity
destroyed, Catholics were politically quiescent for most of the eighteenth century;
even in Ulster, local conflict was agrarian more often than religious.[6]

The limits of the Catholic (and dissenting Protestant) military capacity and the
cost of unsuccessful rebellion were evident in 1798 when the rebellion of the
United Irishmen ended in defeat and retribution and in a political outcome – the
Act of Union – that was the exact opposite to what had been intended. Catholic
politics in the nineteenth century were more cautious and, within those limits,
more successful. Insurrections were rare and on a minute scale. Instead the
emphasis was on harnessing the weight of Catholic numbers and bringing it to bear
on Parliament, but drawing also on the allure of past revolutions and the threat of
mass disorder.[7] There were failures (the repeal movement collapsed in 1843 in the
face of military threat) and long drawn-out delays, but the gains were real: Catholic
emancipation (1829), tithe reform (1838), disestablishment of the Church of
Ireland (1869), land reform (a succession of increasingly radical acts from 1870 to
1903), local government reform (1898), a National University under Catholic
control (1908) and finally Home Rule (1914).[8] The Catholic recovery may suggest
a single-minded project consciously and consistently pursued. In fact, for much of
the period Catholic politics was grievance-driven rather than project-led. But
Catholics had an enormous store of grievances, and no sooner was one met than
another one emerged. Also, the more they acquired the means to address their
grievances, the more they discovered they had. This happened in a geographically
uneven way: in Protestant-majority east Ulster, and in particular in industrialising
Belfast, the Catholic economic and demographic position was weakening.[9]

The confrontation between nationalism and unionism in the early twentieth century was no mere clash of constitutional preferences: it was a power struggle between two culturally and religiously distinct communities with different historic identities pursuing radically opposed political projects. Relying on their numbers and a disciplined political party to exploit the balance of power at Westminster, nationalists finally secured a limited form of Home Rule in 1914. Only the unionists of Ulster had any hope of resisting this, and then simply its application to the north-east of the island. They dismissed claims about its constitutionality and threatened armed rebellion if any attempt was made to impose it on them. The First World War changed the situation, allowing unionists to reaffirm their loyalty and militant nationalists to escalate the demand for Home Rule into a political and military campaign for independence.

The persistence of conflict

The partition settlement of 1921 represented a radically new departure for nationalists in the South; in the North the new geopolitics bore a distinct resemblance to the old. The major difference was that Protestants were now the majority community and could control the state through the ballot box. But their state – and therefore their dominant position – survived only because it had the support of the British state. Initially this was primarily political; later it was also economic. As their predecessors had done before them, they defended their position by restricting Catholic access to power and to the leading sectors of the economy. The Irish government denounced partition and discrimination, but offered no solution other than reunification. The British government was ill-disposed to intervene on the matter of discrimination, and there was no question of forcing unionists into a united Ireland.[10]

For four decades Northern Catholics sought a solution to their situation but made no impact in the face of unionist resistance. Then in a very short period of time – between 1968 and 1972 – they succeeded in destabilising the Northern state and then having it abolished altogether. It was achieved by new forms of politics, new levels of mobilisation and effective use of the new medium of television. The new tactics included a focus on 'civil rights' rather than on the traditional goal of Irish reunification, non-violent demonstration, the renewal of nationalist party politics in the form of the SDLP, communal rioting, and the campaign of violence of the Provisional IRA. Structural changes also played a role. Higher levels of education among Catholics produced more effective leaders while an expanded urban working class provided a plentiful supply of rioters and political and logistical support for the IRA. In contrast, the unionist position had been weakening. In particular the decline of traditional industry increased dependence on the British exchequer and heightened susceptibility to British government pressure.[11]

The devolved government set up in 1921 was dismantled in 1972 and the search began for a new one, this time one that would have the support of both communities. It took twenty-six years to secure and the delay cost more than 3500 deaths in a conflict that was at once a political conflict between nationalists and unionists, a civil conflict between two communities, each of which had its own paramilitaries, and a 'war' between the IRA and the British state. Why did it go on so long? An early and initially successful attempt – the power-sharing Sunningdale Agreement of 1973–74 – was brought down by a loyalist workers' strike supported by paramilitaries which brought the province to a standstill and led to the resignation of pro-agreement unionists from the power-sharing executive.[12] Subsequent attempts at a settlement failed until the GFA of 1998. The SDLP deputy leader Seamus Mallon famously described that agreement as 'Sunningdale for slow learners'. This is a widely shared view, but it misses a key difference between the two agreements: the relative emphasis paid to equality.

A major reason for the delay was that critical issues were at stake for both communities and neither could afford a disadvantageous settlement. For unionists the concern was to ensure the survival of Northern Ireland and their dominant position within it. Their greatest fear was of a British withdrawal, but, even if this was avoided, they could still face reforms that would gradually undermine their position. Their goal was to minimise the reforms and regain as much as possible of their previous control. For nationalists the situation was one of unprecedented opportunity, but it was also possible that the crisis would pass without real change. For most nationalists, the priority was to maximise the reforms without sacrificing the long-term goal of Irish unity. For a minority – republicans – the goal was British withdrawal and reunification.

A second factor delaying a settlement was the changing nature of the power balance. The British government was the major power-holder, but it needed local support. This had traditionally come from the unionist community and there were good reasons for continuing with this: unionists were the majority of the population, they controlled the key sectors of the economy, staffed the higher levels of the state, provided the vast bulk of the security forces, and identified with the state. There was also the risk of a full-scale Protestant revolt.[13] But the nationalist community could no longer be ignored. They had articulate and effective political leaders, the active support of the Southern government and of powerful Irish-American politicians, and the sympathy of international opinion. They also had a new capacity for violence, whether the unorganised street violence of stone-throwing and petrol-bombing or the targeted campaign of bombings and assassinations of the IRA. The military capacity of the IRA was tiny compared to that of the state – the British army, the RUC and the Ulster Defence Regiment (UDR) and Royal Irish Regiment (RIR) – and it had also to contend with collusion between the security forces and loyalist paramilitaries. But their campaign was sufficient to disrupt normal life, wreak havoc on the economy, provoke moral outrage, create the international image of Northern Ireland as a battle-zone and tarnish the image of Britain internationally. The campaign divided the Catholic population, alienated much of Southern Irish opinion and provoked a harsh security force and loyalist response. But it proved impossible to defeat.

These factors in combination brought about the single most important political development of the 1980s: British repositioning, away from its traditional alliance with unionists to a more neutral stance. At the end of the 1970s the political crisis was deepening, with no sign of political agreement and evidence that the elaborate security measures being taken against the IRA were further alienating moderate nationalists. The republican hunger strikes of 1981 and the political rise of Sinn Fein alarmed both governments, particularly the Irish one. British repositioning was made easier by the fact that the alliance was now a pragmatic affair that had little to do with identity or empathy. The Britishness affirmed by most unionists was very different from that in Britain itself, and its more vocal expressions – strident marches and flag-waving – were an embarrassment.

The process began with the opening of dialogue with the Irish government in 1980. After a difficult beginning it bore fruit in 1985 with the Anglo-Irish Agreement (AIA). The AIA gave the Irish government a formal consultative role in Northern Ireland's affairs and established an Irish government secretariat in Belfast. Whether the British government fully appreciated its significance at the time is open to debate; unionists certainly understood it and they reacted with shock and anger. They denounced it as a betrayal and tried to bring it down with boycotts, threats, legal action and appeals to the Crown.[14] But the change had been made and was soon given practical expression in the opening of the political process to nationalist viewpoints and in policies to reduce the extent of Catholic cultural and economic inequality. This included the repeal of the Flags and Emblems Act in 1987 and a much more effective fair employment act in 1989. Though equality legislation was not the only factor, it contributed to a narrowing of the gap between Protestants and Catholics across a range of socio-economic variables, in particular demography, employment and education.

All of this made for a very different political conjuncture in the 1990s and also made possible one of the principal differences between the GFA and the Sunning-dale Agreement: the emphasis on equality. Apart from political power-sharing, this had not been emphasised in the earlier agreement and any attempt to deal with it subsequently would have been blocked by the need for unionist agreement. Unionists had traditionally seen equality as a threat – as giving power to the 'enemy within' – but they could now amply find reassurance in the demonstrated British commitment to remain in Northern Ireland until a majority of its population decided otherwise; the vacillations of the early 1970s were a thing of the past. They got further reassurance: an end to the Republic of Ireland's territorial claim on Northern Ireland and to the IRA's armed campaign. Catholic reassurance about equality, and Protestant assurance of the security of the union, made agreement possible, and provided the building blocks for the Good Friday Agreement.

Peace without reconciliation

The GFA was a major achievement and the best – or close to it – that could be achieved in the circumstances. But it did not end conflict or bring reconciliation. Fringe republican groups are still engaged in violence; loyalist paramilitaries maintain a shadowy presence; there are sectarian attacks and controversies and commotions about flags and other issues.[15] Some commentators explain this in terms of the difficulty of transition: it will take time for the wounds to heal, the memories to become less painful, the situation to normalise and the new rules to gain universal acceptance. Others point to problematic aspects of the Agreement, in particular the insistence that members of the Assembly and the Executive identify themselves as 'nationalist', 'unionist' or 'other'. This, they argue, channels most elected representatives into the first or the second of these and sets politics on an oppositional course.[16]

Neither of these interpretations offers a sufficient explanation for current problems. There is a difficult legacy but it extends back farther than the past thirty years. The problem of difference is not simply one of institutional canalisation; it is the fact that it involves deep-rooted oppositions born of past religious war and colonial displacement. There is also the still contentious matter of inequality. Indeed this has now taken on a new level of complexity, with sharp differences as to whether it still exists, what form it takes, who suffers from it, how it should be addressed and what the Agreement implies in respect of it.

There is a tendency to downplay the difference between the two communities, to stress how diverse each is internally, how similar they are in their lifestyles, values and aspirations, and how these similarities are obscured by 'stereotypes', 'prejudices', 'myths' and 'outdated ideologies', which could be overcome by greater contact and communication.[17] The degree of similarity between the communities, particularly when class is factored in, is not in question. But this does not apply to their historic identities: how each understands its history and relationship to the other community over time. These identities include stereotypes and groundless beliefs. They have a mythic structure and were profoundly influenced by nineteenth-century nationalist ideologies. But they also have a rational core, an empirical basis, and their origins are much older than the nineteenth century.[18]

The historical narratives of the two communities are not simply different, they are radically opposed. The Catholic narrative is one of loss and suffering: their ancestors were pushed off their lands by Protestant settlers backed by a foreign power; they were oppressed because of their religion; their culture and language was destroyed; they endured political and economic discrimination; they were cut off from their co-nationals and treated as second-class citizens in a state lacking any legitimacy. The Protestant narrative is one of accomplishment and survival against an enduringly hostile Catholic community that still does not fully accept their right to be there: they came to Ulster in the seventeenth century, immigrants as well as settlers, at a time when the province was virtually a wilderness; they barely survived an early attempt to drive them out; they made the province their home, developed its resources and put their stamp on it; they defended their religion and culture and the United Kingdom against an ascendant Irish nationalism.[19]

The relationship of individuals to their community's core narrative is complex and varied. They differ in how much of it they know or identify with, whether they ever recite it, whether they are aware of its fictive component, how they learned it, whether and how they transmit it to the next generation. The variation depends in part on family and educational background and level of politicisation. Very often the details of the narrative are secondary to its intuitive aspects, its emotional colouring and the cultural and political assumptions on which it rests, and it is articulated only when the assumptions are challenged. Even then it may involve little more than vague references or even a slogan. There are many situations where it will not seem relevant, though an incident may occur which changes that. But whether in the foreground or background, the narratives form key components of communal and individual identities.

The GFA does not rule out identity transformation as a way of reconciling these narratives, but it neither proposes nor anticipates it. Its main concern is to ensure equality and mutual respect between the traditions and to prevent either from imposing itself on the other.[20] It is assumed that this will provide sufficient basis for reconciliation. Achieving mutual respect between identities that are so opposed, politicised and emotionally charged will not be easy. But there is also the problem of inequality, including how to get agreement on whether it exists, what form it takes, who suffers from it and how it should be dealt with.

The flags controversy shows how difficult this is. For the SDLP and Sinn Fein whether the Union Jack flew over City Hall was self-evidently an equality issue: it was the unionist flag, the symbol of a state with which they did not identify, and a (daily) reminder of their past subordination. In their view not flying it would make the building, in symbolic terms at least, a neutral and equal space. Accepting that it be flown on designated days was a serious compromise. In contrast, unionists and loyalists argued that whether the flag is flown is not a matter of equality: Northern Ireland is part of the United Kingdom, it is the national flag and it should be flown on public buildings. On the other hand, it is also the flag of their community and any restriction on its use signalled a loss in their control of public space and a nationalist advance. There were also unionists who were unconcerned about the new restrictions, but objected to the way the decision was made: by majority vote rather than by agreement. For them, there was inequality in the way the change was made.

The flags issue is just one of a multiplicity of similar actual or potential disputes, all of which arise in one way or another from the centuries of Protestant dominance and the heavy British (and Protestant) imprint on the public culture of

Northern Ireland. As far as nationalists are concerned the commitment to equality in the GFA requires some diminution of this. The question is how much. A minimalist version would allow nationalists to express their identity and be protected from the overly aggressive expression of British culture, while the overarching culture remained British. A more radical version is that the Britishness of Northern Ireland would be substantially diluted, if not undone altogether. This could apply to particular spaces or to the culture as a whole, to surface-level features or to its deeper layers.

Loyalists and traditionalist unionists already have difficulty with the minimalist version, both in principle and in practice; they are completely opposed to the radical one, not simply because they want to retain a public culture constructed in their image but because they are convinced that diluting its Britishness would undermine the foundations of the state. They also believe that this is the reason nationalists want it. This is certainly the motivation of some, but by no means all. Some disclaim interest in equality defined in narrowly communal terms. Others want their immediate grievances addressed and are not thinking beyond that. Others are satisfied as long as Britishness is not imposed on them; they may see a flag on a public building as an example of that, but not necessarily. Others want an advanced level of equality, but not as a way of undermining the union.

At the moment it is loyalists and traditionalist unionists who are most concerned about what they describe as the 'nationalist equality agenda'. Their sense of Britishness is heavily symbol-based and public and assertive in style, and the new restrictions have immediate implications for them. The Britishness of other strata has a wider range of references and is more lifestyle and institutionally-based. But more radical change would impact on them as well. The prospect of even greater loyalist violence might discourage nationalists from pushing things to that point, though it could have the opposite effect, and they could respond in kind. The root of the problem is that what loyalists see as an attack on their culture and community, nationalists see as an attempt to recover from decades, indeed centuries, of subordination and marginalisation.

Any hope of agreement depends on the willingness to compromise. The problem is that it tends to be the uncompromising 'extremes' rather than the 'moderates' who set the political agenda. The DUP and Sinn Fein are no longer at the extreme ends of the political spectrum but they are some distance from the centre, and there are systemic as well as party strategic reasons why this will continue. One proposal is to refashion the political institutions so as to allow a more diverse range of political opinion to express itself. However, this underestimates the tendency to division and the extent to which the positions adopted by the 'extremes' also resonate with the 'moderates'. A different hope is that a 'Northern Irish' identity will come to replace the polarisation of 'British' and 'Irish'. This is already a tendency but its stability and significance are unclear – whether it will continue, whether those who identify with 'Northern Irish' mean the same thing by it and whether it co-exists with or replaces the other identities.[21]

Conclusion

Viewed in the light of the historic conflict, the Good Friday Agreement was a breakthrough in one very important respect: the role of the British state, which moved away from its traditional alliance with the Protestant/unionist community and committed itself to establishing communal equality. This has opened up new possibilities. However, this has not undone other embedded sources of conflict – in particular the depth of the cultural oppositions and the conflicts of identity; and the principle of equality on which it is hoped to build a permanent peace is now another source of conflict. For the moment the hope for reconciliation has dimmed and there is increasing concern about the future. The challenge is to find ways of containing current conflicts while searching for new points of possible intervention.

Notes

1   For links to newspaper articles from this and other periods, see the archives section of www.irishcentral.com/news/nuzhound.

2   For a comprehensive annual survey of the state of Northern Ireland, see Paul Nolan, *Northern Ireland Peace Monitoring Report, Number Two* (Belfast: Community Relations Council, 2013), www.community-relations.org.uk/. For academic assessments, see Michael Cox, Adrian Guelke and Fiona Stephen (eds), *A Farewell to Arms? Beyond the Good Friday Agreement*, 2nd ed. (Manchester: Manchester University Press, 2006), 'Symposium on Northern Ireland: Special Edition', *Political Quarterly*, 83:2 (2012) pp. 201–98.

3   Nicholas Canny, *Making Ireland British 1580–1650* (Oxford: Oxford University Press, 2003); John P. Montaño, *The Roots of English Colonialism in Ireland* (Cambridge: Cambridge University Press, 2011).

4   Liam Kennedy and Philip Ollerenshaw (eds), *Ulster since 1600: Politics, Economy, and Society* (Oxford: Oxford University Press, 2013).

5   Joseph Ruane and Jennifer Todd, *The Dynamics of Conflict in Northern Ireland: Power, Conflict and Emancipation* (Cambridge: Cambridge University Press, 1996).

6   Sean J. Connolly, *Religion, Law and Power: The Making of Protestant Ireland 1660–1760* (Oxford: Oxford University Press, 1992).

7   Tom Garvin, *The Evolution of Irish Nationalist Politics* (Dublin: Gill and Macmillan, 1981).

8   D.G. Boyce, *Ireland, 1828–1923: From Ascendancy to Democracy* (Oxford: Blackwell, 1992).

9   A.C. Hepburn, *A Past Apart: Studies in the History of Catholic Belfast, 1850–1950* (Belfast: Ulster Historical Foundation, 1996).

10 For good analytical overviews of the history of Northern Ireland in the twentieth century, see Jonathan Tonge, *Northern Ireland: Conflict and Change*, 2nd ed. (Harlow: Longman, 2002); Paul Dixon, *Northern Ireland: The Politics of Peace and War*, 2nd ed. (Houndmills: Palgrave Macmillan, 2008).

11 For a detailed study of the 1969–73 period, see William Beattie Smith, *The British State and the*

Northern Ireland Crisis 1969–73 (Washington, DC: United States Institute of Peace, 2011).

12   Don Anderson, *14 May Days: The Inside Story of the Loyalist Strike of 1974* (Dublin: Gill and Macmillan, 1994).

13   Anthony Craig, *Crisis of Confidence: Anglo-Irish Relations in the Early Troubles* (Dublin: Irish Academic Press, 2010), p. 194.

14   For a recent assessment, see Arthur Aughey and Cathy Gormley-Heenan (eds), *The Anglo-Irish Agreement: Rethinking Its Legacy* (Manchester: Manchester University Press, 2011).

15   On dissident republicans, see P.M. Currie and Max Taylor (eds), *Dissident Irish Republicanism* (New York: Continuum, 2011).

16   See Robin Wilson, *The Northern Ireland Experience of Conflict and Agreement: A Model for Export?* (Manchester: Manchester University Press, 2010).

17   For an example, see Brian Walker, *Dancing to History's Tune: History, Myth and Politics in Ireland* (Belfast: Institute of Irish Studies, 1997).

18   Joseph Ruane, 'The Core of Reason in Irish Reversions', *Anthropology Today*, 12.6 (1996), pp. 1–2.

19   For nationalist and unionist narratives and references, see Ruane and Todd, *Dynamics of Conflict*, pp. 87–89, 146–8, 175–7, 200–3.

20   See 'Declaration of Support' section of the Agreement: http://cain.ulst.ac.uk/events/peace/docs/agreement.htm.

21   For the changes over time, see Northern Ireland Life and Times reports, www.ark.ac.uk/nilt. Survey data of this kind have to have to be handled with caution since the questions asked change over time and provide no information on the meaning of the terms for the respondents.

# 17

Irish language, Irish nation

Iarfhlaith Watson

Nearly half the country speaks Irish. Erroneous as this statement may appear, results from the 2011 Census indicate that 42 per cent of the population of the Republic of Ireland can speak Irish.[1] The figure has been this high since the 1990s and had doubled since the 1970s.[2] Most people in Ireland would suspect the accuracy of this figure and would believe that few people can speak Irish. Why then do so many people claim to be able to speak Irish? The answer appears to lie in the connection between the Irish language and the Irish nation.

The high percentage in the census claiming to be able to speak Irish is an indication of the symbolic importance of the Irish language. The situation of Irish provides an opportunity to examine a symbolic aspect of the nation. Across the world, language and nation are intertwined, reinforcing each other. In most contexts the 'national' language is used in daily communication. In these contexts the practice and its symbolic importance for the nation are intertwined. For the Irish nation, the English language is the dominant means of communication. Despite this, Irish is given a prominent position within the nation. This symbolic position of Irish, in contrast to the reality of its limited use in daily communication, provides an opportunity to examine this symbolic aspect of the nation.

What is the relationship between the Irish language and Irish nation? This question will be addressed in this chapter by unravelling the concept of nation and discussing the emergence of the Irish nation. I will then consider the benefits of that relationship for the speakers of the language and for its continued use.

What is a nation?

Defining a nation from the objective stance of a researcher can provide lists of characteristics based around language and religion, as well as around characteristics such as music, sport, literature or even food. Research into the subjective views of members of the nation provides deeper insight into the nation. In clarifying what a nation is, Walker Connor argued that a nation is a group of people, and what that group of people believe to be the case is more important than what a researcher might consider to be the reality.[3] For this reason a nation can be understood from the subjective position of its members.

Research into subjective perspectives of members of the nation allows the researcher to understand how a nation is self-defined and how emotions around identity and belonging are important. This also helps to clarify some of the confusion which arises around the relationship between the nation and state, as well as the confusion around ethnicity and the origins of the nation. With an understanding of subjective perspectives, the researcher comes to recognise how culture is important to the nation, and how culture relates to notions of homogeneity, common descent and consanguinity. Finally, the researcher can gain an understanding of who the 'other' is against whom the nation is defined.

Perhaps the simplest way to define the nation is to say that a nation is a group of people who claim to be a nation because they share some characteristics which they can employ in an argument that they are entitled to some level of political autonomy within some territory. The emphasis here is primarily on the people, and, through them, on the culture, the state and the land.

A number of important points issue from this definition. As the nation is the source of legitimacy for the nation-state, gaining the support of the people depends on the idea of the nation resonating with them. This is particularly important at the time of a nationalist movement for independence, when the nation is defined. This is a time when those definitions of the nation must resonate with the masses to encourage them to participate in the nationalist movement. This is a time when the resources of history are employed to assemble the nation; to determine the ancient origins of the nation; to identify the cultural components of the nation in opposition to a significant other; to argue that this nation has an ancient connection to the landscape and is therefore entitled to some level of political autonomy over that specific territory.

What is the Irish nation?

The resources of history were garnered and used to create an Irish nation during the long nineteenth century, which was the peak period of the initial emergence of nations and nationalism in Europe. There are three phases in the emergence of the Irish nation from the eighteenth to the twentieth centuries, which we can discover in the work of John Hutchinson.[4] In the eighteenth century there was a Celtic revival, in the nineteenth century there was a wider ethno-cultural revival, which, in the late nineteenth century, was developed into cultural and political nationalist movements.

In the eighteenth century some individuals from what might be called the 'colonial' Protestant minority of English and Scottish descent – particularly from among the prelates, country gentleman, professional men, lords and so forth – engaged in a kind of Celtic revival in Ireland. During that time organisations, such as the Royal Irish Academy, which were concerned with the study of antiquities were established. At the heart of this revival was the love of ancient heritage. This revival could promote Ireland's cultural distinctiveness from Britain and perhaps also help to unite the people of Ireland despite religious difference. The Celtic revival had the potential to unite both Catholic and Protestant in the love of ancient Celtic antiquities and culture. This was a kind of colonists' patriotic nationalism, in which there was an identification with Ireland and an objection to London's efforts to subordinate the Irish Parliament and Irish trade to British interests. Even after the Acts of Union (1800) efforts continued to try to uncover evidence of the former high civilisation – a source of dignity for the elite in Ireland (in rivalry with their compatriots in England).

In the nineteenth century there was a wider ethno-cultural revival. During this time many artefacts were discovered, such as the Tara Brooch and the Ardagh Chalice. The focus of this revival was on a perceived golden age which had occurred from the eighth to the eleventh centuries and which had been destroyed by the Anglo-Norman invasion. The focus on an earlier golden age is a common feature of nationalist movements. In Ireland, in the middle of the nineteenth century, this was a cultural, and not yet a political, nationalism. Its main objectives were to protect Irish culture from Anglicisation and to unite Catholics and Protestants. An important element of this outlook came from German Romantic nationalism (e.g. the work of Johann Gottfried von Herder, 1744–1803), in which there was a belief that the landscape can shape national personality, culture and nation and that there is a national life force which must be regenerated in each generation. In Ireland (as in other emerging nations) the project included archaeologists, historians, painters, poets and so forth, to re-create the culture which had existed in the sacred time of the pre-Norman golden age and the sacred place of the West of Ireland, especially the Aran Islands, where the sacred culture still existed. The discoveries of round towers, Celtic crosses, brooches, chalices and manuscripts all provided new symbols for the emerging Irish national identity. The English language and British socio-political values would be maintained, but infused with a Celtic heritage. In the mid-nineteenth century there were local antiquarian societies throughout the country which used these new Celtic symbols, but they were local symbols used in a wider British patriotism.

The religious cleavage continued and, although some Protestants were involved in nationalist movements in the late nineteenth century, forming cultural nationalist movements in crafts, agriculture and the arts (for example, Yeats's literary revival), the Catholic majority became increasingly involved in nationalist movements, thanks to their increasing liberty, both democratic (for example, in local government) and intellectual (for example, in the Catholic University where there were professorships in archaeology, in Irish and so forth). The new national-ist project aimed at constructing a nation which would be Irish-speaking, rural and Catholic. This nationalist movement took over the Celtic revival symbols, myths and heroes to imagine this new Irish nation. Hutchinson argued that this project influenced the emerging small-town, lower-middle-class intelligentsia, who were the main organisers of the newly established Gaelic Athletic Association and the Gaelic League, rather the urbanites. In the early twentieth century the movement for political independence intensified and employed this newly constructed idea of the nation.

In 1922 the Irish Free State was established (following the war of independence, 1919–21). In the period since then there are three identifiable phases.[5] The initial phase from the 1920s to the 1950s was a period of the mass nation. During this time the state attempted to impose the characteristics of the new nation on the population. This was a continuation and an intensification of the project of constructing the nation. Irish, as an aspect of this new nation, was imposed on the children in school, and the population as a whole was exposed to an increasing number of radio programmes in Irish. The effort was clearly to teach people to speak Irish, rather than providing education or radio programmes for those who could already speak Irish.

The second phase, from the 1950s to the 1980s, was a period during which the emphasis on the mass nation began deteriorating and elements of minority rights began to emerge. By the 1950s it was apparent that the major political, economic and cultural elements of the new nation had not been successful. As a result of this, many of these elements were de-emphasised and minoritised during the 1960s and 1970s. This was a shift from the idea of making the nation anew which had been evident in Ireland and many other countries at various times since the late eigh-teenth century. Although elements of the mass nation continued to be in evidence, the emphasis shifted to regarding these as national symbols which, although still of national importance, were embodied within smaller groups.

The minority-rights phase meant that the individual was considered a member of a group with a particular characteristic. Since the 1980s there has been a shift in emphasis to individual rights, in which the individual can practise national charac-teristics. Although the previous two phases, of the mass nation and minority rights, continue to be in evidence, the current phase has introduced more individual choice in the matter of practising these national symbols.

What is the relevance of the Irish language?

The Irish language has been one of the principal aspects of the Irish nation since its construction in the nineteenth century. This connection between language and nation can be found in nation after nation across the world. As the idea of the nation spread across the globe, language has been one of its primary components.

In Ireland, although Irish was spoken only by a minority, it became part of the evidence of the existence of an Irish nation. Part of the objective of making the Irish nation anew was to create an Irish-speaking nation.

By the eighteenth century Gaelic culture had declined to the extent that it was no longer a political threat. In that context an antiquarian interest in Gaelic culture was relatively innocuous. During the nineteenth century, however, as a political movement emerged, first in the form of Catholic emancipation, and later in the form of secession from Britain, the various historical, archaeological, folkloric and other discoveries could be employed as symbols in the construction of a new, but seemingly ancient, Irish nation.

Irish was employed as one of the key symbols of the Irish nation in opposition to Britain and to the English language and nation. However, as the Irish nation was being constructed in the late nineteenth century the number of Irish speakers was continuing to decline. Irish had survived as a native language in the remotest impoverished western extremities of Ireland. These are the areas where emigration was seriously reducing the population. By the beginning of the twentieth century there were perhaps only 250,000 Irish speakers in these areas. Despite an industrialisation plan in the 1970s, emigration continued to reduce the population in these areas (called the *Gaeltacht*). Explaining the situation at the time, the Minister for the Gaeltacht said 'no jobs, no people; no people, no Gaeltacht; no Gaeltacht, no language'.[6] In recent decades there have been only about sixty thousand Irish speakers remaining in the Gaeltacht areas (and only about 35,000 have the opportunity to speak Irish on a daily basis).[7] The connection between the Irish language and nation is primarily symbolic and has not been particularly beneficial for the native speakers.

Does the Irish language benefit from its connection with the nation?

The movement to revive Irish gained strength in the last decades of the nineteenth century, but had already begun to wane only five years into the twentieth century. Despite the waning of mass public participation in the revival of the language, the symbolic connection between the language and the nation resulted in the institutionalisation of language revival, particularly in education (for example in the National Universities of Ireland Act 1908 and in the school system, especially after 1922).

Thanks to its symbolic position Irish has spread throughout the rest of the population, particularly because of its central role in the education system. This means that, for several generations, virtually the whole population of Ireland has been exposed to many hours of learning Irish every week of every school year, with the result that there is a widespread ability in the population which ranges from people who can understand and speak a few words, all the way through to people who can speak Irish well. In that latter group there are at least 400,000 people. This has been confirmed by surveys by the Committee for Irish Language Attitude Research in 1973 and 1983, the Linguistics Institute of Ireland in 1993 and the International Social Survey Programme in 2003 and 2013.[8]

The intergenerational transmission of Irish within the family or the community in the Gaeltacht areas has been disrupted by emigration as well as by the increasing immigration into those areas of people who cannot speak Irish. Meanwhile, outside the Gaeltacht, the number of secondary bilinguals, for whom the principal means of the intergenerational transmission of Irish has been the education system, has increased to more than 400,000 people. Most of these Irish speakers do not live in Irish-speaking families or communities. This means that the survival of Irish from generation to generation is now dependent largely on the education system to produce non-native speakers with minimal opportunity to speak the language.

There are two ways in which the connection between Irish and the nation has helped to produce Irish speakers. The first, institutional way, as mentioned above, is the strong position of Irish in the education system. The second, individual way, is the strong attitudinal support for the language. This support, which emerged with the construction of the Irish nation in the nineteenth century, is still evident in many surveys over the last forty years, but is most evident in the census figure with which this chapter began. The evidence suggests that about 10 per cent or even 15 per cent of the population can speak Irish well, and yet about three times that many people are returned on the census as being able to speak Irish. The census figure includes not only those who can speak Irish well, but also those who can participate in bits of conversations or those who have only a few words, as well as those who are learning Irish at school. The other questions on the census about how often people speak Irish demonstrate, however, that many of them never speak Irish. Of course it is also the case that many of those who can speak Irish well rarely have the opportunity to speak Irish. The point here is that the high percentage in the census is an indication of a positive attitude towards the language. The positive attitude to Irish, and the hundreds of thousands of people who can speak Irish well, are in no small part thanks to the connection between the Irish language and the Irish nation which was made when the Irish nation was being constructed in the nineteenth century.

What benefits arise from the connection between the Irish language and nation?

Many authors who study nations and nationalism point to the importance of intellectuals in the emergence and construction of nations.[9] The particular intellectuals involved were mainly young middle-class men. Because of their Western secular education, they were in a position to discover, appreciate and promote national culture, history, archaeology, folklore and so forth. Their unearthing of the national culture was central to the construction of the new nation. They looked back to a former golden age for that nation and attempted to construct a version of it in the present. Their education, however, also separated them from those who were perceived to be the living embodiments of the national culture which had been passed down to them through the generations.

The promotion of national characteristics meant that those who had or who could adopt these characteristics could be in a position to gain an advantage. In the case of Irish the institutionalisation of its revival in state examinations, in promotion in the civil service and in entry to university implied that Irish speakers could gain an advantage. These advantages, however, are mainly in the domain of the middle class. It is not an Irish-speaker advantage, but rather a middle-class advantage. Middle-class students who can attend good schools and get good results in examinations can do well in all their subjects including Irish.[10] Most of these Irish speakers, even most of those in all Irish schools, do not come from Irish-speaking families.

These advantages have diminished since the 1970s. For example, in 1973 the requirement to pass Irish in the leaving certificate examination was removed and in 1974 the requirement for proficiency in Irish for recruits to the civil service was removed. These were vestiges of the period of the mass nation. Another vestige of the mass nation was extensive education in Irish, but by 1970 many of the schools which had provided education primarily in Irish had closed or had changed to providing education primarily in English. Since then the number of Irish-language schools established, mainly by groups of parents, has increased dramatically (particularly primary schools).[11] Although this increase has been mainly in middle-class areas, there have been a number of Irish-language schools opened in working-class areas since the 1980s.

Being able to speak Irish had advantages in state examinations, entry to university, public-sector employment and promotion and so forth, but this advantage, while not evident in the Gaeltacht, where Irish is the language of family and community, has not required a high level of fluency. Furthermore, the advantages that were there for those who could acquire the rudiments of the language have diminished since the 1970s. In the late twentieth and early twenty-first centuries the advantages of speaking Irish are more symbolic than practical.

Are the Irish different?

The uniqueness of the Irish is a central aspect of the nation. This uniqueness became part of the school curriculum and has been taught to school children for generations. It has also become part of everyday life. This is what Michael Billig called banal nationalism – the way the nation is 'flagged' in national news, in national weather forecasts or in everyday national symbols such as flags and coins.[12] The education system and the mass media help to sustain the image of the Irish as a unique nation.

The world is full of nations, and the Irish are not unique for being a nation. The uniqueness of any nation lies in the content or the characteristics of the nation. This is one of the main points about nations: they are simultaneously universal and unique. Nations are universal because there is a general expectation, in this world of nation-states, that everyone should be a member of a nation. At the same time, nations are unique because, while each individual is expected to be a member of a nation, everyone in the world is not expected to be part of the same nation, and each nation is expected to contain different characteristics.

Groups of people as large as nations tend to be quite diverse. An important aspect of the construction of nations is to homogenise that group of people, to establish a set of characteristics which can differentiate that nation from an 'other'. The state (except for stateless nations) can (through legislation, education, communication etc.) facilitate the members of the nation to embody national characteristics. This sharpens the difference at the cultural border between nations. Consequently, national characteristics, such as the Irish language, receive support from nationalist mass movements and from the state. In most nations a national standardised language is imposed on all its members, even if they speak a dialect of that language or a different language altogether. The situation in Ireland is different because, although Irish has been imposed on children in school, Irish has not been fully standardised and the English language has remained the main language of the nation.

Nations use the resources of history, particularly symbolic resources, and in this case a minority language, to emphasise their difference from other nations. This opens up the interesting question of symbolic differences and differences in practice. The uniqueness of the Irish in terms of the Irish language and Catholicism appears to be connected to the nation in terms of their symbolic value rather than the actual practice of the language or religion. The uniqueness of the Irish nation is established primarily on symbols. The continuing value of the nation rests on national identity or the emotional attachment or belonging to the nation. People gain personal feelings of dignity and respect from the achievements of their nation or the achievements of individuals as embodiments of the nation, as well as from the positive image they believe their nation has in other parts of the world. These achievements can be in the past or the present, in a wide variety of arenas, such as art, literature, sports, economics or science. This dignity and respect, however, can also lead to pride and shame, which, in a tense international context, can be troublesome.

Recent developments in social-scientific research

Over the past decade or so a number of scholars have begun to examine the nation in everyday life.[13] They are beginning to uncover the various ways in which members of a nation identify with, or have a sense of belonging to, that nation.

There are not only differences between nations but also differences within nations. There are different patterns in the ways people deal with national pride and shame, which lead to different relationships with the nation or different manifestations of national identity. For some, in Ireland, Irish, as a kind of national treasure, is a source of dignity (regardless of their own level of fluency), but for others, as a symbol of a restrictive Irishness, it is almost a source of ignominy. This approach provides insights into how members of the nation identify with and reproduce the nation and how they compare that to what they presume to be the ideal of the nation. This can give us a more nuanced understanding of nations and national identity and can allow us to examine the subtleties and diversity of nations as they exist and as they change.

There has also been a growing interest in cosmopolitanism over the past decade.[14] From this perspective, Irish could be considered a cultural treasure of the world, rather than an exclusive symbol of the Irish nation. At the heart of cosmopolitanism is the belief in the equal moral worth of each human being. This clashes with the exclusivity of nations and nationalism. An interesting development to watch is how the tension is resolved in everyday life between the exclusivity of nationalism and the inclusivity of cosmopolitanism, without losing the solidarity and cultural preservation achieved within nations. Although nations have been the source of exclusion and conflict, they have also been a source of sufficient solidarity to facilitate democratic nation-states. Moreover, through processes of homogenisation, nations have devastated cultural diversity, while their preservation of national cultures has resulted in a global cultural patchwork. In a cosmopolitan world, what would be the source of solidarity, dignity and identity? Can we identify with humanity as a whole? What would be the source of the desire for cultural protection? Would the Irish language continue to exist if detached from the Irish nation?

Conclusion

The situation of Irish today is largely influenced by the relationship it has had with the nation. This relationship goes two ways: there can be an advantage for the Irish nation and an advantage for the Irish language. Initially the Irish nation gained most of the advantage. As the Irish nation was being constructed in opposition to Britishness and Englishness, the Irish language was a useful component. Central to the idea of nationalism is the proposition that each nation has its own language. Irish, despite its marginal status, was useful because it was something which could be used to distinguish the Irish nation from other nations. Efforts to revive Irish in the late nineteenth and early twentieth centuries were more symbolic than practical. In that context the Irish language provided symbolic support for the new Irish nation.

As a result of its relationship with the Irish nation, the Irish language gained symbolic importance as well as a number of practical supports. After Independence the Irish state undertook to support Irish in areas such as public-sector employment, radio and, particularly, education. The principal advantage here was increasing employment and educational opportunities mainly for the middle class. At the same time, despite efforts by the state, Irish continues to decline in those areas in which it had survived. Although the number of Irish speakers has increased over the past century, the number of fluent Irish speakers from Irish-speaking families in Irish-speaking communities has continued to decrease and is being replaced by people who have limited opportunities to speak the language.

Nations are a focus of identification; a source of solidarity, pride, dignity and inclusion; a cause of cultural – and in this case linguistic – preservation. Nations have also been a focal point of exclusion, shame, hatred, and cultural and linguistic destruction. With the advance of the forces of globalisation the consequence at the national level will require continuing research. Reactions in opposition to globalisation could mean support for nationalism and cosmopolitanism. Support for nationalism could mean the continuing symbolic importance of the Irish language for the Irish nation, but that would not necessarily translate into the practice of speaking, or even being able to speak, Irish. Support for cosmopolitanism could mean that Irish would be considered a linguistic treasure which belongs to humanity, but that might undermine the relationship between the Irish language and the Irish nation which appears to be supporting the continued survival of the language.

It is neither correct to say that nearly half the country speaks Irish, as the census suggests, nor correct to say that only one per cent or two per cent of the population speak Irish, as Gaeltacht figures would suggest. The Gaeltacht is the symbolic heart of the Irish language, but, unnoticed by most of the population, the number of Irish speakers outside the Gaeltacht have come to dwarf those within it. Thanks to its relationship with the Irish nation, the Irish language has considerable symbolic support, which has resulted in hundreds of thousands of relatively fluent speakers of the language.

Notes

1   Outside Ireland the Irish language is sometimes called Gaelic, but within Ireland it is always simply referred to as Irish.
2   Irish census figures are available from the Central Statistics Office at www.cso.ie/en/census both in reports and in interactive tables.
3   Walker Connor, 'A Nation Is a Nation, Is a State, Is an Ethnic Group, Is a …', *Ethnic and Racial Studies*, 1:4 (1978), pp. 377–400.
4   John Hutchinson, 'Archaeology and the Irish Rediscovery of the Celtic Past', *Nations and Nationalism*, 7:4 (2001), pp. 505–19.
5   Iarfhlaith Watson, *Broadcasting in Irish* (Dublin: Four Courts Press, 2003).
6   Patrick Commins, 'Socioeconomic Development and Language Maintenance in the

Gaeltacht', *Language Planning in Ireland: International Journal of the Sociology of Language*, 70 (1988), p. 14.

7 These figures were produced from Central Statistics Office's interactive tables at www.cso.ie/en/census.

8 The ISSP data on the Irish language results from questions I added to the questionnaire used in Ireland, therefore, the data are not available in the international dataset.

9 For a discussion of the role of intellectuals, particularly artists, in spreading the idea of the nation, see Anthony D. Smith, 'National Identity and Vernacular Mobilisation in Europe', *Nations and Nationalism*, 17:2 (2011), pp. 223–56.

10 For further discussion of the advantages of speaking Irish, see Iarfhlaith Watson and Máire Nic Ghiolla Phádraig, 'Is There an Educational Advantage to Speaking Irish? An Investigation of the Relationship Between Education and Ability to Speak Irish', *International Journal of the Sociology of Language*, 199 (2009), pp. 143–56; and Iarfhlaith Watson and Máire Nic Ghiolla Phádraig, 'Linguistic Elitism: The Advantage of Speaking Irish Rather than the Irish-speaker Advantage', *The Economic and Social Review*, 42:4 (2011), pp. 437–54.

11 A graph of the increasing number of Irish-language schools in the Republic of Ireland can be found in Iarfhlaith Watson, 'Identity, Language and Nationality', in Sara O'Sullivan (ed.), *Contemporary Ireland: A Sociological Map* (Dublin: University College Dublin Press, 2007), p. 367.

12 Michael Billig, *Banal Nationalism* (London: Sage, 1995).

13 There are interesting developments in the area of everyday nations in several places, e.g. Jon E. Fox on Hungary and Romania, Cynthia Millar-Idriss on Germany and Susan Condor on England see Jon E. Fox and Cynthia Miller-Idriss, 'Everyday Nationhood', *Ethnicities*, 8:4 (2008), pp. 536–76; Susan Condor, 'Temporality and Collectivity: Diversity, History and the Rhetorical Construction of National Entitativity', *British Journal of Social Psychology*, 45:4 (2006), pp. 657–82.

14 Although publications on cosmopolitanism have grown dramatically over the past decade, the idea has existed for millennia – in ancient Rome, Greece and perhaps even Egypt, but more famously in the work of Immanuel Kant (1724–1804). A comprehensive book on the topic is Garrett Wallace Brown and David Held (eds), *The Cosmopolitan Reader* (Cambridge: Polity, 2010).

18

The difference of Irish music

Martin Dowling

> The only thing to which I find that this people apply a commendable industry is
> playing upon musical instruments, in which they are incomparably more skilful than
> any other nation I have ever seen. For their modulation on these instruments, unlike
> that of the Britons to which I am accustomed, is not slow and harsh, but lively and
> rapid, while the harmony is both sweet and gay. It is astonishing that in so complex
> and rapid a movement of the fingers, the musical proportions can be preserved, and
> that throughout the difficult modulations on their various instruments, the harmony
> is completed with such a sweet velocity, so unequal an equality, so discordant a
> concord, as if the chords sounded together fourths or fifths.
>
> Geraldus Cambrensis, 'Of the incomparable skill of the Irish in playing upon
> musical instruments', chapter XI of *Topographia Hiberniae* (1187)

It is a peculiarity of the long historical encounter of foreigners with Ireland that,
however barbaric the Irish appeared, their music was always admired for its beauty
and intricacy, and their musicians for their skill and dexterity. In his study of the
performing arts in Ireland before Cromwell, Alan Fletcher found many observations on the peculiarly high musicality of an otherwise barbarous race, beginning
of course with the famous quotation from Giraldus reproduced above.[1] However,
this commentary tells us next to nothing about what Irish music sounded like in
the Gaelic epoch. We do know that some musicians were exalted and held
positions of power within society, acting as historians, propagandists, mediators
and educators, as well as entertainers. This explains why they attracted the
attention of the political and military enemies of the Gaelic aristocracy. But with
the incorporation of Ireland into an archipelago of kingdoms under the English
monarchy, the position of the harper gradually evolved, in Fletcher's estimation,
from a dangerous 'inciter to Gaelic sedition' to a domesticated 'cultural trophy'.[2]
While the culture surrounding it was destroyed and its players scattered across

Europe, the harp itself was paradoxically transformed into a symbol of monarchical rule, of the incorporation of the Irish polity into a large kingdom-wide structure and, eventually, into the British Empire. Irish musical excellence thus evolved from a marker of otherness (the curiously civilised characteristic of an otherwise barbarous other), to a symbol of difference within the unity of the kingdoms under the Crown. In this chapter, I will sketch the trajectory of Irish musical difference since the eighteenth century, and suggest why it is that the generally homogenizing forces of modernisation produced a peculiar outcome for Irish musical culture.[3]

Eighteenth-century music: modern or 'ancient'?

Throughout this long period of social change, music as a marker of Irish difference was preserved, even enhanced. In the eighteenth century, with Irish society under renegotiation at every level and settling itself on 'new foundations', a transition in attitudes towards the wild appearance and sounds of the countryside and its inhabitants began.[4] The stability and self-confidence that emerged in eighteenth-century colonial society afforded a more romantic and celebratory attitude toward the wild landscape and the inhabitants of remote districts. A new marvelling at the simple elegance of the other's lifestyle began to compete with the long-established habit of hectoring about 'improvement' of a barbaric culture. Historians find among educated Protestants 'a new attitude to the Gaelic portion of their cultural inheritance' resulting in a flood of evidence of the growing Anglo-Irish curiosity for, in the historian Toby Barnard's pithy abbreviation, 'crags, cliffs, and culture'.[5]

When the forces of economic and political modernisation of the late eighteenth century began to take hold in Ireland, the urge to articulate a distinct and competitive national cultural history fuelled a discourse on the distinctiveness of Ireland's 'ancient music'. Giraldus's observations became a touchstone for further elaboration. Works such as Charles O'Conor's *Dissertations on the History of Ireland* (1755), Joseph Cooper Walker's *Historical Memory of the Irish Bards* (1786) and Charlotte Brooke's *Reliques of Irish Poetry* (1789) pioneered the engineering of an Irish identity which had an essential musicality. O'Conor wrote of ancient Irish civilisation: 'All their systems, philosophical, metaphysical, and theological, were conveyed in the harmonious measures of sound and verse'. It was O'Conor who elevated the triumvirate of 'geantrai, golltrai, and suantrai' (music that provoked joy, mourning and calmness respectively) into a peculiarly Irish musical system of emotional expression. Walker's work, with its appendices of provincial cries and other 'ancient' material, endeavoured to clean up the tarnished reputation of the Irish bardic tradition, comparing it whenever possible to the nobility of ancient Greek civilisation, without effacing its uniqueness. This is the predicament of the late modernising culture: the requirement to be the same, that is, to be one of the modern nations, but also to be different from the others.[6] This period established a longstanding habit of characterising relatively recent creativity as ancient and timeless in character. The famous tune *Eibhlín A Rúin* (or *Ellen A Roon*) is a good example. A popular eighteenth-century item on both sides of the Irish Sea, this song was 'one of the few Irish tunes which successfully spanned three Irish music genres: that of the aristocratic courtly harp tradition, the Anglo-Irish tradition, and the folksong and folk music tradition'.[7] Modern scholarship attributes the poem to the early eighteenth-century Clare poet Cearbhall Ó Dálaigh. It is a typical instance of more complex medieval poetry refigured in popular song metre ('amhran metre') by the modern generation of Jacobite poets. Yet Ó Dálaigh, like his song, was transformed into an ancient figure soon after his death. Joseph Cooper Walker gave an account of the folklore surrounding the man and the song which erroneously placed him two centuries earlier in history. The late nineteenth-century music historian William Grattan Flood put him even further back, to the fourteenth century. Like Ó Dálaigh, the harper and composer Turlough Carolan began to be celebrated as an ancient bard, and his music characterised likewise, within a couple of decades of his death in 1738.

The 'difference' of Irish musical culture had therefore become, in the generation after Carolan's death, a complex and multifaceted phenomenon. A core problem was that Irish musicality, in its blunt empirical actuality in the eighteenth century, was undeniably different from its ancient origins. Many of the elements that eventually congealed into a coherent tradition, and that we now see as integral to the tradition, had yet to come into existence in 1760. One finds only the faintest of imprints in the written record of earlier musical culture on this formative period. A handful of 'ancient' harp tunes and Irish love songs, along with the output of Carolan and a few of his near contemporaries, were all that remained.[8] This predicament led to a century-long tradition, sponsored mainly by Anglo-Irish elites, which emphasised the preservation of ancient repertoire. When the actual musicians, singers and dancers of the country no longer served as the repository of that ancient repertoire, tradition was invented.[9] According to Joep Leerssen, who studied the nineteenth-century antiquarians in detail, when elites involved with the construction of Irishness faced 'a choice between the return to the pristine example of antiquity or the vigour of a living demotic tradition', they plumped for the former every time. 'The cultivation of the ancient, pre-Norman past,' Leerssen writes,

> with its aristocratic society and refined culture, intersects with ... the cultivation of the contemporary peasant, with his homely humours and artless charm. Despite their great differences, these two elements – past and present – become linked and even conflated because both represent an un-Anglicized, ideal Ireland ... past and present also meet because both are imagined as situated outside factual history: the one in a mythical prelapsarian past, the other in a dehistoricized chronotope situated in the margins of the world as we know it.[10]

This is not to deny cultural continuity across the ruptures and setbacks of the seventeenth century. The direct evidence of this continuity is not plentiful, but we can safely assume that a number of historical constants supported the continuity of musical practices which continued to be recognised as central to social life. Ireland's geographical and geopolitical position, its habitats and agricultural habits, the voices of its languages etc. all contributed to continuity. My point is to question, as Leerssen has done, the validity of the conception that Irish culture is somehow bifurcated, with one part constantly assimilating and accommodating itself first to the Empire and later to a broader globalised culture, and another part which never changes, serving as a repository of ancient essence. It is helpful to conceive 'tradition' as a modern phenomenon, not a phenomenon which predates or counterposes itself to modernity, as many commentators on Irish music do. Modernity, in this view, has the character of what the French *Annales* historians called a *longue durée*, where phenomena such as globalisation, secularisation, social differentiation and the expansion of commercial culture all have a history long predating the twentieth century.[11] Irish traditional music did not fortuitously survive from the ancient past in the periphery and on the margins of commercial civilisation. Rather, it was enlivened and expanded by the peculiar way in which Irish society responded to the dynamics of the age. Traditional music is not the survival of some ancient and timeless manifestation of the essence of Irishness, nor is it the shared symptom of a population mysteriously infected by and obsessed with its own 'Celtitude'. Rather, it is a modern pursuit that kept time with the dramatic modernisation of Irish society. The trajectory of Irish modernity runs simultaneously with the trajectory of the formation of what we now call 'Irish traditional music' as a constellation of forms and practices.

The modernity of the nineteenth-century tradition

The core problem I have been discussing is actually more difficult than the music being different from its ancient self. It was also continually developing throughout the modern epoch. Irish elites obsessed with preservation tended either to ignore or to misdiagnose these developments, often viewing the actual contemporary practice of music, song and dance by Irish people as *all too* modern. Let us return to the examples of Carolan and Ó Dálaigh, both operating in the gloaming just before the dawn of Irish modernity. Ó Dálaigh's song, along with a large repertoire of similar material, was produced in the combustible milieu in which Jacobite and Anglo-Irish cultures confronted each other.[12] Contrary to his first hagiographers, Carolan was in reality Ireland's first modern professional musician, composing in styles as eclectic and varied as his patrons, who spanned religious and class differences. He was 'a master-operator in an assortment of musical dialects, while still being seen as the arch-representative of the peripatetic harper'.[13] At the other end of the century, the United Irishmen saw literary and musical fields as important battlegrounds. The radical milieu in Trinity College which produced them also produced flute players, singers and poets like Henry Hudson and Wolfe Tone himself.[14] Another legacy of this milieu was Thomas Moore, who crafted a distinctively Irish repertoire of song by joining the 'ancient' melodies (many of which were drawn from 'modern' Jacobite song and dance melodies) with romantic lyricism.

At the end of the eighteenth century, one travel writer reported that 'the manners of the ancient Irish have been very much done away by the increase of English commercial civilisation; such of them as survived the lapse of time, or escaped the restraints of law, have prevailed chiefly in places remote from towns, and seldom resorted to for the purposes of traffic'.[15] This clearly Romantic viewpoint was not borne out by the evidence. The songs and their melodies produced within eighteenth-century Jacobite culture were incorporated into a greatly expanding corpus of music, invented by imaginative pipers and balladeers in both English and Irish in the following generations. The invention and refinement of the Irish pipes (later called the Uilleann pipes), the importation from Scotland of the reel dance form and the adaption of its fiddle techniques by Irish players, the invention of characteristically Irish steps and gestures by itinerant dancing masters – these are some of the significant new developments of the revolutionary period. If we are searching for Irish musical uniqueness, then we should look closely at this crucially formative period, characterised by importation, incorporation and development of various European forms, gestures and instruments. At the heart of these developments was the musical and social ascendancy of the Irish pipes and the pipers. They inherited the repertoire and the social function of the harpers who operated in close contact with dancing masters, singers in Irish and English, and fiddle players with Scottish tunes and techniques. On the eve of the Great Famine, George Petrie and James Goodman were collecting tunes almost exclusively from pipers. It is only after their repertoire began to be published in the late eighteenth century that we have a clearly and distinctly identified Irish in style of dance music, recognised today by session players across the globe.

Political defeat, the trauma of the Great Famine, the failure to industrialise and Ireland's off-the-chart demographic profile all helped to produce a unique musical culture which continued to develop in the nineteenth century. From the middle of the nineteenth century the pace of innovation was hectic. The quality of instruments rose while their price declined, and both virtuosity and music appreciation blossomed. There were other developments, including the incorporation of new free-reed instruments and new styles of ensemble playing. There were also rapid developments in dancing – even though the steps were regarded as unpalatably foreign and provoked ire from pulpit and op-ed column alike. When traditional music severed itself from its original context as accompaniment to dance, it did not only open up the development of musical material within the strict confines of its form. It also opened up the autonomous development of dance itself. Here perhaps lies the basis for the great flowering of creativity reflected in collections of dance music published in the late nineteenth and early twentieth centuries. Moving closer to the present, we have yet to place in meaningful perspective the creative revival of the third quarter of the twentieth century when composers such as Ed Reavy and Paddy O'Brien, amongst others, pushed back the boundaries of the form of the music, opening up terrain upon which contemporary composers Tommy Peoples and Liz Carroll have blossomed. This period is also characterised by important innovations in individual and ensemble playing: harmonic filling-in, creative use of both key changes and rhythm changes, new scenarios for perform-ance and a general elevation in the technical rationality of the instruments themselves and in the standards of the techniques used to play them.

Many of these developments were captured by the first recording technologies, and all were occurring in a transatlantic and increasingly urban context. This, after all, is the era of the 78 rpm recording. The dominant performance arrangement in Irish traditional music of three tunes played twice each, or two tunes played three times, corresponding roughly with one figure of a set dance, was devised to suit the 78 and has proved to be incredibly durable and marketable, lasting for decades longer than the 78 rpm format itself, and manifesting itself in a wide variety of live performance contexts from early vaudeville and radio to Riverdance-era specta-cles. Perhaps the most influential single recording in the history of Irish traditional music was one such three-minute selection, the renowned Sligo fiddle player Michael Coleman's recording of the three reels 'Tarbolton', 'The Longford Collector' and 'The Sailor's Bonnet' for Decca Records in 1934. Seventy-five years later, it is still not possible to play the first tune in a session without the other two following, nor is it possible to be recognised as a competent traditional musician without knowledge of these tunes.[16] In Ireland, the musical culture seemed to be neither 'modern' nor 'contemporary', and by the end of the century was given a new name: 'traditional'. The significance of this was generally not appreciated by elites whose sights were set on the ancient past, the impoverished western Irish seaboard and the possibilities for catching up with international art music by deploying new musical strategies such as gapped scales and peculiarly Irish intervals.

If the antiquarians of the revolutionary period were largely oblivious to the formative changes then in train, their descendants of the Revival era and after certainly were not. David Lloyd observed the confrontation between the hybrid and fragmented character of the enormous repertoire of ballads collected in the nineteenth century and the requirement of cultural nationalists that the culture should be 'monologic in its modes of expression'. Some demanded that the adulter-ated repertoire be purged of its foreign and plebian accretions.[17] An analogous complaint was heard with regard to the even more vigorous proliferation of dance tunes in the nineteenth century, as evidenced in volumes like Captain Francis

O'Neill's massive and now canonical *O'Neill's Music of Ireland: Eighteen Hundred and Fifty Melodies: Airs, Jigs, Reels, Hornpipes, Long Dances, Marches, etc.*[18] One pundit feared that clever fiddlers might pawn their creations off on collectors as 'ancient' folk music. 'Given the Gaelic spirit and the knack of melody construction,' Annie Patterson complained, 'one could go ahead with this sort of thing ad libitum'.[19] There was a deep distrust among cultural elites of the creativity and inventiveness exhibited within the field of what became known as traditional music in the late nineteenth and early twentieth centuries.

A nation lacking its own art music

Joe Cleary has argued that Ireland's unique culture comes from a peculiar combination of peripherality and proximity to the dominant forces of historical change in Europe and the globe. Ireland was too remote from the institutions of the Roman Empire and European feudalism for these to find a proper footing. It nevertheless found itself disturbingly close to a state destined to break out of that medieval mould earlier and more dramatically than any other in Europe. The result was that 'Ireland was the only country in that geographical area to be subjected to a sustained, thoroughgoing, and culturally traumatic experience of colonisation'.[20] The European modernist impulse was to react against the cultures of the ancient aristocracies with their deeply entrenched artistic classicism and academicism. In England the court culture typical of Continental states was diluted by the precocious rise of the more philistine merchant and industrial classes. In Ireland aristocratic culture had never fully developed. The landowning aristocracy had been in irreversible decline in Ireland for over a century. In the era of 'the invention of tradition' and international cultural rivalry which fed the outburst of violence of the First World War, Ireland shared with the rest of the United Kingdom anxieties over not having the properly developed aristocratic aesthetic cultures against which modernism was opposed. Yet at the same time it remained peripheral to the urban and philistine Anglo-American context. Even as its immigrants populated its cities, and the rural population at home shrank, Irish culture kept one foot on the farm.

Cleary provides the context for one of the key ingredients of Irish musical difference: the complete failure of its art music culture beyond the baroque and classical periods. Whatever the potential may have been generated by the vigorous musical culture of Georgian Dublin, the nineteenth century saw the collapse of this elite musical culture and the isolation of plebeian culture from its influence. The Act of Union had a devastating, though not immediately apparent, impact, the shifting of the centre of gravity of the Irish politics to London inevitably dragging the cultural focus of the enfranchised and their representatives along with it. The harp was once again symbolic, but this time because of the near complete extinction of its practitioners.[21]

Admittedly, elite musical culture carried on in Dublin with the same vigour of the Georgian period for a couple of decades after the Act of Union.[22] But one is reminded of those cartoon episodes where the protagonist, having run off a cliff, hangs in the air until he finally grasps where he is, and only then does gravity take effect. The depressed 1830s and 1840s delivered a knockout blow. By the 1860s, nothing remained but a threadbare fabric of the classical tradition in Ireland, held together by 'that slender continuity of commitment' of a small handful of Dublin musical activists, all of whom died before the century's end.[23] The case of the Dublin-born Protestant composer Charles Villiers Stanford is exemplary. Stanford abandoned Dublin and late in his career spurned the attention of Irish audiences and musical revivalists, even though he had profited greatly from the reception of his 'Irish' symphonies and operas.[24]

Looking back from the 1890s, it was easy to construct a narrative of the degrada- tion and decline of Irish musical high culture. Catholic Emancipation and tithe wars of the 1820s and 1830s, the bankruptcy of large sections of the landed class in the 1830s and 1840s and the failure to industrialise outside of Belfast, the Fenian uprising, the disestablishment of the Church of Ireland, the Land Acts and the Home Rule movement all signalled the irreversible decline of the Irish aristocracy as a cultural force. Commentators easily found likely scapegoats in the philistine and English-infected Irish petit bourgeoisie, who appreciated only 'Balfe-like ballads, military bands, and that indescribable thing called a Promenade Concert'.[25] The quest for a national musical culture was therefore apparently thwarted at every level of society. With the aristocracy having absented itself from the project, the middle classes were left to follow their own debased inclinations, while the peasantry polluted what was left of the ancient and essential music of the nation with their wild inventiveness and eclecticism.

The integrity of the present

Francis O'Neill, the great collector who had spent a lifetime among practising musicians on both sides of the Atlantic, offered the following persuasive diagnosis of the Irish character in 1918: 'There certainly must be a defect in the Irish character, always glorifying the legendary and historical past, and leaving to the future the realisation of their dreams. The present – the only time within the compass of our energies – gives us but slight concern as long as our leaders dope us with vainglorious praise and holiday oratory.'[26] I have been arguing that elite discourse and vernacular music have, since the eighteenth century, mostly gone their separate ways. Obsessed with preserving the past, or, alternatively, with building towards a utopian future, few recognised that there was something unique and exciting happening in the present which has made Irish music different. While the country missed out on the excitement of the Romantic period of art music and the modernist reaction to it, the vacuum left at the top of the culture may well have facilitated the development of a uniquely rich vernacular culture, which I have briefly documented in this chapter. Certainly an immense store of innate musical talent that might otherwise have been moulded in conservatories was cultivated in the DIY pedagogical context of traditional music. One only has to think simultaneously of flute players James Galway and Matt Molloy, or violinist Nigel Kennedy and fiddler Liz Carroll, to see the point.

There is a further point, linking the musical culture to Cleary's theme of the juxtaposition of peripherality and proximity, of isolation and absorption. This point can be clarified by comparing Irish music to some of its close cousins (Scottish, Appalachian or Breton), with which it shares many fundamental forms, instruments, habitats and linguistic voices. How is the Irish tradition different from these cousins? I have mentioned the Irish pipes, Ireland's only truly indigenous instrument. The unique structure of this instrument combined with the cultural centrality of the pipers in the nineteenth century are surely crucial elements of Irish difference. Yet the story is not so much about the centrality of a unique instrument as it is about the Irish capacity to absorb and incorporate a great variety of instruments without fundamentally altering the stylistic template laid down by the pipers. Here the contrast is clear. Breton music remained centred on the bombarde and biniou, Scottish music on highland pipes and fiddle, and Appalachian music on fiddle and banjo. But in the century after 1870, a whole range of instruments were brought into the centre of the Irish tradition: concert flutes, concertinas, accordions, banjos and more. The point is not that new instruments are absent from other traditions. Rather, the point is that Ireland produced virtuoso performers on these new instruments, who literally reinvented the way the instruments were played in order to conform to and yet subtly expand the palette of the tradition. And recently the tradition has seen the reincorporation of the harp, in the hands of a growing number of extremely talented, and mostly female, practitioners. Irish musicians also provocatively brought the bouzouki and guitar into the tradition. At folk festivals today, bands employing these new instruments tend to all sound the same, whether they are Scottish, Irish or Breton. But the fact is they are all sounding Irish, because the instruments and the arrangement strategies were first introduced by Irish musicians in the 1970s.

Irish musical difference is therefore linked to this hybrid quality of porosity and incubation, whch has given it a capaciousness of difference within its own sameness. This is true not only of the instrumentarium but of the pronounced regional differences on the island and between Ireland and its diaspora, and also regarding the range of expression extending from the solo *sean nos* singer to the Riverdance-style spectacle. We might finally connect this characteristic to the phenomenon for which Irish traditional music is most widely identified and celebrated: the pub session. The diverse instrumentarium is what makes this gregarious and infectious ritual so attractive across the globe. Perhaps it is just a happy historical accident, but Ireland is associated with a ritual of musical social practice that is in multiple ways liberating and therapeutic. The peculiar aesthetics and micro-politics of this form of music making has yet to be properly articulated, but its capacity to cultivate an unfolding and open-ended musical conversation, potentially never the same, is worthy of further reflection. When the discourse of national musical identity has become boring, irrelevant, incomprehensible to all but a shrinking cadre of disciplinary experts, and/or – as occasionally in Northern Ireland – downright dangerous, we can still meet on common ground and in our own style have a conversation drawing on the vast repertoire of tunes and songs created and preserved by our contemporaries and their modern ancestors.

This is not to say, finally, that Irish traditional music has always been and will always remain a permanent marker of difference or a field within which difference is creatively and positively negotiated and celebrated. In some phases of its history, the modernity of Irish traditional music is synonymous with its homogenisation. This can be seen in the present conjuncture. An eclectic spectrum of dance tunes has been boiled down to jigs and reels. The institutionalisation of pedagogy is dampening regional and individual difference. The time and space for *sean nos* song is shrinking. The revolutionary ideas for ensemble playing of the 1970s have been routinised into the formulaic trad-pop sound that now saturates broadcast media. And the pub session has evolved from a subaltern site of musical discourse to an integrated branch of drinks marketing, marked by repetition and boredom. All this diverts one's eyes and ears from the present, and fuels the longstanding habit of celebrating and cultivating what once was. However, there is probably something very interesting happening beneath the discourse, as there has been since the eighteenth century at least.

Notes

1 Alan J. Fletcher, *Drama, Performance, and Polity in Pre-Cromwellian Ireland* (Cork: Cork University Press, 2000). For an account of Giraldus and Irish music, see Leith Davis, *Music, Postcolonialism, and Gender: The Construction of Irish National Identity, 1724–1874* (Notre Dame: University of Notre Dame Press, 2006), pp. 1–4.

2 Fletcher, *Drama*, p. 232.

3 The themes in this chapter are elaborated in Martin Dowling, *Traditional Music and Irish Society with Historical Perspectives* (Farnham: Ashgate, 2014).

4 David Dickson, *New Foundations: Ireland 1660–1800*, 2nd ed. (Dublin: Irish Academic Press, 2000).

5 Toby Barnard, *A New Anatomy of Ireland: The Irish Protestants, 1649–1770* (London: Yale University Press, 2003), p. 292; Sean Connolly, 'Ag Déaneamh Commanding: Elite Responses to Popular Culture, 1660–1850', in James S. Donnelly, Jr, and Kirby Miller (eds), *Irish Popular Culture 1650–1850* (Dublin: Irish Academic Press, 1999), p. 6.

6 Davis, *Music, Postcolonialism, and Gender*, pp. 42, 62.

7 Nollaig Casey-McGlynn, 'Eibhlín a Rúin and the Impact of Fashion in its Dissemination in Eighteenth and Nineteenth Century Ireland', MA dissertation, Queen's University of Belfast, 2011, p. 4.

8 Adrian Scahill, 'Irish Traditional Music and the Seventeenth Century', in Barra Boydell and

Kerry Houston (eds), *Music, Ireland and the Seventeenth Century* (Dublin: Four Courts Press, 2009), pp. 40–61.

9   Here I am drawing on Eric Hobsbawm's distinctions between invented and genuine tradition, and between constructed tradition and organically evolving custom. See Eric Hobsbawm, 'Introduction', in Eric Hobsbawm and Terence Ranger (eds), *The Invention of Tradition* (Cambridge: Cambridge University Press, 1983), p. 8.

10 Joep Leerssen, *Remembrance and Imagination: Patterns in the Historical and Literary Repre-sentation of Ireland in the Nineteenth Century* (Cork: Cork University Press, 1996), p. 225.

11 For fuller statement of this view, see Michael Böss and Eamon Maher (eds), *Engaging Modernity: Readings of Irish Politics, Culture, and Literature at the Turn of the Century* (Dublin: Veritas, 2003), p. 10. The editors adopt a concept of modernity articulated by Peter Wagner in *Theorizing Modernity* (London: Sage, 2001).

12 See Éamonn Ó Ciardha, *Ireland and the Jacobite Cause, 1685–1766: A Fatal Attachment* (Dublin: Four Courts Press, 2000).

13 Frank Lewelyn Harrison, 'Music, Poetry, and Polity in the Age of Swift', *Eighteenth Century Ireland / Iris an dá Chultúr*, i (1986), p. 62.

14 Mary Helen Thuente, *The Harp Re-Strung: The United Irishmen and the Rise of Literary Nationalism* (Syracuse: Syracuse University Press, 1994), pp. 1–16, 46–63.

15 Robert Bell, *A Description of the Conditions and Manners of the Peasantry of Ireland* (London, 1804), p. 17.

16 Of course the so-called 'new ballad' with its stable quatrain structure and pulsing stresses has been as resilient as the dance tune.

17 See Hugh Shields, *Narrative Singing in Ireland: Lays, Ballads, Come-All-Yes, and Other Songs* (Dublin: Irish Academic Press, 1993), and David Lloyd, *Anomalous States: Irish Writing and the Post-colonial Moment* (Dublin: Lilliput Press, 1993), pp. 95–7.

18 Francis O'Neill, *O'Neill's Music of Ireland: Eighteen Hundred and Fifty Melodies: Airs, Jigs, Reels, Hornpipes, Long Dances, Marches, etc., Many of Which are Now Published for the First Time* (Chicago: Lyon and Healy, 1903)

19 'Niamh' [Annie Patterson], 'Music Notes', *Journal of the Ivernian Society*, 7:25 (1914), pp. 40–1.

20 Joe Cleary, 'Towards a Materialist-formalist History of Twentieth Century Irish Literature', *Boundary 2*, xxi:1 (2004), pp. 209, 224.

21 See the letter of John McAdam to Edward Bunting, 30 July 1839, published in Edward Bunting, *The Ancient Music of Ireland Arranged for Piano* (New York: Dover, 2000), pp. 66–7.

22 Derek Collins, 'Concert Life in Dublin in the Age of Revolution', PhD dissertation, Queen's University Belfast, 2001, pp. 44–7, 72–9, 243–78.

23 Harry White, *The Keeper's Recital: Music and Cultural History in Ireland, 1770–1970* (Cork: Cork University Press, 1998), p. 99.

24 Jeremy Dibble, *Charles Villiers Stanford: Man and Musician* (Oxford: Oxford University Press, 2002), pp. 5, 19–47.

25 'Music in Dublin', *Hibernia*, i (1 April 1882), p. 63.

26 Francis O'Neill to Rev. Seamus O'Floinn, 15 October 1918. O'Neill Collection of Irish Traditional Music, Department of Rare Books and Special Collections, Hesburgh Library, University of Notre Dame, Indiana.

19

The GAA and the sporting Irish

Katie Liston

What makes the Irish different, not just in the world of sport but in terms of culture generally, is the Gaelic Athletic Association. It was central to the formation and development of cultural nationalism towards the end of the nineteenth century and to the project of promoting and developing Irish cultural difference. Throughout the twentieth century, the GAA developed local roots that permeated throughout every county and every village. It became central to family and community life. It reached into people's hearts, minds and bodies. It became central to their identity, to the way they saw themselves and related to others. For many people, the GAA was not just a sport, it was a way of being. As Séan Kelly, current MEP and former GAA President, put it when writing about his childhood, the GAA was 'as natural for me as eating, talking or walking'.[1]

But the GAA is not just rural, male and local. It has become urban, female and global. Take, for example, Irene. She is in her late thirties and a civil servant. Like her brothers, when she was young she joined the local GAA club. It was second nature for them. She grew up in Dublin. Not as many girls played camogie (the female version of hurling) but, in the family, school and club in which she grew up, the GAA was for men and women. It was common to see boys and girls walking down the street in her local area with hurls in their hands.

Irene was immersed in Gaelic traditions from a young age, her father having been involved in the same club, Ballyboden-St Endas, in south County Dublin for many years. Born in Kilkenny, a county widely regarded as being at the forefront of hurling on the island, he had moved to Dublin, joined the club and, over the years, became a key figure fulfilling various leadership positions. The club and the GAA became part and parcel of Irene's daily life. It was a way of creating meaning and sustaining bonds. But it was more than that. It was also a moral code. It was about how life should be led.

Irene and her brothers played hurling, camogie and Gaelic football throughout their youth and adult lives. Like many other Irish sporting families, they were involved in the daily routine of cleaning football boots, washing playing clothes – often those of other team players –preparing food for visiting teams, going to home and away matches to support club teams and making annual pilgrimages to Croke Park. The family immersed themselves in many fundraising activities to extend the facilities (training grounds and playing pitches) needed for the club's growing membership, and particularly when the local clubhouse had to be rebuilt after it was destroyed by fire. The back garden of the family home was a space for practicing hurling, using the walls as a backdrop against which to endlessly strike and catch the *sliotar*. Their heroes were not just the international pop stars of the day – Michael Jackson, Madonna, Take That and the Spice Girls – but also hurlers such as Liam Fennelly, D. J. Carey and, latterly, Henry Shefflin and Tony Browne.

Today the club continues to grow. Every Saturday morning up to two hundred school-aged children come to be coached in the basic skills of the game. Over the years, Irene has played her part and coached youth and junior camogie teams. There are strong links to local primary schools in which hurling and football are the main sports. The club and the schools work together as a form of cultural academy. They are part of a network that spreads throughout Ireland and beyond. Each of the estimated 2615 GAA clubs globally has a central role to play in communal bonding and belonging. Many communities and parishes are literally and figuratively built around the GAA club.

For Irene, as for many others, the GAA was more than just a sport. It was, in Séan Kelly's words, about building and developing deep social bonds that embody 'genuine fellow feeling, generosity without thought of cost [and] willingness to do anything for someone you genuinely appreciated and admired'.[2] Being immersed in Gaelic culture not only enabled Irene to form a strong sense of social identity; it was also an opportunity for self-fulfilment, to express her sporting prowess in an era when women's involvement in other sports in Ireland was less prevalent.

Irene took this sense of belonging with her when she relocated to Europe in a professional career move. She found a new psychological home in Belgium GAA. The club brought a sense of the familiar in an otherwise unfamiliar European multicultural environment.[3] There, as in many other Irish corners of the world, Gaelic games take place amid emblems and rituals that reflect and maintain Irish cultural difference. For more than a hundred years, the GAA has provided a platform for the preservation and articulation of ethnic Irishness within and beyond the island.[4] It is stitched inexorably into family, community and parish life like no other sporting or cultural organisation.

What follows is a brief historical examination of some of the processes by which Gaelic games became the cultural heartbeat of the nation. I then consider the uniqueness of Gaelic games set against the broad outline of patterns of participation in sport across the world more generally. Here, the focus is on the distinctive commitment to an amateur ethos as reflected in the importance of community, or what Tovey and Share have termed the 'urge to community'.[5] In this context, I argue that the GAA is the dominant marker of Irish cultural identity and difference, not only because of the objective reality of it as an institution and how it permeates families and communities but also because of the images and identities it conjures up, and the thoughts, emotions and actions it inspires.

From cultural protectors to cosmopolitan patrons

The GAA was founded in 1884 with the objective of promoting interest in Irish sporting and athletic pastimes, particularly Gaelic football, hurling, handball and athletics. From its inception, through its formal rules of membership, it also embodied an explicit opposition to British cultural imperialism. In its organisational infancy and reflecting the political mood of the time, the Association passed a rule (21) prohibiting its members from participating in those sports most closely associated with British colonialism – rugby union, association football (soccer), hockey and any other 'garrison' game. The GAA was an ideological movement and there was a constant struggle to maintain the purity of the movement and avoid all potential sources of contamination. There was extreme vigilance. For example, in 1930, Seán O'Ryan, the President of the Association, wrote to the National Athletics and Cycling Association of Ireland complaining of the organisation's decision to send an athletics team to the inaugural British Empire Games to be held that year.[6]

But towards the end of the twentieth century, the fundamentalist dimension of the movement began to wane. Rule 21 was repealed in 1971. And in 2005, during Séan Kelly's presidential tenure, a motion on another rule (42) was passed by the GAA Congress which paved the way for so-called garrison games – soccer and rugby union – to be played in Croke Park. The amendment to rule 42 was widely heralded as a public demonstration of the degree to which a historically protectionist and culturally reactionary association had become more confident and outward-looking and, increasingly, embodied a global outlook. The GAA began to capture the contemporary cultural *Zeitgeist* and expressed (publicly at least) a clear sense of organisational and cultural cohesiveness, and national confidence. This was not always the case. In fact, objective and perceptual expressions of Irish culture have been historically contested, and sport, notably Gaelic games, has played an important role in the shifting dynamics of sameness, difference, bonding and belonging.

In the late nineteenth and early twentieth centuries, it was unclear whether, in the midst of national debate between various competing elements of Irish culture, a cultural accord could be achieved. This was a hothouse of often confusing cultural and political contradictions in which changing constituencies of educated working, middle and upper-class Catholics and Protestants sought to conserve and cohere their particular notions of Irish identity. While the GAA banned policemen and soldiers from playing Gaelic games and pastimes, some of its own members – including Michael Cusack, a founding member of the Association – competed in, and attended, many other sports such as cricket, soccer and rugby union matches.

This period, described by Elias and Dunning as the second phase of sportisation, was an era in which the co-mingling of sporting, political, economic and social processes led to the establishment of many of the modern sporting associations we know today.[7] In Ireland, there emerged the Football Association of Ireland and the Irish Football Association, the Irish Rugby Football Association, what we know today as Athletics Ireland (a modern antecedent of the bifurcation of athletics and cycling, and subsequently of partition), the Irish Cricket, Hockey and Golfing Unions and many others.

In the midst of this, a cultural revolution was led by the GAA and the Gaelic League.[8] The GAA sought to democratise Irish athletics, to revive traditional games like hurling and to harness the nationalist movement. While advocates of the GAA and nationalism portrayed the early development of the association as something of a prairie fire, in reality there have been peaks and troughs in its development over the past 130 years or so. For instance, a late nineteenth-century collapse of the GAA in many areas was followed by its sporting revival in the first decades of the 1900s. The popularity of Gaelic football and hurling have also ebbed and flowed such that, today, the former is an island-wide sport while hurling is confined to a much smaller number of counties.

The GAA went on to become one of the chief platforms for the expression of cultural nationalism in the twentieth century, being influenced by, and influential in, political issues of the day. For example, the GAA supported the Irish Volunteers after they were founded in 1913. The Association became increasingly radicalised during and after the 1916 Easter Rising. The massacre by the Royal Irish Constabulary of fourteen people in Croke Park on 'Bloody Sunday' in 1920 came to be a crown of martyrdom in the promotion of sportive nationalism. Because it did not recognise Irish partition, operated on an all-Ireland basis and banned foreign (English) games, GAA became the largest 'national' sporting organisation in the Irish Free State. It also became a major political force closely aligned with government figures, neo-traditionalist Catholic clerics, teachers and civil servants. All of this was buttressed over the course of the 1900s by an emerging nationwide network of clubs built on, and across, parish boundaries. But as an ideological movement it was often divisive. In Northern Ireland for instance, the GAA became central to the formation of a nationalist 'state within a state' in which the dream of a united Ireland was not just imagined but realised in matches and participation in island-wide committees, sporting structures and competitions. Today, the GAA story is decidedly different. It has been heavily influenced by the realities of operating in a partitioned island and a divided society.[9] By the late twentieth century the cultural heartbeat of the Irish nation had morphed into an organisation characterised by an alluring mix of cosmopolitanism and neoconservatism. Today, there is a tangible commitment to standards of governance and administration that resemble a professional sports organisation. The ethos is maintained through a rigorous enforcement of rules within every club. At the same time, the Association has become a highly successful commercial organisation, particularly in relation to marketing Croke Park as a tourist spot and for holding meetings, conferences and weddings. The modern GAA espouses the principles of inclusion and diversity in which the opportunity to participate in Gaelic games and culture is afforded to all irrespective of nationality, religion, ethnicity, age and ability. This is also reflected in the increasing number of immigrants playing Gaelic games.

All of this sits alongside the palpable desire by the Association to preserve Irish uniqueness, to maintain the amateur status of its games and, latterly, to celebrate cultural and ethnic difference within its membership. What makes the GAA and Ireland unique in modern sport is that it is an amateur organisation. With the exception of those employed full-time in the running of commercial aspects of the stadia and conference facilities at Croke Park, the GAA functions as an island-wide organisation of unpaid volunteers working at local parish, club, county and provincial levels.

As Dónal Óg Cusack – one of the icons of the GAA who as a gay man epitomises the new cultural diversity of the Association – put it, 'all that energy and progress to move on is a part of the character of the GAA clubs everywhere, of the organisation which built Croke Park and a network of massive grounds as cathedrals to amateur games'.[10] It is the abiding amateur ethos, and its roots in the distinctive Irish 'urge to community' – be that at parish, club or county level – that distinguishes it from most modern sports worldwide. The Association has become one of the key components of the collective self-representation of Irish society. Gaelic games set apart and give unique expression to particular notions of Irish community described by Séan Kelly as simply 'the way of things'.[11]

The urge to community

Research reveals the importance of place in everyday life in Ireland. Despite being economically and socially transformed over the previous thirty years, fictional villages like Peace's 'Inveresk' and Inglis's 'Ballivor' retain a strong and pervasive sense of their own distinct identity, 'of being special places in the world'.[12] There are many factors involved in the lasting importance of family and community in Ireland. Besides the GAA, there was the dominance of agricultural production throughout most of the twentieth century. This was linked to family farms which, in turn were linked to the dominance of the Catholic Church in civil society and everyday life. All of these factors led to a unique form of modernisation.

This brings us to the issue of perceived and real identities and the interaction between them. *Objectively* speaking, Ireland has been transformed, socially and economically. Everyday life in Ireland today is structured far more by market and media forces than was the case fifty years ago. The emphasis is more on self-realisation and liberal individualism than on self-denial. Yet one of the enduring *perceived* differences between modern Ireland and the rest of the world is that many of the Irish believe – partly because of the cultural attachment to the GAA and the Catholic Church – that they do community not just differently but better.

Whether real in nature, these perceived differences are real in their consequences. Not by coincidence, then, adherence to communal values in sport has also persisted for longer on the island of Ireland. As an Irish Catholic national identity was developed and consolidated in the late nineteenth and early twentieth centuries, the GAA was at the heart of a moral doctrine that stressed the importance of mutual identification, mutual dependence and collective solidarity, particularly in rural life. In this regard, the GAA is both the literal (i.e. real) and figurative (symbolic) heartbeat of Irish communities and culture today. Not only does it co-exist with other forms of civil life in Ireland but it is to the forefront in espousing amateur values. That amateurism was at the heart of modern sport around the world is well recognised. But it is the particular form of Irish amateurism that stands apart, encompassing as it does strong forms of communal reciprocity, bonding and belonging that are rooted in the local.

That the GAA is the largest voluntary association on the island means that it represents a not insignificant sphere of social relations based uniquely on trust and reciprocity. In the face of increasing individualisation, the relationships between GAA members and supporters endure, whether on the basis of parish and club, county and province. There is a unique blend of solidarity and rivalry. Involvement in the GAA is, above all, about identity, bonding and belonging. And while there are often intense rivalries, sometimes leading to violence, these are relatively insignificant and perhaps more a reflection of the intense commitment and loyalty that members have to their clubs and counties.

In parishes, clubs and everyday family and community life, the GAA is one of the dominant ways for people to create meaning, a sense of identity and a sense of belonging. Irish people talk of being a Kerryman, a Galway woman or from established GAA towns, villages or clubs like Cloyne, Young Irelands, Crossmaglen Rangers, Bellaghy and Clann na nGael. They distinguish themselves by wearing club and county colours, not just on the day of a match but on many other social occasions and in their everyday lives. As Roy Keane, the former Irish soccer international, put it:

> It's about local pride, that's what GAA is – people representing their parishes and the streets where they grew up ... Gaelic football in Ireland is different. They all come from their local parishes. They don't move clubs when they get fed up. They represent the people they're brought up with. The supporters are brilliant, they mix well, there's a good atmosphere and they take defeat well.[13]

The rooting of Gaelic games as part of the urge to community is also evident in other ways, e.g. in the naming of various GAA competitions after 'ordinary' Irish people and in the ways in which GAA activities and their outcomes become deeply embedded into the folklore and history of Irish people and Irish places, to be relived as part of the creation and maintenance of collective memory. Heroes of Gaelic games – Jack Lynch, D. J. Carey, Mick O'Connell, Dónal Óg Cusack, Angela Downey, Mary Jo Curran and others – are people who share more or less the same sort of daily lives and lifestyles as those who pay to watch them. Being able to engage in Gaelic practices (or to associate with them) can be used to attain social acceptance, social status and honour – just like being a 'good Catholic' used to do.

This sense of bonding and belonging is maintained despite the fact that many GAA members participate in other sports that have gained popularity across the island. And while Gaelic sports might be exceptional as markers of identity, bonding, belonging and collective memory, when it comes to the broad outlines of modern sport more generally, and the way sport has become a central aspect of everyday life for many people, the sporting Irish are, in many ways, similar to the rest of the world. This is because there are common patterns to the ways in which modern sports have assumed economic, cultural and political significance throughout the world.

The wider significance of modern sports

Irish participation in sport might be distinctive in terms of the literal and figurative distinctiveness of Gaelic games but, as a nation, Ireland is located more or less within the typical European parameters of participation in sport and physical activity. When taken to incorporate the full spectrum of activities involving physical exertion and skill in which individuals or teams vie against themselves, another or others for leisure or competitive purposes, sport has become a major social and cultural activity in Ireland.[14]

Gaelic football is the most popular sport, attracting between 30 to 40 per cent of all sports attendances followed by hurling, soccer and rugby union. The All-Ireland football final is the most watched sporting event in Ireland, the 2012 game having been viewed by more than a quarter of the island's total population of roughly 6.2 million people. The most popular participation sports and physical activities in Ireland involve indoor and outdoor spaces and include swimming, golf, aerobics, soccer, cycling, Gaelic football and snooker/billiards.[15] In economic terms, the Federation of Irish Sport estimates that sports tourism, including horse racing, generates in excess of €800 million annually. Sport stimulates €1.8 billion of Irish household expenditure annually and supports in excess of 38,000 jobs or two per cent of the workforce in the Republic of Ireland.[16] In Northern Ireland, in 2006 it was estimated that sport-related activity added £452 million to the economy, corresponding to almost two per cent of total value added in the region, while

13,700 people were in sports-related employment there (1.99 per cent of total employment).[17]

The economic impact of this cultural practice is signalled even further by the contribution of sport to gross domestic product. In the Republic and Northern Ireland, sport contributes approximately 1.4 per cent to gross domestic product and two per cent to gross value added, while the related fiscal return from sport is estimated to be almost one a half times that invested.[18] Sport is also the largest single source of volunteering in Ireland having over a quarter of a million volunteers each week according to some conservative estimates.[19]

As is the case in other European countries, these more tangible economic dimensions of sport are closely intertwined with culture, tradition and history. Beyond the island-wide Gaelic games community, modern sports and leisure lifestyles are equally embedded in the social fabric of everyday life. Brighid and Michael, fitness instructors in Cork city and Belfast respectively, observe this entangling in the pattern of people's lives, in the idea that sport is good for physical and mental health and in the increasing awareness of health and lifestyle choices on the island. What we might call personal exercise is one of the most popular types of wider sports-related activities. Irish men and women, young and old, make the daily or weekly trip to the local gym where they put their bodies through a series of activities designed, primarily, with physical fitness and health in mind, but that also reflect a growing investment in contemporary physical culture across the island. Beyond immediate sporting competition *per se*, going to the gym and 'working out' have become an equally important source of physical and social capital.

Still, competitive sport enshrines the value of achievement in upholding a standard of excellence and building an achievement-orientated national character. It is the context in which collective identities are crystallised, whether it is at parish, club, team, county, provincial or national level. Therefore, while I have argued for the unique contribution of the GAA, it is important to recognise the complexity and status of Irish sport as a whole, reflected in the myriads of sports throughout the island, in rugby union, soccer, cycling, hockey, bowling and athletics, all with their own clubs and teams.

As well as being a strong form of collective identity, sport has become a significant form of social and political capital. Sport is a major form of social integration and networking. It has become an important ideological mechanism of social integration for migrant and minority peoples. At a micro level, success in sport is often a pathway into local and national politics. At a macro level, sport galvanises national identity and is used by the Dublin and Stormont governments as a means of maintaining loyalty and commitment to the state.

There is some tangible basis then to the claim that sport is a new religion of sorts for the Irish. As we have seen, the full significance of sport in any one cultural context can be found not in its popularity or economic return alone but in the manner in which it imparts key social meanings about identities and ways of being. Sport is seen as central to the richness and depth of Irish culture. For example, it is claimed that Ireland's ancient Brehon laws featured Gaelic games, and the Celtic legend of Cuchulainn is specifically associated with hurling.[20] This folklore is fused with contemporary Irish rural and urban sporting lifestyles, celebration and rituals so much so that some would even say that sport, including exercise and health lifestyles, is the new drug or opiate of a more secular and modern Ireland.[21] The empirical question then is not whether sport has wider social significance in modern Ireland than in other societies. This is patently not the case irrespective of which measures are applied.

Rather, in the context of studies of cultural difference, the focus is on those social dynamics that become important in distinguishing between 'them' and 'us', between the Irish and 'others'. The emphasis is on beliefs, feelings and action tendencies that are loaded on to these identities and distinctions, and on the ways in which Irish people take these to be true about themselves. Perceptions of cultural difference have real consequences for Irish personality structures and in how the Irish describe themselves.

Consider, for example, the role of modesty. It is not that other people are not modest, but rather that it is more of a cultural trait or strategy among the Irish. The champion jockey A. P. McCoy was described by his peers as 'very easy to get on with. You don't hear him shouting or squealing – he doesn't think he's better than anyone else ... he's a very modest fella and has always been like that.' The Olympic and world champion boxer Katie Taylor is also lauded for her 'modesty in front of camera' and 'unassuming nature'.[22] Irish sports stars are recommended not to 'get above their station' for being Irish is a 'way of being in the world that shuns and shows disdain for ambition, selfishness and materialism'.[23]

> We like our heroes humble in Ireland, strong, silent types who keep the head down and go about their business in an uncomplicated manner. It is an unattractive trait, this Irish begrudgery which clicks into gear when our stars get 'above themselves' and can lead to a sense of satisfaction when they eventually, and inevitably, have an off-day.[24]

Where, historically, modesty, prudery and humility penetrated further into Irish bodies and, particularly women's bodies, sport has become a major form of self-fulfilment and realisation in contemporary Ireland. Historically, Irish women were mothers above all else but, since the 1900s, they have participated in hockey and camogie, and they have become boxers, Gaelic footballers and rugby players. In the last forty years or so Irish women have also led the way in terms of challenging patriarchal norms in, and through, contact sports in particular.

In contemporary Ireland sport represents, then, a particular mix of continuity and change and one means by which we can observe culture, in its real and symbolic guises. We see Irish culture at many different levels in the ordinary lives of millions of individual Irish people and in the ways in which they engage in all kinds of sports and leisure activities that make them similar to other people, particularly in Western societies. We observe it in the wider significance of sport as an autonomous cultural field in modern societies. But in terms of Western sport, it is the GAA and the spirit of amateurism, voluntarism and the urge to community that make Irish sport different.

Conclusion

From the perspective of broad patterns of sports participation, the Irish love their sport, no more or less significantly than many other Europeans. Whether or not sport has become the new religion in Western society, it is certainly not a cultural epiphenomenon. It has moved centre stage in social and cultural life. It is not simply escapism or insignificant spare-time activity. Sport permeates all aspects of social life and has achieved economic, cultural, historical, political and symbolic significance. Sport, then, is an important lens through which Irish culture can be observed and analysed.

On the island of Ireland, sport demonstrates diversity in terms of how people see and understand themselves and others. However, what makes Irish sport different, perceptually and objectively speaking, is the GAA. And what makes the GAA different is the way that it is stitched into family, community and parish life. In a world of mass media and globalised sport, it has remained the dominant sport in Ireland. While the Association is becoming increasingly cosmopolitan and, in so doing, reshaping the connection between the local and the global on the island, it is still characterised by the dominance of amateurism and volunteerism.

The traditional fear of contamination still persists in many quarters of the GAA, but there is also an increasing acceptance of difference and sporting cosmopolitanism. The importance of community is enshrined in Gaelic games and in continued representations of familial and communal reciprocity that were adopted, historically, as one marker of Irish difference. In this regard, markers of identity work not only because of the objective reality they capture but also because of the images, identities and associations they conjure up and the thoughts, emotions and actions they inspire. It is this which remains at the heart of the sporting Irish and what makes the Irish different.

Notes

1 Séan Kelly, *Rule 42 and All That* (Dublin: Gill and Macmillan, 2008), p. 44.
2 Séan Kelly, *Rule 42 and All That*, p. 197.
3 In a related sense, Seán Kelly's 2009 election to the European Parliament was also intimately tied to his GAA profile.
4 See Paul Darby, *Gaelic Games, Nationalism and the Irish Diaspora in the United States* (Dublin, UCD Press, 2009) for an in-depth study of GAA communities in the US.

5 Hilary Tovey and Perry Share, *A Sociology of Ireland* (Dublin: Gil and Macmillan, 2003), p. 116.

6 Seán O'Ryan, 'Empire Games: Letter from President, GAA', *The Kerryman*, 2 August 1930.

7 See Norbert Elias and Eric Dunning, *Quest for Excitement: Sport and Leisure in the Civilising Process* (Dublin:University College Dublin Press, 2008).

8 The latter was established in 1893 by Douglas Hyde to foster Irish culture and the Irish language, including particular notions of sobriety and conduct.

9 See, for example: Adrian Devine and Frances Devine, 'The Politics of Sports Tourism in Northern Ireland', *Sport & Tourism*, 9:2 (2004), pp. 171–82; Alan Bairner, *Sport, Nationalism and Globalization* (New York: SUNY Press, 2001); David Hassan, 'Sport, Identity and Irish Nationalism in Northern Ireland', in Alan Bairner (ed.), *Sport and the Irish: Histories, Identities, Issues* (Dublin: University College Dublin Press, 2005), pp.123–39.

10 See Donal Óg Cusack, *Come What May: The Autobiography* (Dublin: Penguin, 2009), p. vii.

11 Kelly, *Rule 42 and All That*, p. 37.

12 See Tovey and Share, *A Sociology of Ireland*, p.111.

13 http://www.irishexaminer.com/sport/gaa/keane-all-ireland-bigger-than-world-cup-final-131391.html.

14 The Council of Europe defines sport as 'all forms of physical activity which, through casual or organised participation, aim at expressing or improving physical fitness and mental well-being, forming social relationships or obtaining results in competition at all levels' (www.coe.int/t/dg4/epas/resources/texts/Rec(92)13rev_en.pdf).

15 Arthur Aughey and John Oakland, *Irish Civilization: An Introduction* (London: Routledge, 2013), p. 125.

16 See http://irishsport.ie/wpress/index.php/about-us/background/. In 2009, an estimated 1.24 million people attended horse race meetings throughout Ireland: http://hripressoffice.ie/assets/2013/03/Racing_The_Irish_Way.pdf. This equates to approximately one-fifth of the island's population.

17 See www.sportni.net/NR/rdonlyres/789790EE-73AC-42E3-AECC-CC9E42D397C3/0/EconomicImpactofSport.pdf. Here Sport NI included the following sectors in its economic analysis: sports clothing and footwear; sports equipment; health and fitness; other participant sports; boats; spectator sports; sport gambling; sport TV and video; sport-related publications and sport-related travel.

18 Interestingly, most estimates of the economic return on sport exclude any analysis of the costs associated with the immediate diagnosis and treatment of sports-related injuries, the related impact on absenteeism from work and the longer-term health consequences for overall quality of life. See Rupert Kisser and Robert Bauer, *The Burden of Sport Injuries in the European Union* (Vienna: Kuratorium für Verkehrssicherheit KFV), available at www.eurosafe.eu.com/csi/eurosafe2006.nsf/wwwAssets/9F41F776F8CE8F25C1257849004134D4/$file/WP4%20Sport_Burden_Report%20FINAL.pdf.

19 Irish Sports Council, *Irish Sports Monitor 2011 Annual Report* (Dublin: Irish Sports Council).

20 Cuchulainn also appears in Manx and Scottish folklore.

21 See, for example, *Irish Independent*, 24 August 2013, 'On dark days, we rejoice in sport as opium of the masses'.

22 www.bbc.co.uk/sport/0/horse-racing/22311838, accessed 14 August 2013; http://thecorknews.ie/content/'million-dollar-baby'-george-hook-salutes-inspirational-irish-boxer-katie-taylor; http://www.morganmckinley.ie/article/katie-taylor-olympic-champion, accessed14 August 2013.

23   Tom Inglis, *Global Ireland: Same Difference* (New York: Routledge, 2008), p. 5.

24. www.irishexaminer.com/archives/2004/1217/ireland/damn-the-begrudgers-oaposdriscoll-is-the-greatest-343632132.html.

20

Feeling at home in contemporary Ireland

Ethel Crowley

A well-known advertisement for Irish butter shows a young Irish emigrant and his pregnant German wife visiting his mother at home in rural Ireland. Before he leaves, he extracts a sod of earth, placing it in a shoebox to take with them. He says of their baby, 'He'll be born in Germany, but his feet will touch Irish soil first'. This clever advertisement touches our hearts and raises many issues surrounding identity and migration that are very pertinent in contemporary Ireland. This chapter discusses the new complexities of our increasingly multicultural society that result from migratory ebbs and flows.

'Home'

The young man in the aforementioned advertisement still sees rural Ireland as his 'home', despite living in Germany, probably permanently. We associate the idea of 'home' with a comfortable place where we feel happy, relaxed and deeply familiar with our surroundings. It is where we feel naturally connected or *locked in* to a place and its people, on the basis of shared memories with family, friends and loved ones. It gives us a sense of wholeness and stability. The German word for home, '*heim*', is derived from the Indo-European notion of '*kei*', meaning 'something precious'.[1] It is our own feelings about that place that really matter, as no physical place has inherent meaning until people themselves attach meaning to it.

In Ireland historically, the idea of home has not been one to be taken for granted, because of painful memories of poverty, emigration and war. For example, to some extent, artistic representations of the poverty of the peasantry in rural Ireland still resonate with our historical memories. A painting like James Brenan's *News from America* (1875) still somehow speaks to our souls. In it, the family in a nineteenth-century one-roomed cottage gathers around a young girl reading a letter, clearly from emigrant kin in America. She is the only one in the family who can read, so she is the cultural conduit from the outside world, the most powerful person in the room. The emigration to which this painting refers has remained a constant theme in Irish society, creating social, cultural and economic links between many thousands of Irish homes and other parts of the world.

Of course, our home extends beyond our houses to the areas in which we grew up and/or reside. When asked to write about her own home, the travel writer Dervla Murphy muses:

> to me west Waterford, south Tipperary and east Cork are incomparably satisfying. Everything is congenial: every curve of the hills and valleys, every bend of the rivers and streams, every distinctive seasonal scent of fields and woods. This territory is my natural habitat, where I'm at ease in all weathers.[2]

Despite all of her travels, this region is still the most significant place in the world for her, and, because of its early imprinting, it surpasses all others in its power over her. For others, it is not so simple. The writer Brian Keenan embarked upon an adventure to Alaska in recent years. A very thoughtful person who has endured unimaginable trauma in his life, he admitted that 'a part of me has always been looking for a place of belonging, a spiritual homeland that has nothing to do with ownership but a place where authenticity can be found and affirmed. Carl Jung called it a "psychic observation post" from where we might understand the deepest parts of ourselves and recalibrate the trajectory of our life.'[3]

For some people, the sense of connection with their home is very strong and they have no desire to move anywhere else. Others, like the nomadic Irish travel writer Mary Russell, say that their home is simply where their toothbrush is.[4] However, your home usually means most to you after you have been away from it. To return to your house or neighbourhood after an absence changes your perspective on it. Depending on where you have been, you might love being home or abhor it. It also depends on the circumstances of your leaving. If you have chosen to leave, the idea and reality of home is not as poignant and painful as if you have been forced to leave.

People often speak of being 'homesick' when abroad. They experience feelings of nostalgia and loneliness, missing what is familiar and comfortable. In eighteenth- and nineteenth-century psychiatry, 'nostalgia' was defined as a psychological disorder, with the word derived from the Greek term *nostos* (return home) and *algos* (pain). The term was first used in 1688. It was found to be a common complaint among soldiers, and the only effective treatment for it was to return to their homes.[5] While it is no longer formally defined as a psychiatric problem per se, we all still know what homesickness feels like.

One of the many old songs addressing the idea of home is 'The Homes of Donegal'. This story is told from the perspective of a tramp who finds shelter and company in people's houses as he travels around County Donegal. He paints a scene of traditional domestic bliss. The people are friendly, the fire is lit, a meal is prepared and ultimately there is a 'shake-down by the wall', a bed upon which he can lay his weary head. It was first sung by the recently deceased Bridie Gallagher, but Paul Brady has popularised this old song in more recent years. It is certainly evocative as a piece of social history but it belongs firmly in the past. Imagine the scene in Ireland as we now know it. Firstly, tramps are no longer a well-known social category. Secondly, any door the man might knock on would be unlikely to be answered, as the house might either be a holiday home or simply empty all day because the occupants are out working to pay off their mortgage. Thirdly, even if somebody did open the door, what are the chances of a 'weary wanderer' receiving anything like a welcome? It is my impression that he would be more likely to be greeted with suspicion. Maybe life was never as pleasant a picture as that depicted in the song, but it provides us with a self-image that pleases us, and the song still gives us a rosy glow. Is it the case that the image of home portrayed in this song is still very close to our hearts? Is this unique to Irish people because of our colonial past or is it connected to our history of emigration?

Emigration

The experience of global movement has become part and parcel of being Irish. We have always been a nation on the move, with emigration serving as a socio-economic safety valve. The most recent statistics available show that 40,200 Irish people emigrated between April 2010 and April 2011, with 57 per cent of these male and 43 per cent female. This compared to 13,100 in 2007.[6] It has even been suggested that it could be fruitful to view Ireland as a place of 'pure mobility, dominated by movement and fluidity'.[7] A huge sense of loss is often felt by out-migrants, as they have to sacrifice their sources of support and perhaps their sense of membership of a local community because of economic pressures.

The idealised view of family and community life expressed historically by de Valéra is a far cry from the realities of most Irish people throughout the decades since. In MacLaughlin's emigration survey in the 1990s, 13 per cent of the families analysed had three or more members abroad. He asserts, the 'sanctity of the family as enshrined in the 1937 Constitution is in stark contrast with a reality which sees emigration, often of quite young teenagers, embedded in the economic landscape and political system of this country.'[8] Being set up as pawns to be moved around a global economic chessboard is nothing new to us. For parents and loved ones left behind, this aspect of globalisation touches them too. One oft-quoted effect of this is that some small places in Ireland find it difficult to compose a GAA football or hurling team because of the emigration of the young players.

When migrants return to their Irish homes after a long absence, they may experience feelings of confusion, disappointment or displacement. The place they encounter has probably changed perhaps quite drastically from the one they left years before. It is at once familiar and strange, a bittersweet experience. Peter

Creedon, an emigrant interviewed by *The Irish Times* on these issues, raised some interesting points. He finds that when he comes back to Ireland, his friends who have stayed here tend to keep him at an emotional distance: 'you become part of the community that has travelled away'. He said that he considers New York home now because he did a lot of his growing up there. He muses, 'I think I came of age there'.[9] Peter, as well as every other person who has followed the same path, suffers from what Pico Iyer terms 'the immigrant's bifurcation – torn between the home he carried in his blood and the one he had on paper'.[10] Returned emigrants do not take home for granted any more, because they have seen and lived among difference in other places.

Salman Rushdie is one of the most notable authors on the subject of migration and exile. He left India for the UK as a teenager and only remembers his Indian childhood in fragments. He argues that these fragments become all the more special because they are incomplete, comparing them to the bits of pottery found by archaeologists. These vessels were very ordinary at the time of their using, but acquire great significance many years later. He says that 'the shards of memory acquired greater status, greater resonance, because they were *remains*; fragmentation made trivial things seem like symbols, and the mundane acquired numinous qualities'. It is our very humanity that shapes our memories, as 'we are not gods but wounded creatures, cracked lenses, capable only of fractured perceptions'. We build meaning from 'scraps, dogmas, childhood injuries, newspaper articles, chance remarks, old films, small victories, people hated, people loved' and 'perhaps it is because our sense of what is the case is constructed from such inadequate materials that we defend it so fiercely, even to the death'.[11]

Remembered places have often served as symbolic anchors of home and community for dispersed peoples. Although the 'homes' that connect various identities can be denied people physically by exile or migration, they still continue to resonate imaginatively among the displaced. This may lead to an absentee nationalism being expressed by emigrants, supporting causes back 'home' that those who actually live at home may abhor, especially those movements who have used violent political strategies. However, ultimately, emigrants can never properly return to the place where they grew up, as both themselves and the place itself have changed. It is possibly not the place itself they miss most, however, but their own younger, more innocent selves. Maybe when they leave, they ultimately buy an emotional one-way ticket, as they can never re-create the way things were, and other people move on with their lives, without them in it. They have also had experiences in their own lives that those at home could not even imagine. So emigrants ultimately inhabit a shadow-land between insider and outsider. Being 'worldly' has its downsides as well – part of the messy ambiguity of modernity. The emotional cartography of emigrant families stretches from Cork to New York, from Charlestown to Cape Town. There is a weary familiarity about the new wave of Irish emigration. Ireland has once again become the kind of place that people want to get away from, rather than the kind of place they want to go to. Here we go again.

Irish music, literature and poetry are suffused with stories about emigration and movement. Much of our national cultural catalogue is of course as much *of* other places as it is of Ireland. The power of the Catholic Church stymied so much Irish creativity throughout the years. James Joyce, for example, might never have been published in the early twentieth century if he had not gone to live in other European cities like Paris and Zurich, or the series *Father Ted* might never have seen the light of day if it had been left up to our own national broadcaster to produce it. Those who have had the faith and courage to back some of our best writers and performers have often come from elsewhere, evidenced of course by the huge success of so many Irish actors in Hollywood. Colin Farrell might still be an underpaid exotic dancer if he had never left Dublin. Colum McCann's novel *Let the Great World Spin* is lauded as the quintessential work about the identity of New York City, post 9/11. His novel *TransAtlantic* is a beautifully imaginative evocation of the connections between Ireland and North America over the centuries. As well as this, the market for Irish cultural products is huge internationally, most especially in the United States. As Honor Fagan argues, 'the spectacle of Riverdance, the music of the Chieftains and the "new" Irish films cannot be understood as national cultural forms. They may be partly constituted locally but it is with reference to a global cultural market: they are local cultural keys turning global locks.'[12] So it is not just the subject matter of these cultural products that is based on the major tropes of movement, adaptation, exile, loneliness, but the very conditions of their making, and indeed selling.

Immigration

The immigration of different nationalities in recent years has made Ireland much more diverse than previously. Official estimates of immigrant numbers are usually much lower than estimates by those who work with immigrants. This is due to a proportion of them who are in the country illegally and therefore may not fill in the census. However, these statistics are the only relatively reliable statistical source one can access. At the time of the 2011 Census of Population, 544,357 non-Irish nationals lived in Ireland. The top ten nationalities were 122,585 Poles, 112,259 UK citizens, 36,683 Lithuanians, 20,593 Latvians, 17,642 Nigerians, 17,304 Romanians, 16,986 Indians, 14,699 Irish-Americans, 12,791 Filipinos and 11,305 Germans. Other very significant groups were US citizens, Chinese, Slovaks, French, Spanish, Italians, South Africans, Czechs, Hungarians, Pakistanis and Brazilians.[13] It is impossible to generalise about these immigrants, as they are an extremely socially heterogeneous group. They work in all economic sectors, from manual to professional. They made a huge contribution to every sector during the boom years of the Celtic Tiger.

While moving to Ireland no doubt constituted a positive new start for some immigrants, there has also been proven exploitation of vulnerable immigrant workers. In 2004, the Migrant Rights Centre of Ireland published a report documenting widespread exploitation and maltreatment of foreign domestic workers in Irish middle-class homes. One of their female interviewees said, 'the problem with parents who don't respect foreign workers is that they pass these attitudes on to their children – treating us without any respect becomes normal'. Neither were male immigrants off the hook. The exploitation of the GAMA road construction workers during the Celtic Tiger years was another case in point. This group of Turkish men were often paid as few as €2.20 per hour and accorded few or no basic workers' rights.[14]

As well as this, some non-EU immigrants are placed in segregated temporary accommodation, which serves to cut them off from the rest of the population. This serves to perpetuate social inequality, especially in the context of the continued 'suburbanisation of Ireland [which] has also meant that many individuals have withdrawn into exclusive enclaves, devaluing public spaces and reproducing class and racial segregation'.[15] There have been many racially motivated attacks in Ireland. While there have been many verbal attacks, beatings and stabbings, these have sometimes culminated in death. For example, two young Polish men, Pawel Kalite and Marius Szwajkos, were viciously stabbed to death with screwdrivers on a Dublin street in February 2008. Another young Polish man, Lukasz Rzeszutko, was savagely beaten to death in Dublin in October 2010.

Many of Ireland's immigrants have been returning to their home countries since the onset of the recession. In 2009, 30,100 people from the East European accession states left Ireland, over two-thirds of whom were male. Among the immigrants, this group was the one that was most heavily affected by the downturn in the construction sector. Of the 118,000 foreign nationals aged fifteen or over who were assigned Personal Public Service Numbers (PPSNs) in 2004, only 33 per cent worked in 2009. Ireland may no longer be an attractive destination for immigrants seeking work.[16]

Hybrid identities

The ways in which various types of immigrants adapt to the expectations of their host communities and develop their own cultural confidence lead to the emergence of different forms of hybrid identities. There is a constant movement of people and ideas throughout the world, generating cultural meaning in the interstices and flows *between* physical locations.

This is especially true of young people and the next generation, who change significantly as a result of assimilation. One school, in Balbriggan, County Dublin, has a majority of African pupils. The principal says that 'we have great ambitions for these children – they have great potential and they are as bright as buttons ... some speak several languages and are learning Arabic at weekends. Irish is no problem to them.'[17] I recently witnessed the young teenage daughter of German immigrants translating some Irish for her parents at a west Cork St Patrick's Day Parade. She, and many thousands like her, is well able to negotiate both worlds, that of her parents and of her school and wider society. One would wonder if she feels that her two cultures are conflicting or harmonious. A disadvantage of this hybridity could be that she feels different to everyone else, and therefore not fully at home in either place. A major advantage is that she speaks at least two languages fluently, she has a close affinity with another country and therefore could make more options available to herself in her later life.

Narrow national identities are challenged by such cultural difference, where minorities are not just melted into the host culture but are a source of social, cultural and economic innovation. As Salman Rushdie says, 'to migrate is certainly to lose language and home, to be defined by others, to become invisible or, even worse, a target; it is to experience deep changes and wrenches in the soul'. He then qualifies this: 'but the migrant is not simply transformed by his act; he [*sic*] also transforms his new world. Migrants may well become mutants, but it is out of such hybridisation that newness can emerge.'[18] Diaspora communities, whether of the Irish abroad, or, for example, of German or English people in Ireland, develop new cultural forms which are a mix of the old and new world, the old and new ways. This idea is threatening to some and exciting to others, but, regardless, we must live with the social effects of cultural difference, transition and displacement. There is no room in today's world for ideas about cultural purity and authenticity. Cultural purity is a myth, as mixing has always occurred. In trying to understand the complexities of cultural hybridity, it may be instructive to examine the experiences of other ethnic groups like those of the Asian and Afro-Caribbean communities in Britain.

Probably the most sophisticated and influential attempt to make sense of cultural hybridity to date has been Paul Gilroy's *Black Atlantic*. In trying to understand the 'doubleness and cultural intermixture' of the experiences of British Blacks, he deems it necessary to rise out of the strictures of national boundaries and write their movements across the 'Black Atlantic' into the heart of his analysis. This serves to highlight the connections between British Blacks and those in the Americas and the Caribbean, foregrounding their agency as political activists and cultural producers and not just as passive victims of slavery. He suggests that cultural historians should 'take the Atlantic as one single complex unit of analysis … and use it to produce an explicitly transnational and intercultural perspective'. He finds the image of the slave ship useful in thinking about this. These ships, as well as being symbols of racial terrorism, were ultimately, in the long run, a means of connecting black people globally and a conduit for political dissent and the creation of new hybrid cultures. He unearths little-known Black people who excelled in politics and the arts, and who used their experiences of exile and displacement as sources of inspiration 'in the difficult journey from slave ships to citizenship'.[19] Gilroy argues convincingly that such inputs are best analysed as transcultural products, born out of movement and travel between fixed nation-states.

Music has always been a cultural medium that lends itself very readily to expressing hybridity. It is impossible to build walls around genres, styles and types of music. While it might appear trivial in the bigger scheme of things, cultural products like music, food and language can help enormously in integrating minorities into the broader community and in breaking down racist ideologies. Unpredictable mixing and cultural hybridisation are often reflected in the composition of real places, where the arrival of particular ethnic groups or nationalities can dramatically alter neighbourhoods that might have been quite homogenous in the past.

In Dublin, the Moore Street and Parnell Street area has become an urban hybrid site in recent years. For many decades, the traditional street market traders on Moore Street have been the cultural guardians of this market's distinctiveness. Behind these stalls, there are now a variety of nationalities doing business, providing the tastes of home for Dublin's immigrant communities. There are East European, Nigerian, Vietnamese and Chinese food stores, restaurants, Internet cafés and hairdressers operating cheek by jowl. In the last few years, the Moore Street Mall has opened, offering a multicultural shopping experience to consumers, with various types of African, Asian and East European produce on offer. One could have one's hair done in an elaborate African style, buy some Hungarian wine or Polish pierogi and eat some authentic Chinese Hoisin duck for lunch, all under one roof. Immigrants have been attracted to this area by low rents, and many of the shop fronts are basic and cheaply constructed. The Dublin Civic Trust, while it welcomes the renewed vibrancy of the area, feels that proper planning needs to be put in place to raise its profile and to restore the traditional façades on the buildings. It recommends the creation of an 'oriental enclave' in the area that would showcase Asian culture without impacting on the streetscape nearby.[20] This shows that different versions of a sense of place are not always harmonious. However, more positively, in nearby Smithfield, Chinese New Year is celebrated every year with a dragon-bedecked colourful festival. This has become one of the major events in Dublin's cultural calendar.

As Fanning has described in Chapter 15 above, Gort in County Galway is one of the success stories of Irish immigration. If all Irish immigration stories were like Gort, then Ireland would be really different. According to the 2006 Census, one-third of all 4,388 Brazilians then living in Ireland lived in County Galway. The Census shows that 40 per cent of the town's residents were non-Irish, with 83 per cent of these Brazilian. Gort became a model of cultural integration. That is not to deny that exploitation probably took place too, as some of the Brazilans worked only on a casual basis and for low wages. One could usually see the men standing on a particular corner of the town square, hiring themselves out for casual work on local farms and businesses. Since the recession began in 2008, many of them have gone back home to Brazil, as their lives in Ireland became less viable with increasing unemployment and poverty. One Irish journalist visited the southern Brazilian city of Anápolis, where many of the Gort immigrants originated. He found evidence of new wealth, with extravagant housing amidst the poorer, older accommodation. He met children there who spoke with Galway accents, played hurling and pined for Ireland. One house was even painted in the green, white and gold of the Irish flag. The connection is so strong between Vila Fabril (the suburb of Anápolis where many of them came from) and Gort that it is 'talked about as if it were a neighbouring townland'.[21]

Cosmopolitan values

No matter where one lives or where one moves to around the world, one is never fully removed from the operation of global socio-economic forces. It is productive and useful to use the following as a guideline:

> Rather than view home as rooted, located and bounded, and often closely tied to a remembered or imagined homeland, an emphasis on 'routes' invokes more mobile, and often de-territorialized, geographies of home that reflect transnational connections and networks.[22]

Each town, city, region and country has a place in the global order and is a product of socio-historical change. Massey argues that 'a large component of the identity of that place called home derived precisely from the fact that it had always in one way or another been open; constructed out of movement, communication, social relations which always stretched beyond it'.[23] This is not just a recent phenomenon, but stretches back hundreds of years. The cultural differences between people are a product of a shared historical process that differentiates and connects the world at the same time, producing endless variations.

The core question is how we can live in such a complex world and create for ourselves a sense of self, a sense of connection with our places, as well as being informed by a sense of social justice. Cosmopolitanism is a key philosophical idea that can help us to live lives that are other-centred rather than self-centred.[24] The origin of the word 'cosmopolitan' is from the Greek *kosmos*, meaning 'world' and *polis*, meaning 'city'. To say that someone is cosmopolitan is to say that he or she is first and foremost a citizen of the world, over and above being a citizen of any state. One is not born, but rather becomes cosmopolitan. It is not the product of social class or status, but is something to be *worked at*. We can invent and reinvent it on a daily basis. It is not a cultural resource that is passed on by one's forebears, and it does not exist in pure form. *Webster's Dictionary* defines 'cosmopolitan' as 'not bound by local or national habits or prejudices; at home in all countries or places'. The cosmopolitan can be in her comfort zone in many parts of the world and among many types of people. She can find some essential feeling of connection with people from cultures that are very different to her own culture of origin.

Conclusion

Society is always changing as a result of human migration, and to feel comfortable with that is often a challenge. The cosmopolitan welcomes immigrants into her community, viewing them as an enhancement of the local cultural mosaic. This is the complete opposite of the xenophobic perspective, which ultimately fears 'different' outsiders and views them as a threat to the local culture. A crucial point is that the cosmopolitan *seeks out* the distinctiveness of local cultures, so local cultural guardians perform a huge service in working at maintaining these, for the cosmopolitan to enjoy. To be able to feel at home in contemporary Ireland requires of people that they stretch themselves, adopt a cosmopolitan attitude and welcome difference into their homes and communities. When we sneak backstage in other people's lives, it gives us a great sense of perspective on the value of cultural uniqueness. This also means that we can make learning a life long process, rather than something associated with limited formal schooling. The hybridities that result from the mixing of people from different cultural backgrounds serve to enhance and enrich social life, rather than threaten some mythical cultural 'purity'. The movement of Irish people around the world has created a strong diaspora community, so cultural mixing is nothing new to us.

Notes

1   Jan Willem Duyvendak, *The Politics of Home: Belonging and Nostalgia in Western Europe and the United States* (Basingstoke: Palgrave Macmillan, 2011), p. 27.
2   Dervla Murphy, 'Swept Away on My Own River of Life', *Irish Times*, 8 August 2011.
3   Brian Keenan, *Four Quarters of Light: A Journey through Alaska* (London: Black Swan, 2005), p. 112.
4   Mary Russell, *Journeys of a Lifetime* (London: Simon and Schuster, 2002), p. 105.
5   Trevor Turner, 'Homeworld', *New Internationalist*, 296 (1997), pp. 28–30.
6   Central Statistics Office, 'Population and Migration Estimates: April 2011' (2011).
7   Honor Fagan, 'Globalised Ireland, or, Contemporary Transformations of National Identity?', in Colin Coulter and Steve Coleman (eds), *The End of Irish History? Critical Reflections on the Celtic Tiger* (Manchester: Manchester University Press, 2003), p. 119.
8   Jim MacLaughlin, *Ireland: The Emigrant Nursery and the World Economy* (Cork: Cork University Press, 1994), p. 60.
9   Fiona McCann, 'There's No Fantasy Place Like Home', *Irish Times*, 14 March 2009.
10 Pico Iyer, *The Global Soul: Jet-lag, Shopping Malls and the Search for Home* (London: Bloomsbury, 2001), p. 18.
11 Salman Rushdie, *Imaginary Homelands: Essays and Criticism 1981–1991* (London: Granta, 1991), p. 12.
12 Fagan, 'Globalised Ireland', p. 117.
13 'Highlights from Census 2011', *Irish Times*, 29 March 2012.
14 Carl O'Brien, 'Time to Clean up Migrants' Rights', *TIrish Times*, 18 December 2004; Kieran Allen, *The Corporate Takeover of Ireland* (Dublin: Irish Academic Press, 2007), pp. 94–9.

15 Carmen Kuhling and Kieran Keohane, *Cosmopolitan Ireland: Globalisation and Quality of Life* (London: Pluto Press, 2007), p. 191.

16 Central Statistics Office, 'Population and Migration Estimates: April 2011'.

17 Susan McKay, 'Welcome to Our World', *Irish Times Magazine*, 25 May 2008.

18 Rushdie, *Imaginary Homelands*, p. 210.

19 Paul Gilroy, *Black Atlantic* (Oxford: Blackwell, 1993), pp. 4–31.

20 Olivia Kelly, '"Oriental Enclave" Recommended for Dublin', *Irish Times*, 13 October 2011.

21   Ruadhan Mac Cormaic, 'Brazilian Thoughts Turn to Home', *Irish Times*, 28 April 2008.

22 Alison Blunt and Robyn Dowling, *Home* (London: Routledge, 2006), p. 199.

23 Doreen Massey, *Space, Place and Gender* (Minneapolis: University of Minnesota Press, 1994), p. 171.

24 For a very detailed discussion of this concept and a new approach to it, see Ethel Crowley, *Your Place or Mine? Community and Belonging in 21st Century Ireland* (Dublin: Orpen Press, 2013).

21

Searching for and explaining difference

Tom Inglis

There is always a danger in studying Ireland that, instead of questioning the stories and myths about Irish cultural difference, we end up reproducing them. In the absence of appropriate theoretical frameworks that help shine a light on where to look for difference and, at the same time, the absence of rigorous methods that enable the gathering of empirical data, those of us involved in Irish studies may perpetuate the very differences that we are studying. For example, consider the absence of positive empirical methods and, in particular, the absence of quantitative social survey data. In the wealth of generalisations about the Irish, and what makes the Irish different, it might be useful to produce some verifiable, reliable facts about Irish difference that can be compared with survey data from other countries. From these data, it should be possible to say with some statistical accuracy to what extent the Irish are different in relation to a variety of cultural beliefs, attitudes and practices, including personal characteristics such as happiness and well-being. However, there seems to be little use of such comparative data within Irish studies. Indeed, what is even more remarkable is how little the human sciences are included in Irish studies. The two issues are interrelated. The dominance of literary theory and criticism in Irish studies has meant that, when it comes to understanding the Irish, there seems to be a preference for soft hermeneutical understandings rather than positive empirical truth. The problem with hermeneutical understandings is that, even if there is agreement that there is something different about being Irish, we can never know the significance of the difference. In some ways, the argument about national cultural difference is similar to biological explanations of human behaviour. They are obviously a factor, but the question is to what extent.

And herein lies one of the key issues in understanding Irish studies and how it has come to be the way it is. It would seem that one of the epistemological assumptions behind the discipline is not just that the Irish are different, but that the difference is significant. If the Irish were much the same as the rest of the West, if survey data and other empirical indicators revealed that there was not much difference in how they lived their lives compared to those in other Western societies, there might not be as much point in studying them. Indeed, it may well be that focusing on insignificant cultural difference inhibits an understanding of the real conditions of Irish society and culture. So there is an assumption within the core of much of what constitutes Irish studies that somehow, over generations, the Irish have developed a *habitus*, a way of seeing and being in the world, that differs from the *habitus* and practices of other nationals. It is this national *habitus*, shared at least in part with all Irish people wherever they are, which helps explain not just Irish cultural difference but also perhaps Irish social, economic and political behaviour.

If then, we are to make the argument that the Irish are culturally different, and that this difference is significant, and if we do not insist on making statements that can be empirically tested, there is at least a need to develop coherent analytical concepts, theories and methods that can help illuminate what these differences might be and how they have been created and maintained. It may well be that some of the cultural and personality traits identified and described in the chapters in this book are more prevalent among the Irish. However, the question is how and where we look for evidence of this difference. This is where theories and methods from within the human sciences, particularly sociology, anthropology, psychology and philosophy, could be useful. They may point to empirical clues to the wider social and cultural whole and help explain how the Irish came to be the way they are.

It is, of course, no coincidence that certain perspectives, theories and methods are dominant in the field of Irish studies while others are excluded. The discursive formation of Irish studies is a study in itself. However, any search for an explanation might usefully look to Foucault's notion of governmentality and, in particular, his notions of the technologies of separation and division.[1] There seems to be a taken-for-granted orthodoxy of what constitutes Irish studies, of what theories and methods, are appropriate and relevant. The constitution of an academic discourse does not come about spontaneously: it is an act of exclusion and symbolic domination that is written into technologies of separation and division manifested in institutes, centres, job appointments, conferences and publications. What needs to be investigated is how this exclusion takes place. How many human scientists hold appointments in Irish studies? How many papers from human scientists are presented at Irish studies conferences? How many papers at Irish studies conferences have had tables of social scientific data?

Exalting difference

One of the central questions for all human beings is: how did we come to be the way we are? We can ask this question of ourselves as individuals. What were the social agencies that disciplined and controlled our drives and affects for us to become emotionally controlled, critically reflective human beings? We can also ask this question of social groups and societies. What social structures and long-term processes changed the relationships between organisations and institutions that changed their policies and practices? Making links between the micro-world of personalities and emotions and the macro-world of social structures, institutions and discourses, and the combination of these into long-term processes of change, has been central to the human sciences. One of the key contributions of Norbert Elias was to make links between the rise of nation-states and the emergence of polite, well-mannered, emotionally controlled, self-disciplined citizens. He also recognised the importance of national sentiment.[2] Creating a sense of 'we-ness', of collective consciousness, is central to the state maintaining its symbolic domination, its right to pass laws and raise taxes and maintain its monopoly over the means of violence. The great cultural revolution of modernity was that people who could never meet and communicate with all their fellow members of a nation deemed themselves to be the same on the basis of common culture, language, history and territory.[3] A conception of Irish difference was historically inculcated in the minds, bodies and souls of each successive generation, in a perfect storm of cultural nationalism propagated by priests, nuns, brothers, teachers and writers, reinforced by compliant parents.[4] However, it would be wrong to interpret Irishness as simply a social construction; an illusion or myth that, in creating a sense of 'we', conceals inequalities in power and acts as a form of symbolic domination. Being Irish has become central to creating and maintaining a sense of bonding and belonging. In order to maintain this sense of belonging, it is necessary to live the illusion, to embody what are believed to be certain cultural traits.

Talking up Irish difference can be seen as central to creating and maintaining a sense of collective consciousness. In this view of social action, Irish people are voluntarily committed to the Irish nation and the nation-state. It is something they value. On the other hand, a coercive view of social action would see Irish cultural difference as a myth, a form of symbolic domination that creates an illusion of collective responsibility and papers over social and economic inequalities. In reality, these two views are not either/or, but two ends of a spectrum. However, it is very easy to recreate myths about the Irish and to make them into a collectively responsible group as the Taoiseach Enda Kenny did when he said: 'What happened in our country was that people went mad borrowing.'[5] There is a danger in talking up national difference. If people believe that the Irish are culturally different, and if this belief becomes hegemonic, there is a danger of it contaminating rigorous, scientific analysis. In many respects, being Irish revolves around the belief that the Irish are not just different but in some ways superior. Those investigating Irish difference need to be on guard against popular concepts and beliefs infiltrating their scientific endeavours. They need to be careful about uncritically endorsing the types of mythical beliefs about the Irish developed and reproduced within the media, often as part of marketing strategies. The logic of being Irish may be living out the myth that the Irish are good-humoured, charming, drunk, lazy, creative, imaginative and so forth.[6] However, the logic of rational scientific investigation, and indeed the possibility of freedom and emancipation, should not be contaminated by mythical thinking.

The notion of cultural difference is more than semiotic distinction; it is rooted in power. It revolves around transforming something arbitrary into a form of hierarchical differentiation. Cultural difference, then, is the embodiment of symbolic domination. As Pierre Bourdieu has demonstrated, at the level of individuals, people in higher social classes develop cultural tastes, preferences and lifestyles that distinguish them from lower social classes and through embodying these accumulate higher levels of cultural capital through which they reproduce their social positions.[7] Does such cultural distinction operate at the level of nations? Do some nations, because of the globally recognised forms of national cultural capital, have higher social positions than others? If this is the case, then we can look at Irish studies as part of a struggle to make Irish national cultural capital a valuable form of global cultural capital?

Theories

When engaging in Irish studies we need to be careful that our arguments are based neither on an enthusiasm for Irish difference nor on arguments about regulating or policing 'Irishness'; rather we must concentrate on those arguments whose strengths lie in their analytic rigour and empirical validity. For various reasons, mostly related to the dominance of literary criticism, postcolonialism has been the dominant theoretical model for interpreting the Irish, their cultural practices and their products. There are various strands of postcolonialism, some more Marxist than others, but the general theory is that being Irish – the experiences, expressions and forms of Irishness – are best understood and explained in terms of Ireland being a former colony of England. The legacies of colonial rule can be still seen in discourses, texts, the arts, everyday life and personal traits.

The problem with postcolonial theory as applied to Ireland is that it tends to conflate all forms of global influences and economic and symbolic domination with the legacy of British imperialism[8] It tends to overlook other external forms of symbolic domination, particularly from America and the Catholic Church and internal forms that emanate from gender, class, religious, ethnic and racial differences. It may well be, for example, that if the Irish are different this may be related more to the nature of the internal class structure, the dominance of the Catholic Church and the oppression of women and children than to having been colonised by England. If we are to understand continuing Irish difference, it may be time to look beyond the narrow arguments of postcolonial theory and examine other forms of cultural imperialism. However, there is also a need to examine other global cultural influences and how they are integrated and assimilated into Irish culture. Finally, it would be wrong to only read these global influences as forms of domination. In many respects, they are voluntary and strategic. The globalisation of Irish society and culture is not necessarily passive and oppressive. What needs to be examined is the way Irish people creatively mix and match, borrow and blend elements of different cultures from around the world in their everyday lives and into their knowledge and understanding of themselves. In this way, instead of looking at Irish culture through a postcolonial lens, it might be better to conceptualise it as a variety of global culture. Moreover, many forms of postcolonial theory tend to emphasise structure over agency: they do not capture the vibrant, dynamic ways in which individuals, as part of their own struggle to attain cultural capital and social position, continually reinvent what it is to be Irish in their everyday lives.

There is, as suggested, a need to link structural transformations and long-term historical processes with the micro-world of the struggle by individuals to develop and maintain their identity, sense of distinction and social position. Embodying perceived beliefs, myths and practices about being Irish can, then, be seen as a strategy to obtain cultural capital. Being Irish, being a citizen, having Irish cultural products, being able to engage in Irish cultural practices can be used, as being Catholic once was, to attain social position, honour and respect. Following Bourdieu, we can say that people are socialised into an Irish *habitus* which, as part of developing their identity and sense of self, they make their own. While there is a shared, inherited, predisposed way of being Irish, it is flexible and adaptable to different social interactions and the strategic interests of the people involved. In constructing their Irish identity, individuals mix and match from the whole array of Irish beliefs, practices and products. The display of their Irish identity will depend on the particular social interaction – there is a time and a place to be Irish – and how much being Irish is an important part of their cultural distinction.

Methods

One tried and trusted method of discovering what is different about the Irish is to undertake a reading of the way in which Irish culture has been expressed and represented in books, films, television programmes and other forms. Writers, artists and other cultural producers shift through events, experiences and emotions to create an understanding of everyday life and what it is to be Irish. They can provide rich, thick descriptions of the moods and modes of being Irish.

It would seem that many people involved in Irish studies, who are readers and analysers of Irish cultural difference, do not study culture directly themselves, but rather rely on their readings of these cultural producers. We get readings of readings. What makes the readings different is the way they are theoretically filtered. Nevertheless, there is the danger that, in this never ending circle of readings of readings, any chance of making empirically valid and reliable statements about Irish cultural difference disappears into a hermeneutical fog. It may well be that what is needed is greater interdisciplinarity. As much as the reading of texts can be informed by the human scientific descriptions and analyses of Irish society, so too could human scientific explanations be informed by examples from literature, films and other cultural products.

Most of the attempts to get closer to the empirical world, to try to make statements that are valid and reliable, come from within history. There has been a positive-empirical tendency in Irish historiography – to stick as closely to the facts as possible. Any understanding of Irish difference is built up from a detailed analysis of empirical material, mostly found in archives, most of which are documents. The underlying epistemological assumption seems to be that, whatever the cultural traits of the Irish, they can be deciphered by gathering valid and reliable information about particular aspects of Irish history and, as much as possible, by linking these little pieces of history together so that they contribute to an overall picture of how the Irish came to be the way they are. Within this method, there is a reluctance to be guided by abstract theories, particularly those that focus on long-term processes of social change. There are also epistemological assumptions, rarely revealed or discussed, as to how the interests of the present determine which items from these documents are selected and read. On the other hand, in comparison to literary criticism, there are studious attempts made to avoid wandering into the realm of readings of readings – hence this form of historiography avoids using novels, films and other cultural products. However, the danger of relying on archival material is that any questions about Irish difference are confined by the method; if there are no archives, there may be no history. As suggested, it may be that what makes the Irish different is the way they interact in social life, the way they present themselves, the stories they tell and how they tell them. The problem is: how can we investigate this?

It could be argued that the availability of sources and the use of particular methods of historiography have influenced the questions that are asked about Irish difference and how they are answered. There appears to be a hierarchy of primary sources, starting with public archives and official records. However, all these sources tend to give a top-down interpretation of what makes Ireland different. It is difficult to build a picture of the *habitus* of the time, the practices of ordinary people in everyday life and the way they physically and emotionally interacted and constructed their identities, their sense of self and difference. Diaries, memoirs and more personal material from everyday life may provide important clues and could be used more often. And the task, in an interdisciplinary approach, is to find ways in which these more qualitative methods could be combined with methods in which there is a greater emphasis on assessing the validity and reliability of any statements or claims.

For example, the Ryan Report into clerical child sex abuse provides rich material of what some Irish people did to each other in industrial and reformatory schools which can help shine a light on Irish cultural difference.[9] However, there are dangers in reading the normal from the pathological. But there are other methods of investigating ordinary people and everyday life. Sociologists and anthropologists have developed a variety of reliable methods. It is, for example, possible to interview people who are in their seventies and ask them about sex, marriage and gender relations. It is also possible to use memoirs, diaries, letters and advice columns.[10] More radical perhaps, it is possible for researchers into Irish difference to write their own diaries and memoirs, and try to capture their emotions and bodily experiences. These could become rich archives for historians in years to come. It could be argued that a theoretically informed critically reflective description of an academic's own emotions, intimacies and sexuality would be unrepresentative but it would be no more so than any novel, film or political autobiography.

Conclusion

I have argued that when it comes to describing and analysing Irish difference there is a limited range of theories and methods used. I have suggested that greater emphasis be given to the body, emotions and the strategies in which people use Irishness to create their own identities, sense of self and cultural distinction. There is also a need for a long-term historical perspective linking bodies and emotions to national cultural difference and for a greater variety of methods to be used in investigating the origins and everyday reproduction of these differences.

Instead of seeing the Irish as indigenously different, it might be better to focus on how Irish people construct their sense of difference through combining global cultural elements that they acquire through the market, the media and travel with local and national elements of culture. Irish cultural difference has always been created and maintained through mixing and matching the local with the global.[11] In moving towards the notion of glocalisation, of how the global and the local become mixed into varieties of cosmopolitanism, we may begin to realise that the creation and maintenance of Irish difference does not take place just within Ireland, that what it is to be Irish is being continually reinvented by the diaspora and others in many different countries. Many of the places in which this continual cultural reinvention is happening are in new social media, on blogs, in Facebook and Twitter. These are the new sites, the new texts, which have to be studied, read and analysed. If we are to tell the story about Ireland we need to have greater hybridity, particularly in developing alternative theories and methods and more inter disciplinary approaches that include the human sciences.

Notes

1   Michel Foucault, *Discipline & Punish: The Birth of the Prison* (New York: Vintage Books, 1979).

2   The links between psychogenesis and sociogenesis were central to Elias's theory of the civilising process: see Norbert Elias, *The Civilizing Process: Sociogenetic and Psychogenetic Investigations* (Oxford: Blackwell, 2000).

3   Benedict Anderson, *Imagined Communities* (London: Verso, 1983). The links between national senses of belonging and micro-solidarity are developed in Siniša Malešević, *Nation-States and Nationalisms* (Cambridge: Polity, 2013).

4   Jim MacLaughlin, *Reimaging the Nation State: The Contested Terrains of Nation Building* (London: Pluto Press, 2001).

5   Derek Scally, 'Taoiseach Blames Crash on "Mad Borrowing" Frenzy', *Irish Times*, 29 January 2012.

6   Loïc Wacquant, 'For an Analytic of Racial Domination', in *Political Power and Social Theory* (Greenwich, CT: JAI Press, 1997).

7   Pierre Bourdieu, *Distinction: A Social Critique of the Judgement of Taste* (London: Routledge & Kegan Paul, 1979).

8   For a more thorough analysis of postcolonial theory in Irish studies and of the field of Irish studies generally, some of which I have touched on in this chapter, see Linda Connolly, 'The Limits of "Irish Studies": Historicism, Culturalism, Paternalism', *Irish Studies Review*, 12:2 (2004), pp. 139–62.

9   The Commission to Inquire into Child Abuse, *Commission to Inquire into Child Abuse Report* (Dublin: The Stationery Office, 2009).

10 There are pioneering examples of how the history of intimacy in Ireland can be produced through combining oral history with analyses of popular culture within a theoretically informed framework such as Paul Ryan, *Asking Angela Macnamara: An Intimate History of Irish Lives* (Dublin: Irish Academic Press, 2012).

11 Tom Inglis, *Global Ireland: Same Difference* (New York: Routledge, 2008).

22

A new vision of Irish studies

Linda Connolly

One of the pervasive concerns in contemporary Irish studies is the core question framing this volume – are 'the Irish' different? Numerous studies, particularly in Irish literature and Irish history, have explored whether or not an authentic, coherent and distinctive Irish identity exists. This is often linked to another question. What, in comparative terms, is it that makes 'the Irish' different and exceptional as a nation and ethnic group? The notion of Irish exceptionalism is a subject that has also prevailed in a range of other fields outside of the Irish studies framework. Sociologists along with social and economic historians, anthropologists, political theorists and economists have invariably investigated the question: is Ireland – that is its people, societal development, prevailing values, histories, cultural norms and so forth – fundamentally 'different' from other Western European societies on a range of socio-cultural indicators? Is Ireland an outlier in terms of demography, economy, politics, society and culture? And, if so, why is this the case?

The wisdom of asking such a potentially loaded and essentialist question – are the Irish different? – is, of course, questionable: a more postmodern approach would reject the very notion that some kind of fixed Irishness or authentic Irish identity truly exists. At the same time, this underlying question about 'difference' is strongly reflected in the intellectual and political fault lines that emerged in the field of Irish studies in the 1980s. Much of the acrimony revolved around the 'right' interpretation of Irish history and society, past and present.[1] Debates about the distinctiveness of Ireland (in particular, the historical trajectory and cultural politics of Ireland) and the Irish formed a very prominent binary conflict between two intellectual categories – revisionists and nationalists – in two particular disciplines – history and literary criticism.

This chapter will outline some of the complex debates and transformations that have since taken place in the field of Irish studies, and will explore some of the ways in which 'the Irish' and 'Irishness' have been framed. In particular, the distinctive turn towards dense, complicated theory in the field will be unpacked and analysed. The analysis provided has its own limitations in that it is not a complete survey of the entire Irish Studies field, nor does it claim to address the true diversity of work and perspective that, in reality, exists right across Irish studies (inclusively understood) in a range of disciplines. Taking this into account, part one provides a critical exploration of some important key debates and controversies that have emerged in recent years and shaped the terrain. The question – what is Irish studies now? – will be explored. Examples of new fault lines that have recently emerged, particularly among postcolonial theorists and feminists, will be mapped and examined. The marginal role of sociology and social science in the field of Irish studies will be addressed in part two. In particular, I argue against the perpetuation of a conceptually narrow, limited and exclusive interpretation of the categories the Irish, Irishness and Ireland, which are in reality contested terms. I will propose potentially more inclusive ways of conceptualising that are more sensitive to research emerging from the social sciences and sociology, specifically.

Are the Irish different?

For some scholars, the notion of Irish exceptionalism (considered to be more aligned with 'nationalism') was the overarching framework in which to best understand and define Ireland. In this perspective, Ireland was broadly conceptualised as an oppressed but rebellious nation both in the past and in the context of political, cultural, social and economic legacies in the present. Ireland was colonised and fundamentally oppressed. As a consequence, it is distinctive in its persistent underdevelopment. What is 'different' about Ireland and the Irish in this framework is a historically constructed colonial relationship with England which was sustained in various forms and legacies in the postcolonial era after Independence (1922) and which was opposed and resisted by social and political movements informed by nationalism. In the more contemporary version of this framework, it is emphasised that Ireland has more in common socially and politically with other postcolonial nations and anti-imperial struggles internationally, particularly in the global South, and less with Western European imperial, liberal nations.[2]

A more sanitised and integrationist interpretation of Irish history, culture and society (revisionism) developed in opposition to this nationalist perspective. Here the commonalities and co-operation that Ireland shared and continues to share with other countries globally (particularly with the UK) are emphasised. The Irish, in this perspective, are seen as not really that different (or certainly are not that different any more). This is evident, it is argued, in the fact that Ireland since the 1970s has undergone a process of social change. Irish society has modernised and globalised and, in doing so, has converged with Europe and Western society. Indicators of this include joining the EU, the profound changes in the arena of family life and sexualities, secularisation, the gains in women's rights and, more generally, the diffusion of global culture. In relation to Northern Ireland, revisionists recognise the need for parity of esteem for unionism and Catholics sympathetic to imperialism. They point to the positive interrelationships that exist on 'these islands' and how an acceptance of Britishness and imperialism is an intrinsic aspect of Irish history and culture that must be understood and incorporated into any analysis.[3]

The dispute about colonialism in Irish studies, and the categories nationalist and revisionist as they were originally conceptualised in prominent exchanges between scholars like Seamus Deane, Roy Foster and others, failed to capture the true complexity of Irish studies as it is more broadly practised. The debate about nationalism and revisionism was, in reality, a very sophisticated but limited arena of dispute between some modern Irish historians and prominent literary critics. This struggle for hegemony at the centre ground of Irish studies excluded many other scholars working outside a revisionist/nationalist binary. Several feminists, for instance, went on to expose the gendered nature and orientation of these early debates and the manifest exclusion of Irish women, in particular.[4] The question 'who are the Irish?' and related debates concerning Ireland and 'the Irish experience', particularly in relation to women and everyday life, tended to be ignored. In addition, other disciplines grounded in the materiality of 'everyday life', and in empirical research, were excluded.

What is Irish studies now?

In the 1980s, the Irish historian Roy Foster controversially declared 'we are all revisionists now'.[5] However, in 2014, in the context of Irish studies: what are 'we' all considered to be now? On the one hand, the so-called centre ground of Irish studies has not changed at all since the 1980s: it is still primarily associated with two overarching disciplines – literary criticism and history. At the same time, the field of Irish studies has undoubtedly changed as the original revisionist–nationalist debate waned. Irish studies today is still centrally concerned with nationalism in the context of postcolonialism but there is less overt conflict about historiography and what is considered the right interpretation of 'the Irish past'. There is also more concern with gender.[6] In addition, scholars from other disciplines, apart from literature and history, are beginning to intervene in the arena – some of whom are included in this volume.[7]

In the centre ground of the field of Irish studies today, it could be argued that there is a new overarching presumption that 'we are all postcolonialists now'. Postcolonial theory originally became enormously influential as a framework for understanding the global South. It is also a school of thought popular because of its rejection of the universalising categories of the Enlightenment. Postcolonialism is an academic framework and intellectual discourse that seeks to analyse, explain and respond to the cultural legacies of colonialism and of imperialism. Substantive concerns in the field include the human consequences of controlling a country and establishing settlers for the economic exploitation of the native people and their land. Drawing from postmodern schools of thought, postcolonial studies analyse the social and political power that sustain colonialism and neocolonialism – the how and the why of an imperial regime's representations (social, political, cultural) of itself as the coloniser and of the colonised people. Social scientists working within a world systems or dependency theory framework have been linking the problem of Ireland's economic underdevelopment with colonial structures for many decades. However, postcolonial theory, as described above, has been largely embraced by literary scholars in Irish studies. Several meticulous interventions extolling the centrality of postcolonial theory for understanding Ireland have been published in the field of Irish literary criticism in recent decades. Eoin Flannery, for example, in a detailed appraisal of postcolonial studies, as it applies to Irish studies, hypothesises Ireland as a 'supreme postcolonial instance'.[8] Irish postcolonial theorising is notoriously difficult to understand and, as a consequence, social scientists embedded in 'real world research' have tended to avoid it. Typically, these studies are written in impenetrable language and in an esoteric style.

Postcolonial theory is not completely dominant in Irish literary studies, however. In particular, feminist literary studies, which emerged in the 1980s, have dominated Irish studies conferences and publications in recent years.[9] A new and important debate and dispute have recently developed in Irish studies about the role of gender in postcolonial analysis. Many Irish feminist scholars have been particularly critical of, or hostile to, the manner in which postcolonialism and nationalism represent women.[10] In response, scholars more aligned with postcolonial theory have directly criticised Irish feminism for not engaging with postcolonial theory and for being 'insular' by not aligning more with 'Third World' anti-imperialist feminist struggles.[11] The typical remedy for this alleged flaw in Irish feminism is a demand for it to focus less on criticising Irish postcolonial theorising for being nationalist and masculinist in orientation, to focus less on privileged (particularly Protestant) Irish women writers, and to engage more with postcolonial scholars and writers in the South (global South, that is). In doing so, Irish feminist theorising will be cured of any dubious politics and deficiencies.

New, complicated debates about feminism, nationalism and postcolonialism in Irish studies highlight a propensity for misrepresentation in a field that remains primarily focused on literary criticism. Prominent interventions to date in the debate about gender and postcolonialism demonstrate a particularly narrow focus on certain authors or texts in Irish feminist criticism and do not reference the true varieties of work that exists in Irish gender studies, more globally understood and practised.[12] Very few substantive studies of Irish feminist politics (including feminist nationalism) and the materiality of women's lives in social science are referenced in the field. As a result, essentialist assumptions can arise about Irish feminism and Irish feminist scholars working outside literary theory. Furthermore, the fact that feminist postcolonial theory internationally is in fact strongly critical of nationalism is not considered equally applicable to mainstream postcolonial agendas in Irish studies that tend to align feminist criticism with nationalism. A very strong critique of nationalism in fact exists in feminist postcolonial studies globally, including in the global South.[13] Irish feminist scholars are not at all unusual in critiquing nationalism for being gendered, nor are they 'insular' or non-transnational as a consequence. The opposite is the case, in fact.

It is significant that many postcolonial Third World feminists have pointed to the oppressive nature characterising the external and the internal processes of postcolonial nationalism in relation to their respective nations' minority groups and women. According to Kim, who herself is sympathetic to a much closer relationship between nationalism and women's social movements, postcolonial Third World feminism literature has tended to emphasise the gendered nature of nationalism and its negative effects on feminism:

> Although this literature acknowledges that feminism at birth was closely related to nationalism, the relationship between feminism and nationalism has not been collaborative in many postcolonial contexts. Even in the case in which feminism constituted an essential part of nationalist movements, feminism was a 'subset' of nationalist projects; the relationship of feminism to nationalism was 'hierarchical' ... To secure feminism in the postcolonial Third World, these feminists argue that gender takes precedence over nation and feminist discourse abandons nationalism. The latter is imperative to achieving a transnational feminist alliance across nations and cultures.[14]

A key point has therefore been missed in postcolonial Irish studies. Many of the Irish feminist scholars who are critiquing the way postcolonialism has been adapted for masculinist and nationalist purposes of creating a canonical 'Irish studies' framework in which women's lived experience and women's writing are marginal entities are in fact directly engaging with postcolonial feminist theory transnationally as it has been applied elsewhere to critique postcolonial nationalism. Internationally, it is not at all assumed that engaging with nationalism is a prerequisite for creating 'a radical twenty-first century feminism', as Emer Nolan has suggested.[15]

Of course, not all Irish feminist studies are hostile to nationalism. Irish postcolonial analysis has been challenged and further developed in Irish feminist studies in recent years, which suggests a more complex situation is evident. Some scholars in the social sciences have, for instance, prioritised a connection between anti-imperial nationalist movements and feminist politics in the context of Ireland.[16] Others have attempted to both integrate and separate nationalism as symptomatic of the dynamism and radicalism of Irish feminism. My own study of the Irish women's movement, for instance, argued that, in the context of Irish feminist nationalism, the relationship between feminism and nationalism in the postcolonial context is not inherently oppositional, but neither does support for nationalism in some sections of the women's movement historically encapsulate the 'entire' women's movement or feminist politics as nationalist. The Irish case in fact reveals how feminism has successfully fought against patriarchal aspects of nationalism while in some expressions continued to embrace nationalist or republican agendas. In other expressions, nationalism was simply ignored by feminism. From the perspective of social science, the recent debate about feminism in Irish studies is therefore a good example of how a narrow interpretation of what is understood to constitute Irish studies as postcolonial and nationalist informs the field – and of how a comprehensive interdisciplinary field of inquiry that straddles literature and social science (Irish feminism) can be simplified.

A new vision for Irish studies?

In light of the above, since Roy Foster declared that 'we are all revisionists now', has anything changed? Yes and no is the answer, it seems. Irish studies is still preoccupied with history and literary criticism, and postcolonialism and feminist criticism, and it continues to evade social science and other critical perspectives in the field. Is Irish studies (still) a discipline and terrain that remain primarily associated with historians and literary critics? Yes it is. Is there a role for social scientists in the field? This is not clear yet. A small group of scholars are trying to make inroads but are succeeding only in a limited manner. Are 'we all postcolonialists now' in Irish studies? No, but there is a clear assumption in the centre ground of Irish studies that the field is equated with postcolonialism, and an argument exists particularly aimed at Irish feminist scholars that 'we should all be postcolonialists now'. Moreover, social scientists have yet to fully interrogate postcolonial theory as it applies to Irish society. And, finally, what could be gained by a new vision of Irish studies more intimately connected with and influenced by Irish social science, in particular? What would we all 'be' then?

The debate about what is Irish studies and what constitutes its canon could be easily resolved by stating that that any intellectual studying and researching Ireland in any arts, humanities or social science discipline is engaged in Irish studies. Many of us are 'doing' Irish studies in a huge range of disciplines despite the intellectual politics that frames the main Irish studies journals, conferences and so forth. In that sense, 'we are all doing Irish studies now'. However, in reality, Irish studies is, as we have seen above, an interdisciplinary arena that has been heavily influenced by at times ferocious intellectual politics and a struggle for intellectual hegemony between literary critics and historians, primarily, since the 1980s. In recent years, as demonstrated above, feminists and postcolonial theorists have constituted another divide or fault line in the field to do with nationalism and 'Third World' feminism. Intellectual politics about colonialism and nationalism therefore still lie at the heart of prominent debates about Irishness and 'who are the Irish?' The institutionalisation of these politics is evident in the fact that resources for Irish studies programmes and prominent academic positions internationally have been mainly garnered in the humanities by literary scholars and historians.

Irish sociology, for instance, (my own primary discipline) has not been absent from Irish studies debates but it has quite clearly not been the dominant player in the field as it has emerged and been conceived and resourced internationally – institutionally or intellectually. Yet Irish studies is clearly more than just literary scholars and historians. I would consider myself, for instance, one of a small group of sociologists or social scientists who work within our own disciplinary boundaries but who also engage very directly with debates more prominent within what we might term the centre ground of Irish studies – i.e. history and literary criticism. I have written quite widely across and engaged with cultural criticism, Irish history, postcolonial theory, migration studies and feminist theory and gender studies as they have been applied in the interdisciplinary arena of Irish studies. Although I am primarily a sociologist, I have tried to bring a sociological perspective into the Irish studies field and to engage in an interdisciplinary and critical manner with the field internationally, as it is currently constituted. Similarly, I would also note Mary Hickman's and others' work as an example of how social scientists have engaged with and shaped the Irish studies field internationally within an interdisciplinary framework – bringing frequently occluded subjects, such as the Irish Diaspora or 'the forgotten Irish', to the fore and transforming the core understanding of 'who are the Irish?' in Irish studies in the process. Likewise, a growing body of literary scholars (such as Conor McCarthy, Joe Cleary and Pat Coughlan) are fruitfully and in different ways drawing on the social sciences to contextualise texts. However, all these examples remain a minority.

Particular problems continue to arise in postcolonial analysis when sweeping statements are made about all Irish studies – and Irish culture and society – without adequate reference to social science as a frame of reference. Problems arise when disciplines that have studied politics and society in depth are ignored and marginalised in such analysis. Leading critics continue to ignore empirically grounded social and cultural studies in ground-breaking texts that make very sure conclusions about Irish culture and society. I have highlighted many examples of this in previous work. David Lloyd, for instance, has spoken with authority about social movements but has ignored the impressive corpus of actual research and theorising that has emerged from Irish sociology on this subject in the last decade. The prevailing manner in which colonialism and postcolonialism are interpreted, and the way in which assumptions are made that are inattentive to the findings of empirical social science, is another case in point. One of the more contentious claims in Irish studies is that contemporary Irish culture and society remain unequivocally determined by postcoloniality. This may well be true and we could have a long debate about that. But, post-colonial theorists have yet to systematically substantiate this rather sweeping assertion with sustained evidence from social science.[17] Alternatively, social and cultural researchers have produced several substantive studies of contemporary Ireland in recent years – such as in-depth analysis of the Irish economy, neoliberalism, cultural globalisation and so forth – but this arena is continually overlooked in orthodox criticism or Irish studies.[18] Instead, the role of the past in the perpetuation of current struggles is consistently given priority over actual contemporary research into Irish culture and society. David Lloyd's *Ireland after History* is a very good example of this; it reifies the continuity of the past in the present to exemplify the continuity of colonialism in contemporary Ireland – with scant reference to actual studies of contemporary Ireland.[19]

In the final part of this chapter, I have drawn on my own discipline to summarise why I think the centre ground of Irish studies has more often than not continued to ignore social science in recent years and why I think it will develop as a limited endeavour as a consequence. Needless to say, work in other disciplines (anthropology, politics and economics for instance) could also be incorporated in such a discussion and a similar analysis could be provided. In the final conclusion, I will outline what we as social scientists might do in order to engage better with and populate the mainstream of Irish studies. A key point is: the interdisciplinary field of Irish studies internationally will remain restricted and flawed if social science is not adequately engaged with to inform debates in Irish studies (such as the wide body of varied work that exists on Irish feminism). However, likewise, nothing will change either if social scientists do not critically and positively engage with Irish studies. I will proceed to make a case for social science engaging more with Irish studies in a way that means 'we' step outside our own disciplinary boundaries and critically engage with debates in fields we might be less familiar with e.g. historical scholarship and literary theory.

By proposing such an agenda, a range of questions arise. Does 'Irish studies' – a.k.a. postcolonial criticism or Irish history – merit theoretical attention by the many other Irish intellectuals working outside its developing framework? Should sociologists bother engaging with 'Irish studies', broadly understood as a transnational, interdisciplinary arena that has, in reality, been more dominated by history and literary criticism than social science – to date? Will we read great papers from the social sciences in this edited collection but in truth continue to reproduce a disciplinary conversation simply among ourselves – and not engage with key debates within the interdisciplinary arena of 'Irish studies' as it has consolidated in recent decades, internationally? Is the purpose to establish a parallel sociology strand in Irish studies that criticises the universality of historical and literary methods? Or should we engage more centrally with interdisciplinary Irish studies as it is currently constituted, thereby transforming the field from within and transforming the methodological limitations of our own traditional disciplinary boundaries and understanding of Ireland and the Irish in the process?

Conclusion

Recently a very revealing public debate in the national newspapers in Ireland and indeed in the corridors of power ensued about the importance of maintaining history as a compulsory subject in secondary school because of 'the need to understand the present'. Yet nowhere (apart from the Minister for Education himself) did I hear a single commentator argue for the validity of Irish sociology or social science as a subject that should be even offered in the first place (never mind be compulsory) alongside history – in order to understand the present. The implications of developments of this kind reiterate the concerns outlined in this chapter about the role of the social sciences in Irish academia. Irish studies continues to make grand claims to understand contemporary Irish culture and society through the lens of history and literature, primarily – while occluding Irish sociology and other social science disciplines in the process.

A key conclusion of this chapter is that a paradigm shift will need to occur if Irish studies is to transform into a truly interdisciplinary and inclusive arena, intellectually and institutionally. In particular, tautological Irish studies which make grand claims about Irish culture and society *tout court* will remain seriously limited and flawed if Irish sociology or social science is ignored or occluded. If Irish studies is to become more cognisant of social science, and indeed other relevant disciplinary fields, a double shift will need to occur. Firstly, the tendency to equate the field exclusively with history and literary criticism will need to fundamentally alter and this will need to be reflected in work that seeks to generalise about substantive subjects such as Irish feminism, nationalism and postcolonialism. Secondly, social scientists themselves will need to engage better with Irish Studies as it is currently constituted and fruitfully interrogate metanarratives like postcolonial theory and feminist literary theory.

There is undoubtedly much to be gained intellectually by a more vibrant conversation between Irish studies as it is currently conceived (history, literature, postcolonialism, feminist criticism) and Irish studies more broadly conceived (to include the social sciences or sociology as well as other disciplines not addressed in this chapter). Two examples of where this might occur have been discussed above – feminism and postcolonial analysis. There is much to be gained in postcolonial theorising by referring to a broader range of literature, including literature internationally which theorises nationalism and postcolonialism more comprehensively and critically in the social sciences. Several other substantive subjects can also be addressed by engaging such interdisciplinarity at the current conjuncture in Irish history and society.[20] However, transforming the ideological and institutional terrain in which the Irish studies field is currently constituted will require significant transformation and new critical thinking if this is to happen. It remains to be seen whether or not Irish studies will draw more deeply on the rich tradition of social science as it has been applied to Ireland or the Irish to further enrich the close readings and interpretation of Ireland as a text or archive. And it remains to be seen whether more social scientists and sociologists will continue to work outside this arena or attempt to transform it from within. The present volume is certainly a good start.

Notes

1 The nationalist and revisionist controversy is well documented in D. George Boyce and Alan O'Day (eds), *The Making of Modern Irish History: Revisionism and the Revisionist Controversy* (London: Routledge, 1996); Brendan Bradshaw, 'Nationalism and Historical Scholarship in Modern Ireland', *Irish Historical Studies*, XXVI:104 (1986), pp. 329–51; Ciarán Brady (ed.), *Interpreting Irish History: The Debate on Historical Revisionism* (Dublin: Irish Academic Press, 1986).

2 See Clare Carroll and Patricia King (eds), *Ireland and Postcolonial Writing* (Cork: Cork University Press, 2003); Joe Cleary, 'Misplaced Ideas?: Colonialism, Location and Dislocation in Irish Studies', in Carroll and King (eds), *Ireland and Postcolonial Theory* (Cork: Cork University Press, 2003), pp. 16–46.

3 Stephen Howe, *Ireland and Empire: Colonial Legacies in Irish History and Culture* (Oxford: Oxford University Press, 2000) strongly challenges the view that Ireland is the same as 'Third World' former colonies. See also Liam Kennedy, 'Post-colonial Ireland or Post-colonial Pretensions?', *Irish Review*, 13 (1992), pp. 107–21.

4 For an extensive discussion see Linda Connolly, *The Irish Women's Movement: From Revolution to Devolution* (London: Palgrave/Macmillan, 2003).

5 Roy Foster, 'We're All Revisionists Now', *The Irish Review*, 1 (1986), pp. 1–6.

6 See various chapters in Colin Graham and Glenn Hooper (eds), *Irish and Postcolonial Writing: History, Theory, Practice* (Basingstoke: Palgrave Macmillan, 2002).

7 Examples would include myself, Tom Inglis, Bryan Fanning and Mary Hickman.

8 Eoin Flannery, *Ireland and Postcolonial Studies: Theory, Discourse, Utopia* (London: Palgrave, 2009).

9 See Moynagh Sullivan, 'Feminism, Postmodernism and the Subjects of Irish and Women's Studies', in P.J. Mathews (ed.), *New Voices in Irish Criticism* (Dublin: Four Courts Press, 2000), pp. 243–51; and The 'Treachery of Wetness: Irish Studies, Seamus Heaney and the Politics of Parturition', *Irish Studies Review*, 13:4 (2005), pp. 451–68. See also Margaret Kelleher, '*The Field Day Anthology* and Irish Women's Literary Studies', *Irish Review*, 30 (2003), pp. 82–94.

10 See several chapters in Patricia Coughlan and Tina O'Toole (eds), *Irish Literature: Feminist Perspectives* (Dublin: Carysfort Press, 2008).

11 See Emer Nolan, 'Postcolonial Literary Studies, Nationalism, and Feminist Critique in Contemporary Ireland', *Éire-Ireland*, 42.1–2 (2007), pp. 336–61.

12 See Nolan, 'Postcolonial Literary Studies'.

13 Cynthia Enloe, *Bananas, Beaches and Bases: Making Feminist Sense of International Politics* (Berkeley: University of California Press, 2000); Kumari Jayawardena, *Feminism and Nationalism in the Third World* (London: Zed Books, 1986); Inderpal Grewal and Caren Kaplan, 'Introduction: Transnational Feminist Practices and Questions of Postmodernity', in Inderpal Grewal and Caren Kaplan (eds), *Scattered Hegemonies: Postmodernity and Transnational Feminist Practices* (Minneapolis: University of Minnesota Press, 1994); Nira Yuval-Davis, *Gender and Nation* (London: Sage Publications, 1997).

14 Hee-Kang Kim, 'Should Feminism Transcend Nationalism? A Defense of Feminist Nationalism in South Korea', *Women's Studies International Forum*, 32 (2009), pp. 109–19.

15 See Nolan, 'Postcolonial Literary Studies'.

16 See Begona Aretxaga, *Shattering Silence: Women, Nationalism and Political Subjectivity in Northern Ireland* (Princeton, NJ: Princeton University Press, 1997); Carol Coulter, *The Hidden Tradition: Feminism, Women and Nationalism in Ireland* (Cork: Cork University Press, 1993); Carol Coulter, 'Feminism, Nationalism, and the Heritage of the Enlightenment', in Timothy P. Foley, Lionel Pilkington, Sean Ryder and Elizabeth Tilley (eds), *Gender and Colonialism* (Galway: Galway University Press, 1995), pp. 195–209; Carol Coulter, 'Feminism and Nationalism in Ireland', in David Miller (ed.), *Rethinking Northern Ireland* (London: Longman Addison Wesley, 1998), pp. 160–78.

17 See Connolly, *Irish Women's Movement*.

18 See for instance Tom Inglis, *Global Ireland: Same Difference* (New York: Routledge, 2008); Hilary Tovey and Perry Share, *A Sociology of Ireland* (Dublin: Gill and Macmillan, 1999); Mary Corcoran and Eamon Slater (eds), *Ireland Unbound* (Dublin: IPA, 2002); Peadar Kirby, Luke Gibbons and Michael Cronin (eds), *Reinventing Ireland: Culture, Society and the Global Economy* (London: Pluto, 2002); Colin Coulter and Steve Coulter (eds), *The End of Irish History? Critical Reflections on the Celtic Tiger* (Manchester: Manchester University Press, 2003).

19 David Lloyd, *Ireland after History, Critical Conditions: Field Day Series* (Cork: Cork University Press, 1999).

20 One example would be the pooling of expertise from literature, history, feminist theory and social science to further understand and conceptualise the role of religion in Irish culture and society, evident for instance in the incarceration of Irish women in Magdalen laundries in the twentieth century.

23

Irish studies between the past and the future

Michael G. Cronin

On 31 August 2013 a commemorative event was held on Dublin's O'Connell Street to mark the centenary of the Dublin Lockout. Specifically the event commemorated 'Bloody Sunday' 1913, when members of the Dublin Metropolitan Police baton-charged a gathering of strikers and their supporters, killing two people and injuring several hundred. The commemoration was presided over by President Michael D. Higgins, and included speeches by An Tánaiste Eamon Gilmore, among others. Along with the political speeches the event also included a re-enactment of the baton-charge, featuring participants dressed in period costume, and a staged reading from James Plunkett's *Strumpet City* (1969).

Plunkett's historical novel has received comparatively little attention from literary critics, whereas it has enjoyed recurring bouts of popularity with Irish audiences. If we look at its popularity we notice an interesting rhythm, in which the novel has risen in the public consciousness at moments of crisis in recent Irish history. Northern Ireland was descending into war when it was published and had its first success. Hugh Leonard's acclaimed television adaptation was broadcast on RTÉ in 1980/81, a particularly tense and bloody period in the North as well as the beginnings of economic recession and a right-wing backlash against social change in the South. In 2013 the Lockout centenary brought renewed attention to Plunkett's novel, it was selected for that year's 'One City, One Book' campaign by Dublin City Libraries for instance, and this, of course, coincides with a series of unprecedented economic, political and ecological crises that are both domestic and global.

This novel – this attempt to use the techniques of prose fiction to imaginatively engage with an acute moment of crisis in the history of Irish capitalism – appears to resonate very compellingly when we are confronted with our own contemporary variations on that old struggle between labour and capital. The public reading from the novel at the 31 August event clearly attests to its power to capture the 'dynamic movement of history', as Georg Lukács believed historical novels always should.[1] A successful historical novel can convey the dialectic of historical development as it is experienced – intellectually, emotionally and sensuously – by the individual in the flux and flow of their life as a social being.

But the juxtaposition of the novel reading with the rather carnivalesque 're-enactment' on that day equally demonstrates the facility with which representations of the past can serve to reduce history to a 'static immobilism', as Lukács terms it. This was history projected as a picturesque panorama, vivid and exciting but serving to reiterate that the past has nothing significant to say about our own moment – except perhaps to reassure us that the present is so much better than the past and that we are on the best possible trajectory of 'progress'. That the organisers suffered somewhat from tone deafness about the ironies of history was most strikingly apparent to some members of the audience as they passed through a tight, heavily policed security cordon to attend an event remembering an act of police brutality. Some of this security at a state event was being provided by a private corporation, which merely added to the surreal atmosphere in which the audience listened to the deputy leader of a government actively committed to neoliberal policies of low pay and reduced welfare provision discussing worker's rights.

All this merely demonstrates that commemoration is never a straightforward business; *how* we remember is always as important as *what* we remember, and ways of remembering can simultaneously become ways of forgetting. This dialectic of remembrance and forgetfulness becomes all the more charged and urgent when the events in questions, such as the Lockout, involve what David Lloyd describes as 'social movements whose potential and formative effects have not been exhausted simply because they were not victorious'.[2] Simply put, any approach to understanding history – or, to put it another way, interpreting the world in which we live – requires of necessity one of the basic tools of literary analysis – narrative; that is, a self-reflexive understanding of how we creatively structure the random flux of experience into a coherent story.

Locating Irish studies

At a symposium, held at NUI Maynooth in June 2012, examining the future of Irish studies in the wake of the 2008 crash, Heather Laird argued that while the current global crisis is clearly economic and political it is also a crisis of narrative.[3] The precipitous collapse of the economy – most acutely in the global 'core' – and the ensuing assault on the basic framework of democracy has undermined the tenets of the prevailing market-oriented orthodoxy, along with the conceptual model of capitalist modernity, historical development and subjectivity underpinning that model. But we have not yet witnessed any notable renaissance of counter-discourses and alternative visions of human freedom – such as those offered by Marxism and feminism – and so these too are experiencing a crisis of narrative; a moment of painful reflection about why these narratives are not proving persuasive and compelling in any sustainable fashion.

Thinking about the future of Irish studies invariably meant considering the past of Irish studies, and Laird was just one of several contributors at that symposium to note that this intellectual project had its beginnings in an earlier period of economic and political crisis. The emergence of Irish studies in the 1980s took place in the context of economic recession and bitterly contested social change in the South and a worsening, bloody war in the North. And these economic and political crises were, of course, also a crisis of narrative; or as Seamus Deane put it at the time, 'in a basic sense, the crisis we are passing through is stylistic. That is to say, it is a crisis of language – the ways in which we write it and the ways in which we read it.'[4]

The formation of Irish studies as a distinctive literary critical project, most visibly through the publication of a series of landmark publications in the 1980s and 1990s, brought together, in a complex and sometimes volatile fusion, various strands of postcolonial, feminist and Marxist theory to formulate new ways of reading, and of thinking about how we read, Irish writing, and new ways of thinking about the relationship between literature and history. Perhaps the most significant innovation was less the new answers this formation provided than the new ways of asking questions it provoked, and most notably its reformulation of the problem of Ireland as another way of confronting the problem of modernity.

Irish studies and Irish difference

Let us consider, for instance, how Irish literary studies might respond to the question, 'Are the Irish different?' The indispensable value of the human sciences is its capacity to empirically test such a question, formulating a comparative analysis of data drawn from different locations to assess the distinctive features of Irish social and cultural adaptations to material conditions. In this volume, for instance, Tony Fahey maps a distinctive Irish pattern of deviation and convergence within a broader pattern of Europe-wide marriage trends, and this is just one exemplary instance of how effectively this model can be used.

We might note in passing that when contemporary Irish social scientists engage in such comparative analysis they are following in a long tradition among Irish intellectuals. To consider just the opening years of the twentieth century we will recall that Roger Casement developed an innovative systemic analysis of colonial exploitation drawing on his experiences in Ireland, Congo and the Putamoyo.[5] Likewise Patrick Pearse looked to countries such as Belgium when conceptualising how a truly bilingual, and thus more cosmopolitan, culture could be developed in Ireland.[6] It is also worth noting that in the twentieth century some of the strongest arguments for 'Irish difference' came from US-based ethnographers, from Conrad Arensberg and Solon Kimball to John C. Messenger and Nancy Scheper-Hughes, whose work invariably emphasised the difference, not to say dysfunctionality, of their Irish subjects; when Arensberg and Kimball looked at the same patterns studied by Fahey they concluded that this represented 'features which are unique among civilised peoples.'[7]

Literary studies will respond differently than the human sciences, not by attempting to answer the question, 'Are the Irish different?', but, perhaps frustratingly, by asking a series of other questions. What does it mean to ask are the Irish different? From what epistemological and ideological perspective can one now ask this question objectively, given the long history of how that question has been formulated as an instrument of colonial and neocolonial power? Is there a way of asking 'is X different' that does not include the corollary 'from Y', thereby always already implying that this difference is from some imputed norm or standard of how things *should* be?

In other words, Irish literary studies has never been interested in affirming, projecting or protecting 'Irish difference' but in analysing the complex historical processes through which *ideas* about Irish difference have been discursively produced, circulated and resisted. Seamus Deane's genealogy of 'national character', in all its taxonomic complexity, through two centuries of Irish writing is perhaps the exemplary instance here.[8] Again, the efflorescence of Irish culture at the beginning of the twentieth century known as the Revival is instructive. Here we see Irish writers repudiating certain nineteenth-century conceptions or stereotypes of 'Irish difference', notably the bestialising discourse that produced such libellous caricatures as the simianised Irishman of *Punch* magazine. At the same time these Irish writers adapted and reworked other metropolitan stereotypes of 'Irish difference', particularly the dreamy, spiritual 'Celt' confected by Mathew Arnold in *The Study of Irish Literature* (1867). In an example of what Michel Foucault would term a 'reverse discourse', a writer like W.B. Yeats poetically transformed the colonial stereotype of the 'Celt' into a symbol of a reclaimed and rejuvenated national culture and, in a further twist, projected that figure as a rebuke to modernity as well as a potential solution to the anxieties besetting European culture. This poetic and political project was, of course, riven with inconsistencies and contradictions; and, just as with Friedrich Nietzsche and D.H. Lawrence who were similarly engaged with the problem of modernity, the line between radicalism and reaction is alarmingly fine in Yeats.

Locating Ireland globally

In an important intervention in the early formation of Irish literary studies, Edward Said significantly recalibrated the lens through which we now read Yeats. Along with Yeats's 'settled presence', as he called it, in Irish and British culture and in European modernism, the poet also presents 'another fascinating aspect: that of the indisputably great national poet who during a period of anti-imperialist resistance articulates the experiences, the aspirations, and the restorative vision of a people suffering under the dominion of an offshore power. From this perspective Yeats is a poet who belongs to a tradition not usually considered his, that of a colonial world ruled by European imperialism during the climactic insurrectionary stage.'[9] More recently, in her innovative mapping of 'world literary space' and its historical formation, Pascale Casanova took the Revivalists and Irish modernists, notably James Joyce and Samuel Beckett, as a paradigmatic case for understanding the various strategies used by writers from dominated or outlying literary spaces to engage with the dominant literary order and enter into what she terms the 'literary Greenwich meridian'.[10]

These examples are a very useful reminder that adapting a postcolonial perspective to think about Irish culture does not mean narrowing one's vision and rigidly interpreting every phenomenon solely in light of the historical relationship between Britain and Ireland. On the contrary, as Said and Casanova demonstrate, this approach requires widening one's vision to encompass that global perspective that is utterly indispensable for thinking about Ireland's situation in the current conjuncture. In a world where so many of the processes shaping our lives – financialisation; outsourced production; ecological destruction and climate change – routinely overflow territorial boundaries, it has, as Nancy Fraser argues, 'ceased to be axiomatic that the modern territorial state is the appropriate unit for thinking about issues of injustice ... the effect is to destabilise the previous structure of political claims-making – and therefore to change the way we argue about social justice'.[11]

Irish studies began as a radical body of work, seeking not just new academic methodologies but a definition of a new object of investigation – best understood perhaps as Ireland's uneven or delayed modernisation as exemplary of the dynamic that drove and created the condition of modernity more generally. Evidently the 'post' in postcolonial does not mean 'after' – as in the suggestion that something called 'postcolonial Irish studies' is somehow belated, preoccupied with the past to the exclusion of the present – but registers that we are in a different phase in the evolution of the capitalist world system. The current global economic crisis underlines the degree to which economic peripherality is not easily overcome. While Ireland may still be relatively privileged in global terms, the austerity programme enforced by the government and the EU/IMF has exposed (as elsewhere in Europe) what had been previously and painfully demonstrated in Asia, Africa and Latin America – that debt and unemployment are constitutive parts of the capitalist system and not one country's peculiar fate or misfortune. Hence, the cultural historian Luke Gibbons has argued that postcolonial theory must continue to be at the forefront of any attempt to understand the Irish past but, crucially, must be equally central to any attempt to analyse the Irish and global present. Without the analytical tools of postcolonial theory how are we to grasp the current dynamic between 'core' and 'periphery' in the European Union, for instance, or to confront the fate that has befallen the Irish and Greek populations?[12]

In this volume, Denis O'Hearn's analysis of Ireland's 'dependency bubble' illustrates very forcefully the urgency of bringing the conceptual tools of Marxism and world systems theory to bear on the Irish situation. Along with Peader Kirby and Kieran Allen (the latter also represented in this volume), O'Hearn has been among the few Irish intellectuals alert to the global, structural dimensions underpinning the events unfolding in Ireland and whose analysis escapes that stultifying adherence to neoliberal orthodoxy so prevalent among Irish economists. In his contribution, O'Hearn also alerts us to the significance of culture, when he observes that so much of the commentary on the current crisis in Europe indulges in 'the usual habit of blaming the victims for the failures rather than analysing the national economic disaster within the framework of regional economic crisis'. In Ger Moane's model of a still pervasive colonial mentality we have a useful analytic tool for grasping that connection between culture, the interpellation of subjects and the structural dynamics of a globalised economy.

Challenges and constraints

Thus far I have been moving rather erratically between the terms 'Irish studies' and 'Irish literary studies' – and by the latter I have mainly meant the study of Irish literature written in English – but this imprecision is also useful. It registers that literary critics and cultural historians played a significant, pioneering role in the formation of Irish studies and that Irish literary studies continues to be a distinctive, and I would say valuable, current in that broader field of Irish studies. Nevertheless even a cursory glance at the various denominated Centres dedicated to Irish studies globally reveals a rich combination of disciplines, from English literature and history to Irish language scholarship, sociology, geography, ethnomusicology, and cultural, media and film studies. Moreover, Margaret Kelleher has recently mapped a flourishing field of Irish studies beyond Ireland and the Anglophone world. This broadening of the constituency for Irish studies, she argues, should generate a welcome broadening of intellectual concerns and methodologies within the field, and a renewed commitment to the principles of inter- and multidisciplinarity.[13]

Viewing this vibrant field of endeavour, it is clear that how Irish studies is, or might be, constituted along disciplinary lines – and related concerns about the dominance of some disciplines – is of less pressing concern than the real challenge confronting the field. Irish studies urgently needs to be a radical critical practice; a critical practice that, as Wendy Brown puts it in another context, 'aims to render crisis into knowledge, and to orient us in the darkness'.[14] The most serious obstacle to achieving this is the institutional ecology which the field inhabits, and specifically the current reshaping of universities along corporate lines.

The Hunt Report was published in 2011 and subsequently adopted by the Higher Education Authority (HEA) as effectively providing the framework for the future development of higher education in Ireland. It merely confirmed what many observers recognised, that the Irish state is as committed as every other Anglophone state to the neoliberal objective of making education a marketable service.[15] As Kathleen Lynch and her co-authors point out in their recent study, this marketisation of education has achieved much greater inroads in third-level than in the primary and secondary levels, not least because of the much lower density of union membership and higher levels of casualised labour among academics.[16]

The stated objective of this 'reform' mission is the much repeated call for higher education to serve the so-called 'smart economy' or 'knowledge society' and for universities to, as Hunt puts it, 'strike a balance between the demands of the market and their academic mission'.[17] In other words, what is being called for is the subordination of knowledge in its fullest and richest meaning (scholarship, analysis, interpretation, critique) to a rigid, narrowly defined and thoroughly instrumental conception of 'knowledge'. And, of course, the obvious question that arises for many in the humanities and the human sciences is: how exactly do you 'strike a balance' between the 'demands of the market' and developing a rigorous, thoroughgoing critique of the 'market' as an ideological construct that serves the interests of a minority while causing the immiseration of the majority?[18]

But, as Lynch and her co-authors remind us, there is also an unstated objective here; making education a profitable business. The obvious sign of this is the expansion of the for-profit education sector, with a proliferating number of accredited private third-level colleges particularly focused on attracting students from abroad. Perhaps the most serious development was the decision by the regulatory bodies to allow the education of teachers to be provided by the for-profit Hibernia organisation, a decision with long-term strategic repercussions for the entire education system. But the universities, while remaining public not-for-profit bodies, are also implicated in this. There is, for instance, the emphasis on 'commercialising' research and on building partnerships between industry and the universities. More importantly there is the drive to attract greater numbers of international students to Irish universities. As Lynch and her co-authors observe, 'selling education as a commodity is now a key component of the services economy'.[19] By attracting such students Irish universities are not only scrambling to make good the shortfall in public funding but are also contributing to exports.

The other pillar of this project, and the one with the most immediate effect on the daily work of academics, has been the implementation of what Lynch terms the 'new managerialism'. This style of governance, adopted from the corporate sector, stresses flexibility, accountability and the continuous measurement of 'performance' through various indices and outcomes. The net effect is university departments peopled with scholars and teachers who are increasingly more regulated and less autonomous.[20] Ironically, given the obsessive concern with 'productivity' in this managerial discourse, the result will also be scholars who are actually less productive, since international research, based on OECD data, demonstrates that 'when staff are given more autonomy, they do more research and are more productive'.[21] The structural effects of these developments are plainly visible, as Irish universities increasingly assume the highly asymmetrical shape of the corporate sector. An exceptionally well-remunerated senior administrative and professorial stratum, along with some well-funded research centres, co-exist with the unacknowledged reality that most university departments depend on a growing army of casualised labour (PhD students and early-career scholars on short-term contracts or, worse, occasional teaching rates) to deliver teaching.

Lynch and her colleagues observe that the new managerialism is 'not a neutral management strategy but a political project'. While it changes the structure of education it will also redefine what counts as knowledge, 'what (and who) is taught and not taught and what types of subjectivities are developed in schools and colleges'.[22] As Wendy Brown argues, to understand what is neo- about neoliberalism we need to grasp this hegemonic formation as something more than a revival of classical or pre-Keynesian economic theory; that is, more than a constellation of economic policies (deregulation, privatisation, financialisation and so on) that cast citizens to the mercy of the market and entrench inequalities within and between nations – though it does, of course, also encompass those elements. We have to also confront the *political rationality* of neoliberalism and its distinctive governmentality.

To comprehend, and to resist, the dominant neoliberal order we must comprehend the various regulatory mechanisms through which 'neoliberalism normatively constructs and interpellates individuals as entrepreneurial actors in every sphere of life'.[23] Where liberalism drew distinctions (albeit unstable and contradictory) between different forums for human action (moral, associational, economic), the neoliberal order deconstructs such distinctions and subordinates all action to the entrepreneurial logic of the market. From employment and welfare to education and health the contemporary citizen is insistently encouraged to conceive of themselves as a 'free' subject, wholly responsible for their own self-care and rationally making choices to maximise the benefits accruing to them. But this rationally calculating individual must also bear sole responsibility for the consequences of their choices, regardless of the actual constraints on their freedom to act and choose. In this way the effects of structural inequalities are translated into the failure to 'manage' one's life successfully. As Brown puts it, 'the ideal neo-liberal citizen is one who strategises for her- or himself among various social, political and economic options, not one who strives with others to alter or organise those options'.[24]

Conclusion

How is Irish studies to confront this diminished conception of subjectivity and citizenship, naming and challenging its distinctive structures of thought and, equally importantly, its distinctive structures of feeling? And how is Irish studies to be a site of radical critique in an institutional framework where the potential for generating such critique is being systematically destroyed? Needless to say, this will not be achieved by playing by the rules of the game; producing easily commodified forms of 'Irish studies' ripe for 'export' and generating types of knowledge that reiterate and enforce the dominant political rationality. Nor will it be achieved by aligning Irish studies with the tempo of late capitalism, endlessly striving to 'innovate' and insisting on a necessary rupture with a supposedly outmoded form of postcolonial and Marxist Irish studies. The tempo of any scholarly field that desires to produce a radical critique has a different rhythm, in which conceptual and methodological innovation moves in tandem with the recognition that we are still grappling with and worrying over persistent problems. As the Lockout centenary reminded us, and as James Plunkett's novel also reminds us very powerfully, it is scarcely news to discover that capitalism and the necessary conditions for human flourishing, and even human survival, are inherently in conflict. But as that history of struggle equally reminds us, we also inherit some of the conceptual and intellectual tools for grappling with those persistent problems. Walter Benjamin writes of those historians who have the 'gift of fanning the spark of hope in the past', and in these dark, hopeless times that is the most urgent task confronting Irish studies.[25]

Notes

1 Georg Lukács, *The Meaning of Contemporary Realism*, trans. John and Necke Mander (London: Merlin Press, 1963), p. 57.

2 David Lloyd, *Ireland After History* (Cork: Cork University Press/Field Day, 1999), pp. 25–6.

3 Seamus Deane, Heather Laird and Susan McKay, 'Roundtable: Prospects and Futures', *Irish Review*, 46 (Autumn 2013), pp. 90–1.

4 Seamus Deane, 'Heroic Styles: The Tradition of an Idea', in Seamus Deane (ed.), *Ireland's Field Day* (London: Hutchinson, 1985), p. 46. This essay had originally been published as Field Day Pamphlet no. 4 the previous year.

5 See Margaret O'Callaghan, '"With the eyes of another race, of a people once hunted them-selves": Casement, Colonialism and a Remembered Past', in Mary E. Daly (ed.), *Roger Casement in Irish and World History* (Dublin: Royal Irish Academy, 2005).

6 Patrick Pearse, 'Belgium and Its Schools', in Séamus ó Buachalla (ed.), *A Significant Irish Educationalist: The Educational Writings of P.H. Pearse* (Cork: Mercier Press, 1980).

7 Conrad M. Arensberg and Solon T. Kimball, *Family and Community in Ireland*, 2nd ed. (Cambridge, MA: Harvard University Press, 1968), p. 99.

8 Seamus Deane, *Strange Country: Modernity and Nationhood in Irish Writing since 1790* (Oxford: Clarendon Press, 1998).

9 Edward Said, *Culture and Imperialism* (London: Chatto and Windus, 1993), pp. 265–6. This essay was originally published as *Yeats and Decolonisation*, Field Day Pamphlet no. 15, in 1988.

10 Pascale Casanova, *The World Republic of Letters*, trans. M.B. Debevoise (Cambridge, MA: Harvard University Press, 2004), pp. 303–36.

11 Nancy Fraser, *Fortunes of Feminism; From State-managed Capitalism to Neo-liberal Crisis* (London: Verso, 2013), p. 191.

12 Luke Gibbons, 'The Empire's New Clothes: Irish Studies, Postcolonialism and the Crisis', *Irish Review*, 46 (Autumn 2013), pp. 14–22.

13 Margaret Kelleher, 'Finding New Partners: Irish Studies and Its International Futures', *Irish Review*, 46 (Autumn 2013), pp. 60–70.

14 Wendy Brown, *Edgework: Critical Essays on Knowledge and Politics* (Princeton: Princeton University Press, 2005), p. 15.

15 In what follows I discuss the situation in Ireland, but obviously the development of Irish studies in other locations will confront different versions of this. For an excellent analysis of these developments and their disastrous consequences for the British university system see Stefan Collini's essays in the *London Review of Books*. 'Brown's Gamble: The Future of the Universities', *LRB*, 32:21 (4 November 2010); 'From Robbins to McKinsey: The Dismantling of the Universities', *LRB*, 33:16 (25 August 2011); 'Sold Out: The Costs of University Privatisation', *LRB*, 35:20 (24 October 2013).

16 Kathleen Lynch, Bernie Grummell and Dympna Devine, *New Managerialism in Education: Commercialisation, Carelessness and Gender* (Basingstoke: Palgrave Macmillan, 2012), p. 21.

17 Cited at Lynch et al., *New Managerialism*, p. 13.

18 See Lionel Pilkington's powerful analysis of the neoliberal challenge to creating radical critique in the humanities in '"Crisis? What Crisis?": The Humanities and neo-liberalism in Ireland', *Irish Review*, 46 (Autumn 2013), pp. 35–40.

19 Lynch et al., *New Managerialism*, p. 14.

20 On the pervasive demoralisation wrought on Irish academic life by these changes, see Mary Gallagher, *Academic Armageddon: An Irish Requiem for Higher Education* (Dublin: Liffey Press, 2012).

21 Cited at Collini, 'Sold Out', p. 12.

22 Lynch et al., *New Managerialism*, pp. 3–4.

23 Brown, *Edgework*, p. 42.

24 Brown, *Edgework*, p. 43.

25 Walter Benjamin, 'Theses on the Philosophy of History', in *Illuminations*, trans. Harry Zohn and ed. Hannah Arendt (New York: Schocken Books, 2007), p. 255.

Index